Tom Mix

Tom Mix

*A Heavily Illustrated Biography
of the Western Star,
with a Filmography*

PAUL E. MIX

McFarland & Company, Inc., Publishers
Jefferson, North Carolina, and London

The present work is a reprint of the library bound edition of
Tom Mix: A Heavily Illustrated Biography of the Western
Star, with a Filmography, first published in 1995 by McFarland.

Frontispiece of Tom Mix, ca. 1922 (author's collection)

LIBRARY OF CONGRESS CATALOGUING-IN-PUBLICATION DATA

Mix, Paul E.
    Tom Mix : a heavily illustrated biography of the western
star, with a filmography / Paul E. Mix.
        p.   cm.
    Includes bibliographical references and index.

    ISBN 978-0-7864-6747-1
    softcover : acid free paper

    1. Mix, Tom, 1880–1940.   2. Motion picture actors
and actresses — United States — Biography.   I. Title.
PN2287.M65M485 2012
791.43'028'092 — dc20
    [B]   94-35404

BRITISH LIBRARY CATALOGUING DATA ARE AVAILABLE

Front cover image: *The Great K&A Train Robbery* poster,
1926 (Photofest)

Manufactured in the United States of America

McFarland & Company, Inc., Publishers
  Box 611, Jefferson, North Carolina 28640
  www.mcfarlandpub.com

Acknowledgments

I would like to thank the late Frankie Barr Caldwell, Vivian Moate Smith, Averille Q. Mix, Richard L. Mix, Muriel Mix Hawkins, Amos Bell Mix, Newell A. Williams, the late Nancy Yoder Rohrbach, Margaret Yeska, Mart Amick Hicks, Maurice E. Mix, and Fran A. Wilson for their letters, comments, and assistance with the Mix family genealogy.

The late Jack Cleo Baskin; the University of Oklahoma, Western History Collections; the Denver Public Library, Western History Department; the National Archives and Records Service; and various departments of the U.S. Army have assisted with pertinent historical photographs and documents.

Dr. Richard F. Seiverling and the National Tom Mix Festival Team promote the spirit and ideals of the Old West in general and Tom Mix in particular. I would like to thank Dr. Seiverling and Merle G. "Bud" Norris for photos they provided and Bud Norris for copies of the Circus Belli and Ralston Purina contracts.

I express my grateful appreciation to Art Evans, the late Francis P. Clark, the University of Notre Dame, Alan Tobin, Bud Norris, and Peter Schauer for movie and filmography data; and to the late Leo Reed, Allen "Slim" Binkley, the Pfening Archives, the Circus World Museum, and the late Jimmie Dodd for circus information and photographs.

My thanks to the Ralston Purina Company, Jim Harmon, John Samorajczk of the Tom Mix International Fan Club, Big Slim's Western Museum, Art Evans, and Andy Woytowich for Ralston Purina information and photos.

Colin Momber, John M. Hall, and Reg Wheatley (England), Janus Barfoed (Denmark), Peter Schauer (Austria), and the late Kurt Klotzbach (Germany) have promoted the Old West and Tom Mix in this country as well as in their own.

I would like to thank Andy Woytowich of Yonkers, New York, for the many excellent illustrations furnished for use with this text.

The unselfish contributions of those Tom Mix fans who are deceased will live in the hearts and minds of all future fans.

v

Contents

Preface

In this book, I have attempted to write the definitive biography and filmography of Tom Mix. For the past 30 years I have been gathering information about Tom Mix, his work, and his films. I have traveled to many locations where he lived, worked, and played, interviewed members of his family and his coworkers, film historians, and just about anyone I could find who would talk about Tom Mix. The initial filmography for this book was researched by Francis P. Clark of the University of Notre Dame. A great deal of additional information, appearing in the appendixes of this book, was compiled by Merle G. "Bud" Norris of Columbus, Ohio. Norris's work includes extensive research by Peter Schauer of Austria, and is reproduced here with Bud Norris's permission.

Tom Mix became a legend in his own time. He was billed as a deputy United States marshal in his very first film, a 1909 one-reel Selig documentary titled *Ranch Life in the Great Southwest*. However, unlike Fred Thomson, Tom Mix was not an overnight film success. His ability to handle livestock and firearms landed him his first job as a stock handler for the Selig Polyscope Company of Chicago, a large pioneer film producer.

Tom's daredevil fearlessness soon earned him a spot as a Selig regular under Bill Duncan, Charles Clary, and Tom Santschi, who were Selig's lead actors. By early 1914, Tom had improved his stature as an actor, writer, and producer, and Selig gave him complete control over his own film crew. Although Selig studios had been established in Hollywood by this time, Tom favored the natural beauty of a variety of outdoor film locations.

The "star system" did not exist in 1914, but if it had, Tom would have been one of Selig's popular draws. Following the demise of the Selig Polyscope Company in 1917, Tom and his cast of players joined the Fox Film Corporation. It was here that Tom clearly rose to star status and set the tone for future generations of western stars.

By 1921, at the age of 41, Tom Mix was at the pinnacle of his career. He was one of the top-ten box office stars during the roaring twenties. Soon he was the highest paid motion picture star in the country, earning $17,500

1

a week for 52 weeks. Money seemed to flow endlessly from the cornucopia. During this period Tom lived like a potentate and spent money almost as fast as he made it.

Tom Mix was the King of the Cowboys, and his horse Tony was a star in his own right. This combination of rider and mount has never been equaled. Perhaps with the exception of Buffalo Bill Cody, his boyhood hero, Tom Mix was the greatest American showman of all time.

The magic, and Tom's career with Fox, ended in 1927 when Fox refused to renew his contract. Tom was beginning to feel the effect of his 48 years and was unprepared for the stock market crash of 1929, which almost wiped him out.

His popularity as a wholesome western star led to a successful three-year engagement, 1929–31, with the Sells-Floto Circus. Following the absorption of the circus by Ringling Brothers, Tom made a successful movie comeback in his first series of "talkie" films for Universal in 1932–33. The series proved exceptionally hard for both Tom, now 52, and his horse, old Tony. Tom retired from pictures to go on the sawdust trail again, this time with the Sam B. Dill Circus in 1934.

Dill passed away in late 1934, and Tom bought the circus and took it back out on the road as the Tom Mix Circus from 1935 through 1938. The Tom Mix Circus was for the most part immensely popular and successful for the 1935 through 1937 seasons.

In 1937, no one could have predicted the problems a circus would face in 1938. Almost all circuses, including Tom's, failed to finish the season. Later, Tom claimed he lost $10 million, the bulk of his estate, when his circus folded. Ironically, the Great Depression, which started in 1929, was believed by many to end in 1939. However, Tom never recovered from the financial defeat of his circus.

One can hardly read this biography and filmography of Tom Mix without realizing that Tom Mix was a man of extreme loyalty and devotion. His friends became his friends for life, and his enemies, likewise. He amassed a considerable amount of wealth and power.

If it was the movies that made Tom Mix popular and the hero of America's youth, it was the Ralston Purina radio program, *Tom Mix and His Ralston Straight Shooters* that made him immortal.

PAUL E. MIX
September 1994

Chapter 1

West Is Where the Heart Is

In the mid–1920s, the name Tom Mix had an almost magical air about it. He was Hollywood's highest-paid motion picture star and top box-office attraction. But who was Tom Mix, and where did his family come from?

Family History

The name Mix may have originated from the name Mixe, an ancient territory of France. Earliest stories tell of three brothers from France; one of the brothers left to make his home in Germany, a second brother went to make his home in England, and the third brother remained in France. English variations of the name are Mixfine, Meek, Meeks, Mexx, and Meekes. German (actually Prussian) variations of the name are Mixdorf, Mixen, Mixiussen, Miz, Mizen, and Mitz. The versions Micks, Mixson, and early contractions of the name Michael appear to be other forms of the surname Mix.

However, Tom Mix's earliest known ancestor appears to be Thomas Mix, a spirited English or Irish youth who attended school in London in the 1640s. For reasons unknown, young Thomas emigrated to the New Haven, Connecticut Colony, in 1643. In London, his name is shown on a list of the first grantees of land in New Haven. It was common at this time for many fathers to arrange passage for their first-born sons to various colonies throughout the world because of the laws of inheritance. Other young men emigrated on their own, seeking fame and fortune.

The New Haven Colony was founded by the middle merchant class under the Rev. John Davenport and Theophilus Eaton. In the year of Thomas's arrival, Captain Nathaniel Turner, a well-respected citizen of the colony, was chosen as the colony's deputy to the English Court of Combination. Captain Turner was known as a proud man and a soldier. He had emigrated to the Colony of New England in 1630, become the constable of Boston in 1632, and was a representative of the colony at the First Court from 1634 to 1636. In 1637, Captain Turner led an expedition against the Pequot Indians and gained a reputation as a brave and gallant soldier.

In 1639, the Civil Government of New Haven was formed and Captain Turner was elected one of its first magistrates. Then in 1640, Captain Turner was chosen chief military officer for the New Haven Colony and he became the agent for New Haven in the purchase of Delaware lands. He was also a wealthy and successful planter.

Thomas Mix was attracted to Captain Turner's beautiful daughter, Rebecca, and he admired her father because of his accomplishments. However, the admiration was not mutual for Captain Turner wrote to his friend John Blake in England, "the Colonies should not be used to dispose of wayward youths. This youth, Thomas, was removed from school in London, for he required more regulation than could be provided." Apparently, Captain Turner was distraught about his daughter's pending marriage to Thomas Mix. The letter reflects more than an overprotective father's concern for his daughter, as confirmed by other Colony reports indicating, "Thomas Mix, though not among the first settlers, was here early, and his first reputation was as a headstrong, obstinate lad, and a vexation to the Colony."

In the 1640s, some of the richer men in the New Haven Colony decided it would be a good idea to build a ship to promote trade with the other colonies and England. In January 1646, Captain Turner was called to London as part of his duties as the colony's deputy to the Court of Combination. Captain Turner boarded the newly built ship, *Phantom,* at New Haven and set sail for London. Neither he nor the ship were ever heard from again. At the time of his disappearance, Captain Turner left his wife an estate of 450 pounds, including a debt of 14 pounds owed to her by Thomas Mix. Two hundred years later, Longfellow wrote a poem about Captain Turner's tragic voyage.

A Vexation to the Colony

After a suitable period of mourning, Mrs. Turner married Samuel Goodenhausen, a Dutchman from New Amsterdam, and Thomas Mix married Rebecca Turner in 1649. Their marriage was the only honorable course of action, in view of the following 1649 New Haven Colony court records:

> Thomas Meekes and Rebecca Turner was called before ye court to answer to their sinful miscariag in matter of fornication with sundry lyes added thereto by them both in grose and hainiouse manner. The matter hauing bine formerly heard before the gouernor in a private way, wch was now declared to ye court in ther prsenc, and they called to answer. Thomas Meekes said he could say nothing against whath bine declared but it is true, and he desires to judge and condeme himself for it in ye

sight of God and his people. And for Rebecca Turner, she acknowledg the things ye charged was true, and thought she had saide Thomas Meekes had to do with her but once, yett it was oftener, as she now saith.

Further testimony indicated that Thomas was not Rebecca's only lover. As the governor told the court:

> Matters being thus prepared, before ye court proceeded sentence, Mr. Goodanhousen desired to speake, and desired the court to consider that Rebecka is weake and hath sore breasts with a forward child, that therefore, if it may be, thay would spare corporall punishment, and if they laid a fine he would see it paid.
>
> The court having heard and weighed what was spoken proceeded, and ordered that Thomas Meekes be severely whipped for his folly of sinful vncleanless, and for lying and misscariages that way be fined 5 pounds.
>
> For Rebecka Turner that she also be whipped, if in refferenceded to her self and child it may stand with due mercy, but upon a view and search and report by midwife sister Kimberly, the court saw cause to forbearthat, and ordered her to paye a fine of 10 pounds, wch Mr. Goodanhousen promised to paye for her.

The Missing Heifer

Unfortunately, Thomas and Rebecca's marriage did not prove to be an end of their problems in the New Haven Colony. About a year after the above court trail, Richard Fido and Nicholas Sloper, indentured servants of one of Thomas's neighbors, were charged with theft, lying, disorderly night meetings, drinking "strong watter," and having feasts at night on food stolen from their masters. According to the trial testimony, Fido and Sloper were influenced by a person named James Clements, who convinced them to steal a pistol from one of their masters. Clements later sold the pistol to an Indian for 12 shillings.

James Clements was a friend of Thomas Mix, and he initially introduced Fido and Sloper to Tom. Clements suggested that Sloper should consider living with Thomas after his servitude expired because it was the best place to live that Clements had ever found. At times, the servants Fido and Sloper would steal meat from their masters and bring it to Mix's house, where Rebecca would cook it, and everyone would eat and drink until late in the night.

One evening, Fido and Sloper stole a heifer. They cut off its ears to get rid of the identifying marks, then sold it to Thomas Mix. Several days later, the heifer escaped and returned to its rightful owner. Thomas knew where it was, but he made no effort to reclaim it.

On being called to court and charged with these indictments, Thomas answered as follows:

It is true that James Clements did bring Fido and Sloper to sundrie meetings at (Thomas') house, to drink strong watter, and eat some meate, also at one time (Thomas) did receive a bushell of corne, and a peece or two of beefe wch Sloper brought wch (the Mix's) dressed for them to supper, and (Thomas) told Sloper that if his Mistress gave him leave (Sloper) might come. As for the heiffer, when James went away (Sloper) told (Thomas) he had a heiffer he would sell (Thomas) wch Richard Fido and he had betwixt them, wch was a poor calf, that Richard's master gave him. So (Thomas) bought the heiffer for 5 pounds and pd James 3 pounds and was to pay 40 shillings to Richard Fido. (Thomas) kept her a whill in his yard, but she gott out and went to Mr. Gibbards, and (Thomas) going thither saw her in ye yard, but because he bought her not of Fido, as well as James, (Thomas) would not speak to Mr. Gibbard till hee had spake with Fido, and when (Thomas) spak with (Fido), he vnderstood that they had stole the heiffer from Mr. Gibbard, yet vpon (Fido's) desire (Thomas) promised to keepe it secrett.

Thomas was told that servants were not allowed to own cattle and since the ears had been clipped, he should have known that the heifer was stolen. Thomas was silent, except for saying that he desired to own up to his sin.

Rebecka Meekes, wife of Thomas Meekes, was called befor ye court and told that amonge severall others, she was charged wth partaking wth them in ther sinn, intertaining mens servants in ye nite season when their gouerners were in bed, tht she had satt and drunke, she hath kept them company, and received other stolen goods, and that it was a great agravation both in her and her husband, that it was so quickly after they were sentenced in this court for other sinnful miscariags. She was bid to speak if she had anything to say to cleare herself. She answered she knew not what to say.

The court sentenced the two servants to be jailed, whipped, and sent to work off their debts and fines. As for young Thomas and Rebecca:

They are guilty of intertaining & inviting mens servants such as they might well suspect came in disorderly sinnful base way, in ye night when ther Gouerners were in bed, to drink strong watter, they also have received stollengoods, and that against ther light, for when Sloper brought the bushell of corne, he said it was not safe for him to receive it, yet did so. They buy a heiffer of 5 pounds price wch they might vpon grounds declared to them, conceit she was stollen, and when it was told them it was stole, yetthen promised to conceal it. The Court considered what a mischievous example this is, and how dangerous it is to nourish vnrighteousness & disorder in a plantation.

Therefore the sentenc of ye court is that Thomas Meekes pays twenty pounds as a fine for these misdemnours and miscarriages, and when Fido and Sloper is whipped, he and his wife are to come to ye whipping post, and stand ther whill ye other are whipped: that they may haue part of ye shame wch ther sinn deserveth.

Mr. Goodanhouse before the court ingageth himselfe, for ye payment of this fine within a moneth; and ingageth himselfe in 10 pounds more, for the appearance of Thomas Meekes and his wife to fullfil the sentence of ye court.

Respectability

Young Thomas Mix and his wife, Rebecca, surely were a vexation to New Haven Colony. Nevertheless, Rebecca's stepfather, Mr. Goodenhausen, stood by the young couple, who grew wiser and more respectful. Thomas soon became a constable, and he and Rebecca raised their family and continued to live in New Haven until Thomas's death in 1692. Rebecca Mix lived until 1731 and died at the age of about 100.

At the time of his death, Thomas Mix was considered a substantial and wealthy inhabitant. His large estate, valued at 868 pounds, 17 shillings, and 7 pence, was divided among his surviving ten children, all of whom raised families of their own and became men and women of good repute.

It is interesting to note that in the New Haven Colony court and land transfer records, Thomas's surname is spelled Meekes. However, at the time of his marriage, his last name was spelled Mix. Also, the baptismal records of his children and will documents probated at the time of his death spell the family name Mix. There appears to be no example where Thomas Mix signed his own name with anything other than a capital *M,* and in one case it is barely legible. The sons and daughters of Thomas and Rebecca Mix were John, Nathaniel, Daniel, Thomas, Rebecca, Abigale, Caleb, Samuel, Hannah, Esther, and Stephen.

The oldest cemetery stones for the Mix family in this country are along the north wall of the Grove Street Cemetery in New Haven, Connecticut. The spelling on all 28 tombstones is Mix.

The early Mix family was also closely connected to Yale University and its history. Among the early graduates of Yale were Samuel Mix in 1720, Elisha Mix in 1724, Timothy Mix in 1731, Jabez Mix in 1751, John Mix in 1778, and Silas Mix in 1829.

From New Haven and other Connecticut towns, the Mix family joined the great migration westward, becoming some of the first settlers in states such as Pennsylvania and Ohio.

Pennsylvania Migration

Each spring in the early 1800s, small bands of husky lumbermen poled rafts up the west branch of the Susquehanna River from Lock Haven to Driftwood, Pennsylvania. Because of the shallow waters and tricky currents, family and friends would remain at home, waiting for the lumbermen to return with their annual harvest of logs from the great woodland forests.

After the harvest, the huge logs would be floated down the Susquehanna River to lumber mills in the Lock Haven area.

As the lumber industry grew, it became more economical to build mills in the harvest areas, and lumbermen were soon homesteading picturesque Bennett's Valley near Driftwood, Pennsylvania. In 1804, Amos Mix and his family and the family of Andrew Overturf came up the Susquehanna River by rafts from Lock Haven to settle in what later became known as the Mix Run area, just a few miles from Driftwood. James, a son of Amos, who had been born in Connecticut in 1791, married one of the Overturf girls, and the young couple had four sons, Hezikiah, Solomon, James J., and Henry, who were born from 1816 to 1826. The sons and daughters of Solomon Mix were Emma, Jean, William, and Edwin, the father of Thomas E. Mix, who became one of the greatest western motion picture stars of all time. Edwin E. Mix was always known as Edward or just plain Ed Mix.

Ed Mix, like his father and his father before him, continued to work as a lumberman in the scenic Allegheny Mountain forests. Ed was a teamster; he used a team of horses to drag logs out of the woods and haul them to nearby lumber mills in Hicks Run. Lumbering in early times was a seasonal occupation reserved for the months from spring through fall. Winter was the time for mending clothes and doing the numerous chores that had been postponed during the working season. It was a time to get together with good friends around the cast-iron pot-bellied stove.

Tom Mix made his entry into the world in the late night hours on January 6, 1880. Mrs. Marshall Barr, the Mix's nearest neighbor, who lived about a half a mile away, was Mrs. Mix's midwife. Tom was born at home, in a little two-story frame house located midway between the Pennsylvania Railroad Line and Bennett's Branch of the Susquehanna River. There were two large rooms downstairs and three or four smaller rooms upstairs. Tom's brother, Harry, five and a half, could not sleep from the excitement of having a new little brother or sister. Little sister Emma, two and a half, was not aware of the big event until late the next morning.

On the night Tom was born, Ed Mix was away at one of the lumber camps, working in the woods and driving a team. Two teenage girls, Emma and Martha Moate, who were also neighbors and relatives of Ed and Elizabeth Mix, walked the five miles to Driftwood in a snowstorm, carrying a lantern for light, to summon the doctor. About a year and a half later, Tom's younger sister, Esther, was born, completing Ed and Elizabeth's family.

The census of 1880 documents the family of Ed and Elizabeth Mix. It is interesting to note that Tom's middle initial is shown as *H*. Various members of the Mix family have surmised that Tom may have been named after his great-uncle, Hezikiah Mix, or his great-grandfather, Thomas

Hollen, or Henry Mix, a Civil War hero. Henry served with Company G of the 84th Pennsylvania Volunteer Infantry (known as the Bucktail Brigade) from November 1861 to August 1862. And, it is also possible that the census taker simply made a mistake. All legal documents, signed by Tom Mix show his name as Thomas E. Mix or Thomas Edwin Mix. Through common usage, Tom legalized his name as Thomas E. or Thomas Edwin Mix.

Tom's mother, whose maiden name was Elizabeth Hiestand, was born in Marietta, Lancaster County, Pennsylvania. She was a small woman of Pennsylvania Dutch ancestry. Her mother's name was Rebecca Smith, and her father's name was John Hiestand. Elizabeth was raised by her grandparents, Mary Feltenberger and Samuel Smith, who ran a tavern called the Halfway House, located midway between Marietta and Mt. Joy, Pennsylvania. During the Civil War, when Elizabeth was about seven, she and her grandparents moved to Shiremantown, just west of Harrisburg, Pennsylvania, where Elizabeth was educated and spent most of her childhood. Her grandmother, Mary, who became a widow, met Driftwood's Rev. Thomas Hollen, a widower, at a religious conference in Harrisburg. After their courtship and marriage, Mr. and Mrs. Hollen decided to make their home in Driftwood. Elizabeth stayed with relatives in Harrisburg for a short time until her grandparents could get settled. Then, at the age of 14, Elizabeth went with her grandparents to live in Driftwood.

Tom's father, Ed, was born and raised in Mix Run, Pennsylvania, a few miles from Driftwood. Eighteen-year-old Ed, of English and northern Irish ancestry, was tall, with broad shoulders and a muscular build. Ed, who knew Mr. and Mrs. Hollen, met and became good friends with Elizabeth shortly after she moved to Driftwood, and the young couple were married within a year. It was reported that the Rev. Thomas Hollen gave Ed and Elizabeth Mix the half acre of property upon which they built their first home. Another year passed, and their first son, Harry, was born.

The mills that Ed worked for were owned by John E. DuBois, an early giant in the lumber industry. When Tom was four and his father 29, the family moved from Mix Run to Driftwood. Driftwood was a larger town, a short distance away, situated more conveniently for Ed's work.

It was in the Driftwood area that Tom Mix had his first riding experience, carrying an open umbrella atop his grandfather's cow in the middle of a rainstorm. As a youngster, Tom was industrious and tended to his grandfather's cow and the cows of his neighbors, earning 50 cents per cow per month. Tom's father helped make life easier for the cows when he bought Tom his first pony—now Tom could be a real cowboy while tending to the livestock under his care.

Tom also attended school for the first time while the family was living in Driftwood. The school was a one-room frame building where reading,

The home of John E. DuBois, DuBois Pennsylvania. (Author's collection.)

writing, and arithmetic were taught in the first through sixth grades. Tom attended school for about two years, until the family moved again, this time to DuBois, Pennsylvania, at the request of the DuBois family. Tom was about eight years old at the time.

The Move to DuBois

Ed's employment in DuBois came about as the result of Mrs. DuBois's efforts to remodel her home, the Mansion. While in the process of putting in lawns and gardens with walks, it was necessary, on one occasion, to back a wagon loaded with topsoil down a gently curved driveway. Whitmarsh, the family coachman, was unable to back the wagon that distance without getting either the wheels of the wagon or the horses on the grass. This greatly displeased Mrs. DuBois, and Mr. DuBois promised to get a more competent coachman.

Mr. DuBois went to his woods' foreman and told him to send his best teamster to the house. The foreman sent Ed because he was known to have an almost magical way with animals, especially horses. When Ed arrived, Mrs. DuBois told Ed what she wanted him to do. Ed backed the wagon down the long driveway without touching the grass with the horses' hooves or the wagon's wheels, even though the team of horses was strange to him. This so pleased Mrs. DuBois that she asked Ed if he would move his family to DuBois and become the family coachman.

Mr. DuBois also loved horses, and he owned one of the finest harness racing and driving stables in the country. Eventually, Mr. DuBois promoted Ed to superintendent of the DuBois stables. Much later, after Mr. DuBois bought his first car, a Stanley Steamer, he always made it a point to tell Ed where he was going and when to expect him back. If Mr. DuBois was not back on time, Ed had standing orders to harness up the team and come to his rescue. Ed would rescue Mr. DuBois and his friends by towing them home. Later, when automobiles became more reliable, John E. DuBois Jr. taught Ed how to drive, and Ed became the family chauffeur.

Tom seemed to inherit his love of horses from his father. He hung around the stables, making a nuisance out of himself and always wanting a ride.

Tom continued his elementary schooling in DuBois, but unlike his older sister, Emma, he wasn't a very good student. He would sit for hours daydreaming, staring out the window. Reflecting on his boyhood in later life, Tom remarked,

> My first boyhood dreams were when I was learning to ride a horse. My desire at that time was to be a top-notch sheriff in the West where a man had to be a man. I dreamed and imagined that way of life as far back as I can remember. I imagined all sorts of dangerous traps and I would try to figure out ways to get away from my imaginary enemies. Unknowingly, I was schooling myself from the first grade up, because as a young man, I ended up in the West. I felt ready and was qualified when the time came, and the time did come when I was a sheriff.

In an interview with the *B & O Railroad Magazine*, Tom's mother said, "Tom went to school until he reached the fifth grade. Then he quit school, since he decided that he knew enough." Tom loafed around the stockyards, stables, and racetrack with his friends, did a few chores for the family, and picked up whatever odd jobs he could. In those days, it was common for children to drop out of school before completing the sixth grade. However, most children dropped out of school to work with their parents on the farm. Some members of the Mix family considered Tom a daydreamer and a lazy boy.

The family of Ed and Elizabeth Mix lived in DuBois only a year or so when their oldest son, Harry, was killed in a home accident. In her day, Tom's mother, Elizabeth, was quite a seamstress. She made most of her own clothes and the children's clothing and taught all of her children how to sew. Her only bad habit was using one arm of an overstuffed chair in the living room as a pincushion. One day when no one was home, Harry came in after playing outside and plopped down in Elizabeth's chair. One of the sewing needles went into Harry's arm and a small piece broke off. The broken fragment of the needle got into Harry's bloodstream, and he died

of a heart attack. There was nothing anyone could have done to help Harry, who died before he turned 16.

Harry was buried in the old Rumberger Cemetery in DuBois. At first, a wooden cross marked the grave and the family made frequent trips to the grave site, bringing flowers. However, with the passage of time, the marker was lost and Harry was all but forgotten by everyone except the immediate family. However, the admonition that furniture should never be used for a pin cushion continues to be handed down from generation to generation to this day.

No one knows what effect Harry's death had on Tom or the rest of his family. Most likely, Harry, as an older brother, would have been there to help Tom if Tom needed him. The two boys were far enough apart in age, however, that they appear to have had their own groups of friends. Mrs. Mix undoubtedly felt some guilt over the incident, and it is likely that Ed provided the much-needed support for his wife at this time. No one in the family ever talked much about Harry after his death.

In later life, Tom's mother often mentioned that a circus was the inspiration for Tom's self-taught knife-throwing act and other boyhood adventures. However, according to W. T. "Tone" Evans, who was a year or two older than Tom, the circus that Mrs. Mix referred to was actually Buffalo Bill's (William F. Cody's) Wild West Show, with Annie Oakley (Phoebe Mozee). Buffalo Bill's Wild West Show appeared at the Clearfield County fairgrounds around 1890, when most of the boys in Tom's gang were an impressionable 10 to 12 years of age. This may well have been one of the most important events in the life of young Tom.

Many of Tom's boyhood adventures have been lost in the course of time, but thanks to his proud mom, to numerous newspaper and magazine interviews with the family in later years, and to a few taped interviews with boyhood friends of Tom's, the following boyhood adventures of Tom Mix have survived. The consensus is that Tom and most of his friends were set afire by the action, adventure, and romance of the Old West as portrayed by Buffalo Bill's Wild West Show.

Shortly after the show, all the youngsters in town fashioned their own lariats from whatever rope they could find. According to Tom's mother, his first lasso was made from her clothesline, and the first cow he ever roped and threw was his grandfather's milk cow. According to Mrs. Mix, "After that, we were constantly receiving complaints about Tom lassoing cows in the pasture field."

According to Tom's friends—Tone Evans, Keppy Jody, Dick Clusterman, Pee Wee Harris, and Denny Dwyer—the boys also walked down

Opposite: **Tom's third-grade class, DuBois, Pennsylvania. Tom is in the front row, third from right. (Author's collection.)**

North Brady Street, lassoing hitching posts and all sorts of inanimate objects. One of their favorite lassoing spots was the Dubois Racetrack, where the boys rode their imaginary ponies and roped each other. Tone Evans thought these lassoing games were great fun until the day someone tore a large patch of skin from his neck with a rough rope: "As boys, we played real hard and we were probably just plain lucky that we didn't break our fool necks."

Tom learned to ride anything that could walk during those formative years in DuBois, including workhorses, mules, and stable ponies. He practiced mounts and dismounts, bareback riding, and standing on a galloping horse. Neighbors frequently complained about Tom's daredevil riding of the workhorses in Mr. DuBois's pasture field, but Tom's father made sure he never practiced his horsemanship with Mr. DuBois's trotter stock.

Tom and his friends did manage to perfect one riding stunt. They would stand on the back of a galloping horse as it raced toward an open barn door. Horse and rider were too tall to clear the barn door opening, so the rider would jump into a stack of hay piled next to the door just as the horse entered the barn. It was great fun, but the timing had to be just right.

According to Tom's mother, one of the acts that impressed Tom involved a knife thrower whose beautiful female assistant stood in front of a plank wall as he pinned his knives around her. After seeing this act, Tom went to the DuBois tannery and got some old buffing knives. Then Tom and his friend, the DuBois blacksmith, reworked the buffing knives into throwing knives, and Tom practiced throwing them until he became quite proficient.

However, the worst scare Mrs. Mix ever got was when she caught Tom throwing knives around his younger sister, Esther, as she stood with her back against the wooden barn door. "I can tell you that I put a stop to that show quickly."

Mrs. Mix often talked about Tom's love of guns and said that he was deeply interested in them as far back as she could remember. It was not surprising to her when Tom bought an old revolver with the money he earned from tending cows and Tom spent most of the rest of his hard-earned wages buying ammunition for target practice. Tom soon became a crack shot with both pistol and rifle. Tom's younger sister, Esther, also became his assistant again as more than once he shot cans off her head. Tom's mother and father were always fearful that he might hurt himself or someone else, but as his mother once remarked, "Tom was very fortunate. He was hurt only once."

Tom's mother also described her son as just "a big devil, too busy playing with guns to learn much." Tom was 12 years old when he felt the sting of his first bullet. Tom and his pal, Denny Dwyer, were shooting at old cans, nail heads, and bottles when one of the bullets stuck going into the chamber of an old single-shot pistol. Denny pulled out his pocket knife to

According to Tom's mother, this is a photograph of Tom with his first homemade cowboy suit. (Author's collection.)

free the chamber, and as the two boys were bent over the gun, it discharged. The bullet entered the fleshy part of Tom's leg above the left knee. The boys tried to find the bullet and remove it with Denny's pocket knife, but it soon became apparent that they were doing more harm than good. Denny helped Tom tie an old rag around his leg, and Tom went home and told his mother what had happened. She looked for the bullet, but could not find it, so she cleaned the wound and bandaged it. Tom's leg healed, and it was not until 16 years later, in 1928, when a lump appeared in his leg and started to give him trouble that the bullet was found and removed in a Los Angeles hospital. In later life Tom remarked, "A bullet is more merciful than a knife. It sears the flesh like a hot poker and seals the wound."

According to Tom's mother, Tom was 12 when he made his first cowboy suit using her sewing machine. Tom "sewed some old rickrack lace along the legs of his trousers. Then he cut off his coat and made a jacket, which he trimmed with fringe from a red broadcloth table cover."

If Tom lacked common sense as a boy, he more than made up for it with sheer guts, stubbornness, and hardheaded determination. One day when Tom was 14, one of his friends challenged him to lasso a bull at the J. E. DuBois stockyards. Tom knew better, but he never could turn down a challenge. Tom tied one end of his lariat around his waist and proceeded to encircle the bull's horns with the other end. The frightened animal bolted, dragging Tom over the rough ground. Tom was battered, beaten, and bruised before he finally was rescued by a stock man.

A Shooting in Mix Run

Tom's second cousin, Warren, was shot to death in the driveway of Tom's birthplace home when Tom was 14. The shooting embittered many members of the Mix family, including Tom's father, Edwin.

The circumstances leading up to the shooting were as follows: The original Mix farm, settled by Amos, was handed down to his son, James, when Amos died. James kept ownership of the farm until he had grown old and helpless and was deeply in debt. James's sons—Hezikiah, Solomon, Henry, and James J.—cut and sold timber to pay off the debt. Ownership of the farm was then turned over to the sons, who after a number of years again went into debt, this time causing the farm to be sold for taxes.

Two men, Apker and Clark, who lived in Grant, Pennsylvania, bought the farm when it was sold for taxes. Warren Mix, Henry's son, also lived in Grant and wanted to buy the farm, but his home mysteriously burned to the ground. Warren and his wife, Cora, moved back to Mix Run after the fire and rented rooms at the McQuay house. Warren, suspicious about how his house had burned and resentful that he could not now afford to buy the old Mix farm, vowed that he would kill Apker or Clark or anyone else if they tried to "turn a furrow" (plow the land).

Early on the morning of April 27, 1894, Clark visited Marshall Barr of Mix Run and had breakfast with him and his family. During the course of his conversation with them, Clark asked Marshall if he would plow the old Mix farm for him that spring. Marshall said he would not and explained that Warren had threatened to shoot anyone who attempted to farm the land. Marshall said that he did not want to get involved in any sort of dispute with Warren.

After breakfast, Marshall left to help Frank Smith, a neighbor, float some logs across a nearby creek before the spring floods came. Clark left to visit DeGarmo, another neighbor of Marshall's, to see if he would plow the old Mix farm. DeGarmo had bought the house where Tom was born after Tom's family moved to Driftwood.

Clark was walking up the driveway, in front of DeGarmo's house, when he met Warren headed the other way. Warren threw some rocks at Clark, and Clark ran to DeGarmo's house to borrow a gun. DeGarmo, however, would not give Clark a gun, so Clark ran on to the next house, which was owned by Hiram Moate. Hiram did give Clark a gun, and Clark headed back toward DeGarmo's driveway.

When Clark returned to the driveway, Warren was sitting on an old stump fence, waiting for Clark. Warren had a club with a four-inch burr screwed on the end of it. As Clark approached, Warren rushed at him and raised the club. Clark fired at Warren, and Warren fell to the ground dead. Marshall Barr and Frank Smith heard the shot and came running. When they got to the scene, Clark told them what he had done and he showed them the bruises on his face where he claimed Warren had hit him with stones. Clark surrendered himself to Marshall Barr and Frank Smith. Unknowingly, Hiram Moate had loaned Clark a gun to kill his own brother-in-law. Hiram was married to Amanda Mix, the daughter of Henry Mix and half-sister to Warren.

During the trial, Warren's lawyer tried to prove that Clark had shot Warren and committed cold-blooded murder because of the odd location where the bullet had entered Warren's vest. Warren's lawyer contended that Warren had turned away when he saw that Clark had a gun, thus trying to avoid the fight. George Huntley, Clark's lawyer, took Warren's club and raised it as if to strike the jury. When he did so, the buttons on his vest were brought into view at a location similar to the one where the bullet had struck Warren. The jury was convinced that Warren had been the aggressor, and Clark was convicted on a lesser charge of manslaughter. Clark was sentenced to a few years of imprisonment; Warren, after all, had not had a gun, and Clark had not needed to return to the driveway for a confrontation.

Sometime after the trial, Warren's wife, Cora, threatened Clark. Later, Clark was shot from ambush, and Cora Mix became the prime suspect. Clark was taken to a nearby hospital, where his leg was amputated. In order to protect Cora, Newton Mix confessed that he shot Clark and was arrested and sent to prison for a short time. His conviction was later reversed, and he was released from prison. In the meantime, Cora left the area and was never heard from again. After Clark was shot, the old Mix farm was again resold, this time to the Moate family.

The shooting of Warren Mix and Clark made a lasting impression on teenage Tom. He saw his family as poor, hardworking farmers and lumbermen who had struggled to keep the family homestead, and he saw John E. DuBois, a millionaire, as a happy man who had just about everything in life. Tom made up his mind that someday he too would have great material wealth. This desire to be somebody and have the finer things of life became a driving force in his life.

In his midteens, Tom was rough and tough and would not let anyone push him around. He was no bully, but he would stand up and fight for his rights if he had to. Tom was big for his age and a natural leader. Since there were no scholastic requirements for playing football, Tom often played with the DuBois High School team. Tom's mother had one of the few sewing machines in DuBois in the 1890s, and Tom and his mother made uniforms for the team.

Tom's interest in football continued while he was in the service, and he played football whenever he had the opportunity. According to Tone Evans, who was going to school at State College at the time, he and Tom and three other boys from State College, Pennsylvania, played in an exhibition game of the DuBois All Stars when Tom returned home on furlough on November 12, 1900. The game was played on Thanksgiving Day and Tom, who was elected team captain, led his team to victory.

As a teenager Tom also liked to play baseball and ride his bicycle. The bike became Tom's chief mode of transportation and enabled him to visit friends who lived on the other side of town. Bicycle racing was also a popular sport in the 1890s. One day, Tom read that there was to be a big bicycle race in Hartford, Connecticut, on July 4, 1897. The grand prize was a sterling silver coffeepot with a charcoal warmer and matching silver cup. Tom wanted very much to win the set for his mother. For weeks he practiced riding his bicycle up and down the hills around DuBois. When the time for the race came, Tom and his bicycle boarded a train and headed for Hartford. Tom stayed with relatives there, who turned out to see Tom walk away with the grand prize trophy.

After Tom returned home, his mother found a note in his room and learned just how determined her son had been about winning the bicycle race: "Whatever you do, do it better than anyone else." Tom had learned that he could accomplish great things if he set his mind to it and worked toward his goal. He also had learned the value of practice. He rode a horse every chance he had and became an expert horseman like his father. He practiced throwing lariats and knives until he became an expert with them, marksmanship until he became an expert with both rifle and pistol. And finally, he kept at athletics until he excelled in the sports of his choice. While this may have seemed like idleness to adults, it proved to be valuable schooling for the youth who would become a soldier, physical fitness instructor, bartender, freelance lawman, Wild West show and circus performer, and major motion picture star.

Tom's mother, Elizabeth, was his greatest fan. She saw every Tom Mix movie, most of them several times. Apparently, Tom had arranged a lifetime pass for her through the local theater or the Fox Motion Picture Corporation. Mrs. Mix was very proud of her famous son. She talked and talked about him until even some of her closest friends got fed up hearing of Tom and her words began to go in one ear and out the other.

Tom continued to help his family after becoming a Hollywood star. He periodically visited DuBois and sent his mother money monthly. Tom also provided an extended California vacation for his parents and had the Union Bank and Trust Company present a large financial gift to them on their golden wedding anniversary. Later, for Ed's 72d birthday, Tom bought his parents their first automobile. Tom also helped his younger sister, Esther, get a job with the wardrobe section of Metro-Goldwyn-Mayer studios after her husband, Dr. F. H. Bell, died.

With the exception of Esther, all of Tom's immediate family lived out their lives in DuBois. Tom's father, Edwin E. Mix, died on November 29, 1927, at age 73, and his mother, Elizabeth, died July 25, 1937, at age 79. His older sister, Emma Yoder Swartz, died June 19, 1959, at age 82. His younger sister, Esther, died in 1973 at the age of 92.

Mix Family Genealogy, Hollywood Style

In the 1925 *Photoplay Magazine* story entitled "My Life Story," by Tom Mix, Tom relates how he was educated in the school of experience and tells his earliest recollection in life when he was two or three—his mother using a shotgun to subdue a couple of angry mountain lions as they leaped through a partially opened cabin window. He dove under his bed and looked back just in time to see his mom blast the big cats with several rounds of buckshot. Tom was left with a lifetime personal hatred of all cats, big and small.

Tom said he was born in a little log cabin north of El Paso, Texas, in 1879. It was a lonely spot and a long ride to the nearest neighbor. His father built the log cabin with his own hands and he made it snug and tight; it was also small and primitive. Tom felt lucky because he had always heard it was better to be born in a humble log cabin than with a gold spoon in your mouth, if you wanted to be successful in life.

Tom's father was out on the range most of the time, riding herd on the cattle for other ranchers. This left Tom, his mother and sister, and his other half-sister and half-brother alone most of the time. In the winter they were

Ed and Elizabeth read about their famous son in the comfort of their home in DuBois, Pennsylvania. (Author's collection.)

often snowed in and had to dig paths to wherever they wanted to go, but in the summer they had the run of the hills and prairies for miles around. There was plenty of game and plenty of excitement in those good, old pioneering days.

Tom's mother was part Scottish and part Cherokee Indian. Her grandfather lived on the White Eagle Reserve, was well educated, and translated the Bible into the Osage Indian language. Tom spoke four different Indian languages and could testify to the fact that the Osage is the most difficult.

Tom's father was mostly Irish, and that particular combination of Irish, Scottish, and Cherokee, probably accounted for his desire to get into the midst of the action and adventure no matter what it was—war, feud, or territorial gunfight. Of course, all Texas boys were raised that way in the early days, before law and order were well established.

Tom's dad had been a captain in the Seventh Cavalry and was well known and respected in Texas and the surrounding territories. However, when Buffalo Bill wanted to adopt Tom and asked him to take the name Cody, Tom wanted no part of it. He had been born a Mix and he was proud of his name. The name Mix stood for square shooting and fearlessness in Texas. Tom was born a Mix and would die a Mix.

It was while living in the log cabin in Texas that Tom first learned to ride and rope, but Tom did not remember exactly how or when. His mother had always told him he could stick to a horse's back before he could walk. Tom could never conceive of a life without horses. At the age of five or six, Tom rode to town to get his mother groceries and always felt perfectly safe as long as he had a horse under him.

Tom remembered the potbellied stove that seemed to take up more than half of the little log cabin and he remembered one of his more disreputable uncles coming in out of the cold to warm up. Every few minutes, he would open up the door of the stove and spit tobacco on the hot coals. The sight and the smell sickened Tom on tobacco and he had had little use of it since.

When Tom was seven or eight, Buffalo Bill's Wild West Show came to El Paso. Most of all, Tom remembered the knife-throwing act and the lady in red tights standing against the wooden wall. The knife thrower flipped the knives and surrounded the beautiful lady with them, missing her by not more than an eighth of an inch.

After seeing the knife-throwing act, Tom wanted to be a knife thrower in the circus. His dad came home one day to find that Tom had tied his sister to the cellar door and was practicing throwing pocket knives and a big butcher knife at her, despite her screaming objections. Tom says his father laid him out cold, but thinking back, he did not blame him.

At eight, the family moved to Pennsylvania, where his dad worked in lumber and construction, and he went to school for the first time. They lived in a regular house, but the school did not appeal to Tom's idea of life. Tom tended the stables and felt right at home around the horses. Tom loved the owners thoroughbred horses, hung around the thoroughbred barn whenever he could, and was elated when he was made a swipe (stable sweeper) and paid a wage of 50 cents a week, at age nine.

Since ropes for lariats were rather scarce in Pennsylvania, Tom gathered them up whenever he could. However, he got into a heap of trouble with the community and his dad when he commandeered the one on the flagpole at the ballpark. Again, his father explained things to Tom in no uncertain terms.

Tom claims he went back to Texas again at the age of 15 and became the youngest working cowboy on the Texas range. When his folks got anxious to see him again he went back to Pennsylvania to visit them and became a pincove boy at a foundry. He went around with a wheelbarrow, supplying the men with pincoves to put in the red-hot molds when they were needed. Tom learned a new language as the men hollered at him, but he considered it good discipline. He also played football for the first time, as an end because he was on the light side. After leaving the foundry, Tom became a lumberjack.

It was at about this time that the Spanish-American War broke out and changed the whole course of his life.

Author's Comments

Some writers have accepted the William Fox publicity and Sells-Floto circus life stories as gospel; a few writers have added a twist or two of their own.

In his article, "Swashbuckler Tom Mix," by Milt Hinkle, "Uncle Milt" or Mr. Rodeo, as he was known, says, "Tom's real name was Arthur Levanthau, who later became known as Tom Mix. His father was a miner of Jewish, Italian, and French-Canadian extraction. Elizabeth, his mother, was of Gypsy descent.

"Tom was two years old when his father died. His mother then married Ed Mix, a Greek cabdriver of horses who worked for John E. DuBois."

However, according to the *DuBois Courier-Express*, "Mix himself frequently denied the press-agent reports and on one occasion of a visit here several years ago, he said in a curtain speech at the Avenue Theater that all the glory he attained was due to his training and experience he had in DuBois, that he regarded this city as home and that someday he hoped to retire and settle down to the quiet life and probably run for dog-catcher."

The Mix family genealogy presented in this book has been gathered and compiled by the following members of the Mix family: Frankie Barr Caldwell, Vivian Moate Smith, Averill Q. Mix, Richard L. Mix, Muriel Mix Hawkins, Amos Bell Mix, Newell A. Williams, Nancy E. (Yoder) Rohrbach, Margaret Yeska, Mart Amick Hicks, Maurice E. Mix, Fran A. Wilson, and others.

Chapter 2

"I Want to Be a Soldier"

America's involvement in the Spanish-American War started when American newspapers began publishing sensational accounts of Spanish misrule and oppression of the Cuban people. Americans saw the Cuban revolutionaries as freedom fighters and folk heroes. They saw the similarity between the Cuban struggle and their own revolutionary struggle with England; the Cubans deserved their freedom, too.

In November 1897, President McKinley demanded that Spain grant Cuba limited self-government, but Cuban revolutionaries would accept nothing less than total independence from their cruel Spanish overseers. The Cubans continued their fight for independence as pro–Spanish factions in Cuba demonstrated against American intervention and Americans living in Havana. The battle ship *Maine* was sent to Havana harbor to protect American lives, but it mysteriously sank on February 15, 1898, killing 260 persons. The sinking of the *Maine* was the catalyst that solidly united the American people against Spain, and the slogan "Remember the *Maine*," became America's war cry.

Tom and his friends were caught up by the tide of patriotism sweeping the country, and as the rumors of war began to heat up, Tom quit his job as a laborer for John E. DuBois on April 20, 1898, and headed toward Washington, D.C., sometime later. An old rumor alleges Tom rode his bicycle to Washington, but it is more likely that Tom and a friend made the 240-mile trip from DuBois, Pennsylvania, to Washington, D.C., by passenger train, the most common mode of transportation.

Enlistment Papers

Tom was in Washington, D.C., and took his preenlistment medical exam on April 25, 1898, the day America declared war on Spain. He enlisted through the General Recruiting Service at Washington Barracks, D.C., and was assigned to Battery M, Fourth Regiment, U.S. Army Artillery. The best description of Thomas E. Mix as an 18-year-old recruit is given in his preenlistment interview and medical examination. Second

Lieutenant C. C. Williams, Sixth Artillery, interviewed Tom, and First Lieutenant A. N. Stack, assistant surgeon, U.S. Army, gave him his medical examination. His official enlistment papers were signed on April 26, 1898.

Tom signed his name as Thomas E. Mix, stated he was born in Driftwood, Pennsylvania, gave his age as 21 years and four months, and said he was a laborer by trade. A brief description of Tom stated he had brown eyes, dark brown hair, a dark complexion, and listed his height as five feet, eight inches. Tom answered his recruiting interview questions as follows:

> Name: Thomas E. Mix   Age: 21   Birthday: Jan 6
> Birthplace: Driftwood, Pa.   Residence: Dubois, Pa.
> Are you a citizen of the United States? Yes
> Nationality of father: American   of mother: American
> Have you applied before for enlistment? No
> Have you given your true name and not an assumed one? Yes
> Do you clearly understand the oath of enlistment and are you willing to
>   serve the United States honestly and faithfully? Yes
> What is your object in enlisting? Become a soldier.
> Do you understand G.O. No. 68 re. desertion, etc.? Yes
> Do you understand Circular 11, Sept. 17, 1892? Yes
> What sickness have you had? None
> Where does your father reside? Dubois, Pa.
> How old is your father? 45   What is his occupation? Laborer
> How old is your mother? 41
> Are your parents able to support themselves? Yes
> Do your parents know of your intention to enlist? Yes
> Are there any reasons for your parent or others to object to your enlist-
>   ment? No
> Name two reputable persons who know your parents: Captain Truxall,
>   Mrs. Chas. L. Story
> If brother or sister has died, state cause: None
> Have you given up any occupation on account of your health or habits? No
> By what firm or individual have you been employed for the past six
>   months? John E. Dubois
> Was your character good when you left that service? Yes
> Have you ever had a sprain? Yes   A stiff joint? No
>   [Tom answered no to 26 additional questions dealing with possible
>   health problems. He further stated he never had a broken bone or
>   surgery.]
> Do you believe you are sound and well now? Yes
> Is your sense of hearing good? Yes
> Do you drink intoxicating liquors? If yes, extent? Slightly
> Have you ever been convicted of a felony or sent to jail? No

At this point, C. C. Williams signed the application, testifying "the applicant reads, writes, and speaks the English language WELL and his intelligence is GOOD." The applicant "has also provided evidence of good character."

This personal interview portion of the enlistment application was followed by a physical description of Tom. According to the record, Tom had a good figure and good general appearance. He had "brown" eyes and "dark brown" hair coloring. His hearing, eyesight, chest, organs, and extremities were considered "normal." His chest measurement was 36 inches when he inhaled and 33½ inches when he exhaled. He weighed 148 pounds and was 68 inches tall.

Front and back views of his medical body chart showed a 1-inch-deep scar above his left knee, a ¾-inch linear scar above his left thumb, a ¾ by 1¼-inch scar on his right elbow, a ½ by ¾-inch scar on the back of his right calf, and a ½ by 1-inch birthmark under his right shoulder blade. Numerous smaller scars were noted at multiple locations on the front and back of his body.

In Tom's declaration of recruit, he agreed to enlist for three years, stating that he did not have a wife or child, was physically fit, was of good character, and had never been in the service prior to this enlistment. The consent in case of minor form was never completed.

Inconsistencies

The inconsistencies in some of Tom's replies give us a little more insight into his nature and character. I believe Tom told his recruiting officer he was 21 years old for a number of reasons. First, Tom had his parent's permission to join the service but realized he was a long way from home. He knew he could not easily get one of his parents to sign the consent in case of minor form in a time frame he felt was reasonable. Tom had a rugged outdoor complexion that made him look older than his actual age.

Tom listed Dubois as his place of residence and Driftwood, instead of Mix Run, as his birthplace, an understandable alteration of the facts. Driftwood was a larger town, only three or four miles away, and Tom had lived there from age four to about age eight. His earliest recollections were probably those he had of the Driftwood area.

It seems a little unusual that the answer "none" was given for the conditional statement "If brother or sister has died, state cause." Why didn't Tom reply that his brother, Harry, had died as the result of an accident? Harry certainly must have had a strong influence on young Tom's life. The inquiry appears aimed at trying to determine if there were any hereditary or transmitted disease problems. Perhaps Tom reasoned that the cause of Harry's death was unrelated to the question. Or perhaps Tom did tell the recruiter about Harry's death and the recruiter wrote "none" because he did not believe the question was pertinent in this case.

It is also somewhat puzzling that a young man of Tom's age would say that he drank "slightly" or infrequently. We can only surmise that some of

Tom's working friends, who may have been considerably older than Tom, offered him a shot of hard liquor every once in a while. On the surface, it would appear that Tom gave an honest answer.

Tom's enlistment papers were signed by Tom in three locations. Most of the handwritten interview answers appear to have been written by the recruiting officer, Second Lieutenant C. C. Williams. He inferred that Tom read, wrote, and spoke the English language quite well, however.

Friends remember Tom as tall with broad shoulders and a muscular build. His medical exam, which lists his height as five-foot-eight, weight as 148 pounds, and chest measurement as 33½ to 36 inches, paints the picture of a somewhat smaller Tom Mix than we have come to expect. His reenlistment medical exam, three years later, confirms the fact Tom was still a growing young man when he enlisted in the army artillery.

Tom's Tour of Duty

Tom's first assignment with Battery M was to guard the DuPont powder works at Montchanin, Delaware. During the Spanish-American War, the DuPont powder mills were the major producer of "cocoa," or brown gunpowder, for the U.S. government.

At the start of hostilities, DuPont was asked by the government to produce 5 million pounds of brown prismatic gunpowder as quickly as possible. Smokeless gunpowder was not yet being produced in large quantities. At the outbreak of the war, production in the Brandywine mills was 3,000 pounds of powder a day; during wartime production, this figure increased within 60 days to a daily output of 25,000 pounds. Within four months, the DuPont powder mills had delivered 2.2 million pounds of gunpowder, most of it going to the navy. DuPont powder shipments were usually sent to the Frankford or Schuylkill arsenals and protected en route by military escorts.

DuPont's series of gunpowder mills stretched along the Brandywine Creek, which emptied into the Delaware River. Each mill had three thick rock-wall sides with a thin wooden roof and an open front. The open front faced Brandywine Creek, so that in the advent of an explosion, the debris would blow out into the creek while the other mills and workers on the site would be protected. The brown prismatic gunpowder was produced by eight-foot-diameter stone grinding wheels that were turned by even larger waterwheels at the side of each mill.

For protection the workers wore special boots and aprons and the walkways were wooden. The tools used inside the mill, such as shovels and scoops, were wooden or copper, and the powder was hauled from one location to another in buggies with rubber tires or on wooden rail cars. Spark-producing metals, such as iron and steel, were not allowed in the mill. As a result of these pioneering safety precautions, today only the ladies' garment industry has a better safety record than explosives.

Beginning May 1, 1898, Battery M guarded the powder mills against the possibility of sabotage by Spanish sympathizers. There was also the possibility that an attacking naval force might attempt to sail up the Delaware River to attack either Wilmington, Delaware, or Philadelphia, Pennsylvania.

Battery M made their camp in the upper powder yards, known as the Upper Yards or Eleutherian Mills. It is easy to picture small groups of young soldier sitting around a campfire at night, talking about their families and the girls they had left behind. They probably shared a plug of chewing tobacco and drank coffee as they discussed the routine duties of the day that had just passed. Late in May 1898, Battery M was relieved of guard duty by the First Battalion of the Second Regiment of Pennsylvania Volunteers.

Because of the fear and near panic of an attack on Philadelphia by Admiral Pascual Cervera and the Spanish fleet, Battery M was ordered to take up stations at Battery Point, Delaware (later known as Fort DuPont), and Fort Delaware on Pea Patch Island. The Delaware River was protected by eight-inch guns at Fort Mott, New Jersey, and Battery Point. Three 12-inch disappearing guns at Fort Delaware on Pea Patch Island were aimed directly downriver. Each battery of guns was manned by 30 soldiers, with another platoon of the same size manning smaller guns outside the forts. There was no way for a Spanish ship to come upriver without coming under devastating fire. It was a nerve-racking vigil, waiting for an attack that never came.

The 8-, 10-, and 12-inch disappearing guns used to guard the Delaware River were new developments that the army had completed just before the outbreak of the Spanish-American War. The disappearing guns consisted of a simple counterbalanced gun-carriage mechanism. A large counterweight connected to two pair of steel arms quickly raised the 50-ton gun barrels. The guns could be presighted by soldiers tracking a target in the Delaware River. The gun would rise quickly, fire, and then disappear behind the emplacement walls as the recoil kicked it back into the loading position. Regardless of the angle the guns were fired at, they would recoil to the same position on the loading platform, making reloading much safer and quicker than it had been with earlier designs. Well-trained gun crews could fire two half-ton projectiles a minute at targets up to seven or eight miles away.

Tom continued to perform his routine drilling and practice firing of the 12-inch guns at Battery Point until November 23, 1898. He had been on assignment at the Washington Barracks and Battery Point with detached assignments to the DuPont Powder Works at Montchanin and Fort

Delaware. Tom was promoted to the rank of corporal on July 1, 1898, while stationed at Battery Point.

On November 24, 1899, Battery M took up stations at Fort Constitution, New Hampshire. Tom was promoted to the rank of sergeant on December 31, 1898, and he continued to perform his routine battery and post duties until April 1899, when he transferred to Battery O of the same regiment and reported for duty at Fort Monroe, Virginia.

Tom's outfit, Battery M of the Fourth Regiment, U.S. Artillery, was a heavy artillery unit and as such saw no action during the Spanish-American War. These units were used only to guard the eastern coast against the possibility of attack by Spain or retaliation and sabotage by pro–Spanish sympathizers. On the other hand, light or field artillery units, such as Light Battery B, could be mobilized quickly enough to support ground actions. Light battery B of the Fourth Regiment, under the command of Captain William R. Anderson, did participate in the landings and skirmishes in Cuba and Puerto Rico in June and July 1898.

For all practical purposes, the Spanish-American was over before the end of July 1898; the fighting had ended in less than three short months. America had won its 90-day war with Spain.

On May 1, 1898, Commodore George Dewey, who had sailed from Hong Kong to Manila Bay, destroyed a Spanish fleet of ten ships. There was no loss of life or serious injury to the American sailors. At the same time, Rear Admiral William T. Sampson began a partial blockade of Cuba and continued searching the Carribean Sea for a second Spanish fleet, which had left Spain under the command of Admiral Pascual Cervera.

In less than a month, Cervera's fleet was located at landlocked Santiago Harbor. Sampson successfully blockaded Cervera's fleet on May 28, 1898. On July 3, 1898, Admiral Cervera made the mistake of trying to break through the American blockade and outrun the American fleet. As a result, all of Cervera's ships were quickly beached or destroyed by the pursuing American fleet.

The big land skirmish of the Spanish-American War was the battle for Kettle and San Juan Hills, which took place on July 1, 1898. The Spanish defenses on these hills had to be taken in order to completely isolate Santiago. By nightfall of the same day, there were about 1,600 American casualties, but the defenses had been captured. American newspapers quickly heralded Colonel Wood and Lieutenant Colonel Theodore Roosevelt as America's heroes of the conflict, but it was not until July 17, 1898, that the besieged city of Santiago surrendered.

As a result of the war, Spain granted Cuba its freedom and the United States established itself as a world power. Under the Treaty of Paris, signed on December 10, 1898, Spain ceded Guam, Puerto Rico, and the Philippines to the United States, and in return, the United States paid $20 million dollars to Spain for public lands in the Philippines. Despite our victory, many Americans disapproved of our so-called expansionist policies.

The Spanish-American War ended as abruptly as it had started. Just as the wheels of industry began to gear up, they had to be brought to a screeching halt. Government orders for supplies were canceled and most soldiers found themselves with two additional years of service to fulfill before their three-year enlistments were up.

On April 17, 1899, Sergeant Thomas E. Mix was stationed at Fort Monroe, Virginia, which had been the receiving center for the wounded returning home from the war. Fort Monroe was now the primary training center for the artillery. The National Soldier's Home, which had served as a hospital during the war, was located about a mile from the fort. Tom helped train recruits, visited with the old-timers at the home, and assisted in the remodeling activities for the next several months: making the fort's living quarters more habitable and upgrading and testing the armament. Tom was appointed quartermaster sergeant on July 12, 1899.

While Tom was at Fort Monroe, the Philippine Insurrection began, and Tom's training activities were drastically accelerated until August 5, 1899, when the fort had to be evacuated due to an outbreak of yellow fever at the National Soldier's Home. Battery O left Fort Monroe by steamer and headed for Fort Terry, New York. The battery returned to Fort Monroe a month later, after the threat of yellow fever had subsided.

Because of his hard work and dedication to duty at Fort Monroe, Tom was promoted to first sergeant on November 18, 1899, and became the highest-ranking noncommissioned officer in his battery. Battery O consisted of a captain, first lieutenant, second lieutenant, first sergeant, three regular sergeants, and approximately one hundred enlisted men. The enlisted men under Tom respected him; most of them considered him a natural leader. One of his comrades later remarked, "Tom was all man, and you'd better stay on the right side of him."

Duties at Fort Monroe returned to normal until February 8, 1900, when Battery O went by steamer to Washington, D.C., to attend the funeral of Major General Henry Lawton. The battery returned to their posts two days later. Then on July 25, 1900, Battery O left Fort Monroe to take up permanent stations at Fort Hancock, New Jersey. On November 13, 1900, Tom took his first furlough and returned home to DuBois.

The Philippine Insurrection ended in March 1901, and First Sergeant Thomas E. Mix was honorably discharged at Fort Hancock on April 25, 1901. However, since the Boer War had started in January and was still going strong, he immediately reenlisted.

While at Fort Monroe, Virginia, Tom was promoted to the rank of First Sergeant on November 18, 1899, making him the highest ranking noncommissioned officer in his battery. (Courtesy of Tom Mix Museum, Oklahoma Historical Society.)

Tom's Second Enlistment

Tom had his reenlistment medical exam by Captain and Assistant Surgeon D. E. Howard on April 25, 1901, and effectively reenlisted on April 26, 1901. Tom's recruiting officer was Second Lieutenant David McCruch. In Tom's reenlistment papers, he listed his occupation as "horseman." Prior to becoming a soldier, Tom had stated that his last employer was "John E. DuBois of DuBois, Pa.," and that his last date of employment was "April 20th, 1898." Tom indicated that he was in excellent health and he stated that he drank intoxicating liquors "in moderation." His recruiting officer signed a testimonial statement certifying that Tom "speaks, reads, and writes the English language FLUENTLY, his intelligence is VERY GOOD," and his character is "EXCELLENT."

A comparison of Tom's enlistment and reenlistment medical exams show some interesting changes in his physical appearance. When Tom enlisted, his hair color was dark brown; when he reenlisted, it was black. Tom's height was five feet, eight inches when he enlisted and five feet, ten inches when he reenlisted. Tom's weight rose from 148 pounds to 174 pounds. His chest measurements also increased by three inches. Tom was a growing boy when he enlisted and a full-grown man when he reenlisted.

A comparison of Tom's front and rear body charts also show a few interesting differences. For example, some of his earlier scars, such as those above the knees, seemed to disappear on his reexamination. Other scars and birthmarks appear to be inconsistently identified, although the birthmarks on the back of his neck, left side, and under his right shoulder blade appear to be consistently identified. Also, many more small scars, front and back, appear to be identified on his reenlistment exam. Some of these apparent differences could be attributed to the techniques used by two different medical examiners.

One significant difference appears to be that Tom picked up a couple of gold teeth sometime between his first and second enlistments. Tom's "2nd and 3rd, upper lateral, left, incisors" are listed as "gold."

After Tom reenlisted, he took a 15-day furlough to return to Fort Monroe to visit with old friends. While stationed in the Norfolk, Virginia, area, Tom had met an attractive schoolteacher named Grace Allen. Grace was Tom's first real love, and he felt she was the right girl for him. Tom's furlough soon ended, and for the first time, he found himself hating to return to Fort Hancock.

Little is known about what actually happened to Tom Mix for the next year. There were rumors that the army let some of their regulars go to volunteer to help the Boers in the Boer War. However, there are no entries in Battery O's history-of-events records to indicate this actually happened. Officially, Tom performed the routine battery and post duties at Fort Hancock until July 12, 1902, when he took his next furlough.

Tom returned to the Norfolk area to see Grace. The young couple had been separated for a little over a year, and it must have seemed like an eternity. They had written to each other, of course, but letters could not fulfill the yearning they shared for each other. Tom and Grace decided they should not postpone their marriage any longer. They went to Louisville, Kentucky, to announce the good news to Grace's parents.

Thomas E. Mix and Grace I. Allen were married on July 18, 1902, by Ed Meglemry, justice of the peace. Grace's mother and sisters, Belle and Bernice, were witnesses to the ceremony. Grace's father, a furniture dealer in the Louisville area, did not attend the wedding; if his little girl was happy, that was all that mattered. Tom had about 12 days left on his furlough, and the young couple went on their honeymoon, leaving friends and family behind.

Tom returned to Fort Hancock and was there for about three months when Grace began having second thoughts about being married to a professional soldier. She soon learned that absence did not make the heart grow fonder. Grace could not understand why Tom was such a dedicated soldier when there was no war. Grace told Tom he would have to make a choice— her or the army.

War Games

In July 29, 1902, the 48th Company Coastal Artillery, with three officers and 99 enlisted men, left Fort Hancock, New Jersey, by steamer and headed for Fort Terry, New York, to participate in joint army-navy maneuvers. Fort Terry is situated on an island in Long Island Sound. The troops arrived at Fort Terry on July 30, 1902, and began to take up stations. This was the first time realistic drill maneuvers of this magnitude were ever agreed upon by both the departments of the army and the navy. These large-scale maneuvers were deemed necessary by military officials as the result of what the United States had learned from the Sino-Japanese, Spanish-American, and South African Wars.

For the 1902 army-navy maneuvers, the theater of operation included the Coastal Artillery districts of Narragansett and New London, extending from Vineyard Haven, Martha's Vineyard, to the mouth of the Connecticut River. Forts along this coastal stretch guarded the entrance to Long Island Sound and the enemy's number-one strategic target, New York City. To gain entrance to Long Island Sound and capture New York City, other enemy targets such as the race (entrance to Long Island Sound), two possible Narragansett Bay entrances, Martha's Vineyard, and Block Island might have to be immobilized or captured.

The first objective of a hostile fleet was thought to be to take Nantucket Sound, east of Martha's Vineyard, or Vineyard Sound, on the north side, in order to acquire a general base of operations. Block Island would be the next logical objective of a hostile fleet. From Block Island, hostile operations could be conducted against both Coastal Artillery districts, which were commanded by Army Commander Major General Arthur MacArthur, whose headquarters were at Fort Trumbull, Connecticut. The "hostile enemy" fleet was under the command of Rear Admiral Francis J. Higginson.

At this point in history, the consensus of military leaders was that the navy had the advantage in these war games because it was familiar with the coast and this particular line of defense. It was believed that the joint maneuvers would provide a stiff test for the Coastal Artillery because a hostile foreign fleet would not have this knowledge of the coast or its defenses and would probably not concentrate all of its fire power in one region. In addition, the navy, which was always ready for war, recently had won two decisive battles. By contrast, the Coastal Artillery was defensive in nature and never fully prepared for war. In addition, the Coastal Artillery had never been tested under fire, and several of the forts had never been garrisoned.

General Concept of the Game

The general concept for the maneuvers was as follows: Anticipating a declaration of war, a strong enemy fleet, without torpedo boats, decides to make a sudden attack on Newport, or the eastern entrance of Long Island Sound, to obtain a naval base, taking advantage of the absence of a declaration of war and hoping to find the land forces somewhat unprepared.

Special problem for the Navy: A naval base may be established at the discretion of the commander in chief of the naval force. The attacks of the fleet should include a day attack and a night attack and if possible, a bombardment and the forcing of a passage to the target.

The hostile enemy fleet will consist of the battleships *Kearsarge, Alabama, Massachusetts, Indiana,* and *Puritan;* the armored cruiser *Brooklyn;* the protected cruisers *Olympia* and *Peoria;* the unprotected cruisers *Montgomery, Mayflower,* and *Aileen;* the gunboats *Gloucester, Scorpion,* and *Peoria;* the tenders *Nina* and *Leyden;* and the converted merchant steamer *Supply.*

Special problem for the Coastal Artillery: The districts of Narragansett and New London will be organized and prepared to resist any naval attacks made before the declaration of war. Prior to the period of preparation, August 30, midnight, to August 31, midnight, no channels can be mined or blocked with obstructions. After the period of preparation, mines and obstructions can be used. Floating defenses and torpedo boats are excluded.

All forts in the Narragansett and New London districts will be mobilized on a war basis, permitting two reliefs of artillerymen. Landing parties are allowed only on government or military reservations, with the exception of signal stations and outlying range-finding stations; these will be subject to capture by boats' crews.

Organization of Fort Terry

At Fort Terry (Plumb Island, New York), Major C. L. Best was made the combined company fire commander. The garrison consisted of the 43d, 100th, 39th, 90th, 122d, 48th, and 35th companies of the Coastal Artillery; and part of Company M of the Third Engineering Battalion; the First and Second Sea Coast Companies of Connecticut; a small detachment of the First Signal Corps of New York; and a similar detachment of the Connecticut Signal Corps.

The Action Begins

On August 31, 1902, the fleet, under Admiral Higginson, rendezvoused at Menemsha Bight, Martha's Vineyard, and set about to secure bases at Martha's Vineyard and Block Island. The fleet was divided into two main squadrons and two reserve squadrons as follows:

FIRST SQUADRON
1. *Kearsarge*
2. *Massachusetts*
3. *Alabama*
4. *Indiana*

SECOND SQUADRON
1. *Brooklyn*
2. *Olympia*
3. *Montgomery*
4. *Mayflower*

FIRST RESERVE
SQUADRON
1. *Panther*
2. *Supply*
3. *Nina*
4. *Leyden*

SECOND RESERVE
SQUADRON
1. *Puritan*
2. *Aileen*
3. *Peoria*

SCOUTS
1. *Gloucester*
2. *Scorpion*

The *Supply, Gloucester,* and *Lebanon* (coal supply ship) were dispatched to Block Island after dark on August 31, 1902. They anchored off the entrance to Great Salt Pond, waiting for the arrival of the fleet. The *Olympia* and its tender, *Nina,* landed a company of Massachusetts' Naval Militia at Gay Head, where they occupied an abandoned signal station. The *Olympia* then proceeded to Woods Hole, where they cut all the cables connecting Martha's Vineyard to the mainland. Then the *Olympia* and *Nina* anchored off Gay Head.

The fleet arrived at New Harbor, on the west side of Block Island, at dawn on the morning of September 1, 1902. The second batteries of the *Brooklyn, Massachusetts, Indiana,* and *Puritan* shelled the Coastal Artillery signal station at Beacon Hill, and the *Alabama* landed two companies of sailors, who captured the facility. One sergeant and four signalmen were captured, but one man escaped and sent messages for several days afterward. Then, marines from the *Kearsarge, Alabama, Massachusetts,* and *Brooklyn* landed and established a camp under the fleet marine officer. The fleet anchored off New Harbor, with the small vessels inside Great Salt Pond. With a naval base on Block Island, the fleet could attack any point on the line of defense.

At 10 A.M. on September 1, the *Scorpion* was sent on a scouting mission around the south end of Gardiner Island, but she ran into a sunken barge filled with stone and was put out of action. She returned to Block Island before dark for repairs.

After dark, another scouting squadron consisting of the *Panther, Supply, Montgomery,* and *Mayflower,* under Commander Wilson, left to scout the coast from Price's Neck to Fisher's Island. The fleet was spotted at midnight and fired on by mortars at Fort Adams, using the horizontal-base system of range finding. Two battery salvos, or sixteen shots, were fired at the leading ship at ranges of 6,725 and 7,185 yards. Four battery salvos were fired at the third ship, the one with the tallest mast. The two vessels were easily put out of action.

At 9 P.M. on September 1, 1901, Admiral Higginson launched a bold and determined attack on Fort Terry and Gardiner's Point. The armored cruiser *Brooklyn* and the battleship *Massachusetts* left the base at Block Island to run the Race at Gull Island Passage and take Fort Terry in reverse. By getting behind the fort, the fort would be virtually defenseless and at the mercy of the ships big guns. However, at 10:12 P.M., the ships were simultaneously spotted by Forts Terry, Michie, Wright, and Gardiner's Point. At 10:15 P.M., Forts Terry and Michie opened fire with mortars and 10- and 12-inch guns. The range from Fort Terry was about 4,500 yards when the ships were first discovered. Both ships passed to within 3,000 yards of Fort Terry and later anchored beyond the field of fire. The action ceased at 11:15 P.M.

At 1:40 A.M., September 2, the *Kearsarge, Alabama, Indiana,* and *Puritan* got underway and proceeded to attack Fort Gardiner and Fort Terry from the other side. At 4:45 A.M. they were detected by the forts, moving in a column in the order named above. The *Puritan* was some distance behind. The three leading ships fired at Fort Gardiner as they came in range, silencing the six-pounders there. Fort Terry opened fire on them with mortars and 10-inch guns. Meanwhile, the *Brooklyn* and *Massachusetts* rejoined the fight and opened fire on Fort Terry. Two groups of mines were fired by judgment firing, and it was claimed that the *Alabama* was put out of action. A few minutes later, the *Indiana* struck a contact mine in crossing the minefield and was also put out of action. About an hour later, the *Puritan* crossed the minefield and, it was claimed, put out of action by judgment firing.

The ships passed on close to Plum Island and circled there, firing on Forts Terry and Michie, taking the later in reverse and joining with the *Brooklyn* and *Massachusetts* on the other side of Plumb Island to provide a heavy cross-fire on Fort Terry. It was claimed that the cross fire would have put Fort Terry out of action and allowed the fort to be taken.

At 5:56 A.M., the four ships passed eastward again and moved on to Block Island. The *Brooklyn* and *Massachusetts* joined the squadron on its return to their home base.

The Coastal Artillery claimed that the admiral, who obviously had an accurate knowledge of the forts at the Race, would have been successful if the weather had favored the ships a little more and allowed them to cross the minefield with little loss and get closer to the forts before being detected. The attack, which was splendidly conceived and executed, brought out several weak points of our coastal fortifications.

Other Action During the Week

- September 3   —Run through the Race and day attack and bombardment of Fort Wright.
                              —Bombardment of Fort Rodman.
- September 4   —Attack on Montauk Point.
- September 4 and 5—Run past the forts at the Race and night attack and bombardment of Fort Wright.
- September 5   —Day attack and bombardment of Fort Adams and Wetherill.
- September 5 and 6—Run past the batteries in the eastern passage of Narragansett Bay and night attack on Forts Adams and Wetherill.

The 1902 joint army-navy maneuvers ended at noon on September 6, 1902.

Lessons Learned

The maneuvers provided some valuable lessons.

1. The 10- and 12-inch Coastal Artillery guns have an advantage at extreme ranges due to the instability of ship gun platforms at sea. At midranges there is no advantage.
2. The navy was caught by surprise by the location of some minefields.
3. If a ship could get behind a fort, the fort was at the mercy of the big ship's guns.
4. The searchlight towers were more of a handicap than help under wartime conditions; they should never be used to search for a target. They should be used only to illuminate a target once it is detected. Even then, their usefulness would be questionable if the ships were painted a dull color.

These joint maneuvers appear to be the closest thing to real action that Tom encountered while in the service. The 48th Company Coastal Artillery left Fort Terry on September 14 and arrived back at Fort Hancock on September 15, 1902. (Information pertaining to the joint army-navy maneuvers of 1902 was supplied by Cornell student Matthew Adams and by Thomas J. Hoffman, Park Historian, National Park Service, Sandy Hook Unit, Gateway National Recreation Area.)

Desertion

On October 20, 1902, First Sergeant Thomas E. Mix took his last furlough. He gave his expected destination as Pittsburgh. It is doubtful that he went there, and even more doubtful that he ever expected to return to Fort Hancock.

On October 25, 1902, Tom's furlough ran out and he was listed as absent without leave (AWOL). The AWOL period ended on November 4, 1902, and Thomas E. Mix was officially listed as a deserter in his regimental returns. Tom was never apprehended or returned to military control, and he therefore never received a court-martial for the offense or a discharge for his second enlistment.

Tom's commanding officer never issued a warrant for his arrest. During this time in history, the army seems to have been content merely to let the matter drop. Regimental records show that desertion did increase after the war and fewer entries are made with regard to deserters being returned to army custody for prosecution.

However, Tom's desertion had a great impact on his life. Initially, he was never quite sure whether the army was looking for him. Partly because he had always wanted to go West, and partly because he was on the run, he and Grace moved into the Southwest late in 1902. They settled in Guthrie, Oklahoma, which was the capital of the Oklahoma Territory. For a short time, Grace continued her work as an English teacher and Tom taught a physical fitness class. Tom also tended bar in the Blue Belle Saloon.

Grace's father found out that Tom had gone AWOL and eventually succeeded in having his daughter's marriage to Tom annulled. For the next 10 years, some people described Tom as the type of person who never volunteered much information about his past. Tom did not keep a low profile for long, however.

On January 5, 1928, long after Tom had gained fame as a motion picture star, he applied for membership in the United Spanish War Veterans. Quartermaster General James J. Murray wrote to the adjutant general of the U.S. Army requesting information pertaining to Tom's service in Batteries M and O of the Fourth Artillery. On January 7, 1928, the adjutant general's office replied, giving the pertinent facts relating to Tom's service to the United Spanish War Veterans. Tom was granted a life membership in the USWV and joined the Joe Wheeler Camp no. 5, USWV, Prescott, Arizona.

The question of Tom's desertion came up again at the time of his death. His estate tried to secure an American flag from the Veterans' Administration for his casket during the funeral. The VA hesitated to supply the flag, and John Ford of Hollywood fame intervened for the family and wrote to the VA and the USWV. Ford was a relative of the quartermaster general of the United Spanish War Veterans. The USWV replied to Ford's letter on October 18, 1940: "Confidentially, I wish to advise that Tom Mix evidently, in the days of his youth, was a soldier of fortune and just seemed to want to be in everybody's war. He had an honorable discharge from the war service and was mustered out in 1901 as a First Sergeant. He enlisted again a few days later and then, as you remember, the Boer War was starting and Tom left without saying 'Good-bye' to Uncle Sam."

Tom's marriage to Grace Allen and the circumstances leading up to his desertion are not known. His flight appears to have been excused on the basis that "he was off to fight another war." A simple check of the paperwork would have revealed that he did not desert until October 1902, long after the Boer War was ended with the Treaty of Vereeniging, signed at Pretoria on May 31, 1902.

With regard to Tom's foreign service and the possibility that he was wounded in action, the National Archives and Records Service wrote, "Nothing has been found to show that Sergeant Mix served in any troop of the 1st Regiment United States Volunteer cavalry, which was popularly known as Colonel Theodore Roosevelt's 'Rough Riders' or served beyond the continental limits of the United States. Medical or other records do not show that he was wounded in action. His name does not appear on the Index to the Decoration and Awards Correspondence of the Quartermaster General's Office. This indicates that he was not awarded any decorations or medals." A similar check of army records in England revealed that no documentary evidence exists to indicate that Tom Mix ever served officially or unofficially in any capacity in the Boer War.

Over the years, several possible reasons have been given for Tom's desertion. The most likely is that Tom was bored and wanted a life of his own with his wife, Grace. The army never knew he was married. Perhaps Grace wanted to continue her career as a schoolteacher until Tom could get out of the service. In any case, Tom was unable to spend much time with his wife, which probably created a stressful situation. This reason for his desertion appears to be the most plausible.

A second possible contributing factor, mentioned by Tom himself in the legendary aspect of his military career, is that he may have grown tired of firing artillery guns at imaginary enemies and playing nursemaid to a bunch of army horses and mules. As a first sergeant, Tom had reached a plateau in his career; he was the highest-ranking noncommissioned officer in his battery and could not advance further in rank; he could only accumulate more time in rank.

It is also possible that the 1902 mock attack on Fort Terry left Tom with a new sense of vulnerability. The big guns on both sides of a real war would have wreaked havoc and destruction, killing many people. The forts and the targets they guarded may not have been sitting ducks, but they certainly were not impenetrable.

And finally, a wild tale, which I have heard and hesitate to repeat, was related to me by W. T. (Tone) Evans, a boyhood friend of Tom's. According to Evans, Tom explained his desertion on a return trip to his hometown of DuBois in the late twenties. According to Evans, Tom claimed that he was accused of stealing some horse blankets. Tom knew he was not guilty of the charges, but he could not prove his innocence, so he headed north into Canada to give the situation time to cool off. Later, two officers admitted that they were responsible for the missing blankets, and the charges against Tom were dropped, but Tom did not know it. By the time Tom found out, he was listed as a deserter. Evans did not know that Tom was married to Grace Allen at the time of his desertion.

All attempts to confirm any part of this story have been futile. Apparently, there are no official or unofficial records of any missing property or of any charges against Tom Mix, other than his desertion. Aside from moving to Oklahoma Territory, Tom seems to have done little to evade the army.

Persons and organizations who have written to the adjutant general prior to December 19, 1961, about Tom's military records and desertion are as follows:

Spanish War Veterans	March 12, 1927
Spanish War Veterans	January 7, 1928
Congressional inquiry	March 12, 1934
Veterans' Administration	October 15, 1940
Unknown	November 5, 1942
Congressional inquiry	August 7, 1957
Sam Henderson	January 27, 1959
Sam Henderson	December 18, 1961

The second inquiry was made when Tom applied to join the United Spanish War Veterans. The two congressional inquiries were probably made by congressmen on behalf of constituents seeking information about Tom Mix. The 1940 VA inquiry was made when Tom's family asked the VA to furnish a flag for his funeral. The two Sam Henderson inquiries were made by the well-known Oklahoma western writer. Apparently, after December 18, 1961, the army stopped making notations in Thomas E. Mix file #5257. My own inquiries in the midsixties are not noted.

War, Hollywood Style

It might be said that the pen is mightier than the Truth when it comes to stories about Tom Mix. A good example of this is found in a two-part story entitled, "My Life Story" by Tom Mix, in the February 1925 issue of *Photoplay Magazine.* Tom states that he was a cowboy, soldier, scout, sheriff, law enforcement officer, U.S. marshal, and Texas Ranger. According to the *Photoplay* story, Tom was born in a little log cabin north of El Paso, Texas, in 1877. The story then goes into great detail about his ancestry. For details about Tom's actual and legendary birth and boyhood, see chapter 1.

The *Photoplay* story claims that Tom was working as a lumberjack in the Pennsylvania forests when the Spanish-American War was declared on April 25, 1898. He was swinging an ax and chopping down trees on a mountaintop when a little tram car arrived with the news that changed his life. Tom knew something exciting had happened when the men began yelling and dancing around. Then, one of the lumberjacks hollered to him, "Hi, Tom, America's declared war on Spain and the president has issued a call for volunteers."

When the news of the war sank in, Tom threw his ax as far as he could and started running down the mountain as if a pack of wolves were after him. Tom says that he wanted to enlist in the navy because of the sinking of the *Maine.* Being in the Navy would be a new challenge and put him close to the action. Tom's only problem was he did not have enough money to get to the navy recruiting headquarters in Philadelphia; he had spent it all making time payments on a racing bike. Bike racing was very popular in the nineties and Tom had won a number of local races. Tom decided to sell his bike back to the original owner to get money enough to go to Philadelphia.

When Tom arrived in Philadelphia, the navy would not let anyone enlist who had never been to sea before. Suddenly, Tom found himself aboard a big navy warship, arguing the point with some of the navy's top brass. All the arguing in the world did not do any good; he still was not allowed to enlist in the navy. Tom was disappointed; he wanted to get into some branch of the service where he would see action, not get stuck marching around a parade ground with a musket on his shoulder or playing chambermaid to a bunch of army mules while the other boys were out hunting Spaniards in Cuba.

With the five or six dollars he had left, Tom headed to Washington,

D.C., to interview the adjutant general, who, after all, should know where the action was going to take place. The adjutant general was sympathetic to Tom's desire and sent him to see Captain Grimes, whose battery of artillery was expected to see service at once. Tom became a full-fledged member of Grimes's battery.

They went to Tampa, Florida, and set sail for Cuba on June 21, 1898. Shortly after they landed, they saw action in the Battle of Guaymas. Then Grimes's battery saw action with the Rough Riders at the Battle of Cristabel Hill. There, Tom became a scout and courier to General Chaffee because of his knowledge of the Spanish language. Tom managed to get into all the action he wanted: "It was pretty much hand-to-hand fighting, raiding nests of Spaniards that were hidden in all sorts of places. We fought hard and the climate was hell, and the living conditions were terrible, but nobody cared. We came to do a job and we did it."

Tom says that he only saw Teddy Roosevelt once at Cristabel Hill, but the memory was indelibly etched in his mind. It was a great experience and great training for any man.

Tom's next assignment was to round up Spanish snipers and sharpshooters. As he was climbing a quiet-looking hill, a shot rang out from a mango tree. The bullet blew a hole in Tom's sleeve, but he could not tell where it came from. Tom shot at the mango tree and the sniper popped his head out. Tom tried to tell the sniper that the war was over, but as he was shouting another shot rang out and Tom was hit in the roof of the mouth by one of the sniper's bullets. The bullet exited through the back of his neck.

Tom toppled over as some of the other scouts came to his rescue and shot the sniper out of the mango tree. He was sent to the hospital in Santiago, where he spent more than a month recuperating from his wounds. He never fully recovered from his injuries and ever after had trouble pronouncing half a dozen or so words. Often, he would hesitate and quickly come up with a substitute word that he could pronounce.

Tom returned to the States in September, but he could not settle down. A few months went by and then Tom joined the provisional army artillery unit headed for the Philippines. As he crossed the ocean a second time, he never realized he would become involved in fierce, desperate fighting in the Boxer Rebellion before his next return to the United States.

The Boxer Uprising was a religious war that pitted the Boxers against all others. All foreigners were to be driven out of China. A few American missionaries, French priests, and British officials became the official targets. To escape the Boxers, the foreigners had to hide in their embassies and the nearby hills. The foreign powers, seeing their people in trouble, sent military aid to rescue them.

Tom was put in charge of a Gardiner (rapid firing) gun during the siege of Peking and watched as the victorious allied armies marched into the city. But the real excitement came when the allies were laying a new railroad between Peking and Tien Tsing. It was flat, open country with a little brush and an occasional tree. Tom's job was to guard the workingmen with the Gardiner gun. Snipers, behind bushes, harassed the railroad workers every mile of the way. There were many skirmishes, and many men died, but the work was finished.

It was outside the city of Tien Tsing that Colonel Listenn was killed and Tom was seriously wounded a second time. Tom's Gardiner gun had been pounding away on one of the gates of the city when a shell exploded right in front of him. It blew up the gun's carriage, and one of the wheel spokes was blown in two. The spoke splinter flew through the air like a tomahawk, neatly scalping Tom. It peeled the top of his head and skinned his forehead down to the bone. Tom's eyebrows were left hanging over his eyes. Tom was hurled into a ditch along with several others who were hit by the shell. Later he was carted off to the hospital for repairs and finally shipped home on a hospital transport.

After the Boxer Rebellion, Tom sought a quieter lifestyle, breaking horses in Denver for the British government at the start of the Boer War. However, he still wanted to be in the action. Tired of breaking horses, he hitched a ride with a shipment of horses to South Africa to see what the fuss was all about.

Tom and the horses landed in South Africa as trouble was starting in Ladysmith. The horses, who were only partially broken, went berserk when the British, rattling their brass buttons, sabers, and all kinds of hardware, tried to mount them. After rounding up the horses, they were properly broken and finally ready for service.

After being in South Africa for a while, Tom's sympathies soon turned to the Boers, who were the underdogs, so he got off the sidelines and joined the Boer Army. Tom was immediately impressed by the fact that almost all the Boers had beards. To him, it seemed like Boer rankings in the army were established by the fullness of a man's beard. General Cronje and Oom Paul Kruger, president of the Dutch Transvaal Republic, had two of the finest beards that Tom had ever seen. Both men were short and round but grand fighting men with the courage of lions.

Tom was taken prisoner in his very first skirmish with the Boers, at the Battle of Spinecob. This posed a real problem for the British, who had captured about one hundred American citizens along with the Boers. To solve their problem, the British decided the best thing they could do was transport the Yanks back to the States to get rid of them.

When Tom landed at the Philadelphia navy yard, he showed them his honorable discharge papers. Some of the boys had left the U.S. Army "without stopping to say good-bye to Uncle Sam." Tom headed back west to join up with the Miller Brothers 101 Wild West Ranch outfit.

Author's Comments

Tom's legend was created by publicity writers before 1925. The 1925 *Photoplay* story is a good summary of the legend, however, and a masterpiece of fabrication created by Fox publicists. At first Tom objected to and fought the creation of the yarn because he had spent hours talking with his publicists about his real life. When Tom first saw some of the early Fox publicity, he was furious about the distortion of the facts, especially about his birth and boyhood, and he did not think the public gullible enough to believe the war-hero image created by Fox.

Stuntman Scotty McPherson, a friend and co-worker of Tom's at the Fox Studios, who specialized in falls from horses, recalled that

> Tom used to have a running gun battle with the Fox studio chiefs over the "born in Texas" publicity. It got so bad at one time that there was some question about whether Tom would sign a new contract with Fox. Finally, the Fox executives worked out an agreement with Tom which said that the studio could put out all the Texas publicity they wanted to, but Tom was free to deny the Texas birth story and confirm his Pennsylvania birth and boyhood if he was ever directly asked about it. This was the agreement that Tom had with Fox for many years.

The bottom line is that the Fox studio executives convinced Tom that it was in his best interests to leave the publicity stories to the publicists. Tom was free to tell anyone anything he wanted to on a one-on-one basis. However, by going along with the Fox agreement, Tom condoned the legend that would continue to grow and survive to this day.

Chapter 3

Freelance Lawman and Daredevil

Go West, Young Man

Late in 1902, after Tom's hasty departure from the Coastal Artillery, he and his wife, Grace, moved into the Southwest for the first time. Grace became an English teacher in Guthrie, Oklahoma, and Tom taught a physical fitness class in the basement of the old Carnegie Library. Tom also coached the Guthrie football team and became the athletic director for the high school. To earn a little extra money, Tom also tended bar at the Blue Belle Saloon and broke horses at a little corral located near the Santa Fe Railroad depot. It was his skill in breaking horses that led to his being hired for the first time by the Mulhall Ranch.

While in Guthrie, Tom met and became friends with Zack Mulhall and Thompson B. Ferguson, governor of the Oklahoma Territory. The governor shared Tom's enthusiasm for working with young people and developing a physical fitness program to help strengthen youth. Tom impressed the governor with his winning smile and Tom Sawyer flamboyance; his personality was his greatest asset.

Tom's marriage to Grace was eventually annulled, due in large part to the efforts of her father, who had discovered that Tom had deserted the Coastal Artillery. Tom was deeply depressed, but with the help and encouragement of Zack Mulhall, he accepted a job as drum major of the Oklahoma Cavalry Band, in 1904, despite the fact that he was neither a member of the militia nor a musician. However, he proved to be a proud, colorful, handsome figure as a drum major bedecked in gold braid.

Oklahoma Cavalry Band

Tom and the Oklahoma Cavalry Band attended the St. Louis World's Fair in 1904 to help dedicate the laying of the cornerstone of the Oklahoma Building. Local newspapers described Tom: "The handsome drum major, marching in the foreground, was a gallant figure who attracted a great deal of attention, especially from the ladies."

Will Rogers was also at the St. Louis World's Fair as a rodeo clown for the Colonel Zack Mulhall Wild West Show. There was one year's difference in the ages of Will and Tom, and the two men became great friends. It was at the fair that Will Rogers introduced a young girl of 14 to Tom Mix. Olive Stokes was an attractive young lady who would one day become Tom's third wife.

Will Rogers started down the road to fame at the World's Fair. During the show, a runaway steer from the Mulhall Wild West Show went up an aisle into the grandstand crowd. Will ran into the stands, twirling his rope, and caught the steer. He slid the steer down the aisle and back into the arena. When the announcer asked Will why he pulled the steer out of the grandstands, he replied, "He doesn't have a ticket." Stories about Will and the steer were widely publicized, and Flo Ziegfeld hired Will to spin his rope and tell his yarns at the Ziegfeld Follies.

For the World's Fair, the Mulhall Wild West Show combined with the Colonel Cummin's Show, and almost immediately a storm of jealousy and contention arose between the leaders of the two shows. It was at the 1904 World's Fair that Zack Mulhall shot three men in the midway. On June 18, 1904, the *Mulhall Enterprise* carried the following story:

> Zack Mulhall, livestock agent of the St. Louis and San Francisco railroad, tonight shot three men. One of them an innocent bystander named Ernest Morgan, is believed to have been fatally wounded. He was shot in the abdomen. The other men are Frank Reed, boss hostler of the Wild West Show, and Johnny Murray, one of the cowboys. They are being cared for at the emergency hospital set up on the Fairgrounds.
>
> The doctors say that Morgan will die. He lives in St. Louis and is 18 years old. Frank Reed, 50 years old, was shot in the arm and right side of the neck. Murray, 35 years old, was shot in the abdomen.
>
> The shooting was the culmination of trouble between Mulhall and Frank Reed over the question of authority. The shooting occurred at the entrance of the show just after the conclusion of the performance and while the Pike was crowded with people. Mulhall was locked up and bail was refused.

After the St. Louis World's Fair, Tom returned to Oklahoma City with the Oklahoma Cavalry Band, where they appeared at the Delmar Gardens. Tom stayed in Oklahoma City after the band left, but he had a hard time finding a job. As he put it, "I came down here with the band to appear at the old Delmar Gardens and I stayed after the band left. The only thing that I could find to do was be a bartender, and I was always trying to find something else to do."

Seth Bullock's Cowboy Brigade

In March 1905, Seth Bullock of Deadwood, South Dakota, formed the Cowboy Brigade to help celebrate the inauguration of President Theodore Roosevelt to a second term. The cowboys started at Edgemont, South Dakota, and traveled by train to Washington, D.C., and the White House. Tom joined the brigade in Omaha, Nebraska, as the train picked up horses and riders on its way east. The cowboys arrived in Washington on March 4, 1905, inauguration day. The Mulhall Wild West Show provided western entertainment for the president and his guests at the inauguration. For Tom, it was an opportunity to renew many of the friendships he had made in St. Louis at the World's Fair.

After the inauguration, Tom returned to Oklahoma City and his job at the bar on Robinson Avenue. Tom lived in the Perrine Hotel, and it was there that he first met Kitty Jewel Perrine, the owner's daughter. Tom and Kitty were soon engaged, but Tom postponed their marriage several times in hopes of finding better employment.

It was while tending bar that Tom finally got one of his big breaks. Early in 1905, Colonel Joe Miller overheard Tom complaining of the inside work and expressing his desire to work outdoors. Miller, along with his brothers George and Zack, owned and operated the famed Miller Brothers 101 Real Wild West Ranch near Bliss, Oklahoma. He had heard about Tom's expertise with horses and hired Tom to break horses and handle the livestock for the 101 Ranch Show when it was scheduled to appear at Madison Square Garden in New York in April 1905.

Breaking Horses for the 101 Ranch

Tom told how he was hired by the 101 Ranch in testimony given during his 1929 breach of contract suit with Zack Miller. In the trial transcripts, Tom recalled: "They [the 101 Ranch] had a Buffalo Chase in 1905 and I went up there and broke horses for the Oklahoma cowboys to ride. Earlier in 1905 [April], I went to Madison Square Garden, the old one, and Zack Miller was there and he made arrangements for me to come back to his Buffalo Chase, and I went back with him to the [101] Ranch." Tom was hired as a full-time cowboy for $15 per month, including room and board.

There is some question as to whether a runaway steer act was staged at the 1905 101 Ranch Show in Madison Square Garden. Some believe a steer was pushed under a rope fence near the grandstands; others say that

Opposite: **Tom Mix as drum major (back center) with Oklahoma Cavalry Band, 1905. (Courtesy of Western History Collections, University of Oklahoma Library.)**

what happened was a freak accident that was coincidentally similar to the
steer incident at the World's Fair. In any event, the *New York Herald* of
April 28, 1905, carried the following story:

> Panic prevailed at the afternoon performance of the horse fair at
> Madison Square Garden yesterday, when a wild Texas steer leaped out
> of the arena and climbed two flights of stairs. Tom Mixico, a celebrated
> rope thrower, ran up the 27th Street side and tried to head off the steer;
> he missed with his lasso, but caught an usher by the leg, bringing him
> down with a thud.

This time, the steer ran away.

Sam Henderson, noted Oklahoma writer, believes that Tom Mix used
the name Tom Mixico to avoid possible Army prosecution for his 1902
desertion. Tom may not have been aware that charges were never filed
against him by the army.

In 1905, the National Editor's Convention was held in Oklahoma
City. The 101 Ranch joined forces with the Colonel Zack Mulhall and
Pawnee Bill Wild West Shows to put on a great Buffalo Chase. Hundreds
of Indians were brought to the 101 Ranch to add to the authenticity of the
event. The editors and their friends were entertained at an arena set up
in the buffalo pasture on the 101 Ranch. Fifty-three trainloads of editors
and their guests came to the show, to swell attendance to over 60,000
people.

One of the big stunts for the show was to be an authentic Indian
buffalo hunt. Colonel Joe Miller had arranged to have Chief Geronimo
released from prison at nearby Fort Sill. The Indian chief was supposed to
shoot and kill a buffalo bull with a bow and arrow during the chase. He shot
the buffalo with an arrow, but the buffalo was still alive, and the enraged
animal nearly knocked Geronimo off his horse. Geronimo drew his rifle
from a saddle scabbard and shot the animal again. This time the frightened
animal headed for the arena fence next to the grandstands.

Before the angry animal could reach the crowd, Stack Lee, the world's
champion rifleman for the 101 Ranch, shot and killed the tormented
animal. Other buffaloes were killed during the chase and some of the more
"savage" Indians ate the raw flesh of the dead buffaloes, much to the
dismay of some of the editors and their guests. The remainder of the
carcasses were cooked and served in sandwiches to the editors later in the
day.

After landing the job with Miller, Tom and Kitty were married in the
Perrine Hotel on December 20, 1905. The Reverend Thomas H. Harper,
pastor of the Pilgrim Congregational Church, performed the ceremony.
H. M. Tittoin and Mrs. S. A. Eldridge were witnesses. Tom was 25 years
old and Kitty was 22.

Labor Camp Peace Officer

In the fall 1905 and spring of 1906, industrialist Lee Hunt of the Hunt Construction Company began building the Western States Cement Plant in Kansas. The town that sprang up where the plant was built was named Le Hunt. Ellis Soper was the construction engineer for Hunt and needed someone to restore law and order to the labor camp. By this time, Tom had built a reputation for keeping law and order in Oklahoma bars and bawdy houses such as the Blue Belle Saloon. Ellis Soper hired Tom and had him deputized as a labor camp peace officer. The construction of the cement plant was a vast enterprise involving a great deal of money.

The town of Le Hunt, Kansas, is now less than a ghost town. Only concrete rubble reminds residents of the one-time community that flourished and died in a nine-year period, from 1905 to 1913. In its heyday, Le Hunt had a large Portland Cement plant with rock crusher, 10 large rotary kilns, railroad access, two general stores, a 40-room hotel, a pool hall, a drugstore, 75 houses, and two-room school for 40 children, and medical care. Tom Mix was there when this early-twentieth-century local experiment started, and he was more than just a deputy sheriff.

When the cement plant was about two-thirds complete, local Independence, Kansas, reporters wrote:

> The Reporter representatives took dinner at the camp as guests of Major Thomas Mix (who had general supervision of the camp) and were surprised at the bill of fare. Few hotels set a better or cleaner table. It cost the company $10,000 to equip the cook house and arrange quarters for the men before a lick of work had been struck on the plant.
>
> Major Mix has adopted stringent rules to keep the camp clean and in good sanitary condition. The company hired Dr. Butler, who attends the men without charge. A hospital tent is equipped for the care of the sick and injured. A drug store, in charge of a registered pharmacist, furnishes medicines.

Le Hunt was a boomtown, a tent city that swelled to several times the local population. Gambling, drinking, knife fights, gunfights, thievery, and prostitution were common, but it was well known that Tom ruled the camp with an iron hand.

The only additional evidence of Tom's activities as a law enforcement officer in Le Hunt is found in a short Independence newspaper article dated April 23, 1906, which reads: "Deputy Sheriff Tom Mix arrested some 'woollies' at Le Hunt; they had made off with a horse and buggy and were drunk and hard to handle." One can only imagine what Tom may have done to bring these "hard to handle" boys in, but it is not difficult to believe that he could have handled any "woolly" that "got out of hand." Tom returned to the 101 Ranch after the spring of 1906 and worked there for the rest of the season.

What did Tom's wife, Kitty, think of Tom's work as a freelance lawman? She once confided to a friend, "If this is what it is like to be married, I don't much care for it."

Tom was again called upon by his old friend Ellis Soper to protect the interests of industrialist Lee Hunt when a new, Dixie Portland (later renamed Penn Dixie) Cement Company plant was built in Marion County, Tennessee. Richard Hardy was the founder and first president of the Dixie Portland Cement Company. Soper was his brother-in-law. Old-timers remembered that Tom Mix arrived on the site accompanied by Hardy and Soper.

Almost overnight another town sprang up not far from South Pittsburg, Tennessee. The town was named Richard City, after founder Richard Hardy, and incorporated in 1907. Again, new homes, a hospital, stores, and a school were built and a boomtown atmosphere flourished. Gamblers and prostitutes moved in, hoping to take advantage of the situation and creating additional work for law enforcement officers.

Again, Tom had several duties. He was a yard foreman, Richard City marshal, and the employment agent for foreign workers, who were mainly Greeks and Italians, who earned their living with picks and shovels, laying the foundations for most of the structures. They slept in so-called bull pens, long bunkhouses. One of Tom's coworkers remembered that "Tom broke horses, kept the peace, and never forgot his old friends once he became famous." Horses were brought in from Missouri and broken for the workers to ride; others were sold to the general public.

Tom's friends, such as Ben Case and Milo Hamill, say that Tom always wore a cowboy hat, carried a pearl-handled .45 six-gun, and occasionally wore chaps. Milo Hamill remembers Tom as "a very likable man, a man who had lots of friends." The date July 4, 1907, sticks in his mind: "Mix put on an exhibition that day with his wife (who lived in Richard City) using his pistol and rope. He also did some stunt riding." Milo does not recall much trouble at the time, but he remembers, "Some of the workers from Penn Dixie went to a movie downtown and started making trouble. N. J. Haskew, the chief of police, warned Mix that unless he could do something, the workers would have to be locked up. Tom talked to the men and herded them back to Penn Dixie," thereby defusing the situation. Ben Case, John "Cappy" Holden, and Maurice Patton, who were also expert horsemen, often rode the mountains with Tom. Case says, "Mix didn't stand for any foolishness. He tended to stick to his own business and expected everybody else to do the same." For the most part, Tom had a good disposition and usually wore a friendly smile. Tom returned to the 101 Ranch in mid-November 1907, where his star continued to rise.

Old friends recalled that Tom Mix and Tony returned to South Pittsburg in 1928, entertaining the children with gun twirling, rope spinning, and fancy horse stepping at the Richard Hardy Memorial School.

History of the 101 Ranch

The Miller Brothers' 101 Ranch was established by Colonel George Washington Miller in the late 1800s. His three sons, Joe, George, and Zack, managed and maintained the property. The 101 Ranch—which got its name from the Bar-O-Bar cattle brand—was 110,000 acres.

In the early days, at the end of a cattle drive, the cowboys would let off steam by staging various sports events that were later used in frontier day celebrations, Wild West shows, and rodeos. The 101 Wild West Shows developed as a natural sideline from these rodeo-type sporting events after the cattle business began to wane.

The Wild West shows were spectacular affairs, too large to be housed in a three-ring circus tent. The show featured as many as one thousand performers including troops of cowboys and Indians, covered wagons, stagecoaches, Russian Cossacks, musicians, and just about everything else imaginable. The shows were put on in open air arenas comparable in size to a modern football stadium. Grandstand seats were on one side of the arena and a row of tents housing animals, actors, coaches, and other paraphernalia were on the other side of the arena.

The Wild West show might consist of a historic enactment, cowboy and Indian battle, horse-thief act, sharpshooting act, trick ropers, or a buffalo hunt. Rodeo events such as bulldogging, bronco riding, and steer roping were also staged. At first the shows were put on to help stimulate the cattle business. Later, the shows became a big business in themselves.

Buffalo were kept on the 101 Ranch as an additional drawing card for the ranch and nearby Ponca City. The buffalo pens at the 101 Ranch became a routine stop for the Santa Fe Railroad line. When the Santa Fe passenger train was due to arrive, the cowboys at the ranch would herd the buffalo from their pastures to specially built pens near the tracks, where the passengers from the train could stop to see what a real ranch was like.

Tom worked his first season for the 101 Wild West Ranch in 1906. His initial job was to break horses, which was a profitable business, and act as a host for "dude" cowboys and cowgirls on summer vacation from the East, Tom looked the part and he proved to be an excellent host for the 101 Ranch.

The cowboys who worked for the 101 Ranch were a rough bunch. They worked hard, played hard, and occasionally fought hard. They were the type of fellows who would trip you coming out of the bunkhouse in order to beat you to the chow hall table. If you made it to the table, you still weren't safe—you had to make sure one of your "buddies" didn't slip your chair out from under you before you could sit down. And, if this were not bad enough, you might be punched in the mouth if you tried to beat someone else to a second helping of chow.

The 101 Ranch was not the ideal place for a young married couple. Many of the ranch hands never knew that Tom was married when he came to work there. They did know that he dated a particular girl quite frequently. In any event, Tom and Kitty could not make a go of it, and they divorced. Kitty had not liked being married to a roustabout cowboy and freelance lawman, and Tom had no intentions of settling down and starting a family.

After the divorce, Tom turned his attentions to Lucille Mulhall, champion cowgirl of the Mulhall Wild West Show. Colonel Zack Mulhall, Lucille's father, did not approve of the roustabout cowboy either, so he ran Tom off at gunpoint. Mulhall thought that a friend of his, a millionaire from Burkburnett, Texas, would make a much better husband for Lucille. He was probably right.

The sport of bulldogging was invented by Bill Pickett, a black cowboy, and differed somewhat from the present-day rodeo event. The cowboy would ride after the steer, lean out of the saddle, grab the steer by the horns from behind, then twist its head around, trip it to throw it to the ground, and bite the animal's top lip to hold him in the throw position. Using only his teeth, the cowboy had to hold the steer down for the prescribed period of time, sometimes several minutes in the early days. The biting and holding action led to the name of bulldogging. In 1907, Lon Sealy became the first white bulldogger for the 101 Ranch, and Scout Maish became the second.

At first Tom played only a minor role in the Miller Brothers' Wild West Show. Sometimes he was the dragman in the horse thief act. The "good guys" would hook a rope to a steel eye in the back of Tom's heavy leather jacket, pull him from the horse, and drag him around the arena in front of the spectators. This roughhouse activity became a preview of the day when Tom would perform his own dangerous stunts for the silver screen. He was an expert at breaking horses and handling livestock, and he soon mastered the new rodeo sports such as bulldogging and steer wrestling.

Night Marshal of Dewey

Shortly after coming to work for the 101 Ranch, Tom made Dewey, Oklahoma, his home. For a short time, he also worked at the cement plant there.

Oklahoma became the 46th state on November 16, 1907, and documentary evidence shows Tom Mix was a deputy sheriff and night marshal in Dewey, Washington County, Oklahoma in 1908. Tom knew Mayor Earl Woodward and Joe Bartles, the head of the Republican organization in Dewey. Both Bartles and Woodward were rodeo promoters. The mayor asked Tom if he would consider accepting a position as night marshal in Dewey, and Joe Bartles used his influence to help Tom get the job. Dewey was always peaceful and quiet during the day, but at night the gamblers and bootleggers were a problem. Since Tom had no immediate commitments, he accepted a deputy sheriff's commission under Sheriff John Jordan, the Cherokee lawman. Sheriff Jordan had a son, Sid, who was also a deputy sheriff. Sid was a first-rate cowhand who worked with his father for a number of years as a law enforcement officer.

Tom's duties as night marshal were to curb the cheating and gambling by local and traveling card men. Instead of closing the gambling games down, Tom insisted that they be run by honest men, and he proposed that fines collected for cheating be used to help build and maintain the town.

The scope and extent of Tom's work in helping to clamp down on bootleggers in 1908 is best described in the following story. The story appears to have been written in 1920, shortly after the national amendment on prohibition was adopted. The Fox Film Studios used the story as publicity for Tom Mix films such as *The Coming of the Law.*

Fe-Fi-Fo-Fum! I Smell Smuggled Rum
by Tom Mix

Every time I think of prohibition, I feel like a man who is living in the past. Having subscribed to a reserved seat on the water-wagon myself, I have no personal grudge against the constitutional amendment. But, I don't believe in coercing others.

But, I can't help laughing. I start thinking of the wily old foxes who will make life miserable for the law enforcement officers. No matter how watchful these officers may be, some folks are going to keep secret meetings with old John Barleycorn. The constitutional amendment won't make the slightest difference in their habits, except that they will work in the dark. The amendment has forbidden old John Barleycorn to remain in the country. Well, the lovers of the bottle will hide him, even if it means playing dozens of tricks on the law enforcement officers.

I know what I'm talking about. I was an enforcement officer myself once upon a time. Whew, it was a hard job! It was a great job too, because it meant being alert all the time. I tell you the bootleggers led me on a fine chase in those early days in Dewey, Oklahoma.

You know, when that roaring western country became a state, liquor was barred. It was up to me, the law enforcement officer, to help bar it. I think I did help some; but it also required the help of plenty of nerve and six shooters. The schemes that were tried in Oklahoma were many and varied.

Railroad trains, naturally, were ideal hiding places for the demon rum. We used to hold up the trains regularly to find out if there was any booze aboard. So expert did we become in detecting the presence of anything stronger than water that we could walk through a car and learn whether any bottles were concealed in grips, merely by kicking them. You know how a fellow can feel a letter and tell you whether it contains a greenback? Well, that's how expert we became in sighting bottles through leather and carpet bags.

Often the fellows tried to bring the stuff in small casks concealed in trunks. They soon stopped that, because all we had to do was turn a trunk over quickly and then put an ear to it. Oh boys!, we knew the sound of trickling liquor hundreds of feet away. Its gurgling warble is unmistakable!

It is easy enough to tell by a man's face whether he has liquor inside of him. But, I learned the art of telling by a man's face whether he had liquor on him or was more remotely connected with liquor in the baggage car. It's a great sport, finding a "liquor conscience" reflected in a "liquor face."

Another stunt they used to try on trains was to have a couple of bottles in grips. They would come into the car and say to some innocent looking duffer, or some sweet-faced old woman, "May I leave my bag here for a moment?" Then, they would disappear until it was time for them to leave the train. But even that did not work because the person with whom the bag was left disclaimed it the moment the officer asked about it.

We also kept an eagle eye on the trunks that were sent to Dewey. The most innocent looking wardrobe trunk, belonging to the leading lady of the circus, was examined. Many is the time such innocent looking trunks, when tipped over, revealed the presence of liquor. What did we do with those trunks? We cut a hole in the side, allowed the liquor to flow out of the opening, and then let the trunk travel on to its destination.

I had so many odd ways of detecting booze that for a time in Dewey they called me "Pussyfoot Mix."

You can imagine the ingenious stunts that will be practiced under the nation-wide prohibition law. Finally, of course, it will be enforced, but not before the wily old foxes have had their fling at foiling prohibition.

Billy Jenkins, who later became known as "the German Buffalo Bill," was one of Tom's sidekicks at the 101 Ranch and paid a great tribute to Tom as an early law enforcement officer when he said: "Tom Mix was a fighter. Mercilessly he took up the cause of law and order. No wonder he was repeatedly employed as a sheriff at the roughest places in the then Far West. This was no soft job at all that I experienced myself when I was once his deputy in Oklahoma. During all my life I never have had a better friend than Tom. His word was held in high esteem. You could rely on him no matter how difficult and dangerous the situation was."

Champion All-Around Cowboy

By 1908, Tom had improved his overall image as a cowboy and became the 101 Ranch Champion All-Around Cowboy or King of the Cowboys. Tom, as well as other famous cowboys, continued acting as hosts for the 101 Ranch during the summer of 1908, when E. W. Marland came to inspect the property. Marland came to the ranch from Pennsylvania after learning about Oklahoma oil leases from a nephew. He had made over a million dollars with the discovery of the Congo Oil Field in West Virginia, although he lost it in the business panic of 1907.

While at the 101 Ranch, Marland collected samples of rock and shale, looking for signs of oil deposits. He found what he was looking for, formed the Marland Oil Company, and became known as "the Patriarch of Ponca City." George Miller, founder of the 101 Ranch, had convinced White Eagle, the stern chief of the Ponca Tribe, to allow Marland to drill for oil on Indian land near Miller's ranch. This company later became the 101 Oil Company and, finally, Conoco. The familiar red triangle trademark, inspired by Marland's Masonic ring, has survived to this day. As a result of the 101 oil finding, Marland made an estimated $85 million. Tom was now earning $35 a month at the ranch and never considered investing in the venture.

In December 1908, after Tom finished his third season with the 101 Ranch Wild West Show, he went to Dewey, Oklahoma, to see Olive Stokes. Olive had gone to Medora, North Dakota, to buy horses for her parents' ranch. Luke Bells, a foreman for the Stokes's Ranch, and Tom took a train to Medora to help Olive select the animals. Tom and Olive had a wonderful time together that Christmas. Olive stayed at the ranch of Nels and Katrine Nichols, who were friends of the Stokes family. After a farewell dance held in Olive's honor, Olive and Tom were married by Nels Nichols, a justice of the peace. Tom and Olive were married on January 19, 1909, and the newlyweds went to Miles City, Montana, for their honeymoon.

After their wedding trip, Tom and Olive joined the Widerman Wild West Show in Amarillo, Texas. Tom's roping act was one of the top attractions. Unlike most cowboys, who used a 40-foot rope with a 25-foot reach, Tom used a 60-foot rope with a 40-foot reach. Things perked along fine until Tom asked Widerman for a raise and Widerman refused. Tom and Olive decided to quit the show in Denver and organize their own show in Seattle, Washington.

A Wild West Show of His Own

Tom and Olive went to Seattle, where they hired a troop of 60 actors and performers. Charles Tipton and Ezra Black, friends of Tom, joined the show in Seattle. The Alaska-Yukon-Pacific Exposition was being held in Seattle that year, and Tom's plan was to catch the overflow crowds. They rented the Western Washington Fairgrounds and put on their own Wild West show, which included a "Days of Olde" jousting act and mock battle with about 40 Blackfoot Indians.

A publicity photo taken of Tom with a downed steer bore the caption, "Tom Mix, Champion Steer Thrower, A.Y.P.E., Seattle, Was. 1909."

Business proved good when the weather was favorable, but the crowds failed to turn out when it was bad. The show was successful enough that three men attempted to rob Tom and Olive as the show was about to close. They foiled the attempt, but Tom was wounded in the hand during the fracas.

Shortly after Tom and Olive concluded their show in Seattle, they received a letter from an old friend, Will A. Dickey, asking them to meet him in Flemington, Missouri, to make a few western films. Tom was receptive to the idea, and he and Olive headed to Cheyenne, Wyoming, to take part in the Cheyenne Frontier Days celebration, a two-day event, before joining Dickey in Flemington.

The Cheyenne Frontier Days celebration consisted of calf roping, bulldogging, bronco and steer riding, a cowgirl relay race, an Indian squaw race, a cowboy pony race, wild horse races, and military maneuvers. Tom entered the calf roping and bronco riding contests. In the bronco riding contest, Tom drew an "outlaw horse" named Sabile, known for his wicked twists, turns, bucks, and jumps that threw most riders off in the first couple of jumps.

Charlie Irwin, the show's producer, did not think Tom or anyone else could ride Sabile for three jumps, so Olive made a side bet with Charlie for $500. Sabile did everything he could to throw Tom, but Tom stuck to his back like glue and before the ride ended, Sabile was running instead of bucking. In the end, Tom made $100 for winning the event and Olive made $500 on her side bet with Charlie. Later, Charlie Irwin became good friends with Tom and Olive.

It was also at about this time that oil was discovered on the Stokes Ranch in Oklahoma and Olive received her first government check for royalties. Olive, known as "Ollie" by her friends, was well liked by most of Tom's friends because she was "just one of the guys," and she accompanied Tom almost everywhere.

Some western writers believe that Tom completed a stint as a labor camp peace officer during the construction of the Two Buttes Reservoir in Colorado in 1909. However, there appears to be no documentary evidence to confirm his law enforcement activities there.

Tom and Sam Garrett joined the Mulhall Wild West Show in 1910. Sam remembers that Tom was arrested when the show appeared in Knoxville, Tennessee, and was taken back to Oklahoma. It seems that Tom borrowed a horse from the 101 Ranch to enter a rodeo, was injured in the rodeo, and left the horse at the nearby Mulhall Ranch. Supposedly, the horse disappeared and Tom was charged with embezzlement on a trumped-up

Opposite: **Tom Mix, second from left, and his Wild West troupe at the 1909 Alaska-Yukon-Pacific Exposition, 1909. (Courtesy of Dan Hutchins.)**

horse-theft charge. Bond was set at $1,000 but was never paid. Zack Miller was the overzealous head of the Cattleman's Association and wanted to make a name for himself, so he accused Tom of being a horse thief. The Kay County Court knew Zack Miller and never took the charges seriously. Tom, in the hospital at the time, was cleared of all charges. However, to soothe Miller's feelings, Tom agreed to appear with the Miller Brothers' Show when it wintered in Mexico City.

While in Mexico City in 1910, Tom Mix, Stack Lee, and Bill Pickett staged the same stunt that started Will Rogers on the road to fame. The show was held in a Mexican bullfight ring and Tom and Stack turned a bull loose in the grandstands. Bill Pickett, with the aid of his pony, roped the bull and dragged it from the grandstands before it could do any damage.

When the action started, the Miller brothers quickly got up a bet with some Mexican officials that Pickett could not hold the steer in the thrown position for a full five minutes. It turned out that Pickett held the bull for seven and a half minutes, and the stunt allegedly netted the Miller boys $53,000. No one knows what Tom's share of the loot was, but he probably got a bonus that year.

In 1911, Jack Cleo Baskin and a Mexican boy named Machacha were mascots of the 101 Wild West Show. Jack was 10 years old at the time, and both boys lived on 101 Ranch property. Jack's cousin, Mabel Pettyjohn, of Red Rock, Oklahoma, married Colonel Zack Miller in 1906. Machacha had been adopted by Zack and Mabel when the show wintered in Mexico City in 1910. Machacha's parents had been lion tamers for a Mexican circus and were killed by the lions during one of their acts. One of Machacha's arms had been mangled by the lions when he attempted to pull his parents through the cage bars.

Jack and Machacha frequently played near the buffalo pens next to the Santa Fe railroad. On this particular day, the boys were out riding their Shetland ponies and decided to dismount and coax a small buffalo calf to a large alfalfa haystack in order to give him some better hay. The calf frequently crawled under the fence to browse around, anyway.

The mother buffalo became infuriated when she saw the boys pulling and tugging on her calf. In a fit of rage, she knocked down the gate of the pen and charged the boys, who hightailed it to the alfalfa stack with the buffalo cow close behind. Tom Mix, Stack Lee, and Bill Pickett, who were touring tenderfeet around the buffalo grounds, saw that the boys were in trouble.

Stack Lee wanted to shoot the cow, but Tom said, "No, we'll rope her." Tom and Bill roped the cow and her calf and pulled them back to the buffalo pens. Stack had placed himself between the angry cow and the boys. When the episode was over, the three men made temporary repairs to the gate as the boys looked on admiringly at their instant heroes.

Later, the Wild West shows took to the road and toured the United States, Canada, and Mexico. Each show had its list of "world champions." Lucille Mulhall became the Champion Cowgirl for the Mulhall Wild West Show. Bill Pickett, the cowboy who invented the sport of bulldogging, was the Champion Bulldogger for the 101 Ranch Wild West Show. Stack Lee was the Champion Rifleman, and Tom Mix was the Champion All-Around Cowboy. Tom continued to work as an active lawman in Dewey through 1912, before he hung up his marshal's star to become a regular Selig player and spend most of his time making motion pictures.

During the 1909–17 period, the 101 Ranch became the proving grounds for aspiring motion picture stars. Colonel William N. Selig of the Selig Polyscope Company out of Chicago and other movie pioneers used the ranch as a western locale. Some of the ranch's alumni were Tom Mix, Will Rogers, Ed Echols, Buck Jones, Hoot Gibson, Bill Pickett, Milt Hinkle, Pat Chrisman, Ken Maynard, Jack Webb, Billy Jenkins (Eric Rosenthal), and Tex Cooper. While the sheriff's posse hunted the hills for outlaws, the early motion picture pioneers were making films on the 101 Ranch, featuring former outlaws and 101 cowboys turned movie stars.

The Miller Brothers were well aware of how successful Will A. Dickey's connection had become with the Selig Polyscope Company and they courted the Bison Studios near Santa Monica, California. In 1912, the same year that Hoot Gibson became the Champion All-Around Cowboy for the 101 Ranch, the Miller Brothers offered to rent livestock and personnel to the Bison Studios. Some of the regulars for Bison Studios were A. R. "Rawhide Reckon" Sutton, Vess Pegg, and Jack Mulhall. But the real star of the show always turned out to be Rose Helen Wenger, who three years later became Hoot Gibson's wife.

Mythical Law Enforcement Adventures

There have been many stories published claiming that Tom Mix was a sheriff of Montgomery County, in western Kansas; Washington County, in Oklahoma; and Two Buttes, Colorado; city marshal of Dewey, Oklahoma; special enforcement officer in Oklahoma; marshal in Montana, New Mexico, and Arizona; and a Texas Ranger. Although most of the stories seem to be highly exaggerated, there is more than a grain of truth to some of them. The problem lies separating fact from fantasy. Tom was an expert horseman and excellent shot with both rifle and pistol. His services very well could have been enlisted by various law enforcement agencies.

As an Oklahoma bartender around the turn of the century, Tom was also in a good position to meet, talk with, and gather information on outlaws who frequently crossed state lines to avoid pursuit. Many of these outlaws were considered folk heroes by the local population, if not by law enforcement officers. Tom's work with Wild West shows and early movie producers was highly seasonal in nature and left considerable time for him to act as a local law enforcement officer. Tom appears to have worked as a bartender, Wild West show performer, peace officer, and budding Selig star at various times in a 10-year period from 1903 to 1913.

On September 22, 1905, Tom allegedly meandered down to Waco, Texas, and signed up with Company B of the Texas Rangers. Tom gave his birthplace as El Paso, Texas, and his occupation as ranchman. He enlisted under W. W. Sterling, adjutant general, and Tom R. Hickman, captain of the Ranger Force. Tom probably pulled a few strings to get a certificate with a perpetual enlistment. Sterling was reputed to have been a friend of Tom's and a former Wild West show performer. The date on the certificate appears to be forged and is dated about the same time as Tom joined Ellis Soper as a labor camp peace officer in Kansas.

In the February 1925 *Photoplay* autobiographical story, Tom tells how as a New Mexico marshal he single-handedly captured the notorious Shonts Brothers, cattle rustlers who spread death and destruction through Texas and New Mexico. There was a $750 reward for their capture, and they were holed up in a dugout in the Capitan Mountains. Snow was falling as Tom quietly made his way into the corral next to their dugout. Tom tried to arrest the first brother when he came out to water the stock in the morning, but he went for his gun, despite the fact that Tom had the drop on him. Tom wounded him seriously, and the second Shonts Brother came running out of the dugout when he heard the shots; he was blinded by the bright snow and sun and he fired in Tom's general direction. Tom returned the fire and hit him in the leg. Then he dragged both brothers back to the dugout and waited four days for his posse to arrive. Tom gave the $750 reward to the mother of the Shonts boys, a good woman who was unaware of her sons' misdeeds. Tom had arrested and locked up the two sons who were her sole support.

Tom tells the story of how as an Arizona sheriff he was chasing a train robber and murderer when he was shot in the back by the bandit's wife, an Indian woman with a shotgun. Tom had trailed the bandit to his hideout, captured him, and tied him to his horse when the woman came up from behind, firing the shot that ripped a long furrow down Tom's back. When Tom was knocked to the ground, both the Indian woman and tied-up bandit escaped. Tom deputized a friend and found the bandit a short time later, still securely tied to his horse.

Tom says he was a sheriff in Two Buttes, Colorado, when he brought a clever cattle rustler named Blair and some of his Mexican ranch hands to justice. Blair owned a small cattle ranch named the Lone Tree. When Tom thought he had enough evidence to arrest Blair, he went to the ranch. As he arrived, Tom was shot by Blair from ambush with a shotgun loaded with buckshot. Tom put an end to Blair with his six-gun as Blair cautiously approached to check Tom's "lifeless" body. Tom's faithful horse during this period of his life was Old Blue.

Tom seems to contradict himself in a 1932 article entitled "Bad Men I Have Beaten," by Tom Mix. In this story, Tom tells how he and his faithful horse, Star, first ran into the Shonts Brothers when Tom was a Texas Ranger. He found the two brothers in a saloon that they planned to hold up that afternoon. As soon as they saw Tom, they shot at him and barricaded themselves in the saloon. It took Tom and his men 10 minutes to break down the door and, in the meantime, the men escaped. Tom trailed them to a rough log hut built against the side of a mountain.

As he approached the door of the log cabin, he heard a shot fired behind him and remembers his left shoulder feeling as if someone had stuck it with a red-hot poker. He pulled open the door of the cabin and rushed inside. As he did, he caught the face of an Indian woman with a smoking gun at her shoulder. As Tom rushed in, both Shonts boys fired at him. One missed, the other blew his hat off. Tom fired simultaneously, hitting Al Shonts in the shoulder, putting him out of action. The second Shonts brother rushed him and the two were soon locked in a life-and-death struggle. Finally, Pete Shonts passed out; Tom had choked him into unconsciousness. Tom tied up both of the brothers as the old woman escaped on foot. Tom started walking the boys out of the mountains on the end of a rope when he was met by the other members of his Ranger company.

This time in Two Buttes, Colorado, Sheriff Tom Mix brought Dandy Tex O'Dowd to justice. On the surface, Tex was a respectable rancher who liked to gamble. He always seemed to have more money than his spread seemed capable of earning, however. His two boys were also absent many evenings, and prime cattle always seemed to disappear when the boys were out of town. Tom began to observe the ranch and the comings and goings of Tex and his boys.

One night as Tom was watching the O'Dowd gang rustle some prime cattle, he sent Star, his range pony, back to the sheriff's station to round up help. Finally, the boys were ready to leave, but the posse had not arrived yet. Tom jumped out of the darkness and shouted to the gang, "Hands up!" They answered Tom with pistol and shotgun fire. This time, buckshot ripped into Tom's right shoulder. Tom fired his pistols, dropping one or two of the rustlers in their tracks. At about the time that Tom thought the gang was going to finish him off, his posse came to the rescue. Dandy Tex O'Dowd had built a secret corral at Lone Tree.

Tom claims he was a government marshal in Arizona when Joe Creedy, half Apache, swore to kill the next marshal he came across because a marshal had once produced evidence that had sent him to the penitentiary. Later, a cowboy came to Tom claiming that one of their hands had been filled full of lead at the Arrowhead Ranch, Boss Kinney's outfit. The cowboy offered to act as a guide and take Tom out to the ranch. Since most of the deputies were out at the time, Tom took the only deputy he had, an English lad named Jim Wilson, nicknamed Molly because of his innocent face.

As they rode through a cleft in the rocks, shots rang out and the traitorous guide galloped off into the darkness. Tom and Molly tried to make their way to higher ground, but Tom was shot in the left bicep during an exchange of gunfire. As they were about to be surrounded, Molly shouted, "This way, boys." Then other rangers appeared to answer his call. Creedy's gang of seven or eight men, believing themselves surrounded, jumped down into the rock basin, surrendering themselves to Tom and Molly. It turned out that Molly was a ventriloquist—there were no other rangers.

There is one more version of the Shonts Brothers' story worth retelling. It appears in Olive Stokes Mix's book, *The Fabulous Tom Mix*. This time, the notorious Shonts Brothers brought death and destruction to eastern Oklahoma.

Tom was serving as an honorary deputy sheriff when he tracked them to a Mexican woman's sod hut deep in the prairie. Tom waited patiently in a mesquite corral until one of the brothers emerged at daylight to feed the horses. Tom shouted, "Get your hands up!" but Shontz went for his gun, and both men fired simultaneously. Tom was shot in the knee as the first Shontz brother dropped to the ground, dead.

The second Shontz brother rushed out of the hut, firing at Tom. Tom shot him in the leg. In a great deal of pain, he managed to get the younger Shontz brother onto his horse.

As Tom was strapping the younger Shontz to his saddle, a Mexican woman came out of the hut with a double-barreled shotgun. She blazed away at Tom, riddling his back with pellets. Tom managed to get the younger Shontz brother back to town, where he spent many years in prison.

The reward for the capture of the Shontz brothers was $2,500 which Tom turned over to the bereaved mother, a fine old lady whose life had been turned into horror from worry over her outlaw sons.

Curiously, this version of the Shontz Brothers' saga was related to Olive, Tom's third wife, in a letter from Tom's mother, who had lived her entire life in Pennsylvania. Olive, who spent a large portion of her own life in Oklahoma, seems to have had no firsthand knowledge of the story or events surrounding it.

Texas seems to have forgotten about the Shonts Brothers in general and Tom Mix in particular. With regards to the incident, former governor and secretary of the treasury John Connally wrote: "Tom Mix was never employed as a Texas Ranger, in fact, he was never a resident of the State of Texas. It is my information, however, that he did hold an Honorary Ranger Commission that was given to him by Governor James V. Allred." Allred was governor of Texas from 1935 to 1939.

However, in June 1992, a new convention center was built in Austin, the capital of Texas. On the west side of the building, a Walkway of Stars was paved to honor the famous native sons of Texas. And there, along with former president Lyndon B. Johnson and some of the astronauts, is Tom Mix, one of Texas's famous sons—and so the legend continues to flourish.

Stories crediting Tom with being a former deputy United States Marshal are equally puzzling. Tom was billed as such in the picture *Ranch Life in the Great Southwest*, a 1910 Selig documentary. However, there is no evidence to indicate Tom was anything more than a city marshal or deputy sheriff. These were sufficiently tough jobs in themselves at the turn of the century. Regarding inquiries about Tom's career as a deputy United States Marshal, archivist Robert H. Bahmer of the National Archives and Records Service replied:

> An examination of the pertinent records in the National Archives has revealed no reference to any service by Tom Mix as a deputy United States Marshal, in Oklahoma or elsewhere. The chief records examined were the records of the Department of Justice that relate to the services of deputy United States Marshals in the Eastern District of Oklahoma, 1908–1921; Oklahoma Territory, 1896–1907; Colorado 1896–1912; the various districts of Indian Territory, 1896–1907; Kansas, 1896–1912; Wyoming, 1896–1912; and New Mexico, 1896–1912. These are the areas in which persons who previously have written to us about Tom Mix indicated that he may have been a deputy United States Marshal.

This letter does not rule out the possibility that Tom may have been deputized by a United States Marshal to help clean up a gang of local outlaws in Oklahoma or elsewhere. Tom had a deputy United States Marshal certificate, probably honorary in nature, issued by J. R. Wright on March 15, 1934.

Wounded in Action?

A question frequently asked is how many times Tom Mix was wounded in his job as sheriff or law enforcement officer. According to the *New York Times*, "Tom Mix was critically wounded four times; and, at the time of his death, still had three slugs in him as mementos of his law enforcement days."

A former circus aide of Tom's once told me: "One evening, Tom took off his shirt and showed me 21 different knife and bullet wounds where he had been hit in his job as sheriff. They were all in his upper torso, and he explained in great detail how he acquired them. Tom explained, that in his opinion, a bullet was more merciful than a knife—it was like a tiny hot wire searing the flesh." Later, a chart showing Tom's wounds was published for Ralston Straight Shooters.

Stories about Tom being wounded have undoubtedly been exaggerated by various publicity agents. However, in all probability, Tom was shot, accidentally or deliberately, a number of times. Many of the scars on his upper torso probably resulted from wounds inflicted during his career as a Wild West show performer and motion picture star. Tom's back, for example, was badly torn up by a premature dynamite explosion during the filming of a William Fox feature. In Tom's own book, *Roping a Million*, Tom claimed he made over 370 films and never used a double. As a result of doing his own falls, he had to have over 150 stitches sewn into his hide, not to mention the 33 broken bones and cracked ribs he had suffered.

Chapter 4

Early Selig Films

Sid Jordan and Tom Mix, former deputy sheriffs from Dewey, Oklahoma, became trusting friends for the greater part of their lives. Sid was a cowpuncher born in Muskogee, Oklahoma, and educated at the Vanita Oklahoma Indian School. Sid and Tom both worked for the 101 Ranch and in 1913, Sid joined Tom while Tom was making pictures for Selig in Prescott, Arizona.

Flemington, Missouri

According to Olive, Selig made most of his money in westerns. Their first movie was to be a two-reel Selig epic titled *The Range Rider,* filmed in Flemington, Missouri. Selig's first unofficial western star was George "Bronco Billy" Anderson, who made *The Great Train Robbery* in 1903. Anderson had recently left Selig to start his own production company, which turned out to be a bad move on his part. Because of Tom's experience breaking horses and bringing outlaws to justice, Selig thought Tom could bring authenticity to the screen.

Even in this early age of movies, the plot for a good western story had already been formulated. The cowboy was the good guy and hero, the villain was the bad guy, and the leading lady was the ranch foreman's daughter, who had to be rescued from the clutches of evil. In the end, Goodness always triumphed over Evil, and the cowboy won the hand of the ranch foreman's daughter as his reward. In *The Range Rider,* Tom was the good guy, William V. Mong was the bad guy, and Myrtle Stedman was the damsel in distress. Tom did all of his own stunts in the movie, which favorably impressed both Selig's director and Will A. Dickey.

There is a little controversy as to which film was Tom's first motion picture for the Selig Polyscope Company of Chicago. Some people believe that *Ranch Life in the Great Southwest* was Tom's first film; Johnny Mullins, who also appeared in that movie, recalls that *Ranch Life* was also made in Flemington in 1909. Tom was filmed bronco busting and bulldogging a steer, and Olive roped a calf.

According to Harvey Hazeleaf, a clarinet player for Will A. Dickey's Circle D Wild West and Indian Congress, a number of Selig films were made along the Des Plaines River, near Chicago, in 1909. Most of the cowmen with the Dickey show were from Montana. The one rider from Oklahoma, who was hired to handle the show stock and throw a rope if an animal got out of hand, was Tom Mix. Hazeleaf recalled:

> Tom Mix used to chum around some with our bunch, but you could never say he believed in tooting his own horn. Ask him a question, and he'd answer it honestly, though he wasn't much on volunteering information about his past.
>
> His wife, Olive Stokes Mix, was with the Dickey outfit too. They were married before the show opened in January.
>
> We made at least a half-dozen films along the Des Plains (river), some titles included *Up San Juan Hill, The Millionaire Cowboy, An Indian Wife's Devotion,* and *Briton and Boer.* All were short films, for which Selig was noted.

Students of western films should exercise extreme caution when it comes to determining the release dates of early movies; the dates they were advertised or appeared in local newspapers may or may not be close to the date they were released by the film company. Also, the working title of a film may bear little or no resemblance to the title of the released film. It is possible that it might take one month to produce a short film and an additional six months to bring it to market. Then it could remain in circulation for another six months or more. Even a one-reel Selig western might have been seen in a theater a year or more after its official release date.

Also, after some popular movie personalities like Tom gained fame, their movies were re-released at a much later date under the original title or a new title. For example, *Single-Shot Parker* was combined with *The Heart of Texas Ryan* and re-released by Exclusive Films after Tom left the Selig company.

After making films in Flemington, Tom and Olive went to Medora, North Dakota, for rest and relaxation with their old friends Nels and Katrine Nichols. After the visit, Tom joined Bill McCarty to help with the fall roundup.

Tom was elected head of the drovers by the ranchers, made roundup assignments, checked out the provisions, and then he and 50 men, with half-a-dozen wagons, set out on the roundup with five hundred head of horses. The 16-hour days in the saddle required frequent horse changes. The men rounded up strays, branded new calves, and separated the herd by brand; it was a cooperative effort. The roundup was successful, with only a couple of minor stampedes and no major injuries.

First Selig Contract

In 1910, Tom signed his first film contract with Selig. Tom had no visions of becoming a great movie star, and he reluctantly signed the contract because he felt the movies provided a better, more steady source of income than the ranch (Wild West) shows. However, if Tom lacked enthusiasm in the movies, Will A. Dickey certainly did not. Dickey said, "Westerns are the biggest moneymakers. The romance of American life comes right out of what happened in the winning of the West." American films were soon being shipped abroad, and foreign audiences were thrilled by the reenactments of the winning of the West—a unique American experience.

Tom made about 12 films for Selig in 1910 and according to Olive, *The Range Rider* was barely released by this time. Tom and Olive did some bit parts in Chicago while they waited for the script to Tom's next western film, which was filmed in Tennessee. In that film, Tom's most dangerous scene occurred when he jumped his horse off a 30-foot cliff into a lake; Tom broke one tooth and two ribs. Tom's western film career was off and running.

Shortly ater making the Tennessee film, Tom appeared as a star performer with Zack Mulhall at the Appalachian Exposition in Roseville, Tennessee. Theodore Roosevelt was in the audience at this performance of the Mulhall Wild West Show and chatted with Tom after he had made his grand entrance. The audience was thrilled to see Teddy talking with his old friend, Tom. After the show, Tom and Olive dined with Roosevelt, and Roosevelt presented them with an autographed set of his volumes *The Winning of the West.*

Tom's next films were shot in Florida with leading lady Kathlyn Williams. The Florida films were probably shot at Selig's permanent studio in Florida; Selig also had a permanent studio in Prescott, Arizona, known as the Diamond S Ranch.

Kathlyn Williams was the first serial queen of the silents. Her series was the forerunner to later, more popular serials such as *The Perils of Pauline.* In Florida, Tom Persons was the animal trainer hired for jungle films; he also owned one elephant, one camel, one lion, and three leopards.

During the filming of the movie, a leopard had been trained to pounce on a chicken. However, a gust of wind caught Kathlyn's long blond hair, and the leopard was distracted and pounced on Kathlyn. She was knocked to the ground and scared speechless as the leopard towered over her, waiting for her next, and perhaps last, move.

Tom told Kathlyn to lie perfectly still as he quietly drew his revolver. Tom fired one shot, killing the leopard instantly. Kathlyn was badly shaken but uninjured except for a few scratches. The movie camera had captured

A young Tom Mix as a regular Selig player. Tom had a long way to go to perfect his image as "the Good Guy in the White Hat." (Author's collection.)

the unplanned adventure on film, and the scene turned out to be one of the film's highlights. This movie could be either *Taming Wild Animals, Lost in the Jungle, Back to the Primitive,* or *Rescued by Her Lions,* part of *The Adventures of Kathlyn* or the *Captain Kate* series.

In her book *The Fabulous Tom Mix,* Olive describes her feelings about that first hectic year under contract to Selig: "After we left Florida, we hopped around various states for the filming of the [remaining] moving pictures Tom made for Selig in 1910. I was constantly packing and unpacking, it seemed, but at least we always spent from two weeks to a month in each location. We would have moved much more frequently had we been involved in ranch shows [Wild West shows] that year." Olive creates the impression that only one film was made in each of several locations. However, I believe that more than one film was probably made at each location.

Tom's contract came to an end in 1910 and no effort was made to renew it. Tom could not understand why because he felt his films were quite popular and well received at the box office. What Tom did not realize was that Selig and other major movie producers were still embroiled in litigation with Edison on patent rights infringements. This led to the formation of "the Trust," an alliance formed to help alleviate patent litigation.

According to the Pike National Forest file, Tom also worked for a short time as a cowhand for the Crescent Cattle Company at Four Mile Ranch in 1910. The company owned land all over South Park, in the Four Mile country, and in the Divide country.

Canon City, Colorado

Early in 1911, Selig asked Tom to come to Chicago to sign a new contract, which he did. The traveling western film crew of William Duncan, Myrtle Stedman, Josephine West, Joe Ryan, and Tom Carrigan left for Canon City, Colorado.

At one time, Canon City was the western terminal of the railroad and became a major shipping point for cattle going to market. Later, when the railroad was extended westward through the Royal Gorge, Canon City remained an important shipping point from the South Park and Fremont County areas. Thousands of head of cattle wintered along the Arkansas Valley and were driven to Canon City for fall shipments.

The cattle were driven to market or the rail heads by drovers, or "hands." Large herds would be started north with several experienced drovers and a "bossman," or foreman, in charge. Many pioneers of the cattle country were anxious to get their sons out and working, hoping to get them away from the table as soon as possible. At about 12 years of age, they would be "let out" to the drovers, working mostly for their board, keep, and experience. This would keep the youngsters away from the family feedbag for months at a time. These nonpaid youngsters were called "cow boys" to differentiate them from the experienced drovers. Somewhere along the way, the name "cowboy" became respectable.

Tom once wrote to a friend that he had broken horses, participated in a cattle drive, and tended bar at George Yowell's saloon in Lamar,

Colorado, sometime around 1906. If so, he may have taken part in one of the fall drives and tended bar for a spell that winter.

After the fall shipments, the cowboys who had been with the herds for months would let off steam with racing, roping, and riding exhibitions that first became a part of the early Frontier Days celebrations and, later, ranch shows. These cowboy sporting events became rodeos (Spanish for round-up) at a much later date. Canon City became a favorite spot for these Wild West exhibitions and may have been one of the factors that lured the Selig Polyscope Company into the area.

There was some wishful thinking in 1911 when the *Canon City Record* reported that, "there is some thought that Canon City may become the movie capital of the country." Selig was the largest motion picture producer by far with headquarters in New York and Chicago. And, for a while, the western film crew and the not-so-well-known Mixes enjoyed the sunshine, wide-open spaces, panoramic views, and clean mountain air. With a little coaxing from his friends, Tom found it socially fulfilling to sit around the campfire and tell tales of his days as an Oklahoma lawman.

Local residents remembered Tom as just another one of Selig's troupe of actors when the crew came to Canon City. Bill Duncan was the leading man and Myrtle Stedman was the leading lady. Duncan could be a good guy, bad guy, producer, or director, depending on where he was most needed and later became a top-notch serial star. Josephine West was remembered as a dark-haired beauty who liked to overact; Joe Ryan was a villain who also made his mark in Hollywood later. Myrtle Stedman was the diminutive heroine from a poor but honest family who had only pure thoughts—in other words, sickeningly sweet by today's standards. Myrtle also gained greater fame playing matronly roles in later years.

Tom did get some leads in the early westerns, which were about all the Selig studios or anyone else made at the time. The Selig studios were located in a rented two-story building on the southwest corner of Third and Main Streets. He was allegedly paid $100 or $150 a week, but many old-timers think this figure was somewhat inflated. Charles Canterbury Sr. and E. C. "Woody" Higgins were two of his closest friends from the Canon City area.

Tom Mix was remembered as "a rugged cowhand who had done some acting, and had served some time as a regular poke on the ranges. He was deeply tanned and his legs were a little bowed. He had a wife who tried, sometimes without success, to keep him close to the home corral. He had an eye for a pretty filly." Tom's wife was "from Oklahoma, part Indian, and extremely jealous. She could never quite condone the love scenes Tom had to enact with his various leading ladies. On one occasion, she grabbed a six-gun, broke up the love scene, and then went out gunning for Tom after dark. The old ranchers and extras here took the thing as a lot of fun, but they seem to agree that Olive was very serious about it."

Tom stops a runaway buggy to save the life of Myrtle Stedman, his leading lady. (Author's collection.)

Friends recalled another story when Tom was chased by his angry wife. According to the story, Tom ran into the Smith Hall Elks Club and up the stairs. His wife followed close behind him. As a doorman temporarily barred her way, Tom climbed out a window and hid in the awning. Olive finally gained admittance and stalked through the club rooms, looking for her man. "He's in here someplace and I'll wait for him," she was quoted

Tom Mix in an early gunslinger pose. Some say his legs were slightly bowed. Who can tell? (Courtesy of Frank Galindo.)

"Old Blue" was Tom's Wild West Show horse and first movie horse. He was superbly trained by Tom. (Author's collection.)

as saying. She then parked herself outside by the front door and waited. According to the tale, another employee of the Elks Club came on duty and rolled down the awning. Tom was dumped unceremoniously on to the walk, next to where his wife sat biding her time.

It was also while making films in Canon City that Olive played the part of Tom's mother on more than one occasion. Her early makeup for the part consisted of a thin coating of lard on her face covered with flour; more flour was worked into her hair and the lines in her face were accented with charcoal. Tom had fun teasing Olive at first, but she no doubt tired of this sort of fun in a hurry.

Many residents hoped that Canon City would indeed become the next motion picture capital of the United States. There was ample housing for the actors and crews and plenty of horses for hire. Extra cowboys could be rounded up on relatively short notice to play good guys, bad guys, or whatever the script required. Selig rented horses, livestock, saddles, wagons, buckboards, and other paraphernalia from Woody Higgins. Charles Canterbury Sr., and the local livery stable. For a really spectacular production, a whole herd of cattle and their drovers might be hired for one dramatic scene.

Local people were hired as extras for five dollars a day, which was good money in those days for eight hours' work. In addition to Higgins and

Canterbury, Jack "J. P." Donahoo, George Green, Clyde Chess, Frank Steinmeier, W. A. McKenzie, and John I. Williams were numbered among the local actors. Youngsters used in the films made a dollar a day, but they did not have to work for eight hours. It should be remembered that a dollar would buy a heap of groceries in those days.

At the tender age of 16, Lonnie Higgins, Woody's son, frequently played the part of an Indian. Many a time he bit the dust by falling off a horse running at full gallop. No trick cameras or faked scenes were used because the limited shooting budget would not permit it. If the script called for a runaway team to be stopped, the horses were whipped up and one of the actors rode after them and stopped them. Most of the time, the actors received injuries no more serious than scratches or bruises.

Canon City residents recalled that J. P. Donahoo appeared in almost every picture; at one time or another, he was a good guy, bad Indian, bailiff, and even a suave gangster. Later Donahoo became Canon City's chief of police.

The film crews seldom worked on Sunday because many members of the cast believed that the Sabbath belonged to the Lord and felt that everyone should go to church on Sunday. At first, the movie people made quite a stir around town. They got invited to teas, dinners, and Sunday drives to the Royal Gorge. Later, they were matter-of-factly accepted as part of the local economy.

When not in church or entertaining prisoners at the Colorado penitentiary, Tom loved to go to Fremont's Hell's Half Acre Saloon, where beer was a nickel and lunch was free. It was a great place to socialize and play pool after a hot day on the range. Tom and E. C. "Woody" Higgins frequently displayed their shooting prowess by blasting lemons out of a row of empty shot glasses. The bullet holes were still in the walls when the old Fremont Saloon was torn down.

The early movie industry recognized that pleasant community relations were good for business, and Tom and the Selig crew usually spent one hour every Sunday entertaining inmates at the Colorado penitentiary in Canon City. Tom frequently demonstrated his abilities with a lasso, and Myrtle Stedman, who had a lovely voice, sang. The Selig crew were a big hit with the imprisoned men. Tom promoted charitable work throughout his movie career.

The filming season was primarily from spring through summer and into fall during the 1911 and 1912 seasons. The Selig crew did not return in 1913. A typical early Selig film took four or five days to shoot.

However, when Selig decided to leave Canon City, some of the actors and technicians liked the area so well that they decided to stay behind. Those who remained put up some of their own money and helped attract more money from Canon City and Denver to form the Colorado Motion

Picture Company. Their new leading lady was Grace McCue, a former Selig bit player, and the head cameraman was Owen Carter, who had also been the head cameraman for Selig.

The Colorado Motion Picture Company had only made a few pictures when tragedy struck while filming near the scenic Hot Springs Hotel on the east side of the Royal Gorge. Ms. McCue, the leading lady, became frightened when her horse stumbled while attempting to cross the Arkansas River. She tried to rein him to shore, but the animal stumbled again and threw McCue into the river, where she was rapidly swept downstream.

Carter, the head cameraman, failed to recognize the seriousness of the situation at first. When he realized McCue was in trouble, he dropped his camera, raced 40 yards downstream, and dove into the water in an attempt to rescue her.

Carter reached Grace fairly quickly and, fighting her panic and struggles, managed to pull the two of them to a sandbank and temporary safety. Both McCue and Carter stood up in the waist-deep water for about 30 seconds, then McCue, still somewhat hysterical, took a few steps toward the shore. She dropped off a ledge into deep water, and Carter grabbed her again, but this time they were both exhausted and swept downstream. Both Carter and McCue rapidly disappeared from sight, and their bodies were not found until several days later.

Although it was widely publicized that the Selig crew went to a little-known spot named Hollywood after they left Canon City, their real reason for not returning could have been the tragic deaths of Owen Carter and Grace McCue. After the accident, McCue's family sued the Colorado Motion Picture Company and won a court judgment against them.

Apparently the Selig crew did return to the Canon City area for one film in 1916, however, as the *Canon City Record* carried the following story on November 2, 1916:

> The Selig Motion Picture Company wants to get a film of some couple getting married while going through the Royal Gorge on the observation platform of a passenger train.
>
> If any local couple is interested, the Selig Company will take care of all the marriage fees and also provide a little honeymoon trip.

Author Raymond M. Beckner, aka Milton LeMoyne, a longtime Colorado resident, leaves us with these positive thoughts about Tom.

> I do remember that he was a generous man, perhaps generous to a fault. He helped many people when down on their luck, most deserving and some, I suppose, not so deserving. He could spot a phony a mile away and he felt at home with real, honest-to-goodness, down-to-earth people, those who were sincere. We had one thing in common; we both came up the hard way. Whenever I met him in Colorado, he would always mention Lamar and Canon City. I finally uncovered the Canon City end of it,

but have never been able to learn about his cow-punchin' days around Lamar.

Later, after Tom came to Colorado Springs with his circus, Beckner recalled:

> I remember spending most of an entire evening with him, going over some advertising stunts and ideas. He handed me two box passes to his show at Colorado Springs and when the grand entrance was made, he stopped his beautiful horse, Tony, in front of our box, then doffing his hat, he announced to the crowd that this was a very special salute to Mr. and Mrs. Ray Beckner. He was just that kind of guy, one of the most likable and appreciative of all the show people that I have ever known.

Ray, a Columbia Broadcasting executive, was in radio and show business for more than 40 years had occasion to meet and interview Tom Mix several times. The last time he introduced him to a Columbia Network audience was during the peak of his career with the circus in the mid-thirties. Ray recalls,

> He came down Tejon Street in Colorado Springs, dressed as was expected of him in those days—huge white hat, polished black boots, white western suit with black trim—and was perhaps the most striking figure western pictures or the circus has ever seen. Following in his wake were literally hundreds of youngsters, just ready to touch or shake hands with him. They would all meet at our studios, and Tom would shake hands with all the youngsters and have a word with them. I distinctly remember him shaking hands with one little urchin who turned and said, "Boy, oh boy, I'm not going to wash this hand for a week."
> I would always personally introduce Tom to the radio audience, and on the last occasion, shortly before his death, I said, "And now, ladies and gentlemen, insofar as Hollywood is concerned, here is the world's greatest cowboy, Mr. Tom Mix." With an introduction like this, Tom came on the mike and drawled, "Well Ray, I never figured to be the world's greatest cowboy or greatest anythin' else. Fact is, I am an old cowpuncher from down here at Lamar, Colorado." And, after the broadcast, he told me about his cow punching days around Lamar and his moviemaking days at Canon City.

Apparently Tom did not renew his contract with Selig in 1912, but he may have made a few pictures that year. As shown in the Selig filmography, only three films are listed for 1912.

The Calgary Stampede

It was very early in 1912 that Tom received a letter from Guy Weadick in New York, who was planning to put on a show in Calgary, Alberta, and invited Tom to join him. Tom and Olive went to New York and met with Weadick to discuss the plans for the show and then went with him to Calgary. The so-called Oklahoma delegation which gathered that March in Calgary hoped to convince local promoters they could put together a Wild West show of immense scope and historical significance. While they were there, they put on a little show of their own for the potential backers.

A history of the Calgary Stampede, reported in the *Calgary Herald* of July 9, 1949, explains the purpose of Guy Weadick and Tom Mix's trip as follows:

> In March 1912, Guy Weadick went to Calgary to promote the Calgary Stampede. Tom Mix made the trip west with Weadick to fill in time before opening with a new Wild West show that Fred T. Cummins was launching in April for a tour of the United States. Weadick helped Mix obtain the position of Arena Director for the new Cummins show. Tom stayed in Calgary for a few days and then left for Minneapolis to visit friends.

Guy Weadick is given the credit he deserves as the originator of the Calgary Stampede. Little mention is made of Tom Mix. It is curious, however, that two early news clippings tell different stories.

On March 25, 1912, the *Alberton,* in an article entitled, "A Calgary Frontier Week Is Proposed," stated:

> The syndicate which is in Calgary promoting the affair is headed by [Micks], of Bliss, Oklahoma, who holds the world's record of 14 seconds for roping and tying a steer, and an Australian buckjumper named Frank Brown. They state that they can get 500 experts in Calgary to take part in the affair, which will become an annual national event that will mark the last stand of the picturesque western cowboy on the outer edge of civilization which is gradually, but surely, sounding the deathknell of the law of the Colts 45 and the rough and ready riders, who are now rarely seen or heard of, except in Russell pictures or western novels.

The second article, published in the *Calgary News Telegram* on March 27, 1912, was titled "Cattle Barons Willing to Back Frontier Week in Calgary If Cowboys Can Deliver the Goods." An excerpt from this article stated:

> If the Oklahoma cowboys, headed by Tom Mix, Champion Roper of the World, can show Col. Walker, George Lane, Pat Burns, Robert L. Shaw, M.L.A., and a number of old time cattlemen that they can deliver the goods and put on a Frontier Week in Calgary two weeks after the Provincial Fair, they will receive all the backing they want and be given "carte blanche" to go ahead and make arrangements to bring to Calgary the best aggregation of ropers, riders, and general all around cowpunchers that has ever been gathered together on the American continent.

The article also noted that "live stock agent McMullen of the C.P.R. [Canadian Pacific Railroad], who has known Mix and his men for years, says that they can deliver the goods."

It is interesting to note that in these early newspaper articles Guy

Weadick's name is not mentioned. While in Calgary, both Mix and Weadick supposedly worked for A. P. Day, a prominent rancher with a newly acquired string of bucking broncos. Day was interested in promoting the first Calgary Stampede and getting his stock in shape for the big event. Day also may have furnished the stock for Weadick's show while it was in Canada. Tom was hired as a working cowboy to help handle the show stock for both Day and Weadick.

While the show was being rehearsed in Calgary, Olive learned that she was pregnant with their first child. Tom was the proud expectant father, treating his wife as if she might break if he touched her. Olive assured Tom that she didn't need to be treated like an egg; pioneer women had had it a whole lot harder in childbirth.

Shortly after leaving Calgary, the relationship between Mix, Weadick, and Joe Miller became strained to the breaking point after Tom received a letter from Joe Miller and Tom wrote the following letter to him at the 101 Ranch.

March 31, 1912

Mr. J. C. Miller
101 Ranch, Bliss, Okla.

Friend Joe:

Received your letter and was glad to hear from you and sorry I did not get to see you in N.Y. when you [were] there.

Joe—Guy Weadick and I came up here and Guy told me a lot of junk you said about me and I passed it up as nothing. Now to show you where I stand—If you intend to make Calgary this year, you [should] write [to] Mr. H. C. McMullen, General Live Stock Agent, C.P.R. and cut Weadick's knocking off for he is sure sore on you and is knocking the [101] show right and left. [Guy] has Mr. McMullen [in an] abused sort of condition [because of the] so-called discourteous treatment on your part towards Mr. McMullen on the show lot when you [were here] last.

Now I should advise you to write—to some Shriners at Calgary, Col. Walker Pat Burns [packing house and big cattleman], R. L. Shaw, M.L.A. [Guy] has been talking along the lines—the show is nothing like it was when here before and said that they ought to stick you up for the $1000 license, etc.

Now, I don't know what you and Guy's troubles are, but I know this much, that you gave him work when no one else would have him and as far as I know, treated him with more consideration [than] he retaliated with.

Trusting you consider this confidential.

From yours as ever,
[signed] Tom Mix

Tom's letter was handwritten in fancy cursive style on stationery from the Assiniboia Hotel, Medicine Hat, Alberta. However, it incorporates poor sentence structure and the slang of the period, which makes it difficult to read and understand. Words in brackets, primarily in the second paragraph, are added or changed to improve the overall readability of the material. The contents of Joe Miller's initial letter to Mix is not known.

Joe Miller was apparently taken by surprise by Tom's letter, and he quickly replied to Tom as follows:

Hanford, Cal., April 10, 1912

Mr. Tom Mix
Medicine Hat,
Alberta, Canada

Dear Sir:

I beg to acknowledge receipt of your letter of March 31st and [to] say that I was very much surprised at what you say about Guy Weadick's roast about me, is putting it mildly.

In the first place, I have always considered Guy a very good friend of mine and have held up for him when other people have knocked him. I met him recently in New York and we had a long conversation in regard to putting on a vaudeville act which he was to manage and take to Europe next winter. I told him in Billie Burke's office, the vaudeville agent in New York, that any deal they would fix up, I would not only furnish the stock but would finance it and left it up to them to frame the act. What could have possessed him to have made these remarks that you mentioned is more than I can understand.

As to my discourteous treatment of Guy's friend, the live stock agent in Calgary, I do not think that needs any comment or explanation. The people that know me and know my way of treating people and doing business, know that I was never discourteous to anyone around the show, and if the gentleman, for any reason, felt that he did not receive the consideration or attention that he should have, it certainly was not done intentionally on my part and I do not feel that I owe any explanation whatever in regard to this.

While ordinarily I do not pay any attention to things of this kind, still it hurts me to a certain extent to think that a person would misrepresent facts without any occasion to do so whatever. I note that you say that I gave him work when he could not get it anywhere else. As far as that is concerned, he worked good for me and I paid him all that I promised and when he got ready to go, he left with no ill feelings, as far as I knew, either on my part or his.

While you ask me to treat this letter as strictly confidential, I feel that in justice to myself, it is nothing more than right that I should send the letter to him and ask for an explanation.

Everything is going along very nicely with the show and I feel that we may have the best show this season that we have ever had and as to any statements of Guy Weadick to the contrary, the show, when it gets to Canada will speak for itself, and if it is necessary to pay [a] $1000 license, I expect we will come as near having $1000 in the safe as any show of a similar character on the road. However, I feel that nothing of this character will be exacted, and hope to see the same courteous treatment and patronage through Canada that we [saw] on our last visit.

I trust that everything is going nicely with you, and with kindest regards, I am

Yours very truly,

J. C. Miller's letter was on Miller Brothers and Arlington 101 Ranch Real Wild West stationery. This copy was unsigned and apparently attached to the next letter in this series. Joe Miller tended to write everything as one long, continuous paragraph. His letters have been rearranged into conventional paragraphs.

The final letter in this series was written to Guy Weadick by Joe Miller:

Hanford, Cal., April 10, 1912

Mr. Guy Weadick
c/o Billboard
Cincinnati, O.

Friend Guy:

I enclose herewith a letter from Tom Mix. I am certainly at a loss to know how to take this letter. However, [I] must say that somebody is either a damned fool or crazy. I enclose you a copy of a letter that I have written to Mix, that I think goes far enough into detail and explains matters as far as I am concerned.

If I mistreated your friend, Mr. [McMullen], while in Calgary, the matter was never called to my attention. I remember you introducing me to him and telling him that I extended all the courtesies of the show, and I cannot think that either you or he felt that he was not treated right around the show. Had it been any other way, I believe you would have mentioned it to me and [would] have given me the opportunity to make proper apologies which I am always glad to do under these conditions.

As I said in my letter to Mix, your acquaintance, [people who know me] know how I treat people and [discourteous treatment] would be so foreign from my custom that [the accusation] is simply absurd. However, I will be glad to have an expression from you in this regard.

As to the show being rotten this year, or not being as good as former years, I do not understand why you would make this assertion, as you have not seen the show nor [talked with] anyone who has. From my several years of experience in show business, I think we have the best show this season that we have ever put out, regardless of the fact that there are some features that we have been unable to [do that we have done in the past], but taking the show as a whole, I think it will compare very favorably with any similar organization.

I will say that I think so little of the remarks in regard to Mr. [McMullen], the [General] Stock Agent of the C.P.R.R., that I will not take the trouble to write him personally because I do not think that he feels toward me in the manner in which Mix's letter states. With kindest regards, I am

Your friend,
J. C. Miller

The above letter has been rearranged and the terminology modernized to improve its readability without changing its meaning.

The three letters, presented above, have been furnished courtesy of the Glenbow-Alberta Institute, Calgary, Alberta. The final outcome of this series of letters is unknown. One wonders why Tom would write such a letter to Joe Miller in the first place, unless it were true. Tom should have realized that serious repercussions might occur. At this late date, we can only wonder if the apparent dispute might have been one of the reasons Tom did not appear at the first Calgary Stampede, given the great press coverage he received on his initial trip to Canada.

After the Weadick show left Calgary, it went to Dominion Park, Montreal. While Tom was bulldogging a steer at a Sunday night performance, it turned quickly, hooked Tom on the base of his jaw, and knocked him out. Tom was carried from the arena to his dressing room, but he refused to see a doctor. Later during the same show, Tom was thrown from a bucking bronco, knocked unconscious again, and this time was talked into going to the hospital with Johnny Mullins as his escort.

Apparently, Tom left Weadick's show in Montreal, made two films for Selig, then joined Vernon Seiver's Young Buffalo Show in Peoria, Illinois. Seiver's show made a number of appearances and at about midyear ended up back at Dominion Park. At this time, Olive's baby was almost due, so she went back home to Oklahoma, where the baby was born about a week early, on July 13, 1912. After finishing the Montreal show, Tom returned home to find that he was the proud father of a three-day-old baby girl, Ruth Jane. The birth of Ruth Jane Mix is probably another reason that Tom did not appear in the first Calgary Stampede.

The first Calgary Stampede was held during the week of September 2–7, 1912. The event opened with a six-mile-long parade in town. Exact replicas of a Hudson Bay trading post and old Fort Whoop-Up were erected on the exhibition grounds. A cast of over 1,000 played to 75,000 spectators. It featured a complete History of the West pageant.

Guests of honor were His Royal Highness, the duke of Connaught (son of Queen Victoria), governor-general of Canada, his wife, the duchess, and his popular daughter, Princess Patricia. The duke was accompanied by a large staff from England and many friends of the family. There was a musical ride by the Royal Northwest Mounted Police, including Z. T. Wood, the commissioner.

Eddie McCarthy, of Cheyenne, Wyoming, thrilled the audience when he conquered Tornado, a previously unbroken bronco, known as the worst bucking horse in the state of Colorado. Some of the other thrill riders were "Tex" McLeod, Hazel Walker of California, Bertha Blanchette, Annie Schaefer, Ed Echols, and Lucille Mulhall. Echols bested Joe Gardiner's steer roping and tying record by 2.8 seconds; it was a new Calgary record, but the performance was about 4 seconds shy of breaking the world record of 19 seconds.

"Bud" Pollack surprised the audience by living through his bronco riding experience aboard Redspur. Bud's bronco jammed him against the fence, knocked him out of the saddle, and dragged him about the arena by one foot, amid flying hooves, for 50 yards or more. Amazingly, Bud was able to free his foot, and survived the event with a few bumps and bruises.

Hazel Walker's bronco fell with her three times, pinning her on the last fall. She too walked away with minor injuries. Later, the same afternoon, she rode Rooster, another bronco who liked to jump sky high and land stiff legged. After three minutes of wild bucking, the horse ran into the fire fence, knocking Hazel beneath him and injuring her arm as he fell on her. Hazel remounted the bronco and finished her ride amid the cheers of the crowd. Bertha Blanchette won the cowgirls' relay race.

At the night program, the grand entry was led by Stampede management, Florence LaDue and Elberta McMullen. Leading the cowgirls were Goldie St. Clair and Lucille Mulhall. Some of the favorite cowboys were the Weir brothers, Clay McGonigill, and "Tex" McLeod. President Madero of Mexico and a delegation of Mexican cowboys were also present and took part in the cowboy sports. And, finally, the Reverend John A. McDougall supervised a contingent of about two hundred native American Indians.

Colonel Felix Warren, a veteran stagecoach driver, put on a demonstration ride using a six-team hitch. Indians from six nations did their famous Peace Dance to the beat of tom-toms. The night lighting was particularly effective, displaying their fancy headdresses, lances, and long rifles. A demonstration of fancy Cossack trick riding was put on by Arline Palmer, Jason Stanley, and Otto Kline.

Frank Walker beat "Booger" Red in the wild mule ride, to the delight of the audience. As a boy, Booger was helping his father dynamite tree stumps. One charge failed to explode, and Booger went to investigate. As he got to the stump, it exploded in his face. Since there were no plastic surgeons in those days, Booger's face was badly disfigured; thus giving him the self-proclaimed title of Ugliest Man, Living or Dead.

There was a fancy roping exhibition by Florence LaDue, Lucille Mulhall, George Wells, Stanley Whitney, and Tex McLeod. Whitney spun an 80-inch loop around himself and an assistant lady rider. McLeod demonstrated his skill by roping five horses abreast as they passed him.

Some of the night bronco riders were Eddie McCarthy, Red Parker, and Henry Webb. Booger Red put on a nice exhibition of bareback bucking horse riding. However, he was somewhat outdone by Ed Parker, who rode bareback on a bucking buffalo. Some of the women bronco busters were Annie Schaefer, Blanche McCaughey, and Goldie St. Clair.

Finally, some of the Mexican cowboys put on a mock Mexican bull-fight; many narrowly escaped being gored by the bulls. They also delighted the audience with a colorful Mexican roping demonstration. Other Americans who competed in various events were Ad Bradston, O. K. Lawrence, G. H. Johnson, Ellison Carroll, Doc. Pardee, and Charlie Tipton. Guy Weadick was general manager of the first stampede and was credited with the general idea and its promotion. H. C. McMullen was director general. Local ranchers Pat Burns, George Lane, A. J. McLean, and A. E. Cross financed the event and guided its early development.

Because of the birth of his daughter, Ruth, Tom apparently spent the rest of the year in Oklahoma. To make a little money, Tom again became a Dewey marshal and special state law enforcement officer. Olive was probably very happy to have Tom at home for a while.

In 1912, the oil business was still booming and there was plenty of lawlessness, including moonshine payola. Tom's job was to crack down on the bootleggers who were selling moonshine to the Indians and paying off county law enforcement officers. When the payola ceased, Tom, figuratively speaking, hung up his guns and turned in his star.

Prescott, Arizona

Late in 1912, Tom's contract with Selig came to an end, and he received a letter from Selig asking him to come to Chicago again to sign a new contract. After making a film or two in the Chicago area, Tom and his little family moved to Prescott, Arizona, where the Selig Company surprised Olive by supplying the Mixes with their first real home.

In 1913, most of the Selig western films were shot near Selig's Diamond S Ranch at Prescott. The ranch got its name from the Selig trademark, a large *S* in a diamond-shaped border. The Diamond S may have also been Tom's inspiration for his world famous Diamond TM Bar trademark.

By mid–1913, Sid Jordan also grew tired of his job in law enforcement. As far as he was concerned, Oklahoma had been tamed, so he headed for new adventures in South America. However, by the time he got to Colorado, he read in the newspaper that his old friend Tom Mix was making pictures in Arizona. Sid went to Arizona to visit with Tom, and Tom promptly gave Sid a job. Sid stayed with Tom for the rest of Tom's career and never did make it to South America.

Sid recalled that the movies were pretty rough in those early years. Scripts were meager at best, and the costumes and wardrobes were shared by the actors and stored in trunks. Producers, directors, and cameramen had little if any schooling and learned mainly from experience. Mix's Selig films gradually improved with time, but it was a long, hard, fast-paced struggle.

Both Tom and Sid did their own stunts; they used live ammunition on some occasions, blanks on others. Sid frequently used a rifle to shoot holes through the knot in Tom's ties. By the same token, Tom frequently shot holes in Sid's hats, sometimes so close to his head that strands of his hair were pulled out through the exit hole. Both men would do a horse fall or ride a stage over a cliff, or whatever the script called for. Tom and Sid literally put their lives on the line for each other; it was the ultimate test of trust. Luckily for both men, there were few accidents in these early Selig films.

Officially, William "Bill" Duncan was still in charge of the western film crew, but during the 1913 season, Bill and Tom more or less took turns appearing in the leading role. By mid–1914, Tom was ready to take over all aspects of his western productions, and Bill Duncan moved on to other things.

Tom continued to take part in local Frontier Days celebrations while in the Prescott area. On July 6, 1913, the *Prescott Miner-Journal* carried the following story:

> The Grand Entry [July 5th] on the field of sports was headed by Mr. and Mrs. Tom Mix of the Selig Polyscope Company. First Event—Cowboy Trick and Fancy Roping: Harry Knight proved victor over Tom Mix. Steer Bulldogging: Harry Knight 12½ seconds, Tom Mix 18½ seconds. Steer Riding: Tom Mix first, Nip Van second.

The next day, the paper reported, "The potato sack race was won by Tom Mix, Captain. His team included Nip Van, Nick Frick, and Harry Loverin." The account also mentioned that "Mrs. Tom Mix put on an exceptionally pretty stunt in the Cowgirl Race in which Mrs. Henry Ritter outdistanced her by about 20 feet. It was a quarter mile dash, time 30 seconds.

"Bulldogging: all entrants of the previous day entered. Won by Tom Mix, 16½ seconds, Harry Loverin, second, 20½ seconds." This was the first time that the *Prescott Miner-Journal* ever recorded the results of a Prescott Frontier Days celebration, even though it had been a paid attendance event since 1888. It is now a major tourist attraction.

Most of Tom's films made in Prescott were western comedies, and the main criticism of them appears to deal with camera placement, camera angle, and the lack of good close-ups. These were typical shortcomings of early film, and filming techniques continued to improve with time. It was also during this period that Tom begin to build up his own stock company of handpicked cowboys and cowgirls.

Some of Tom's favorite leading ladies were Kathlyn Williams, Bessie Eyton, Goldie Colwell, and Inez Walker. Popular male actors were Sid Jordan, Pat Chrisman, Leo Maloney, Tom Santshi, Joe Ryan, Wheeler Oakman, Joe King, Frank Clark, and Roy Watson.

Tom's first range pony and movie horse, Old Blue (born July 14, 1897, chloroformed January 29, 1919), was retired or put out to pasture in 1914, leaving Tom with an immediate need for another good horse. Pat Chrisman, another Selig actor and one of Tom's regular crew, discovered a colt trotting beside a vegetable wagon on the streets of Los Angeles. Pat bought the animal, shipped it to an Arizona ranch for training, and sold it to Tom Mix for six hundred dollars late in 1914. Mix named the horse Tony Boy, then shortened it to just plain Tony.

Tom continued to make films in the Prescott area until mid–1915. At that time, the film crew was lured to the Las Vegas area for a five-month period. Other Tom Mix films made during the Fox era and filmed in the Prescott area were *The Wilderness Trail* (1919), *Three Gold Coins* (1920), *Sky High* (1922).

Veteran film projectionist Charlie Kendall, who worked at the Elks Theater in Prescott, recalled doing screenings for Tom Mix and other stars in the teens and twenties. "Tom Mix was really a nice guy. He'd come back and ask me to rerun a clip. Most of the stars would send someone else to ask, but not Tom. Once he gave me a $50 tip." During the filming of *Three Gold Coins,* Charlie recalled, "That was a movie where [Tom] really demonstrated some shooting ability. They used buckshot instead of slugs. Made it real easy to break bottles. I'm not saying that's the way Mix did it; I'm just saying he made a good demonstration."

Las Vegas, New Mexico

I had heard that Tom Mix made a series of films in Las Vegas, New Mexico, but the information was sketchy. Some people thought he had been there a year; others thought he had been there three years. No one seemed to have any vivid memories of the Tom Mix/Selig film crew in Las Vegas, and no one seemed to have a clear understanding of the dates he and his film crew were there.

Then, beginning in February 1988 local actor and writer Alan S. Tobin wrote a four-part story about Tom Mix making films in Las Vegas, New Mexico. Alan's boyhood heroes were Tom Mix, Buck Jones, and Wild Bill Elliot. The only singing cowboy that he had any use for was Old Tex Ritter. I met Alan for the first time in 1992, and for a few enjoyable hours we enjoyed each other's company, openness, and honesty. Some of Alan's Las Vegas history is based on Professor Lynn Perrigo's book *Gateway to Glorieta.*

Tom Mix fan and writer Jack Smith, of Albuquerque, New Mexico, notes that Las Vegas, New Mexico, was one of the toughest towns in the early West. It had a reputation as bad as Tombstone's and Dodge City's. Notorious lawmen and outlaws such as Billy the Kid and Doc Holiday once graced Las Vegas with their presence. And it was here that Teddy Roosevelt organized his famous Rough Riders.

The Rough Rider Museum is still one of the town's historic attractions. Today it is also the site of the Rails 'n' Trails festival, held on Memorial Day weekend to celebrate the town's western history and connection to the Santa Fe railroad. Tom Mix's early moviemaking activities are also celebrated as part of the festival.

Alan's story was published as a special feature by the *Victorian Gazette*, in the section "Meet the Places and People of Las Vegas, New Mexico." Alan researched the files of defunct newspapers such as the *Daily Optic* and interviewed a few old-timers who were young men in the 1915–16 period. The men he interviewed had a good recollection of events, but exact dates tended to elude them.

In 1909, a trust was formed by the existing motion picture companies to help settle patent right disputes in the early industry. Shortly afterward, many of these motion picture companies left the East and struck out for more scenic and picturesque western locations.

Sigmund Lubin of the Lubin Film Company headed into the Southwest and made films in Arizona in 1912. Romaine Fielding was a key figure for Lubin, acting as manager, director, actor, and writer. Fielding's half-brother, Robert, worked for a copper mine in New Mexico and convinced Romaine to bring the Lubin film crew to Silver City. In 1913, Fielding began looking for new locations around Albuquerque and Las Vegas. Because of the scenic advantages and encouragement of the Commercial Club, the Lubin film crew moved to Las Vegas, New Mexico. The Lubin Film Company made films in Las Vegas through 1914, then left, leaving a local economic void.

To help fill in economic space, Ludwig Ilfield, a local Las Vegas merchant, invited Tom Mix to come and participate in their first Cowboy's Reunion (rodeo) celebration, to be held in early July 1915. Mix came, was impressed by the scenery, and moved into the old Fielding studio at 920 Gallinas Street. Apparently the Mix/Selig studio was upstairs, Mix and his family lived downstairs, and the wardrobes and props were kept in the basement.

The following newspaper articles were extracted from Alan Tobin's research of the *Daily Optic*. Some of Selig's film crew apparently arrived in Las Vegas on July 1, 1915, with Tom arriving on or about July 4, 1915. According to Tom, Las Vegas had everything a movie producer could want. He especially liked the spirit of cooperation, and he invited the townspeople to park their cars on Gallinas Street and watch the movie action.

> July 2, 1915—Selig Co. gets ready for work. They are using the studio on Gallinas Ave.

*   *   *

July 3, 1915—The secretary of the Commercial Club has received a telegram from Thomas Persons, manager of the Selig Polyscope Company, to the effect that the two producing organizations scheduled to be stationed here during the next year will arrive in the near future. The company in charge of Tom Mix, the noted cowboy motion picture actor and producer, will reach Las Vegas on Thursday afternoon. The Commercial Club suggests that all persons at the Santa Fe station take trains to the Reunion grounds, and as many others as possible, give Mix and his associates a rousing welcome.

Mix wired yesterday that he anticipated great pleasure in attendance at the Reunion. His message came as an answer to a telegraphic invitation from the cowboys to hurry up and get here for the big roundup.

*   *   *

July 5, 1915—Tom Mix's movie men win potato race.

*   *   *

July 8, 1915—Tom Mix and his Selig Polyscope company are at work this afternoon on the production of "The New Deputy," a two-reel motion picture play, written by P. H. LeNoir, secretary of the Las Vegas Commercial club. The play has the promise of being one of the most spectacular pictures that the local Selig Polyscope company will produce for some time.

*   *   *

July 10, 1915—The events of yesterday were interesting. A stage coach race, featuring Tom Mix, the moving picture star, had to be cut out of the program on account of the fact that the coaches, which were on their way here from the coast, had failed to arrive. . . .

As the cowboys circled the track at Gallinas Park at 3:30 o'clock yesterday afternoon, the First Annual Reunion of the Cowboys of New Mexico, the biggest event that has even taken place in the state, passed into history. The four day roundup has been so successful that it will be made an annual event, with Las Vegas as the permanent meeting place.

*   *   *

Wednesday, July 14, 1915—Reception for Tom Mix and His Company: Commercial Club Arranges for an Enjoyable Function Friday Night: The Commercial club will give a reception on Friday evening in its quarters in the Masonic building in honor of Thomas Mix and his company of Selig Polyscope players. Invitations will be issued this evening. It is expected the affair will be highly enjoyable. The entertainment committee had complete charge of the function, and judging from its successes in the past, it undoubtedly will make the Mix reception something entirely worth while. The committee is composed of the following: N. O. Hermann, chairman; Simon Bachrach, George A. Fleming, William Rosenthal, Herman Ilfield and Charles Greenclay.

*   *   *

Friday, July 30, 1915—Mix and Company Working in Country. On the Whitmore Ranch South of Las Vegas a Drama Will Be Finished: Tom

Victoria Forde joined Tom's film crew for the first time in 1915 when they were shooting films in Las Vegas, New Mexico. (Author's collection.)

Mix and his company of Selig Polyscope actors and actresses left this morning for the Whitmore ranch, 30 miles south of Las Vegas. The company will put in two day's work there, returning tomorrow evening.

★　　★　　★

August 7, 1915—Tom Mix, Miss Virginia [Victoria] Forde, Ben Lewis, Simon Lewis and Ludwig William Ilfeld were weekend visitors at the Phoenix ranch near Watrous.

★　　★　　★

August 18, 1915—There will be a basket social for the actor folks.

*   *   *

September 22, 1915—Mix has no idea of moving away. There are no grounds for the rumors that he is moving to Santa Fe.

*   *   *

October 13, 1915—Tom Mix Arrested in Albuquerque: Open Muffler is the Cause of Picture Man's Paying a Fine: Albuquerque, October 13—Ten dollars of Tom Mix's money went into the city treasury this morning. Mix is a director of the Selig Polyscope Company and he is here to take movies of the fair and parades. He has a big [car], and is careless with his muffler. He was warned that the law forbade open mufflers, but he disregarded or forgot the warning in the small hours this morning and drove through town making as much noise as a machine gun platoon in action.

Policeman Schuff arrested him and gave him a ten dollar cash bond for his appearance in court this morning.

*   *   *

November 6, 1915—Mix writes sketch for the Elk's Club Minstrel Show.

*   *   *

November 22, 1915—Tom Mix and Co. were engaged yesterday in taking pictures of the East Las Vegas Fire Dept. The Fire Dept. was worked into the shot of a new Selig film.

*   *   *

November 26, 1915—The East Las Vegas Fire Dept. will buy the Selig film to use for the Department. It will not be used in the Selig film.

*   *   *

December 27, 1915—The Tom Mix Co. is leaving for their winter home in Los Angeles. His company turned out 39,000 feet of film in so many weeks. In one week they made 6,000 feet of film, an amount which has never been made by any other company. Tom Mix says he'll be back by the first of April next year.

*   *   *

From the above series of newspaper articles, it appears safe to conclude that Tom Mix and his film crew were in the Las Vegas, New Mexico, area for about six months before leaving for Los Angeles. And although they apparently intended to return in 1916, Tobin's research indicates they did not.

Some time after the Selig film crew started making films in Las Vegas, *Glitterings from the Diamond S Ranch* was published. The publication appears to be a newsletter of sorts from Selig's permanent facilities in Prescott, Arizona.

Won't be long before the Mix Las Vegas made films will begin to make their appearance. Not only will we be able to reenjoy our own scenery, but millions of others will also. Advertising? Well, we guess, chess!

★   ★   ★

The men folk of the Selig Company are enjoying the swimming up at Hot Springs Nat. The Y.M.C.A. has given the whole company a pass to use the pool whenever desired.

★   ★   ★

Las Vegas has the Mix craze, it seems. One merchant is featuring Mix cravats, while Dave Conway, Murphy's soda dispenser, threatens to get a brand new Mix-ed drink. Yeah, just kill him, he ain't no friend.

★   ★   ★

Pat Fields and Dick Hunters are seen limping these days. So would you if you were shot off a horse going about "thirty [miles] per [hour]." "We don't mind plowing up the earth," Pat said, kind of peeved, "but gee man, them stones. Phew!"

★   ★   ★

Miss Hazel Page, who does characters for the Selig Company, is still mourning the loss of two trunks. The Santa Fe is making strenuous efforts to locate the apparel.

★   ★   ★

Have you seen the Selig dog, Teddy, act? He is a regular canine Thespian, he is. Teddy will appear in the story soon to be shown here, "The Girl, the Villain and the Dog." Teddy did some great work in one of the *Hazards of Helen* the other night. He played "opposite" friend Maloney.

★   ★   ★

The question has been asked a number of times, "Are the Selig cowboys sure enough punchers?" We can positively say they are. Everyone of them has ridden the range and done every bit of work incidental to ranch life. If you want to make the bunch happy, just tell them that you heard the "Major" (their name for Mix) say they were going out camping for a few days. While they tolerate it, city life becomes downright irksome to these sons of the range.

I was told by one Las Vegas resident, who was a wee boy in 1915, that two old wardrobe trunks with costumes were left in the basement of the old Selig studios on Gallinas Street, so perhaps one mystery is solved—Hazel Page's wardrobe trunks never boarded the Santa Fe train.

There is yet another mystery for the Las Vegas folks. The films shot at the East Las Vegas Fire Department have disappeared and never been found. Perhaps they have crumbled into decay by now, or perhaps someone has a treasure of old Tom Mix films and doesn't realize it.

By researching the old newspaper articles, Tobin was able to come up with the following film titles of movies that he believes were made in the

Las Vegas area: *The New Deputy, Never Again, Her Slight Mistake, The Race for a Gold Mine, Athletic Ambitions, Impersonation of Tom, Bad Man Bobbs, Weary Goes Wooing, The Range Girl and the Cowboy, The Foreman's Choice.*

This list adds up to 10 pictures, which would still appear to be far too few, based on the large amount of film shot by the film crew in six months. For example, since Tom made 55 Selig films in 1915, it is more likely that about 27 were made in the Las Vegas area. If the films were all one-reelers (15 minutes long), that would account for 27,000 feet of film and 11,000 feet of cropping. If some of the films were two-reelers (30 minutes long), there would have been less waste. In any event, 39,000 feet of film is much too much film for ten pictures. I have put an asterisk by the films in the Selig filmography that may have been shot in the Las Vegas, New Mexico, area.

While in the Las Vegas area, the Selig film crew and cast were remembered as good neighbors, who, in general, helped the local economy. Although they apparently did not hire many area residents as actors, they did, of course, spend a good deal of money in the Las Vegas area.

From Tobin's interviews, Tom was remembered as a flashy dresser who looked more like a movie cowboy than a working cowboy. Tom did not carry guns, at least into the local bank, and he seemed rather quiet in manner. Some recalled that he still liked to drink a bit. All in all, the Tom Mix/Selig crew and cast were remembered as good citizens who caused no problems. And apparently there were not any accidents or unusual incidents that occurred during the making of their films.

For the entire Selig era, from 1909 through early 1917, it seems that many of Tom's films were shot on location; the more rugged and picturesque the location, the better. The Selig filmography in the appendix of this book indicates the general pattern of filmmaking went at random from Canon City, Colorado; to Prescott, Arizona; to Las Vegas, New Mexico; and, finally, to Hollywood, California. There were probably numerous excursions from these locations as well.

An introduction to *An Arizona Wooing* reads as follows:

> Tom Mix and the motion picture met up in Oklahoma Territory early in the middle of 1910. Mix a United States marshal there, and Colonel William N. Selig had dispatched a crew to the region to film what would today be known as a documentary, *Ranch Life in the Great Southwest.*
>
> The result of this meeting was Mix's start on the road to fame and fortune as a motion picture cowboy. Over the next seven years he appeared in a score of films of various types made by Selig. By 1914, he was a motion picture star.
>
> Two years later, the fortunes of Selig, along with the other production companies that made up the General Film Company, the "Trust" were on the wane.
>
> Mix's last appearances for Selig were early in 1917 and by that spring

During his early days with Selig, Tom was the good and sometimes the bad guy in the black hat. (Author's collection.)

he was under contract to FOX, where in the 1920s, he was one of the most popular and highest paid motion picture stars.

This summary does not explain why Tom left Selig. After all, Selig gave Tom his start in movies, and Tom was grateful to him for it. The truth of the matter was that Selig and the General Film Company trust ran into financial difficulties in 1916. Until that time, Selig had produced about two hundred films a year. Now the total output of the trust was curtailed to about two hundred pictures a year, and Tom's films were alternated with the other films being produced. Instead of making one picture a week, he suddenly found himself making one picture a month. Tom did not have to be hit in the head with a hammer to know his relationship with Selig was nearing an end.

The real end came in early 1917 when Selig sent an efficiency expert to help Tom decide how to cut production costs. Tom knew in advance that the only way to cut production costs was to cut the jobs of his loyal film crew and cast. Rather than do that, Tom and Victoria Forde, his leading lady, guaranteed the wages for the Mix film crew while Tom looked for a new producer. The new producer turned out to be William Fox, who met all of Tom's demands and expectations.

Tom and Olive were divorced in 1917, and the following year Tom married Victoria Forde, who was frequently cast as his leading lady and was a star in her own right. Tom and Vicky had something in common—their movie careers.

Perhaps the reason Tom had so many wives is also best explained by Raymond Beckner:

> I always felt that Tom Mix and the other stars were victims of the times. Hollywood was pretty rugged in those early days—the jazz age, flapper era, et cetera. The film industry was comparatively new, and so many were being swept into sudden success that it caught them unprepared. Most of them had not learned that there were physical limitations. They were still trying to keep up with their popularity and the demands of their fans.

Chapter 5

A 1920s Hollywood Mogul

Unemployed Cowboys

Hollywood and the hundred miles of surrounding countryside provided the ideal climate and scenery for early moviemakers. Within this distance were the snow-capped Sierra Nevada, with their ice, deep gorges and chasms, rivers, mountain lakes, and valleys. There was also Catalina Island, with its varied scenery, and the ocean, with beaches, rocky shores, and an ever-changing coastline.

The cowboy's main attraction to Hollywood and vice versa has best been described by Diana Serra Cary in her book *The Hollywood Posse: The Story of a Gallant Band of Horsemen Who Made Hollywood History*. Cary was a child star known as Baby Peggy in the early twenties, and her father was a well-known double and stuntman, Jack Montgomery. Jack worked with Tom Mix at Mixville during the height of Tom's career and later for Carl Laemmle's fabled Universal City, which supported a number of western stars in the twenties and thirties. Cary's story is about the Hollywood posse of stuntmen and doubles who risked life and limb to help make the stars look good.

Sometime after 1912 the great cattle empires began to crumble, and hundreds of seasoned cowhands and range riders found themselves out of work. By one quirk of fate or another, a sizable band of these out of work cowboys and expert horsemen ended up in Hollywood; they were just what the big producers like Thomas Ince, D. W. Griffith, and Cecil B. DeMille needed to stay in business.

The producers wanted riders who were chronically unemployed and therefore immediately available for work. Second, they wanted experienced, hard-riding daredevils who were crazy enough to risk life and limb on a regular basis to provide entertainment for the early movie patrons. For example, hundreds of skilled riders might be needed for an Indian or cavalry attack or even a biblical film portrayal.

This band of western drifters frequently hung out and played poker, as they waited, at a small café called the Water Hole. Others spent a few hours or even a day or so at the Universal pens just outside the Universal City studio gates. Some of the unemployed cowboys also bided their time at the Sunset Barn, where western stars stabled their horses. The objective was to be seen and be immediately available for work whenever needed. Many of these cowhands, who started out as doubles and stuntmen, later became stars in their own right.

The unemployed cowboys soon became familiar with the western stars, directors, and producers of the twenties and thirties. According to Hank Bell, a former Texas cowboy turned stuntman,

> The cowboys who rode in [the stars'] shadows could read them better than anyone else alive. They observed the hero under fire, confronted by the daily challenge of the job and the nightly pitfalls of fame. They would pursue generations of such big names, eating stardust as they followed each White Hat's fortune from his first big break to the last fade-out in the final frame of a long and precarious career. . . . They had only one yard-stick by which to judge any man, from the greenest juvenile to the most powerful director, and that was, Is he the kind of man you'd want to ride the river with?

Climb to the Top

Tom did not realize it, but his climb to great fame and riches beyond his imagination, as King of the Cowboys, started in 1917 when he signed a new contract with William F. Fox. Tom made only six films for Fox that year, and most of them were two-reelers, 30 minutes long. However, from 1918 on, most of Tom's Fox films were feature-length five-reelers, 75 minutes long. Tom's marriage to his leading lady, Victoria Forde, in 1918 also seemed to further enhance his movie career, pushing him toward that elusive stardom. Tom's greatest film output for Fox was nine films each in 1920 and 1922; by 1921, he reached the peak of his career with Fox and took the title of King of the Cowboys away from William S. Hart. Tom's horse, Tony, was accepted by the moviegoing public as a star in his own right. In Tom's last year with Fox, 1928, he made only four films. However, he also made five six- and seven-reelers, 90 to 105 minutes long, for the Film Booking Office (FBO) in 1928. Unfortunately, the FBO films were rebuked by reviewers and did not help Tom's career.

If the shoot-'em-up westerns were nourished in the teens, then the B westerns were in full bloom in the twenties. The roaring twenties brought a history-breaking number of western stars to the silver screen, including Pete Morrison, Roy Stewart, Buck Jones, Jack Hoxie, Hoot Gibson, William Desmond, J. P. McGowan, Dustin Farnum, Neal Hart, Fred Hume, William S. Hart, William Duncan, Bob Custer, Harry Carey, Edmund Cobb, Ted Wells, Bob Steele, Charles Jones, William Farnum, Art Acord, Yakima Canutt, William Russell, Tom Santschi, Fred Thomson,

Franklyn Farnum, Robert McKim, William Fairbanks, Ken Maynard, Tim McCoy, and Tom Mix.

According to Edgar M. Wyatt, in his book *More Than a Cowboy; The Life and Films of Fred Thomson and Silver King,* the nine highest-paid silent-era cowboys were: Bronco Billy Anderson; the first cowboy star, William S. Hart; Tom Mix; Buck Jones; Fred Thomson; Ken Maynard; Hoot Gibson; Jack Hoxie; Art Acord; and Yakima Canutt. The first six made over a million dollars; Tom Mix led the pack with a top salary of $20,000 per week for 52 weeks—the highest salary ever paid in the history of show business through 1942. Neither Anderson nor Hart had a western background, yet both managed to make a fortune on westerns in the teens and early twenties.

The Big Five

Other writers and the voting public have dubbed Buck Jones, Ken Maynard, Hoot Gibson, Tim McCoy, and Tom Mix as "the Big Five"—the greatest western stars of all time. These men were true heroes of the Old West and the last of the real-life cowboys who eventually became movie cowboys; the guitar-strumming dudes of the "singing cowboy" era could hardly be classified as real cowboys. While this is partially true, they certainly were not the only great cowboy movie stars of the twenties. Tom was the oldest of this group, nine years older than Jones and 15 years older than Maynard; Gibson and McCoy were in the middle of the group. However, Tom had 10 years of early filmmaking experience on the other four members of the so-called Big Five.

William S. Hart

Let's take a look at some of the cowboy stars of the twenties and at the traits that made them famous. To movie patrons who idolized William S. Hart, Tom Mix must have appeared as some sort of comic relief; the two men had absolutely nothing in common. Hart was known as a fine Shakespearean actor when Thomas Ince brought him to the West in 1912 after he appeared as Messala in the original New York stage play *Ben Hur.* Soon, Hart was on the 101 Ranch lot near Santa Monica, where he played the villain in *The Squaw Man* and followed this with an outstanding performance in *The Virginian.*

Hart became obsessed with realism. He killed villains who needed killing, drank rotgut whiskey at the local saloon, chewed tobacco, and spit the juice with unerring accuracy into a brass spittoon. After a hard day on the range or a big cattle drive, Hart and his boys came to town, downed a few shots of old Red Eye and raced their horses down the street, whooping, hollering, and firing their six-guns in the air to let off steam. But when the

Tom as he appeared early in his career with Fox. Note the personal "TEM" monogram on his shirt. (Author's collection.)

sheriff needed a few stouthearted men to ride after the desperadoes, Hart and his gang were usually the first to volunteer, helping to bring the bad men to justice. About the only realistic thing that Hart did not do was spend time with one of the ladies of the night in an upstairs room at the Blue Belle Saloon.

Hart was so obsessed with realism he even tried to convince himself that he was an authentic westerner, claiming he had grown up on a ranch in the Dakota Territory. No one, including himself, was ever able to verify his claim.

Stuntman Hank Bell gave his opinion of William S. Hart:

> Bill Hart's all ham, and melodrama is his middle name. He can put on that dome of a hat and deck himself out in a bandana as big as a Harvey House tablecloth, but he ain't no hand. ... He's got the conscience of a Puritan elder and about as much sex appeal as a Joshua tree. Besides, he's always suckin' on a stick of alum between takes, and that's how he gets his face all puckered up and solemn lookin' come shootin' time.

Fred Thomson

Ed Wyatt has made an interesting comparison between Tom Mix and Fred Thomson in his book *More Than a Cowboy*. Fred Thomson (Frederick Clifton Thomson) was an all-around track-and-field star and a Presbyterian and World War I army artillery minister. He made films from 1921 until his unexpected but natural death on Christmas night in 1928. Thomson may have died as the result of a liver or kidney problem, complicated by tetanus and following several blood transfusions.

By the time Fred Thomson made his third film, he was a star; Wyatt estimates that Thomson made only about 30 films, most of them for FBO. By contrast, Tom had made an estimated 236 films for Selig and 29 for Fox by 1921. By 1914, Tom has been put in charge of his own Selig western film crew, even though the star sysem had not yet been formalized. Tom's climb to the top was definitely not meteoric.

Wyatt also describes Thomson as combining the effortless acrobatics of Douglas Fairbanks with the elaborate stunts of Tom Mix. Thomson was noted for his fine acrobatics, believable plots, and lively action sequences. Like Mix, Thomson also dressed for the movie cowboy's role. Mix loved the spotlight and attention, but Thomson was quieter and more modest.

Wyatt feels that Fred Thomson and his horse, Silver King, were rapidly gaining on Tom Mix and "Tony" in popularity by 1924 and that they would have become more popular than Tom and Tony if death had not claimed Thomson in 1928. This appears to be a fair evaluation because Mix's 1928 FBO films were not well received by the moviegoing public or the critics. Fred Thomson was only 38 years old in 1928, while Tom was 48 years old, and his age was beginning to take its toll.

Even though Tom made a relatively successful movie comeback for Universal in 1932, Fred Thomson would probably have surpassed him in popularity had he lived. Fred Thomson and Silver King have been described as the only serious competition that Tom Mix and Tony had in the twenties.

William F. Cody, "Buffalo Bill," was the boyhood hero of Tom Mix, Tim McCoy, and Billy Jenkins, "the German Buffalo Bill." (Author's collection.)

Colonel Tim McCoy

Colonel Tim McCoy has been described as "the Man of Destiny in Basic Black" and "the Last Plainsman." He had a military bearing and the air of an aristocrat. His icy stare would freeze the hearts and gunhands of his villainous opponents. Tim was reputed to have the fastest six-gun draw of any western star.

Buffalo Bill Cody was Tim's boyhood hero, and real-life Indians became his friends. Tim was a working cowboy, a rancher, a U.S. Cavalry officer, the adjutant general of Wyoming, a performer with the Ringling Brothers and Barnum and Bailey Circus, and head of his own traveling Wild West show.

As a young man, Tim worked on the Double Diamond Ranch for a man called "Irish Tom," and since Tim liked to sing to the cattle at night, he soon became known as "Irish Tom's Canary."

In 1922, at the age of 32, Tim became the technical adviser for the epic film *The Covered Wagon*. Many of Colonel Tim McCoy's fringe, buckskin, and beaded Indian-scout costumes remind us of Buffalo Bill and appear as gaudy as Mix's personal-appearance costumes. McCoy soon became MGM's answer to Tom Mix and Hoot Gibson.

In the early thirties, Tim worked for Columbia pictures. His movie career extended into the early forties, and he made cameo appearances as late as 1965.

Hoot Gibson

Edward "Hoot" Gibson, known as "Hooter" to his friends, has been described as a cowboy's cowboy. Gibson became a rodeo star, stuntman, and movie star. Hoot bought his first horse at age 15 and headed West, where he gained a reputation for breaking horses. At age 17, he won the Pendleton Roundup in Oregon and became Champion All-Around Cowboy. Some people say he was discovered by Buck Jones, others by Tom Mix. One thing is known for sure; he appeared in the following Tom Mix/Selig films: *Pride of the Range* (1910), *The Man from the East* (1914), *The Man from Texas* (1915).

Based on his film appearances, it is more likely Hoot was discovered by Tom Mix, since Buck Gebhart (Jones) was an unknown at this time. Hoot was a terrific cowboy, known for his roundhouse punches and big fight scenes. It has been said that he tended to overemphasize the comic element in his light western films.

Harry Carey, a top western star for Universal in the late teens, and a young director named Jack Ford helped Hoot Gibson get work with Universal. In his early films, Hoot considered himself a stuntman. According to Diana Serra Cary, daughter of famed stuntman, Jack Montgomery, Hoot was once asked by a Universal director if he would allow himself to be dragged by a running horse for an extra five dollar. Hoot's reply was, "Make it ten and I'll let him kick me to death."

Hoot was known as a great horseman and trick rider. He was one of the greatest Roman riders of all time—someone who could stand on the back of two horses galloping at full speed around a Wild West show or rodeo arena. A Roman rider can also ride backward, back the team up, turn

According to some historians, Buck Jones learned the tricks of the trade at the 101 Ranch from none other than Tom Mix. (Author's collection.)

them, and swap the horses while still standing on their backs; it's a good show.

By 1921, Hoot Gibson replaced Carey as Universal's top western star, and Carey's contract was not renewed. At the peak of his career, Hoot's salary with Universal was about $14,500 a week. But in 1930, Hoot's career with Universal came to an end, and Universal signed a contract with Buck Jones for a measly $1,000 a week. Hoot then moved on to Allied Pictures.

Buck Jones

Buck Jones (Charles Frederick Gebhart) looked like Hart but fought like Mix, which turned out to be a successful combination. Jones was a fine actor and a good rider. Buck Jones joined the U.S. Army Cavalry in January 1907, suffered a bad leg wound by the Philippine Moros in late 1909, and was mustered out of service in October 1913. Apparently, Buck learned to ride and shoot while in the service, and he picked up the rest of his Wild West experience working for the 101 Ranch. Buck Jones appeared in the following five Tom Mix/Fox films before becoming a star in his own right:

Western Blood (1918), *The Wilderness Trail* (1919), *The Speed Maniac* (1919), *The Cyclone* (1920), and *Dick Turpin* (1925).

According to Sam Henderson, it was Tom Mix who first came up with the idea of using singing cowboys to increase the popularity of his feature films in 1919. The Tom Mix Quartet, consisting of Buck Jones, Peewee Holmes, Earl Simpson, and Riley Caldwell, was formed to entertain the audience between showings of Tom Mix feature films. Nine years later, a new group of singing cowboys began to replace the old shoot-em'-up stars. Perhaps one could say Tom Mix brought it all on himself.

It has also been said that Buck Jones followed in Tom's shadow. Apparently, William F. Fox was grooming Jones to replace Tom Mix in the event that Mix's salary or other demands got out of line. However, Fred Thomson entered the scene and soon became a threat to the careers of both men.

Buck Jones had small parts in the Mix movies mentioned above and allegedly doubled for Mix in some of his movies. However, after becoming a star in his own right, Jones made over two hundred movies in a career that spanned 25 years.

Buck Jones lived a hero on the screen and died a hero in real life. He was caught in the disastrous Coconut Grove night club fire in 1942 and later died as a result of burns he received while trying to help save others. Jones was on a personal appearance tour at the time of the fire promoting his popular *Rough Riders* series.

Ken Maynard

Ken Maynard was born in Texas and raised a cowboy. He was one of the greatest riders of all time and rode with different Wild West shows as a youngster. Maynard dressed like Mix and tended to overemphasize his trick riding skills. Rooftop chases became a Maynard specialty.

In 1920, at the age of 25, Ken Maynard became the World's Champion Trick Rider and second place All Around Cowboy. A William F. Fox movie scout spotted Maynard while he was performing as a trick rider with the Ringling Brothers' Circus.

Ken Maynard was probably one of the first unofficial singing cowboys because he also liked to strum a guitar and warble a tune, which he did in at least one early film. Ken Maynard made over three hundred films during his movie career before retiring in the 1940s.

Tom Mix

Tom was not a western purist. He did on the screen what he knew best how to do — rode hard, performing daredevil stunts calculated to keep the audience on the edge of their seats. Tony, who knew no master other than Tom, was superbly trained. Tony could untie his master's hands, perform amazing jumps, or pull Tom from a blazing fire. Each stunt was performed with such perfection that horse and rider functioned as one. The lariat and six-guns added to the flashing adventures of the Old West.

Old-timers who knew Tom say that Tom would talk to his horse just like he would talk to another cowboy. If he wanted Tony to do a particular stunt, he would lead the horse through the sequence, explaining the stunt to him in detail. Then Tom would turn to the cameraman and director to let them know he and Tony were ready. Most of the stunts, no matter how difficult, were completed on the first take. People close to Tom and Tony felt that Tony really was a Wonder Horse.

Tom and Tony performed nearly all of their own stunts until they became too valuable an asset to the Fox studios. Even then, Tom would often insist on doing his own stunts and permit a substitute to be used only for Tony. Tom was the one who suffered when the timing of one of his stunts was slightly off. The close-up cameras usually revealed that Tom was the man fighting on the top of the mountain, riding his horse into the swirling waters as a bridge collapsed, and jumping from horse to train and back again. Possible broken arms and legs were risks of the trade as far as Tom was concerned, and he paid the penalty more than once. Several times the shooting schedule of a Tom Mix picture had to be interrupted while Fox's top star lay in a hospital bed recuperating from injuries received on location.

Most of all, Tom Mix and Tony represented the finest showmanship of their time. The cowboy in his broad-brimmed Stetson and the well-groomed, white-stockinged sorrel horse rode together to fame and fortune. The fancy duds and hand-carved boots were never intended to represent the working clothes of the average cowboy, nor the intricate stunts the everyday happenings of his life. The costume and stunts exaggerated the adventure and romance of the Old West, and the audience loved every minute of it. A next-to-impossible stunt was executed with such smoothness that it appeared to be a natural occurrence in a Tom Mix movie.

Tom Mix streamlined the western movie and set the stage for generations of cowboy movie heroes yet to come.

Actor, Producer, Director and Fall Guy

Colonel William F. Selig never fully realized the great potential he had in Tom Mix. He tended to keep Tom's salary down at the same time he made him completely responsible for his own pictures. Selig failed to furnish Tom with any professional help as far as writing scripts and devising plots were concerned. Some early writers have said it is remarkable that Tom and Tony survived the Selig era. Tom was strictly on his own, and he earned every penny he made under Selig. Tom learned the tricks of the trade through his own experiences, and the quality of his pictures steadily improved, despite these early handicaps.

Fox was quicker to recognize the potential of Tom Mix and Tony. Fox used Tom's boyish nature to make a strong appeal to the youthful audience. Pictures such as *Cupid's Roundup, Six-Shooter Andy,* and *Do and Dare* were specifically aimed at the younger generation. Youngsters also appeared in Tom's pictures, and he always proved worthy of their trust and friendship. Tom was a first-class hero for any youngster.

Tom's Golden Years

By 1920, Colleen Moore had become one of Tom's leading ladies, and Tom had replaced William S. Hart as America's most popular western star. In the same year, Tom visited with Jack Dempsey and engaged him in a friendly boxing match. Boxing was part of Tom's physical fitness program, and he maintained his weight at a healthy 175 pounds. It was also in 1920 that Tom's friend Will Rogers appeared in Rogers's first movie, *Laughing Billy Hyde.* He became a popular film star of the thirties, and in one picture, Will did a satire on Tom Mix and western films.

By 1921, Tom was one of the top box-office attractions in the country. Other stars of the period were Douglas Fairbanks, Charlie Chaplin, Mary Pickford, Gloria Swanson, Lillian Gish, Richard Barthelmess, and Constance Talmadge, to mention a few. With Tom's fame came a host of necessary social and promotional engagements, such as Tom and Tony's 1921 visit to President and Mrs. Harding in Washington, D.C. A publicity photo was taken of Tom and Tony on the lawn of the White House. During the same year, Tom and Tony were star attractions at a luncheon at the Hotel Astor in New York City. As the luncheon started, Tom excused himself and reappeared a few minutes later with Tony, much to the delight of the patrons.

On September 22, 1921, Tom sent a telgram to Justin Bootmakers of Nocona, Texas. The telegram read as follows: "PLEASE MAKE TWO PAIRS OF BOOTS SAME AS THE FIRST PAIR. SHIP TO LOS ANGELES. MAKE THESE AS SOON AS YOU CAN AS I AM SORELY IN NEED OF THEM. THIS GRAND CANYON IS SURE GRAND BUT HARD ON BOOTS. OBLIGE. TOM MIX."

The Peak of His Career

Tom Mix reached the peak of his career with Fox in 1922, the same year he hit another milestone, the birth of his daughter, Thomasina, on February 12, 1922. In that same year, his $250,000, Hollywood Hills home was completed and his seven-car garage was filled with fancy imports worth

At age 16, Colleen Moore became Tom's leading lady in *The Wilderness Trail,* circa 1919. (Author's collection.)

about $100,000. His salary with Fox was about $17,500 a week, and he bought his dream ranch in Arizona—11,000 acres he owned and an additional 25,000 acres leased from the U.S. Department of the Interior. Several Fox films were made at Tom's Arizona ranch.

Tom's Hollywood Hills home was a four-bedroom, three-bath home with four thousand square feet of living space. It also boasted a guest house with two bedrooms, a kitchen, and bath. Central air conditioning and Spanish architecture were featured throughout. The entryway of the main house featured large peg-and-groove flooring, Spanish arches, stained-glass windows, and railings that overlooked a large step-down living room with rough-hewn beam ceilings and a floor-to-ceiling rock fireplace. The family room had cathedral and French windows and doors that opened onto a long balcony with a view of the canyon. Victoria's part of the house, the living room, was furnished with an Aubusson rug and delicate Louis XVI furniture. Tom's part of the house, the family room, was furnished with animal heads, Navajo rugs, mission-type furniture, and other western paraphernalia. The formal dining room also had peg-and-groove flooring and stained-glass windows in the dining area. The kitchen had a breakfast area, barbecue, dishwasher, and garbage disposal. The master bath had

Top: Tom's home near Los Angeles. *Bottom:* His Beverly Hills mansion. (Author's collection.)

imported hand-painted ceramic tiles and a private dressing room. Tom's Hollywood Hills home was convenient to the studios, shopping, and Toluca Lake.

It was also in 1922 that Tom Mix and Tony put on an exhibition of stunts at the American Legion Stadium for a show titled "A Presentation of Making the Movies." Many of the famous stars of the period participated in the event to give visitors some insights into the wonderful world of moviemaking. A few months later, Tom also participated in Sacramento's Days of '49 gold-rush celebration. Tony missed out on this event because the railroad would not let Tony's caretaker ride with him.

In 1923, Tom and Tony helped Fox celebrate the opening of a new theater in Oakland, California. This special occasion marked the completion of Fox's coast-to-coast chain of theaters. During the grand opening, Tom rode Tony into the lobby and down one of the aisles to the applause of the audience. Outside the theater, thousands of children lined the streets for a glimpse of Tom Mix and Tony. Tom was not about to disappoint his young fans and, without hesitation, put Tony through his paces with some fancy sidestepping and romping. The same year, a charity circus was sponsored for the Children's Hospital of Los Angeles, and Tom and Tony were featured in the program. Helping children meant more than good publicity to Tom because he believed children were American's future.

Despite the great scenery near Hollywood and his Arizona ranch, Tom often favored filming his Fox spectaculars at locations such as the Grand Canyon, Yosemite Valley, and the national parks. In *Sky High,* Tom and Tony leaped 11 feet across a 1,000-foot-deep gorge, and in *Three Jumps Ahead,* they vaulted over 20 feet across a 90-foot-deep chasm. In *The Rough Diamond,* Tom rode Tony into the water from a 50-foot-high pier; in yet another film, Tom rode Tony up and down several flights of stairs in a hotel scene.

Risks of the Trade

During the filming of *Eyes of the Forest,* late in 1923, Tom and Tony were injured by a poorly timed gunpowder explosion on a narrow trail. In the story, Tom plays an aviation ranger with the U.S. Forest Service. As he battles a gang of forest thieves, their leader plans to kill him. The bandits plant a mine along a narrow trail where they know the ranger must pass. A large charge of gunpowder was used, and the charge was covered with a pile of small rocks.

The charge was supposed to be triggered about two seconds afer Tom and Tony passed the spot, which was calculated to put them 50 feet beyond the explosion. Due to an error in timing, the charge was detonated as Tom and Tony passed the spot. The force of the explosion blew Tom and Tony

50 feet, injuring both and knocking them unconscious. Tony regained consciousness first and nudged his master until he came to. After Tom got his bearings, he noticed a large gash in Tony's side and sewed him up with needle and thread from an emergency medical kit. Tom's back was badly torn, but his injuries were not life-threatening. On November 11, 1923, newspapers noted Tom's and Tony's injuries, and on December 11, 1923, they noted Tony's rapid recovery.

In almost every movie, Tom and Tony risked life and limb. They tempted fate hundreds of times but were seldom injured. It was the elaborate stunting, action, and adventure that made Tom Mix and Tony the idols of America's youth and their parents.

Famous Initials and the Diamond TM Bar Brand

Tom's initials and the famous TM Bar brand were emblazoned on just about everything in sight at his ranch: the electrically operated gate, the doors of his mansion, over his fireplace mantel, and on nearly every piece of gear in sight. Tom had a string of fine horses and a large saddle collection, most of which were silver-studded. Tom had his own permanent sets constructed at Mixville (Tom Mix Rancho), located on 60 acres in the Fox Hills between Hollywood and Santa Monica. Tom's initials were gaudily displayed in lights outside his mansion—there could be no mistake as to where the famous cowboy lived.

Tom Mix had such a fetish when it came to using his brand and initials that he even had the tires of his Rolls Royce embossed so that they would leave the famous "TM" initials imprinted on the numerous dirt-roads in southern California.

Tom had an extensive wardrobe and a vast gun collection. Twenty-eight of his guns are now housed in the Tom Mix Museum in Dewey, Oklahoma. Included in the collection are 14 handguns, 9 rifles, and 5 shotguns. Most of these guns have fancy engraving and the famous Mix name or initials. Many of the handguns have pearl or bone handles. Some of the guns in the collection are:

- Bisley .45 Cal single action with 4.75-inch barrel
- Browning semiautomatic shotgun in 16 gauge
- Colt .41 caliber single-shot Derringer
- Two Colt single-action revolvers in .45 caliber with 7.5-inch barrels
- Matched set of Colt Army Special revolvers in .38 caliber
- Matched set of Colt Police Specials in .38 caliber
- Matched set of Colt Officers' revolvers in .38 caliber
- Iver Johnson double-action revolver in .22 caliber
- Marlin 1894 Saddle Ring Carbine in .38–.40 caliber

- Marlin lever action shotgun in .410 gauge
- Custom German Mauser bolt-action rifle in 8 mm caliber
- William Parkhurst 20-gauge double-barrel shotgun
- Remington Model 11 semiautomatic shotgun in 12 gauge
- S & W Model 3 single-action revolver in .44 caliber
- S & W Model 10 double-action revolver in .38 Spl. caliber
- S & W double-action .357 Magnum with white grips
- Custom Winchester 1890 rifle in .22 caliber
- Two Winchester 1892 Saddle Ring Carbines in .44 caliber smooth
- Winchester 1892 Saddle Ring Carbine in .44 W.C.F. caliber
- Winchester 1892 Saddle Ring Carbine in .38 W.C.F. caliber
- Winchester 1892 lever-action rifle in .38 W.C.F. caliber
- Winchester 1905 semiautomatic rifle in .32 W.S.C. caliber

This list represents only a small portion of the guns owned and used by Tom Mix at one time or another. Many of his guns are currently in the hands of private collectors or other museums, such as the Texas Ranger Museum in Waco, Texas.

Tom also had a roomful of boots and shoes, over six hundred pairs, most of which were embossed with his initials. He had several western-cut dress suits and, for special occasions, a purple tuxedo. He wore a diamond-studded platinum belt buckle and diamond-studded spurs. Tom apparently tried to rival Diamond Jim Brady with regard to his jewelry collection. His fancy dress for personal appearances was often gaudier than the elaborate costumes he wore for the silver screen; he dressed and acted the way the public expected a top star to dress and act in the roaring twenties, when money was plentiful, times were good, and Hollywood gaiety flourished.

Despite the show of great wealth and his extravagance, he was never a snob. His old-time friends remained his friends, and his money seemed to make little difference to him. He was generous to the point of fault and would invest in a hare-brained scheme just to help an old friend. Once, during a visit to his hometown of DuBois, Tom mentioned to a friend that he would like to see one of his boyhood friends again. When the boyhood friend heard that Tom was in town and wanted to see him, he remarked, "Well, Tom knows where I live." Word got back to Tom, and he excused himself and took time to look up his boyhood pal. Tom's buddy was impressed, a little apologetic, and most happy to see that Tom had not changed a bit.

Early Lawsuit

In 1924, Tom was sued by the 101 Ranch and Wild West Show for breaking his contract with them. Tom's movie contract with Fox had

Tom and wife, Vickie, shared the good times. (Author's collection.)

expired, and at the time, it appeared that he would have the 1924 season open. In the meantime, Fox advanced the shooting schedules for Tom's western pictures so that they were to begin work during the 1924 season. Tom had been more or less under continuous contract with Fox. The movie industry paid triple what the 101 Wild West Show could afford to pay, so Tom returned to Fox. To settle the lawsuit, a compromise agreement was reached between Tom and Zack Miller: Tom appeared with the

101 Wild West Show between pictures, in Kansas City, Chicago, Cincinnati, Washington, D.C., and at Madison Square Garden in New York. As it turned out, the lawsuit publicity helped both Fox and the 101 Ranch show. This was destined to be the last "friendly" lawsuit between Zack Miller and Tom Mix, however.

First European Tour

In 1925, Tom and Tony visited Europe for the first time. Tom was accompanied by his wife, Vicky, his young daughter, Thomasina, and Thomasina's grandmother. Tony was accompanied by Pat Chrisman, his caretaker. The party departed Los Angeles on March 28, 1925, heading for New York City, where Tom and Tony drew a large crowd as Tony was walked through the railroad station. Tony was stabled by the city's police while waiting to board the ocean liner the *Aquitania.*

On April 8, 1925, Tom and Tony made headlines when Tom rode Tony up the gangplank as they boarded. A special stall had been built for Tony on one of the lower decks. During the voyage, Tom rode Tony into the dining room and up the grand staircase. On the last day of the voyage, Tom walked Tony back and forth on the passenger deck, exercising him and giving him a breath of fresh salt air.

London

The next day the ship docked at South Hampton, the harbor for all London-bound passengers. This time, Tom rode Tony down the gangplank and was greeted by the deputy mayor of South Hampton and the mayors of Brighton and Howe, then took the train to London, where Tony was stabled at the famed Tattersalls stable at the invitation of the Prince of Wales. Tom looked forward to riding Tony down Rotten Row, a bridle path in Hyde Park where the fashionable people of London rode their horses. Otherwise known as the King's Way, the path is 90 feet wide and a mile and a half long and stretches from Hyde Park Corners to Kensington Gate. Hundreds of children swarmed the bridle path to see Tom demonstrate his ability to stand in Tony's saddle and ride Indian style (sliding down on one side of the horse so that he could not be seen from the other side).

While in London, Tom also visited a rest home for old horses and donkeys at Cricklewood. Tom was happy to see that there was a place for faithful old horses who had served their masters well.

Paris

After visiting London, Tom's party crossed the English Channel by boat to arrive at Paris on April 18, 1925. While in France, Tony was invited by the famous French racehorse Epinard to be his guest at Maison Lafitte, the famous training grounds and racing stable. On their second day in France, Tom and Tony did a benefit performance for the Children's Welfare League at the six-thousand-seat Trocadero Hall. To the delight of the children, Tom rode Tony up into the balcony and back down again. In appreciation, the entertainment chairman kissed Tom on both cheeks and presented him with a silver medal from the French Association for the Protection of Horses.

While in Paris, Tom also attended a Boy Scout conclave and presented deserving scouts with a full set of scout equipment. Tony was still hobnobbing with Epinard and did not attend the conclave. Tom and Tony broadcast their thanks to the people of France and headed for Berlin.

Berlin

On the way to Berlin, Tom and Tony made stops at Brussels and Amsterdam, where they were warmly greeted by large crowds, then boarded the *Amsterdam Express* for Berlin. Tom rode Tony down the Unter den Linden, a famous drive lined with Linden trees. As had happened in London, enthusiastic crowds frequently blocked their pathway. At the Adlon Hotel, Tom was greeted by city officials and several boy scout troops. Tom gave out dozens of white Stetson hats, costing $125 each, on his European trip and in turn he received many gifts, including several medals from various branches of the Humane Society.

Tom's United States and Canadian Tour

After Tom's Berlin engagement, he and his family boarded the *Mauritania* for the trip home. The Mix party arrived back in New York City on July 21, 1925. Pat Chrisman and Tony returned home a few days later aboard the *Aquitania*. While Tom was waiting for Tony to arrive, he visited the Children's Hospital in Boston and several historic sites and was presented with another Humane Society medal by a little boy who said, "Mr. Mix, we have a medal for you to show you how much we like you and because you like animals."

From Boston, Tom went to Toronto, Canada, to attend a luncheon at the King Edward Hotel. Next came a reception at the parliamentary buildings, where Tom was presented with another Humane Society medal. While in Toronto, he was also entertained by the Royal Canadian Dragoons and their thoroughbred horses.

Then, Tom joined up with Tony in New York, and they traveled to Washington, D.C., for the National Horse Show. Tom and Tony cleared the highest hurtle and were presented with a horseshoe wreath of red and white carnations. While in Washington, they were guests of President and

Tom and Vicky Mix visit Berlin on a 1925 European tour. (Author's collection.)

Mrs. Coolidge as the Disabled War Veterans entertained the president and his wife on the White House lawn. Tom and Tony also put on a little show for the crowd.

From Washington, D.C., Tom and Tony's personal appearance tour went to Buffalo, New York, Detroit, Michigan, St. Louis, Missouri, and Denver, Colorado. In each of these cities, they were greeted by thousands of children. Finally, it was back to Los Angeles and a surprise welcome home party for Tom Mix and Tony. As they got off the train, they were greeted by six stagecoaches filled with cowboys and Indians, gold prospectors, and other western characters. Dignitaries and boy scouts seemed to be everywhere. In fact, the whole town turned out for the celebration and, after an exchange of greetings, a parade wound through Los Angeles and on to the Fox Studios in Westwood. At the studios, Tom was greeted by studio officials, schoolchildren, Shriners, and Pal, a little white bulldog with a pink nose. While on his tour, Tony had missed rubbing noses with his old friend Pal.

Chip Off the Old Block

Tom's 14-year-old daughter, Ruth, entered motion pictures in 1927 and made a series of cowgirl films with Rex Bell. She was billed as "a chip off the old block," terminology that Tom was not happy about. After all, the 47-year-old block was still in excellent health and knew that he had a long way to go.

On October 13, 1927, an article titled "The Coconut Grove," by Tom Mix, appeared in *Life* magazine. In the article, Tom or his ghostwriter lionized Ben Frank's Coconut Grove restaurant as a Hollywood institution. After describing the interior of the restaurant and the dance floor, Tom provides some humorous insight about Moving Picture Night, a weekly event.

> A lot of picture stars go to the Grove because they are afraid to stay away. If you miss a few of the players on a picture night, you can lay a good bet on the line that they didn't come because they didn't have anything new to wear. Of course, all have ermine or near-ermine coats. There's probably more summer, winter, spring and fall ermine coats in Hollywood than any other place in the world. I know picture women who bought ermine coats when they didn't have anything to wear under them—not that they wear much more under them now. It's a good thing the styles in ermine coats don't change. If they ever do, it'll work a greater hardship on Hollywood than the bustin' of the only bank in town would do to an Arizona cow settlement.
>
> Most of the men stars get dragged in by their wives, although some of the boys still thinks it's good advertisin' to attend the Coconut Grove an' give the customers from Keokuk, Kalamazoo, Kansas City and Kankakee a treat.
>
> Movin' Picture Night is a great money-makin' event for the Coconut Grove waiters, as they hustle around an' get the stars to autograph menu cards for the visitin' brother an' sisters, receivin' from four bits to a dollar tip for each one. I've written "Tom Mix" on so many menus that now every waiter in the place can imitate my handwritin'. Maybe I ought to be thankful for a-writin' of these autographs, as it's sure improved my penmanship. The men stars sit around with a bored air that is supposed to indicate social manners, although I still believe when a lady or gent does a polite yawn, it's time for 'em to be a-hittin' for the bunk house.

Grauman's Chinese Theater

In December 1927, Tom Mix and Tony were honored by having their names, handprints, and footprints embedded in cement at Sid Grauman's Chinese Theater on Hollywood Boulevard during the celebration of *Forest Ranger's Night,* which showed with Douglas Fairbanks, Sr. in *The Gaucho.* The ceremonies took place in a courtyard named the Forecourt Gallery of Fame. Tom wrote his name, then made his handprints and footprints. He took a couple of Tony's shoes, made his footprints, and signed Tony's name for him. Other imprints made the same year included those of Douglas Fairbanks Sr., William S. Hart, and Mary Pickford.

A Ten-Week Vaudeville Tour

In March 1928, Tom's contract with Fox expired, and he and two other cowboys went on a ten-week vaudeville tour to demonstrate fancy roping, sharpshooting, and western yarn spinning. The show played Denver, Chicago, and the New York Hippodrome Theater. While in New York, Tom awarded boy scouts with the horsemanship medals they had earned.

On June 1, 1928, the following article appeared in the *Brooklyn Eagle.*

> A luncheon party without a speech was held at the Brooklyn Riding and Driving Club yesterday afternoon when Tony was the guest of four horses owned by Mr. C. Prior. Tony was invited to stand up to a horseshoe table bearing the single course of oats and carrots. Tony carried his master into the ring and frisked about a bit to work up his appetite and to open the eyes and mouths of several hundreds of children who were fortunate enough to gain admission. It was not until photographs had been taken that the hosts arrived. Life is just one long round of work for Tony for he seemed more anxious to play for the benefit of everyone present than to pose for the sake of photographs. However it must be admitted that Tony accepted the flashlights during the luncheon with much better grace than did his hosts, perhaps because he was elegantly attired in his silver saddle, while they were very much d'eshabille.

In about the ninth week of the tour, Tom confided to a friend that he and Tony had had about all of vaudeville they could stand for a while. Most people did not know how to pet a horse and were ignorant of the fact that a horse's nose is as sensitive as their own. Tom related the following story to his friend:

> It was while we were on tour that something happened which I shall never forget. This is about as good an example of the ignorance of some people in treating horses as I have ever seen. One night after the performance was over, a man from the audience came back stage. He walked up to Tony and said, "Hello, old boy," and gave him a quick, hard slap

between the eyes. Tony, as you would expect, threw back his head and shied away from him, at which the man turned to me and said, "That's a fool horse you have there. Can't a person get near him?"

I didn't reply in words but gave him what he had given Tony. When he covered his nose with his hands and stepped away from me, I reminded him that he was acting the same as any horse would act if a person walked up to him and hit him on the nose. If he had approached Tony quietly, put his arm up over his neck, and gently stroked him or patted him, all would have been well.

Goodbye, Fox—Hello, FBO

Tom made his last pictures for Fox in 1928. Shortly before the Great Depression struck, Tom felt himself at odds with Fox policies that he felt to be wasteful and extravagant. To a great extent, Tom himself had been largely responsible for the tremendous growth of Fox. As a result of this dispute, combined with the fact that "talkies" were now coming in, Fox refused to renew Tom's contract.

Tom was also getting older and beginning to feel the effects of his years. At 48, he began to find it difficult to keep up the pace of making a feature film in a month or less. Tom's departing comment to his Fox studio bosses was alleged to be, "If all business places were run as poorly as the movie business, failure and bankruptcy would be unavoidable."

In 1928 and 1929, Tom made six additional silent films for the Film Booking Office (FBO) which was then under the direction of Joseph P. Kennedy. Originally, Kennedy had hoped that with Tom's help, he could keep the silent films of the Old West alive. However, he soon realized that westerns were out and family features were in, silents were out and talkies were in. Under this change in direction, the FBO film studios were re-organized as the RKO film studios.

It has been said that Tom's FBO movies were poorly done, and the film reviewers let him know it. About *Outlawed,* the critics said: "Not so hot, Mr. Mix, not so hot. The saddle girths are slipping under the King of the Cowboys. He'll do well to lay low, 'til he gets some new gags under his high hat. Here's the same old thing, only worse, without enough sparks, color or action to keep an eight year old boy awake. Another flop like this and the kids will shout a lusty 'Applesauce'."

About *King Cowboy,* the critics were short and to the point: "Please, Mr. Mix, don't do anything like this again." And about *The Drifter,* they said: "Tom Mix is bowing out. The jingle of his spurs will soon be an echo, the sight of his ten gallon hat just a memory. Vaudeville is calling him. He'll probably break little glass balls with a rifle. *The Drifter* is his cinema swan song—his last picture on his last contract. Unfortunately, it won't emblazon the famous Mix initials in film history. Just another western, but send the kids anyway, just to see the aeroplane."

Other stars who suffered through the FBO series were Sally Blaine, Barney Furey, Dorothy Dwan, Ernest Wilson, Frank Austin, Joe Rickson, and Wynn Mace. Whether the pictures were as bad as the *Photoplay* reviews claim is a matter of opinion. It is doubtful that eight- or ten-year-old boys read reviews before going to see their favorite cowboy star, but reviews of this nature undoubtedly hurt Tom and his career. Nevertheless, hundreds of youngsters, including the Kennedy children, remained loyal and faithful friends and fans right up to the bitter end of the series. I feel, too, that the moviegoing audiences may have been merely tired of the silent western format, ready for the talkies, which were introduced by Al Jolson in *The Jazz Singer* in 1927. Jolson was so thrilled by the fact that he could be heard as well as seen that he prophetically exclaimed, "Wait a minute! Wait a minute! You ain't heard nothing yet!"

The Crash of '29

Like many others, Tom lost his shirt in the stock market crash of 1929. It is said that he lost about one million dollars worth of stock, his Beverly Hills mansion, and his Arizona dream ranch. He temporarily retired from pictures—not to go into vaudeville and break little glass balls, but to appear as a top attraction with the Sells-Floto Circus for three seasons. As a main attraction with the circus, Tom's salary reached a peak of about $20,000 a week.

Tom's String of Horses

About the time Tom started his circus career, his string of horses included Tony, Tony Jr., Taggart, Ponca, Buster, Nina, Doc, Osa, Apache, Banjo, Comanche, King Woodford, Clara Bow, Squirrel, Fox, Crow, Betty Lou, Junior, Chipmunk, and Jasper, a trick mule.

Pat Chrisman bought a colt from a Los Angeles street vendor selling vegetables in 1914. Pat shipped the colt to Arizona for training and sold him to Tom for six hundred dollars. Tom named the colt Tony, taught him many tricks, and groomed him for the movies. Tony has been described as a sorrel with white socks on his hind legs. When Tony grew old, Tom began searching for a replacement. Tom found and bought Tony Jr. from a New York State florist. Tony Jr. was also a sorrel with matching mane and tail and four white-stocking legs. He was part Arabian, first trained by John R. Agee as a circus horse; later, Tony Jr. also became a movie horse.

Taggart was a young black horse; Ponca was a blood bay named after the Ponca Indians and one of Tom's best jumping horses. For parades,

Tom liked to use Comanche, a cream-colored palomino with silver mane and tail. Comanche and Buster were also trained for steer-roping events. King Woodford was a large black horse who had mastered many tricks like prancing and stepping in time with music. Apache was a pinto who liked to perform with Nina, Doc, and Osa, who were ring horses. Banjo was a light sorrel who also appeared as a stand-in for Tony in Mix pictures. Clara Bow, Squirrel, Betty Lou, Junior, and Chipmunk rounded out the Mix herd of magnificently trained performing horses. Jasper, the trick mule, was a favorite of the children and provided the comic element in several of Tom's Universal pictures.

Chapter 6

The Ralston Phenomenon

If the movies of the twenties made Tom Mix the idol of America's youth, then the Ralston Purina radio series *Tom Mix and His Ralston Straight Shooters* immortalized him. What further made it unique was that Tom Mix himself never played the role of Tom Mix on radio.

Early History

The pioneers of what would become the Ralston Purina Company had a humble start indeed. A miller named Will Danforth, from Missouri, believed that good food was the secret to good health, a you-are-what-you-eat advocate long before the term *health food* had been coined. Danforth was seeking a way to keep the wheat germ in cereal from becoming rancid. According to the story, a chance meeting with a miller from Kansas provided the answer he was looking for—he had developed a product known as "cracked wheat." Before long, Danforth was packaging and selling Purina Whole Wheat Cereal in the St. Louis, Missouri, area.

Meanwhile, a nutritionist with the surname of Ralston was making nutritional history through his guide to good health, *Life Building.* The guide was so successful that good-health clubs began springing up everywhere. By the turn of the century, Dr. Ralston had over 800,000 good-health believers. Danforth, realizing the need for a sound marketing approach, contacted Dr. Ralston, seeking his endorsement of the Purina whole wheat cereal. Dr. Ralston agreed under the condition that his name be added to it and in 1902 Danforth changed his company's name to Ralston Purina Company.

The distinctive red-and-white checkerboard design and logo came about as the result of Danforth's memories of working as a boy in his father's store. He recalled that one mother in particular always dressed her children in a distinctive red-and-white checked material so that she would have no trouble locating them when it was time to gather them up and go home. The familiar pattern was put on the cereal packaging so that it, too, would stand out on store shelves.

119

Tom Mix Endorses Hot Ralston

Sales for Hot Ralston began sagging in 1933, and the marketing people began looking for someone to pump life into the merchandizing of their healthy breakfast cereal. After a brainstorming session between Will Danforth and copyrighter Charles Claggett of the Gardner Advertising Agency, it was decided that an endorsement by Tom Mix, America's number-one cowboy hero, would do a great deal to restimulate sales. It should be remembered that Tom Mix had just completed a relatively successful movie comeback with his nine talking features for Universal in 1932 and early 1933.

There are many stories about the existence or nonexistence of Tom's original 1933 Ralston contract. According to Jim Harmon in his book *Radio Mystery and Adventure and Its Appearances in Film, Television and Other Media,* the original contract may have been a hand-scribbled document on the back of a large envelope. Tom undoubtedly agreed to lend his name, photographs, circus, and movie-life backgrounds to the advertisers, as well as to permit himself to be impersonated on radio. The terms of the contract and the amount of Tom's royalties are unknown.

In the middle of Tom's first Ralston contract period, he completed *The Miracle Rider* serial for Mascot studios. The series was popular and profitable. In addition, it renewed Tom's image as a cowboy hero with a new generation of young Americans. This recent popularity also created fresh interest among Ralston executives, who offered to renew Tom's contract in 1938 — this time a three-page double-spaced agreement dated April 11, 1938, signed by Tom Mix and witnessed by Elmer G. Marshutz. Signing for the Ralston Purina Company were Donald Danforth Jr., president, and Lewis B. Stuart, treasurer. Tom granted Ralston the right to broadcast a series of programs known as *Tom Mix — Ralston Straight Shooters* and to use continuity advertisements entitled *Tom Mix and the Ralston Straight Shooters* and other titles as necessary. The radio programs were to be broadcast over the National Broadcasting Company, Columbia Broadcasting Company, or others chosen by Ralston Purina. The radio series was to start no earlier than September 1, 1938, and end no later than September 30, 1939.

Tom further granted Ralston the right to use his name; photographs of him, his horse, and his equipment; and the Diamond TM Bar brand in a series of advertisements in magazines such as *Ladies' Home Journal, Woman's Home Companion, Good Housekeeping, True Story, Child's Life, Parents' Magazine,* and others — the leading periodicals fo the day, heavily emphasizing family values.

There was also a clause allowing Ralston to continuously run the radio series and advertisements without individual show or advertisement

Six-and-a-half-year-old Ken Haag in a 1938 Tom Mix Ralston Purina ad. (Courtesy of Ken Haag.)

approval as long as the same high standards of the previous shows or advertisements were used. All Ralston rights were to terminate after December 31, 1939. Copies of all material were to be sent to Tom's Los Angeles office for his files.

Tom was exempt from making public or private appearances, and the Ralston Purina Company agreed to pay him a contract sum of $5,000. Ralston had the right to extend the contract for one additional year by paying an additional $5,000 before July 1, 1939, and to use the contract rights and privileges forever by paying an additional $5,000 before July 1, 1940. Apparently, these additional extensions were granted and the stated fees paid as outlined in the following letter:

June 4, 1940

Mr. Tom Mix
13753 Osborne
Pacoima, California

Dear Tom:

It is a real pleasure to enclose the draft which completes the payments outlined in the option clause of your April 11, 1938 agreement with the Ralston Purina Company. I wish I had an opportunity to visit with you and tell you personally the feeling of appreciation and satisfaction I have because of our contracts together and our cooperation on the Ralston Wheat Cereal program. It is just impossible for me to express my thoughts properly in a letter.

I do want you to know, however, how happy we have been to have Ralston and Tom Mix as partners all through these past years. In Ralston, we have a worthy product that is building a better and stronger youth throughout America. In you, we have had the man who, through his life and example, has been a constant inspiration to these same youth. Together, it has been a great team.

Working with Elmer Marshutz and the Gardner Advertising Agency, we have constantly attempted and, I believe, succeeded in carrying out advertising on a high plane that has been a credit to you and your famous name. While we have done this, you have continued to lead a life that has been above reproach. It is really an inspiration to follow your career and note how you always stand for the best in Hollywood. Your name has been kept clean and free from scandal which, in itself, is a great tribute.

We hope this next year and in future years to continue this fine association with you and to keep your name constantly before millions of our American boys and girls. I hope that during this period we, personally, can have a much closer contact than just an occasional letter.

With best wishes,

Sincerely yours,

HEP
enc.

Tom Mix Radio Show Outline

Tom Mix lived on the TM Bar Ranch in Dobie Township. His horse, Tony, frequently rescued Tom from outlaws and desperadoes. Tom's friends and cohorts were known as Straight Shooters, and one of the main themes of the program was that "Straight Shooters always win!" Tom usually enlisted the aid of portly, middle-aged Sheriff Mike Shaw in rounding up the outlaws. Other characters included the Old Wrangler, an aging but wise and agile sidekick; Pecos, Tom's young sidekick; Jane and Jimmy, Tom's wards; Wash, the black cook; Doc Green, a crusty old frontier doctor; Amos Q. Snood, a likable villain; Boss of Flying City, a dangerous villain; and additional characters who appeared from time to time to round out the cast and enhance the stories. During Curley Bradley's years as Tom Mix, Dick Good frequently played Wash, Jane Webb played Jane, Leo Curley played Sheriff Mike Shaw, Sid Ellstrom played Amos Q. Snood, and Mike Romano played other heavies.

Originally, the series was based on the "true life adventures" of Tom Mix as a soldier, sheriff, and lawman. Unlike other murderless children's serials, such as *Jack Armstrong,* Tom was usually involved in baffling western murder mysteries. When killing was on the rampage, Tom fearlessly tackled the mystery of a vanishing village. He also tried to track down the source of a mysterious voice that appeared on his commercial recordings and defied all rational explanations.

With the advent of World War II, the emphasis changed and Tom jumped right in to promote the national effort on the home front. In one episode, Tom went to Europe, with foreign agents close on his heels, on a secret V-E (Victory in Europe) Day mission. In another episode, he tracked down a giant to its lair only to discover that it was a Japanese terrorist trick to disrupt the home front. Most of these modern episodes had little, if any, resemblance to western adventure. While the mystery and adventure carried the Tom Mix radio show to the top of the children's shows ratings, the lack of believable plots following World War II may have contributed to the show's ultimate demise.

The *Tom Mix and His Ralston Straight Shooters* show started in September 1933 and ended in June 1950.

Radio Time: Monday, Wednesday, and Friday, 15-minute serial, 1933 until 1936; Monday through Friday, daily 15-minute serial beginning 1936; Monday, Wednesday, and Friday, 30-minute complete story, 1949 to end.

Series Creator: Charles Claggett.

The role of Tom Mix: Artells Dickson, 1933; Jack Holden, 1935–37; Russell Thorson, 1938–42; Curley Bradley, 1944–50; other actors appeared as Tom Mix in single episodes.

Producers/Directors: Clarence Menser, 1933–42; Al Chance, 1944–47; Mary Afflick, 1947–50.

Writers: Roland Martini, 1930s; Charles Tazewell, 1930s; George Lowther, 1944–50.

Opening and Closing Commercials

Opening Commercial
Tom Mix Program #436
Mutual Radio
February 4, 1947

DON *[Use lead-in on script]:* ... but first, Straight Shooters, these *cold* damp winter mornings do you walk across the *cold* floor of your *cold* bedroom, get into your *cold* clothes, and shiver and shake your way down to breakfast? Well, that's the time to dive into a dish of good old steaming Hot Ralston. Hot Ralston warms you up away down *inside*—puts an ear-to-ear grin on your face and gets you off to a flying head start for the day. Made of whole wheat, Hot Ralston is the warm up build up breakfast that's loaded with *cowboy energy*—the kind of energy that helps you get going and keep going these chilly fall mornings. You'll like Hot Ralston. It's a real western breakfast with a delicious nutlike flavor you'll really go for. Ask mother to get you a red-and-white checkerboard package tomorrow for sure. She'll be glad to when you tell her it's the top brand of cereals your pal Tom Mix recommends to help keep you in the top of condition. *[Continue with script]*

Opening Commercial
Tom Mix Program #672
Mutual Radio
December 31, 1947

DON: ... but first Straight Shooters, here's your pal Tom Mix with an important message:

TOM: Howdy, Straight Shooters. With a new year just ahead of us, this is the time when we all make our New Year's resolutions—and this is the time that all us Straight Shooters usually set aside to read over and renew our Straight Shooter's pledge. I want to read this pledge to you again. Here it is. It says:

> I promise to shoot straight with my parents by obeying my father and my mother.
>
> I promise to shoot straight with my friends by telling the truth always, by being fair and square at work and play, by trying always to win, but being a good loser if I lose.
>
> I promise to shoot straight with Tom Mix by regularly eating good old Hot Ralston, the official Straight Shooters cereal, because I know Hot Ralston is just the kind of cereal that will help build a stronger America.

Straight Shooters, if you'll all make this pledge and follow it, I know that 1948 will bring you all the good things and happiness you wish for and all of us wish for you.

DON: Thanks, Tom. And now Straight Shooters, come out to the snow-swept range where we join Tom and Sheriff Mike, who have not seen the mysterious Black Rider. They are moving along together...

BIZ: Sound of horses. Occasional blubber. Sound of cattle in background
[Continue with script here].

Closing Commercial
Tom Mix Program #696
Mutual Radio
February 3, 1948

DON: ... Well, I—I guess we'll all want to listen tomorrow. So be with
us then, won't you, for the next episode in *[still low]* "The Mystery
of the Black Rider." *[Pause ... very sincere]* Straight Shooters—
should tragedy overtake the little pinto colt, which with all our
hearts and soul we hope won't happen, this beautiful daughter of
Tony the Wonder Horse *must not be nameless*. She is entitled to a
name—*must* have a name, and one that is unusual and worthy of
her. That is why Tom is asking for your help. If you name this
colt—that is, if you send in the name that is finally chosen for her—
Tom will reward you with a new Chevrolet four-door sedan that
you can give to your parents, and he'll send you a Monarch Super
Deluxe Bike. To those of you who send in the next best two hundred names, Tom will award Monarch Super Deluxe Bicycles.
And to the next three hundred winners he will give three hundred
pairs of superspeed ball-bearing roller skates—Red Rascal Skates.
There are 501 swell prizes waiting for 501 boys and girls to win in
this great name hunt. Send in your name suggestions right away.
Here's all you have to do. First think up a special name for this
colt. Second, send no money! Simply print your name suggestion
on the back of one Regular Ralston or Instant Ralston box top.
Third, mail it with your name and address to Tom Mix, Box 808,
St. Louis, Missouri. That's Box 808, St. Louis, Missouri. Send in
as many names as you want, but be sure to print each name on the
back of one Hot Ralston box top. If you print more than one name
on a box top, only the first one will be considered. Contest closes
midnight, February 15th. Winners will be announced over the air.
Decisions of judges will be final. In case of ties, duplicate prizes
will be awarded. Families of employees of the Ralston Purina
Company and their advertising agency cannot enter. Hurry! Enter
this easy contest tonight. Tom Mix was played by Curley Bradley.
Don Gordon speaking. This is the Mutual Broadcasting System.

[Note: Omit closing theme and hitchhiker.]

Ralston Jingles

The Ralston jingle, or theme song, was sung to the tune of "When It's
Roundup Time in Texas and the Bloom Is on the Sage."

HOT RALSTON THEME SONG

When it's Ralston time at breakfast
Then it surely is a treat
To have some rich, full-flavored Ralston
Made of golden western wheat.

Wrangler says it is *deeeeee-licious*
And you'll find before your through
With a lot of cream—boy, it sure tastes keen
It's the tops for breakfast too.

Ask your mother in the morning
To serve you up a steaming plate
It's a grand, hot, whole wheat cereal
And the cowboys think it's great.

Once you try it, you'll stay by it
Tom Mix says it's swell to eat.
Jane and Jimmy too, say it's best for you
Ralston cereal can't be beat!

PREWAR THEME SONG VERSION

When it's Ralston time in Texas
And it surely is a treat,
To have some good, home-flavored Ralston
Made of good old western wheat.

Wrangler says it is delicious
And you'll find before your through,
With lots of cream, boy it sure tastes keen!
And it's tops for breakfast too.

Ask your mother in the morning
To serve you up a steaming plate.
It's your grandma's whole wheat cereal
And the cowboys think it's great.

Once you try it, you'll say buy it,
For it's really swell to eat.
Tom and Jimmy say it's best for you,
Ralston cereal can't be beat!

WARTIME THEME SONG VERSION

Eat Hot Ralston every morning,
Boy, that flavor can't be beat!
It's a warmup up, build-up breakfast
Made of golden western wheat.
It's delicious and nutritious
Gives you cowboy energy
Take a tip from Tom,
Go and tell your Mom,
Ralston is tops with me!

SHREDDED RALSTON THEME SONG

Shredded Ralston for your breakfast,
Starts the day off shining bright,
Gives you lots of cowboy energy
With a flavor that's just right.
It's delicious and nutritious
Bite size and ready to eat;
Take a tip from Tom,

Go and tell your Mom,
Shredded Ralston can't be beat!

Ralston Straight Shooter Clubs

Tom Mix and His Ralston Straight Shooters radio program was immensely popular with millions of youngsters in the United States and Europe. It has been said that it was the most popular youth-oriented radio program of all time.

For many Americans, the depression started with the stock market crash of 1929 and lasted until the start of World War II on December 7, 1941. Many Americans were dirt poor in the early thirties, and there was little affordable entertainment for young and old alike. Ralston Purina Company catered to the youth of America and gave them three priceless gifts: (1) wholesome radio entertainment, teaching that Straight Shooters always win and challenging Straight Shooters to build strong bodies and clean minds; (2) the ideal something for nothing or next to nothing in the form of radio premiums that provided countless hours of additional entertainment for them and their friends; and (3) a reasonably priced whole wheat cereal that was good for everyone—and everyone had to eat during the depression.

Ralston Straight Shooter clubs were formed all around the country. The Ralston Purina Company published the *Ralston Straight Shooter News*, the official newspaper of Tom Mix Ralston Straight Shooters. In volume 1, number 1, Straight Shooters of America flooded the Ralston headquarters with mail and were encouraged to become news reporters by sending in photos and news notes about their neighborhoods. A youngster could win a set of Captain's Spurs by sending in his or her name and the names of two friends who wanted to join the SSOA (Straight Shooters of America) along with three Hot Ralston blue seals or three Instant Ralston red seals. Straight Shooters who had the honor of having their pictures in the first issue were Herman Wende, of St. Louis, Missouri; Elizabeth Eckhout, of Detroit, Michigan; Fred Morss, of Oakland, California; and Allen Glidden, of Dover, New Hampshire—the first to join the Ralston Straight Shooters of America. Various Ralston premiums and the Tom Mix Comics were advertised in this issue.

The newsletter also listed the NBC Red Network stations featuring the *Tom Mix Western Air Show* at 5:15 P.M.

New York City	WEAF	Philadelphia	KYW	Cleveland	WTAM
Boston	WNAC	Baltimore	WFBR	Detroit	WWJ
Hartford	WTIC	Washington	WRC	Chicago	WMAQ
Providence	WJAR	Schenectady	WGY	Cincinnati	WSAI
Worchester	WTAG	Buffalo	WBEN	Grand Rapids	WOOD
Portland	WCSH	Pittsburgh	WCAE	Minneapolis/St. Paul	KSTP

Covers of first four Ralston Tom Mix Comics. (Author's collection.)

In volume 1, number 2, young readers read an article titled "The Life of Tom Mix in Pictures." The pictures showed Tom as a first sergeant with Teddy Roosevelt's Rough Riders in the Spanish-American War, as a Texas Ranger hunting outlaws along the Rio Grande, as a circus star of the largest motorized circus in the world, as a cowboy bulldogging champion, and as a movie star daredevil performing difficult and dangerous riding tricks.

Ralston also sponsored and published the *Straight Shooter Roundup,* featuring drawings and poems that had been sent to Pecos by his fellow Straight Shooters. Pecos Williams had these words of consolation in case a child's drawing or poem was not selected:

> Well, Straight Shooters, here's another roundup of drawings and poems sent in to me by your fellow Straight Shooters. And there were lots more of 'em than just these—so many, in fact, that I just didn't have room to print everybody's contribution. It was lots of fun to get them, though, and I sure am sorry that some of you won't find your names on this page. But I know Straight Shooters are good sports—and will understand.
>
> (signed) Pecos Williams

In addition, the Old Wrangler frequently informed Straight Shooters about strange western stories such as driving cattle a thousand miles just to fatten them up; Texas being bigger than Illinois, Missouri, Pennsylvania, New York, and Ohio all put together; the history of western firearms and offered western quizzes with small cash prizes.

Ralston advertisements featured comic strips advertising the latest Ralston premium, which was free when one Ralston Wheat Cereal box top was enclosed with the request. One of the most popular Ralston premiums was the 1936 exact replica of Tom Mix's favorite six-shooter. The pine gun was painted steel black and had pearl-colored handles and a revolving cylinder. The wooden six-shooter was so popular that the Ralston company was unable to keep up with the demand. Just before Christmas, many Straight Shooters received a letter informing them that 200,000 boys and girls had ordered the guns, and the manufacturer could make only a few thousand a day. Rather than sacrifice quality, the factory was working night and day to fill their orders. The letter thanked the children for being good sports and informed them that it might take a while, but that they would get their six-guns.

According to Jim Harmon, *Tom Mix and His Ralston Straight Shooters* program went off the air in 1942 and 1943, during World War II—not, as some people thought, due to the death of Tom Mix or poor ratings, but because of the implementation of Daylight Savings Time. Show promoters worried that children would stay outside later and the ratings would plummet. However, the ratings for *Captain Midnight* and *Jack Armstrong* held up, proving the promoters wrong. In the meantime, the Tom Mix show lost its spot, and Ralston had to wait for an opening on the Mutual Network. When the show returned, actor Curley Bradley became the Tom Mix of radio. The program was put on at 5:30 to 6:00 P.M. as a 30-minute complete story, similar to the revised format of *The Lone Ranger* and other popular children's shows.

By 1947, the Ralston SSOA numbered more than 5 million, with an additional 5 million children in Europe—the strongest following of any children's program.

Straight Shooters' Secret Manual

The Ralston Straight Shooters' manual of the midforties featured Tom Mix with a broad smile and his horse on the cover. Tom is waving his hat from the back of his rearing horse.

On page 2, there is a note from Tom reading:

> Not so many years ago America was a wilderness. Straight Shooters with vision, determination, honesty and courage turned it into the greatest nation on earth.
>
> Today, America needs Straight Shooters—alert, fearless, upright boys and girls who will carry on the ideals that have made our country strong.
>
> By joining the Tom Mix Ralston Straight Shooters of America, you are pledging yourself to build a glorious future for America. Live up to your pledge! Be proud you are a Straight Shooter and America will be proud of you!

On page 3 a youngster filled in his or her name, address, and official membership number. A warning on the bottom of page 3 advised boys and girls to "Keep This Book in a Secret Place! Show this book only to friends whom you want to become Straight Shooters. But do not show anybody except your family the sections marked 'Confidential.'"

Pages 4 through 8 reviewed the life of Tom Mix, soldier, ranger, cowboy, movie star, and founder of the Ralston Straight Shooters of America. Tom's true life story was told in seventeen numbered paragraphs as follows:

> 1. Tom was born in a log cabin not far from El Paso, Texas. A true son of the Old West, he grew up among hard-riding cowboys and bands of roving Indians.
>
> 2. As a boy, Tom grew up in the saddle—learning to ride, rope and shoot. Tom has been called the greatest rider who ever lived. No man ever loved horses better.
>
> 3. Always intensely patriotic, Tom joined the army and went to Cuba during the Spanish-American War. He was badly wounded in a daring charge. But robust Tom recovered.
>
> 4. When the Boxer Rebellion broke out in China, Tom went to serve his country again. Once more he was wounded—when an ammunition wagon was blown up by a shell.
>
> 5. Tom handled horses so skillfully, the British sent him to Africa during the Boer War in charge of cavalry mounts. When the war ended, news from America brought him hurrying home.
>
> 6. Bad men and killers were staging a reign of terror in the West. On his return, the fearless Tom was elected Sheriff and took up the fight for law and order.

7. Tom used his gun only when he had to. His cool courage and daring make him feared by lawbreakers. Recognizing this, the Government named him U.S. Marshal.

8. When trouble broke out along the Rio Grande, Tom joined the famous Texas Rangers. Wounded time and again in gun battles, Tom's rugged health always pulled him through.

9. Having helped wipe out crime, Tom returned to ranching. In the Pendleton, Oregon, Rodeo he won the title, "World's Champion Cowboy" and was given a movie contract.

10. In Hollywood Tom discovered Tony, bought him and trained him to be the world's "Wonder Horse." Tom and Tony braved every danger together to thrill millions.

11. Never using a "double," Tom became the star of stars. For years he was Hollywood's highest-paid actor—made more pictures than anyone on the screen.

12. Always in demand for personal appearances—always eager to show city people the glamour of the West—Tom organized a huge motorized circus and toured America.

13. By now Tom was a hero everywhere. In England, the crowds that flocked to see him blocked traffic for miles. And every place Tom went, Tony went too.

At the bottom of page 7 was a chart of Tom Mix's injuries.

14. Even European Royalty idolized Tom. He began life as a poor boy. But, because he was a straight shooter, he became famous. And his popularity never spoiled him.

15. Firemen and policemen called Tom a buddy. By staging shows, he helped raise money for widows and orphans of firemen and policemen killed in the line of duty.

16. But Tom's best friends were the boys and girls of America. More than anyone else, he wished to help them grow up into fearless, clean-living men and women—the same kind of Straight Shooters as the men and women who pioneered in the winning of the West.

17. To carry out this ideal Tom founded the Tom Mix Ralston Straight Shooters of America—dedicated to building courageous, healthy, sturdy citizens. Through the Tom Mix radio program, the principles and ideals for which he stood are being brought to the boys and girls entrusted with the world of tomorrow.

Page 9 gave the Ralston Straight Shooters' Pledge of Allegiance, with this note from Tom:

All Straight Shooters Take This Pledge of Allegiance. Read Pledge carefully so that you fully understand it. Then take Pledge by reading it aloud in the presence of your father or mother. Finally, sign it in the space provided.

THE RALSTON STRAIGHT SHOOTERS'
PLEDGE OF ALLEGIANCE

As a loyal American and faithful follower of Tom Mix, I pledge allegiance to his Ralston Straight Shooters of America and promise to obey, to the best of my ability, the following rules.

1. I promise to shoot straight with my parents by obeying my father and mother, and by eating the food they want me to eat.

2. I promise to shoot straight with my friends by telling the truth always, by being fair and square in work or play, by trying always to win, and by being a good loser if I lose.

3. I promise to shoot straight with myself, by striving always to be at my best, by keeping my mind alert and my body strong and healthy.

4. I promise to shoot straight with Tom Mix by regularly eating Ralston, Official Straight Shooters' Cereal, because I know Ralston is just the kind of cereal that will help build a stronger America.

I have taken the Straight Shooters' Pledge of Allegiance.

Sign your Name Here _____.

On page 10 was a warning that the information on pages 10 and 11 was confidential:

> *Important*—the information contained on these pages is very confidential. You must never reveal the Secrets of the Straight Shooters to anyone, either by telling anybody about them or by showing these pages of your Manual. Remember to keep you manual in a secret place.

The secret manual then revealed the secret salute, the secret grip, the secret password, the secret knock, the secret whistle, and the secret flashlight signal.

On page 12, Straight Shooters were taught how to be home-front soldiers by buying war stamps regularly, collecting waste paper, helping mother save tin cans and waste fat, not talking about letters from relatives in the service, not wasting anything, and being careful to avoid accidents in the home. On page 13, Straight Shooters were told how to organize a Straight Shooter club in their neighborhood. Boys and girls were encouraged to form teams, elect officers, play sports, and listen to the radio program for special prizes that would be offered. Page 14 told about boys and girls who had grown up to become Straight Shooter heroes, who had fought on every battlefront. The Shredded Ralston and Hot Ralston theme songs were also listed.

On page 15, the likeness of Tom encouraged boys and girls to tell their friends about Ralston, the official Straight Shooters cereal. The back cover of the booklet listed the stations where *Tom Mix and His Ralston Straight Shooters,* radio's biggest western detective program, could be heard on the Mutual Network, from coast to coast every evening, Monday through Friday.

Ralston Premiums

The Ralston Purina Company issued about 140 premiums from 1933 to 1950; no premiums were issued in 1943 because the show was off the air. For the Ralston revival of 1982–83, an additional ten premiums were issued.

The number of premiums issued by year are as follows: 1933—15; 1934—10; 1935—18; 1936—12; 1937—11; 1938—9; 1939—8; 1940—12; 1941—8; 1942—5; 1944—3; 1945—4; 1946—8; 1947—5; 1948—2; 1949—5; 1950—5; and 1982-83—10. Some of the higher-priced 1933 to 1950 mint-condition premiums are listed below:

- 1933 wooden gun with spinning cylinder—$100
- 1934 Tom Mix deputy ring—$1,000
- 1934 paper face mask of Tom—$150
- 1935 wooden gun with cartridge belt—$110
- 1935 Straight Shooters' bracelet—$100
- 1935 cowboy chaps—$100
- 1936 girl's charm bracelet—$100
- 1936 signet (initial) ring—$100
- 1937 target ring (Marlin)—$250
- 1938 mystery ring with picture—$250
- 1939 streamline parachute plane—$100
- 1940 Indian blowgun with four darts—$125
- 1940 elephant hair range finder—$200
- 1940 Tom Mix comic number 1—$100
- 1941 *Tom Mix Manual,* 16 pages—$100
- 1941 Captain Spur medal—$125
- 1942 Tom Mix signature ring—$200
- 1950 magic-light tiger-eye ring—$220

These items represent some of the more valuable Ralston premiums. Prices vary drastically based on the condition of the premium, and even the sale prices for mint condition items may vary considerably depending on the source of supply. Serious collectors should consult *Hakes Americana* catalogs or the *Illustrated Radio Premium Catalog and Price Guide* for complete details.

The 1982 Ralston Revival

In 1982, Ralston celebrated their 50th anniversary and, with the help of Ralston Purina executive Steve Kendall, brought in some new Ralston premiums. Even Curley Bradley, the Tom Mix of radio, was brought back in 1983 by producer Jim Harmon to record a few more Tom Mix radio adventures. Harmon played the role of Pecos Williams in this short series.

Premiums offered during the Ralston revival were

- Commemorative ceramic bowls ($3.75)
- Radio show record album
- Wristwatch postcard

- 50th anniversary Tom Mix watch ($19.95 plus proof of purchase from Hot Ralston)
- Authentic Ralston Purina Straight Shooter Tom Mix Photo ($1.00 plus proof of purchase)
- Membership kit letter and envelope
- Membership card
- Premium poster
- Patch
- Comic book

To get some idea of recent premium appreciation, the following 1982–83 premiums in mint condition are priced as follows:

- Cereal bowl—$30
- Record album—$5
- Postcard—$4
- Wristwatch—$85
- Photograph—$3
- Kit and envelope—$3
- Membership card—$3
- Premium poster—$3
- Patch—$15
- Comic book—$5

Curley Bradley, the Tom Mix of Radio

To the children of the forties, Curley Bradley *was* Tom Mix. He was born on September 18, 1910, to Mary and Thomas Bradley, on a ranch near Colegate, Oklahoma (about 45 miles west of McAlester). Curley had two older brothers, Bill and Gordon, the latter who was called Tom. He did the usual ranch chores during his boyhood years, went to the village school during the day, and learned to pick and sing in the evenings. As a teenager, Curley became a rodeo star in Oklahoma and California. While in California, he found work as a double for John Gilbert. It was also there that he met and worked with Tom Mix in a couple of pictures.

In the early thirties, Curley, Shorty Carson, and Jack Ross formed the Ranch Boys singing group. Their music was published by the M. M. Cole Publishing Company of Chicago. The 96-page 9-by-12-inch book, titled *Ranch Boys (Deluxe Song Book)*, featured 84 complete songs with guitar chords and piano accompaniment, words, and pictures. The book included such songs as "Little Sweetheart of the Ozarks," "Desert Serenade," "Little Puncher," and "My Prairie Rose."

Curley and the Ranch Boys appeared at the Boston Gardens and Madison Square Garden in 1938. In 1939, the group made a cross-country

The great Ralston revival of 1982. (Author's collection.)

trip on horseback. As they rode Red, Blue, Croppy, Lucky, and Teddy, they stopped along the way to camp out and entertain, meeting many radio stars—Janet Baird, Ken Carpenter, and Kate Smith, "America's Sweetheart." Curley became a sought-after master of ceremonies, and the group was popular on radio shows such as *Don Mcneil's Breakfast Club*.

Curley and the Ranch Boys started with *Tom Mix and His Ralston Straight Shooters* radio show in 1934. Curley reluctantly accepted the role of Pecos Williams in 1939. When first asked if he could read a few lines, he replied, "Well, I can read, but I don't know how well." Radio fans soon fell in love with his voice, however, and after the show's two-year absence from radio in 1942 and 1943, he returned as the Tom Mix of radio in 1944. He remained in the leading role until the show went off the air in June 1950.

Children were one of Curley Bradley's main interests, and he devoted a good deal of time to his radio fans. He was never too busy to stop to talk to them, autograph a picture, or pose so their parents could snap a shot. He lived the role he played and frequently gave youngsters advice on playing fair and being good Straight Shooters.

Throughout his life, Curley made many personal appearances as the Tom Mix of radio and he continued to promote the ideals of Tom Mix and his Ralston Straight Shooters. Curley even rode in the St. Louis Charity Rodeo, founded by the original Tom Mix.

In 1947, Curley Bradley dreamed of the days when he could spend his summers entertaining underprivileged city youngsters on his own ranch. He wanted to teach children how to care for livestock, hunt, fish, ride a horse, and paddle a canoe. He wanted to teach a new generation of Straight Shooters how to enjoy the outdoors.

After the Ralston Straight Shooter program went off the air, Curley returned with the Mutual Broadcasting Company in August 1950 to fill in the Tom Mix time slot as the Singing Marshal. At first the show more or less followed the Tom Mix format, but it eventually deviated to a nonsensical, moralistic extreme, where the Singing Marshal would never use his gun against another human being—an impossible task for a lawman. After floundering for about a year and a half, the show went off the air.

Curley Bradley was perhaps the best known and most beloved radio Tom Mix. The following obituary was written by his friend and business partner, Jim Harmon.

CURLEY BRADLEY REMEMBERED
by Jim Harmon

Our friend, husband of Margaret Courtney, stepfather to Elinor, who leaves his sister-in-law, cousins, other family members and friends, was born into this world George Raymond Courtney in Colgate, Oklahoma, 74 years ago. In later years, his God-given voice made him known to others as Curley Bradley, a name many of us still knew him as. And to millions of others he was known by another name—Tom Mix, the name of another real man in motion pictures, but a name that has become a legendary or fictional character like the Lone Ranger.

To generations who couldn't even remember the movie actor, Curley was the great American hero, Tom Mix, on the radio series. To me, as a boy and even a young man, listening still, Curley Bradley was Tom Mix and Tom Mix was Curley Bradley. Just two different names for my hero.

And Curley wasn't just a voice in the air, and his abilities were not all just on the paper scripts written for the show. He was a great horseman. He could train them, ride them, and he loved them. One of his favorite adventures he liked to tell about his riding horseback from coast to coast in 1938, along with Jack Ross and Ken Carson, the other members of the Ranch Boys singing trio he was with at the time. They rode through sunshine and rain, wind and fog, over unpaved roads and highways (although not the superhighways of today). Curley was riding a horse less than three years old, that hadn't gotten its permanent teeth, so he had to hand feed the young animal every day, to see it got its mash properly. When the young horse was nervous, Curley let it suck on his thumb, a task a man like Curley never minded. More than a publicity stunt, Curley and his friends gained a lot of useful information on horse care, and even tested a new horseshoe metal for the U.S. Army for their cavalry mounts. Perhaps Curley's information helped with the cavalry horses that were used in the early days of World War II.

It was Curley's singing voice that first got him into show business in the twenties. He worked with a number of groups but settled in with the Ranch Boys. He may have even helped get together some of the members of that famous group the Sons of the Pioneers, including Roy Rogers and Bob Nolan. For a time, he was a standby singer for that group, on hand in case somebody couldn't make it to the radio studio.

Curley was also a composer of songs, and while he never wrote a song as immortal as his friend Bob Nolan's "Tumbling Tumbleweeds," he belonged to that same generation of men—sons of the first Westerners, born too late to lay the first wagon tracks across this country but still of the same spirit of independence and courage, whose work and songs reflected those attributes.

In those early days in Hollywood, Curley worked as a stuntman, doing horsefalls and other dangerous tricks, and was friends with many of the movies' famous cowboys, including Tom Mix, the man he would portray on radio years later. He was even better friends with Buck Jones, a great personality who gave his life in saving others in a tragic fire back in 1942.

While Curley can be seen in nice moments in films—part of a singing group on a bus in the opening of *It Happened One Night,* as one of the Ranch Boys in the Gene Autry film *In Old Monterey*—it was his voice that took him from Hollywood to Chicago to work there beginning in 1936.

In Chicago he worked on a number of shows as a singer—on *Club Matinee* with Gary Moore, on Don McNeil's *Breakfast Club, National Farm and Home Hour, National Barn Dance,* working with teenaged George Gobel. But it was on the series of *Tom Mix and his Ralston Straight Shooters* that so many of us came to know him.

When he first went there, he had been offered the role of Tom Mix, but though he had a fine voice, he was then basically a singer and didn't have that much experience as an actor. So he was put in the part of Tom's right-hand man, Pecos Williams. That stopgap part went on for seven years, until Curley's character was getting more mail than anybody else on the show.

Finally, after a short hiatus off the air, Curley became the lead in the Tom Mix show on June 7, 1944, postponed by one day because of the D-Day Invasion. We're just two short of that day 41 years ago.

With Curley in the lead, the show became the number one show for children in the afternoon and stayed there consistently. Even when television came in, the show's listeners increased! But the days of radio drama were numbered, and the sponsor went on to something else in TV. But though Ralston took the name Tom Mix, basically the same show continued for a number of years with Curley Bradley now simply Curley Bradley and no longer called Tom. But even that series of *Curley Bradley, the Singing Marshal* came to an end eventually, as did all the great favorites of radio, bowing to the picture tube.

Curley had a few other jobs in radio, and though he had done some interview shows on TV, hosting such radio peers as Brace Beemer, the Lone Ranger, when he was in town for a rodeo appearance, Curley never got deeply into TV.

His parents came from Norwalk, California, when Curley was nine. In the 1960s and early 1970s, Curley came back to Norwalk, getting a job in a small steel factory, living near his brothers, and taking care of his mother, who was in failing health. I never met Curley's mother, but I understand she was a fine woman, and Curley never resented caring for her for one moment, I know.

Curley liked Norwalk and appreciated all his friends there, especially the people connected with the American Legion. Because of his eyesight, he was rejected for service in World War II, but he did USO work and contributed to other activities. Tons of scrap metal and fat were saved because Curley, as Tom Mix, asked us to do it. He was proud that he was accepted as an honorary Legion member in Norwalk.

I know Curley was happy with the life he led—he told me so. He appreciated working in films with men like Buck Jones and Bob Steele. He loved working in radio, loved it so much he was embarrassed to take pay for it. He had a lot of friends—his partners on the *Tom Mix* show, Leo Curley and Forrest Lewis, both gone now. Other friends like Jack Lester, whom he looked upon as a brother, Art Herns, Les Tremayne, Ed Prentiss, and so many others.

Late in life, I approached him about doing some more *Tom Mix* shows. His voice was still wonderful. Frank Bresee, an authority on the subject, once said Curley was one of the two greatest radio actors he had ever heard. Curley not only said it so you believed it, his words were like a subtle painting which could be interpreted in more ways than one. The great screen and stage actor John Abbott joined Curley in his last radio performance, only months ago, and said Curley was an actor of "great weight and authority."

Well, beginning in 1975, Curley worked with me on a series of varying formats which attempted to revive the old *Tom Mix* series. Finally, our efforts were joined by Steve Kendall of the Ralston Purina Company in 1982. That year and in 1983, Curley made several radio episodes of *Tom Mix* which were played on tape around the country and offered in part on a premium record album. He made many other radio interviews and one stage appearance with Frank Bresee in Los Angeles. We had hoped the revival might have been somewhat bigger, but both Curley and I were pleased Ralston realized that there were still a lot of grown-up boys and girls out there who still remembered Curley Bradley as Tom Mix.

Of course, Curley was no more a cardboard hero than was the man he portrayed. He had his human weakness, like all of us mortals. But Curley worked on defeating those weaknesses. I think with the help of his loving wife, Margaret, he had just about trampled down every one of his personal devils.

He was a great man. If he had wanted the kind of wealth and empire of a Gene Autry, he could have gotten that out of life. But Curley was a man who wanted to do the things he loved, and be with the people he loved, his family and friends. Even people he knew late in life—like my late friend Ron Haydock, our friends Dick Gulla, Bob Lynes, my wife, Barbara, daughter Dawn, and myself—meant a lot to him. He asked Margaret that I be notified if he "got worse." She did, and I saw him one last time. He knew me and reached his hand out to me before slipping back.

Curley is with his mother and brothers now, with Buck Jones and Tom Mix, with Leo Curley and Forrest Lewis and Bob Nolan. Somewhere he is singing. We are the poorer for not hearing. But we'll be along bye and bye. Scout's rest, partner.

Chapter 7

A Tired and Aging
Miracle Rider

Following the 1934 season, Tom Mix bought the old Sam B. Dill Circus at a cost of about $400,000. He took the show out on the road as the Tom Mix Circus. It soon became apparent to Tom that circus operations were expensive, and by the end of the season, he realized he needed a financial shot in the arm. Tom also knew he was still popular and had box office appeal. One more film could provide some much-needed capital and a little circus publicity.

Like the answer to his prayer, Tom was approached by Nat Levine in 1934, another self-made man, to star in *The Miracle Rider* serial. Nat, who had started out as an office boy, later became an independent producer and, finally, the founder and owner of Mascot Studios. Nat needed the Tom Mix name and appeal as much as Tom needed the money.

After Tom read *The Miracle Rider* script in Nat's office, an agreement was reached where Tom would spend a month filming the serial for Mascot in return for $10,000 a week, or $40,000 total. This was big money in those days; as a matter of fact, it was the most money that Nat Levine had ever paid an actor. For Tom, the timing was right, and he could not afford to turn down the $40,000 and the publicity the movie would bring to his circus. The total budget for producing *The Miracle Rider* was double Tom's salary, $80,000.

In true Tom Mix style, Tom and the Mascot publicity agents created a much more interesting story to herald Tom's return from retirement to Hollywood's silver screen. Tom was fighting mad "about the conditions I saw and read about every day. Criminals on the loose. Boys and girls learning Communist propaganda in the schools. Crime filling the newspapers. Finally, I figured out a way I could help—by returning to the screen with a picture with some old-fashioned virtue and Western justice!"

As soon as Tom accepted Nat's offer, the advance publicity team was put to work. Mascot Studios promoted *The Miracle Rider* as "Mascot's supreme achievement in chapter plays." Large-format pressbooks, filmed with photos, suggested advertising, and so-called news releases for the local newspapers, were sent to every prospective film exhibitor. Large, 16-by-21-inch lobby cards were printed with a smiling Tom Mix proclaiming that the world's most famous cowboy was about to "ride again" in a thrilling new Mascot adventure—Tom Mix's greatest movie.

By now, Tom was openly promoting the legend that had been born in the twenties at Fox and nurtured to maturity for the Sells-Floto Circus by the start of the thirties. It is alleged that Tom told Nat and his producers, "I've always wanted to make a serial which would depict the everyday problems of the Texas Ranger and U.S. Marshal forces. When Mascot Pictures Corporation showed me the story *The Miracle Rider,* I knew they had the kind of rip-snortin', he-man chapter play which would thrill every kid in town."

When Tom arrived at Mascot and was ready to begin shooting the film, he was so favorably impressed by the cast of native Americans that he said, "I feel at home among the Indians. I'm part Cherokee on my mother's side, you know." Although not a cast of thousands, it was one of the largest casts ever assembled by Mascot.

Nat Levine spent a small fortune to help assure the success of *The Miracle Rider.* Two of Mascot's best director's, B. Reeves Eason and Armand Schaefer, were assigned to the film. The Mascot format was expanded from 12 to 15 chapters and chapter 1 was an unprecedented 45 minutes long. The total running time was 310 minutes. The film was supervised by Victor Zobel and based on an original story by Gerald Gerahty, Barney Sarecky, and Wellyn Totman. The fifteen chapters were titled:

1	"The Vanishing Indian"	9	"The Silver Band"
2	"The Firebird Strikes"	10	"Signal Fires"
3	"The Flying Knife"	11	"A Traitor Dies"
4	"A Race with Death"	12	"Danger Rides with Death"
5	"Double-Barreled Doom"	13	"The Secret of X-94"
6	"Thundering Hoofs"	14	"Between Two Fires"
7	"The Dragnet"	15	"Justice Rides the Plains"
8	"Guerrilla Warfare"		

CAST OF CHARACTERS

Tom Morgan	Tom Mix	Sewell	Tom London
Ruth	Joan Gale	Metzger	Niles Welsh
Zaroff	Charles Middleton	Vining	Edmund Cobb
Carlton	Jason Robards	Morley	Max Wagner
Janss	Edward Hearn	Hatton	Charles King
Stelter	Ernie Adams	Crossman	George Chesebro
Adams	Edward Earle	Chapman	Stanley Price

Tom Mix as he appeared in *The Miracle Rider* series at age 55. (Author's collection.)

Mort . . . . George Burton   Longboat . . . . Bob Kortman
Rogers . . . . Jack Rockwell   Tony Jr. as himself
Black Wing . . . . Bob Frazer

OTHER CREDITS

Screenplay . . . . John Rathmell
Film editor . . . . Dick Fantl
Photography . . . . . Ernest Miller and William Nobles
Supervising editor . . . . Joseph Lewis
Sound engineer . . . . Terry Kellum

OTHER PLAYERS IN THE SERIES

Pat O'Malley   Frank Ellis
Jay Wilsey   Earl Dwire

Hank Bell	Lafe McKee
Art Artigan	Slim Whitaker
Forrest Taylor	Chief Big Tree
Dick Curtis	Fred Burns
Dick Alexander	

Story of the Play

Chapter 1

In the opening chapter of *The Miracle Rider,* youngsters acquired an accelerated history lesson showing how Indian land steadily shrank from 1777, with the formation of 13 states, through 1912, with the formation of 48 states. Finally, a small degree of peace was achieved when the Indians agreed to live on reservations. The Great Chief in Washington promised the Ravenhead that the reservation would belong to them so that they might "live in peace and grow and prosper." The land would be theirs "as long as the grass grows and the water flows"—or until the white man needed more land, whichever came first. Boys and girls learned how the white man's greed for more land and wealth was used by a few evil men to justify genocide in Daniel Boone's time, trapping on Indian land in Davy Crockett's time, and hunting buffalo in Indian territory in Buffalo Bill's time. Our heroes, of course, did not take part in these loathsome escapades.

The opening chapter sets the stage and theme for the entire series. Tom's father, a Texas Ranger and longtime friend of the Ravenhead Nation, comes upon a group of land grabbers trying to stake a homestead on reservation land in 1912. He is shot in the back by one of the cowards, and young Tom rushes to his dying father's side. Tom promises his father that one day, he too will become a Texas Ranger and protect the Indians. True to his promise, Tom becomes the captain of the Ranger force in 1930 and is assigned to his deceased father's territory.

We quickly advance to the present time, 1935, and learn that Tom has convinced the Indians to pool their resources so they can buy farm equipment and improve their lot. Indian agent Adams helps the Indians keep track of their funds until they have accumulated the $28,000 needed to purchase new tractors. Featherfoot and a friend leave the Indian agent's office in a car with the money and head toward town to purchase the tractors. Tom finds out they have left, and fearing for the safety of the Indians and money, hops on Tony and takes off after his Indian friends. Soon he finds the wrecked car and dazed Indians; the money has been stolen. Tom and Tony quickly pick up the trail left by the thieves and ride out after them.

Tom finds the villains counting their loot in a cave. While they are busy, Tom loosens their saddles and ties one end of a lasso to each saddle and the other end of the lasso to a nearby tree. He then builds a fire and tosses a handful of loaded shells in it. The shells explode and the bandits rush out of the cave, jump on their horses, and take off. When they reach the end of their ropes, they are abruptly dumped on the ground. Tom captures the thieves and recovers the tribal fortune.

In appreciation, the Ravenhead prepare a great celebration and feast. Tom drinks out of the sacred cup, making him one with the Ravenheads. Chief Black Wing presents Tom with a chief's headdress and giving him the name Hotan, Spirit Son of the Ravenhead—Hotan, the Miracle Rider. Ruth, the chief's daughter, also gives Tom a beautifully beaded holster and gun belt. "We grew up together and we will always be brothers," says Tom. Zaroff, head of the local Zaroff Oil Company, also congratulates Tom and invites him to his ranch, where Zaroff assures Tom he will be a welcome guest anytime.

On leaving, Zaroff signals Longboat with a car mirror. Longboat nods his acknowledgment of the signal, and Zaroff drives off. This is the first clue that Zaroff, his crew, and Longboat are villains. When Zaroff arrives at the ranch, a flashing light on a large picture signals that a wireless (radio) message is about to be received. A large television-like screen behind the picture scrolls the message, "London is holding an order for two hundred tons of X-94" and "other European orders are pending." As it turns out, Zaroff is illegally mining large quantities of X-94 on the Ravenhead reservation and secretly shipping it out in his oil trucks. The Indians are unaware that they are sitting on the world's largest known supply of X-94, a compound that can be refined into a superhigh explosive.

Zaroff, of course, must drive the Indians off the reservation before they uncover his scheme. He envisions selling X-94 to military forces around the world and becoming the most powerful man in the world; kings and queens will kneel at his feet. Longboat's only aspiration is to become chief of the Ravenhead after he helps Zaroff drive the Indians off their reservation. Zaroff's power over Longboat is based on the fact that he knows that Longboat is a half-breed and therefore ineligible to be an Indian chief.

Meanwhile, Metzger is refining X-94 in the lab, where Zaroff goes to check on his progress. Metzger has loaded one pistol bullet with X-94 to demonstrate its awesome power. He explains that one pistol bullet is as powerful as a three-inch artillery shell, but Zaroff is more concerned with the fact that the X-94 detonations produce too much smoke. Zaroff fires the pistol and compares the results, which are dramatic. However, Zaroff tells Metzger that "there is still too much smoke" and "more work needs to be done" to reduce it.

Longboat calls Zaroff on an outdoor phone hidden in some fake rocks at a small grotto and informs him that Tom Morgan is the main reason the Indians are refusing to leave the reservation. Zaroff sets a series of fires by radio control, and Longboat tries to convince his brothers that the reservation is cursed and that the evil Firebird will continue to strike them until they leave the reservation. To further frighten the Indians, Zaroff's men have built a radio-controlled rocket glider, which they launch at night. The Firebird, with its medium-pitched whirling sound, has the Indians on the verge of revolt. Tom does all he can to convince the Indians that the Firebird is some sort of manmade air ship.

Zaroff convinces his men that they must kill Tom Morgan. To throw blame on the Indians, Chapman disguises himself as an Indian and sets out to kill Tom with a bow and arrow. Several of Zaroff's men go with Chapman; they plan to stay out of sight but will come to Chapman's rescue if needed. Black Wing happens to spot Chapman with the bow and lunges in front of Tom. The arrow strikes and kills Black Wing, and Tom takes off on Tony, chasing the assassin.

Zaroff's men see Tom coming and fire an X-94 rifle bullet at him. The ground explodes in front of Tom and Tony, and Tom is temporarily distracted but continues chasing Chapman to a nearby highway, where one of Zaroff's oil trucks picks Chapman up. Tom chases the truck on horseback, and Chapman and Tom exchange gunfire. Chapman is hit in the hand and drops his gun.

Tom catches up with the truck and manages to climb inside. Tony heads for Ranger headquarters to get help. As the truck is coming down a steep hill, brakes fail and the driver panics and jumps out. Tom grabs the steering wheel and Chapman tries to grab Tom's gun. After a brief struggle, Tom shoves Chapman out of the truck.

Now it is just Tom and the runaway truck full of high explosives. Zaroff's men spot Tom and the truck and decide to get rid of Tom once and for all by firing an X-94 rifle bullet into the truck. A shot is fired, and the truck is blown to bits in a cloud of smoke.

Despite the fact that we have just seen Tom Mix apparently blown to smithereens, we can hardly wait until next Saturday to see how Tom narrowly escapes his brush with death.

Chapter 1 of *The Miracle Rider* seemed to have all the elements of a great serial: good pitted against evil, a villain with a Russian-sounding name and a western superhero, a modern setting, and a sympathetic theme. It had horse chases, a horse-and-truck chase, a running gun battle, and runaway truck. In the secret category, it had a secret high explosive, a secret cave, a secret wireless telephone, a secret wireless radio, and a secret rocket glider. What else could an adventuresome ten-year-old want?

Chapter 2

"The Firebird Strikes" is the title of Chapter 2 and it starts with the following screen introduction:

Zaroff is trying to drive the Indians from the reservation in order to secretly mine a new, powerful explosive known as X-94.

Ruth, daughter of the slain chief of the Ravenheads, has possession of the arrow that struck down her father.

Longboat, secretly working for Zaroff, tells the tribe their land is cursed—and urges them to move.

Emil Janss, merchant, is trying to sell his land to the government for a new reservation.

Tom Morgan, Texas Ranger and staunch friend of the Indians, is after the man who murdered their chief.

Tom's horse arrives at the ranger station and stomps a hoof on the steps to attract attention. The rangers rush out, recognize Tom's horse, and follow Tony back to the site of the truck explosion.

Meanwhile, we learn from a flashback that Tom jumped out of the far side of the truck before it was hit by the X-94 rifle slug. Tom rolls down a steep embankment and comes to a rest as the truck explodes, scattering debris around him.

Tom recovers, whistles for Tony to come, and joins the rangers at the site of the explosion. Tom tells the rangers that a white man disguised as an Indian killed Chief Black Wing, and he sends the rangers out looking for the killer's three accomplices, who are riding bay horses.

The angry truck driver returns to Zaroff's ranch, complaining that he would have been blown to bits if he had not jumped out of the truck when the brakes failed. He convinces Zaroff that Tom was killed because no one could live through such an explosion. However, at about that time, Tom arrives on Tony, and Zaroff takes his driver aside, coaching him on what to tell Morgan.

Carlton meets Tom at the door and invites him in. When Tom confronts Zaroff and the driver, the driver explains that an Indian forced him at gunpoint to give him a ride and that when the brakes failed, he feared for his life and jumped out of the truck. "I would have done the same thing myself," says Zaroff.

Then Carlton drops a hint that maybe Janss is involved in Black Wing's death because he is trying to sell land on the other side of the reservation to the government. Morgan leaves for Janss's office. After Tom leaves, Zaroff conspires with Carlton to make Morgan's impending death look like Janss's fault.

Meanwhile, near Janss's office, Longboat is telling the Indians that Chief Black Wing would still be alive if he had heeded Longboat's warning and left the reservation. Longboat promises the Indians that he will lead them to safety, in a place where the Firebird cannot strike them, if they will follow him and make him chief. Tom arrives and tells Longboat to knock off the idle chatter. Even though the Indians feel that too much time has already elapsed since Chief Black Wing's death, they agree to give Tom two days to bring his killer to justice.

Tom goes to the Indian agent's office, Ruth, holding the arrow that killed her father, joins them shortly. Janss arrives and tells Ruth he is sorry to hear about her father. Adams puts the arrow on his desk. Tom, Adams, and Ruth are talking about her father's death. As Ruth is explaining that the arrow does not belong to the Ravenheads or any tribe she knows, Janss takes the arrow and leaves in his automobile, heading toward his general store. Tom rides off on Tony after Janss.

In the lab, Metzger is demonstrating to Zaroff that he has now perfected the glider operation. Both the model and the real rock glider can be controlled from either the lab or Zaroff's study. He puts the glider model through its paces in the lab.

Longboat telephones Carlton to warn Zaroff that Janss has taken the arrow to his store. Zaroff sends Chapman to retrieve the arrow so that Janss will continue to be a suspect. Chapman wants to retrieve the arrow for a different reason—he realizes his fingerprints may be all over it.

When Janss arrives at the store, he confronts his clerk. Janss knows that the arrow came from his store, and he questions his clerk about Black Wing's death. The clerk denies that he had anything to do with Black Wing's death, and Janss puts the arrow in a quiver and hides the quiver in the closet of an adjoining room.

Tom arrives at Janss's store a little ahead of Chapman. Tom asks Janss why he had taken the arrow. Janss denies any knowledge of the arrow. Chapman arrives at the store, enters through a window, and finds the arrow. Tom, still with Janss, insists on searching the store. Chapman leaves through the open window before Tom searches the room. Tom does not find anything, and as he is leaving, Tony gets Tom's attention and leads him around the building to the open window. Tom looks up just in time to see Chapman riding away in the distance.

Tom rides off after Chapman and rapidly gains ground on him by taking dangerous shortcuts across rough ground. Chapman dismounts and fires a rifle shot at Tom. Tom falls off his horse and rolls down a steep embankment. Tom whistles for Tony, who joins him so the two can continue their pursuit of Chapman. As soon as Chapman spots Tom, he throws the arrow into a nearby bush and rides off.

Tom catches up with Chapman, lassos him, and jerks him off his horse. Chapman glances toward the mouth of a cave that Tom assumes is his hideout. To inconspicuously gain entrance to the cave, Tom changes clothes with Chapman, ties Chapman up, and puts him on Tony Jr. Then, dressed as Chapman, Tom leads Tony Jr. into the cave. The others in the cave congratulate Chapman on catching Morgan.

Tom spots the rocket glider and draws his gun on the villains. A fight ensues around the rocket and its controls. One of the bad guys goes to the rocket and gets a rifle in the glider's cockpit. Tom wrestles for the rifle in the cockpit. A second henchman throws a rock at Tom, hitting him in the back of the head, knocking him unconscious. Tom falls forward and activates the rocket glider's launching controls. The rocket takes off with Tom in the cockpit, and Tom wakes up flying high over rocky terrain.

The men in the cave call Zaroff from a wireless phone in the cave. A crystal ball on Zaroff's desk flashes, and he pulls a hidden telephone out of his desk drawer. The men in the cave tell Zaroff that the rocket glider has been launched and that Tom is in it. Zaroff goes to the lab and decides to destroy both the rocket glider and Tom Morgan. Zaroff nosedives the rocket into the ground, and it crashes with a mighty explosion.

At this point, all loyal and faithful Tom Mix fans must accept on blind faith that somehow our hero has survived this disaster and will reappear in chapter 3, "The Flying Knife."

Chapter 3

This episode starts by showing photos of the main cast and introducing them as follows:

> Ruth, whose father, Chief Black Wing, was slain in a mysterious campaign to drive the Indians off their reservation.
> Janss, trying to sell his land for a new reservation, is suspected of being behind the attacks.
> Zaroff, secretly mining X-94 on the reservation, uses a glider to frighten the Indians into moving elsewhere.
> Longboat, in Zaroff's power, tells his people the glider is a Firebird, sent as a warning to them to move on.
> Tom Morgan, Texas Ranger, staunch friend of the Indians, is trapped in the Firebird, which is radio-controlled by Zaroff.

In this episode, we see Tom strapping on a parachute before the glider crashes and Tom gets hung up in a tree. Tony, who has followed the glider, soon arrives on the scene.

In the meantime, Zaroff calls his henchmen in the cave and tells them to go to recover the glider wreckage. Zaroff hopes to blame Janss for Morgan's death.

A buzzer warns Zaroff that a wireless message is about to arrive. He goes to the hidden screen and the following message appears, "My country declaring war soon—stop—Munitions factories need X-94 badly—Leon."

Zaroff and Carlton discuss the problem. Now they are under additional pressure to get the Indians out of the way so that they can mine the large quantities of X-94 needed. Thinking that Tom has been killed, Zaroff instructs Carlton to radio Leon that he will be shipping two hundred tons of X-94 shortly and will follow this initial shipment with additional shipments of two hundred tons per week. Zaroff gloats at the idea of being the most powerful man in the world.

Longboat arrives at the ranch, and Zaroff orders him to go back to the reservation and tell the Indians that the Firebird is going to strike again—and anything else that will drive them off the reservation. Longboat agrees and again envisions himself as chief of the Ravenheads.

Meanwhile, Tom and Tony find the wreckage of the glider, and Tom finds a manufacturer's tag on a piece of equipment in the glider. Tom rides to Janss's store and accuses him of killing Chief Black Wing and building the glider to frighten the Indians. Tom points out that Janss has everything to gain by selling his land to the government for a small fortune. Janss denies any wrongdoing, then Tom shows him the name tag inscribed "Ideal Mfg. Co., Emil Janss, Distr." Janss points out that anyone could have put his tag on the glider.

Ruth finds Tom at Janss's store and warns him that Longboat is stirring up the Indians again. They decide they should recover the wreckage of the glider to prove to the Indians that the glider is manmade and not the spiritual Firebird of Indian mythology. Tom and Ruth ride off to recover the glider wreckage.

However, Janss does not want Tom to recover the glider wreckage either because he is afraid his land deal with the government will fall through if the Indians find out the glider is a hoax. Janss sends four men to stop Morgan.

Two of the men spot Tom and Ruth and fire at them. Ruth takes cover and Tom rides off after the bushwhackers. Tom takes a shortcut to get ahead of the men, and lassos and hog-ties the last rider. The three others finally discover that they are one man short and backtrack to find him. As they find their hog-tied friend, Tom jumps off a rock onto one of the horses, and two of the bad guys take off in hot pursuit after him. Tom gets ahead of them, dismounts, quickly ties his rope to a tree, and pulls it tight as the riders catch up to him. The two riders are knocked to the ground with a jolt.

In the next scene, Tom catches up with Ruth and finds the glider has been taken. Tom sends Ruth to get help while he goes to the Indian Cave at Dark Mountain. Tom suspects the wreckage of the glider has been taken there.

Zaroff's men find Tom's parachute but no trace of Tom. They give the parachute to Zaroff and Carlton, who now realize that Morgan is still alive. Zaroff anticipates that Tom will return to Indian Cave looking for the glider wreckage. He calls his henchmen at the cave and sets up an ambush for Tom.

Zaroff's men hide the wreckage of the glider deeper in the cave and set up their ambush. Tom leaves Tony outside the cave, and as he approaches the entrance, there is an explosion. One of Zaroff's men staggers out, faking injuries, but Tom quickly discovers the ploy and takes him at gunpoint back into the cave.

Tom's prisoner spots the barrel of a gun and ducks, leaving Tom exposed to gunfire by Zaroff's men. Tom takes cover among the rocks and eventually climbs a ledge, seeking a higher-ground advantage. Unfortunately, Tom knocks a rock loose, and Zaroff's men spot him. They all open fire on him, and Tom, appearing to be hit, falls off the ledge amid dozens of gun shots.

As a boy, I found the ending of chapter 3 a real disappointment. Even the ten-year-olds guessed that Tom faked being hit and merely rolled off the ledge to find a hiding place. Furthermore, what happened to the flying knife? Did I miss something? Chapter 3 had nothing to do with a flying knife or any other kind of knife. Just a catchy title, I guess.

Chapter 4

"A Race with Death," starts with basically the same introduction as chapter 3. As we had anticipated, Tom rolls off the ledge and takes cover behind a rock.

Ruth rides to the Indian agent's office to get help. Longboat is there as she explains Tom's plan to recover the Firebird. Longboat leaves under the pretext that he is going to help Tom. In reality, he calls Zaroff on a hidden phone and tells him about Tom's plans. Ruth sends Featherfoot and other Indians to help Tom. Zaroff calls his men in the cave and tells them to fall back and get out of the cave. One man holds Tom off while the others gather their horses and prepare to escape. They all escape, and Tom cautiously makes his way to the mouth of the cave.

Ruth and the Indians arrive. Longboat joins them as they go into the cave to search for the Firebird. They split up and search the cave but cannot find the remains of the Firebird. Longboat insists that the Firebird is still alive, but Tom and Ruth insist that the Firebird is dead.

Then Tom discovers a strange spiderweb and accidentally uncovers the machine used to spin the strange manmade spiderwebs. Tom brushes aside the web, and they find the remains of the glider. Now, at last, some of the Indians realize the Firebird is a manmade glider.

Tom momentarily alarms the Indians when he energizes the glider's eerie siren. After Tom shows them how the siren works, he has the Indians load the wrecked glider on a flatbed wagon. They head back to the reservation with the glider's remains.

A couple of Zaroff's men who remained behind have observed everything, and they call Zaroff on the wireless phone in the cave. Zaroff sends additional men to attack the Indians and steal the glider.

Zaroff's men ambush Tom and the Indians at a narrow pass, and while Tom is busily engaged in a gun battle, some of the Indians and the wagon

Tom Mix picking up the trail in *The Miracle Rider*, 1935. (Author's collection.)

with the glider take off on an alternate route to the reservation. At Tom's urging, Ruth rides off after the wagon. Some of Zaroff's men also ride off after the wagon.

One of Zaroff's men shoots the driver. They drag the other Indian passenger off the wagon, beat him, and set fire to the wagon. Ruth tries to help by setting off the glider's siren to warn the others that they are in trouble. Tom rides to the rescue, but before he can get there, Ruth is knocked unconscious and the fire spooks the horses. The horses take off at a gallop with Ruth in the burning wagon.

Meanwhile, one of Zaroff's men spots Tom coming, and he lies in wait for him. He shoots at Tom from ambush, and Tom, apparently hit, falls off his horse and rolls down a slight incline.

Needless to say, Tom has been ambushed half a dozen times by now. So far, no one has been able to hit him. Why are the bad guys such poor marksmen? We know that somehow Tom has to survive, if for no other reason than to save Ruth.

Chapter 5

The update for the "Double Barreled Doom" episode reads as follows:

> The Ravenhead Indians are victims of a series of mysterious attacks to drive them off their reservation.
>
> Emil Janss, trying to sell his land for a new reservation, is suspected of being behind the attacks.
>
> Zaroff, secretly mining a powerful explosive on Indian land, deliberately throws suspicion on Janss.
>
> Stelter, a clerk in Janss's store, is actually one of Zaroff's secret henchmen.
>
> Ruth, daughter of a slain chieftain, is trying to convince her people that the Firebird is an airship.
>
> Tom Morgan sees Ruth trapped in the flaming Firebird and races to the rescue.

The bad guy rides off as Tom recovers from his fall. Tom whistles for Tony to come, and he rides off after the burning wagon once again. Ruth regains consciousness and jumps to Tom as Tony pulls alongside the burning wagon. Tom puts Ruth down as the wagon falls apart under the strain of fire and racing horses. Meanwhile, Zaroff's henchmen recover the badly damaged glider.

Tom points out to Ruth that their every move has been known well in advance. Tom tells Ruth that he suspects there is a secret phone somewhere in the Indian cave. Tom returns to the cave to search for the telephone.

Meanwhile, another wireless message is being received by Zaroff. The message says, "Orders for X-94 rapidly increasing—stop—Rush shipments at once—JB." Zaroff meditates on how he will lose a fortune if he cannot make his shipments. Carlton points out that at least Morgan does not have proof that the Firebird is dead.

Back at the Indian agent's office, Tom, Ruth, and Longboat are arguing about whether the Firebird is dead. Longboat leaves and shortly afterward, Emil Janss arrives. Janss tells the Indian agent that he has been receiving complaints from his eastern buyers about the quality of goods that the Indians have been turning out. Perhaps their work has suffered as a result of their recent problems. Whatever the cause, he will have to stop buying their rugs, pottery, and silverware. Janss suggests that the Indians could make more money if they moved to better land and started farming. Tom interprets Janss's suggestion as self-serving, an outright attempt to make himself a rich man. Tom tells Janss that he will help the Indians sell their goods and, as a matter of fact, will take a truckload of goods to town himself.

Janss's clerk, Stelter, asks to borrow Janss's car to make a couple of deliveries. After he leaves, he drives to Zaroff's to inform him of Tom's plan. Zaroff then borrows Janss's car and sends it off with a load of henchmen to hijack the shipment and kill Morgan in the process.

Tom follows the truck on Tony. The truck is stopped by Zaroff's men. Unbeknownst to them, the truck is filled with good guys instead of merchandise. The men pop out of the truck, and a gunfight ensues. Tom joins in and Zaroff's henchmen make a hasty retreat to Janss's car.

Tom recognizes Janss's car and rides cross-country on Tony to head it off. Along the way, the car slows down and lets the henchmen off. Tom follows the car and driver to town, where the driver parks the car behind Janss's store. Stelter lets the driver in and goes upstairs.

Tom arrives, and Stelter lets him in. Stelter denies any knowledge about the car or driver, and Tom decides to make a search on his own. Tom discovers Janss tied up in a closet. Janss claims he was hit in the head from behind and does not know anything. Stelter says he was off running errands for Janss and likewise knows nothing.

Meanwhile, the driver has set up a booby trap upstairs. He has mounted a double-barreled shotgun so that it points to the door and has tied a cord from the trigger to a support and back to the door knob so that the gun will discharge when the door is opened.

The driver watches through the keyhole as Tom approaches the door. He drops a box to get Tom's attention and leaves through a trap door in the floor. As Tom opens the door, both barrels discharge with a blast, and Tom reels backward. Is this the end of Tom Morgan, or will we see him again in chapter 6, "Thundering Hoofs"?

Chapter 6

In the opening scene of chapter 6, we see Tom quickly step aside as he pushes the door open and the shotgun blast goes off, narrowly missing him. Tom looks for the gunman but cannot find him. A ranger outside tells Tom that no one left through the window.

Janss arrives on the scene with Ruth and Stelter, and Tom tells Janss he is taking him in for questioning. Janss reminds Tom that he has been "a respectable businessman for 30 years" and threatens to get Tom's badge. Tom signals Ruth to return to the store and keep Stelter busy so he can come back and look around.

When everyone leaves, Stelter tries to get the driver out of the crawl space, but the trapdoor is stuck. Ruth comes back, and Stelter leaves to see who is in the store.

Tom sends Janss to ranger headquarters with the other ranger and returns to Janss's store to look around. He uses a rake to enter the second-floor window of the room where he was ambushed. Tom hears the bad guy trying to open the trapdoor, and he hides. He sees Sewell getting out of the trapdoor, and a fight ensues when he tries to arrest Sewell. Sewell tries to hit Tom with the shotgun, but Tom ducks and finally subdues his opponent. As soon as Tom leaves with Sewell, Stelter calls Zaroff and tells him that Tom has taken both Janss and Sewell into custody.

Zaroff, fearing that Sewell might talk, sends his henchmen, disguised as Indians, to Janss's store. They wreck the store, nearly inciting a riot among the white, anti–Indian local population. Stelter says he escaped through a rear window to save his life.

At ranger headquarters, Tom fingerprints Sewell, and Janss denies knowing Sewell. Stelter bursts in, saying that the Indians have raided the store and just about destroyed everything. Tom and Janss leave for the store in Janss's car. As they leave, one of Zaroff's henchmen arrives on a motor-cycle with a sidecar.

When Tom arrives at the store, the local citizens are still steaming; they want to run the Indians out of the country. By examining footprints at the scene, Tom quickly learns that the riot was not caused by Indians. "No moccasins made these tracks," he proclaims.

Tony, having seen the motorcycle arrive at ranger headquarters, goes to get Tom. When he arrives at the store, he stomps the floor, getting Tom's attention. Tom hops on Tony, who takes him back to ranger headquarters just in time to see Sewell and the motorcyclist escaping.

Tom and Tony take a shortcut across the hills, picking up the chase again a short distance behind the motorcycle. Sewell borrows the cyclist's gun and fires at Tom. A gunfight ensues. The wheel on the sidecar goes flat, and Sewell jumps out and rolls down a hill. The motorcyclist escapes, but Tom lassos Sewell and walks him at the end of a rope behind Tony as they head back to ranger headquarters.

The motorcycle rider meets up with Zaroff's other henchmen, and six of them ride off to rescue Sewell. They catch up to Tom and Sewell, and Tom puts Sewell behind him on Tony to prevent getting shot in the back. Sewell grabs a low branch to escape, and the bad guys shoot at Tom when Sewell is out of the way. Tom falls to the ground, apparently shot. The thundering hoofs of six horses appear ready to trample Tom as he gains consciousness and chapter 6 ends.

Chapter 7

In chapter 7, "The Dragnet," we see the riders ride up to Tom, assuming he is dead. They then return to free Sewell and notice that Tom has disappeared. One of six riders stays to free Sewell while the others ride out looking for Tom. Tom returns to where Sewell is and throws a rock, knocking Sewell's would-be rescuer off his horse. Tom kicks a gun out of his hand and knocks him unconscious, then unties Sewell and throws him over his saddle.

The bad guy comes to and calls for help. Zaroff's men regroup and ride off after Tom and Sewell. Tom has enough of a head start that he stops and swaps clothes with Sewell, ties Sewell to Tony, and sends them back to ranger headquarters. The bad guys see Tony and Sewell but think it is Tom returning to ranger headquarters and continue their search for Sewell.

One of Zaroff's men spots a piece of clothing in the brush and dismounts to examine it. Tom jumps the villain, takes his horse, and returns to ranger headquarters. Sewell and Tony arrive at ranger headquarters just ahead of Tom. Tom tells the rangers to hurry up and get Sewell inside, but Stelter sees the whole thing.

Stelter phones Zaroff, telling him that Sewell is back in jail. Zaroff, fearing that Sewell might talk, comes up with an ingenious plan. He tells Stelter to leave the country, promising Stelter that he will "take care" of him.

Zaroff and Carlton come up with a scheme to get a message to Sewell before he is pressured into talking. Carlton writes a message to Sewell on a cigarette paper and rolls it into a cigarette. He takes it to ranger headquarters, where he throws it to Sewell. Sewell unwraps the cigarette and reads the message: "Stelter leaving the country. Tell Morgan he is your boss."

Sewell gets Tom's attention, then appears to change his mind. Tom encourages Sewell to talk because it will go easier on him. Finally, Sewell confesses that Stelter is his boss. Tom does not believe a word of it because he still thinks Janss is the chief troublemaker. Tom and another ranger ride off to Janss's store to pick up and question Stelter.

When they arrive at the store, Janss tells Tom that Stelter quit without giving notice and said he was leaving for good. Tom calls ranger headquarters and sets up a dragnet throughout Texas. Stelter and his driver do not get far before they run into a roadblock. To advert suspicion, Stelter escapes on foot.

Stelter makes his way back to Zaroff's ranch, but Carlton refuses to let him in. Stelter suspects Zaroff is in the lab and goes there, overpowering a guard. Zaroff and Metzger hear the ruckus and Zaroff hides in a back room. Stelter gets into the lab, but Metzger will not tell him anything. Stelter makes his way to the back room, and a single shot is fired. Zaroff enters with a smoking gun.

Meanwhile, back at ranger headquarters, one of Zaroff's men learns that Sewell has confessed that Stelter has a hideout shack in the hills. The henchman telephones Zaroff, letting him know this latest development. Then Zaroff sends two of his men with a car to take Stelter's body to the mountain hideout, hoping to make it look like Stelter was killed in a shootout with the Texas Rangers.

The two men hide the car out back and carry Stelter's body to the shack. As the rangers arrive, they engage them in gunfire. When the shooting stops, the rangers assume they have shot Stelter. They enter the cabin, find Stelter's body, believing they have gotten their man.

Tom examines the body and quickly concludes that Stelter has been dead for hours, although his gun is still warm. Therefore, someone else must have fired the shots and escaped out the back window leading down the cliff. Tom gets a rope, and the rangers lower him down the cliff.

Zaroff's men see Tom being lowered and fire a volley of shots at him. Tom is apparently hit, falls from the rope, and drops and rolls into the rocks.

By now, we are beginning to have faith that we will see our hero again in chapter 8, "Guerrilla Warfare."

Chapter 8

There is no similarity whatsoever between the ending for chapter 7 and the beginning of chapter 8. This time after Zaroff's men open fire on Tom, he does not fall from the rope—the rangers merely lower him faster. Tom never lets go of the rope and lands on his feet at the bottom of the cliff. The rangers in the cabin and Tom fire a few shots at the bad guys as they escape in the car. Neither Tom nor the rangers in the cabin recognize the henchmen. Isn't it strange? Everybody knows Tom, but Tom doesn't seem to know anybody.

Sewell, who had accompanied the rangers, still refuses to talk even though Tom informs him that he has known all along that Stelter was not his boss. There is only one thing left to do—Tom puts Sewell back in jail, hoping his memory will improve.

Meanwhile, the henchmen return to reap Zaroff's scorn for firing on Tom, thereby ruining the plot twist of blaming the rangers for Stelter's death. Zaroff begins to worry about what Tom might find if he decides to search Stelter's room above Janss's store. He sends one of his men ahead to look for samples of X-94 or other incriminating evidence.

When Tom, his men, and Sewell get back to ranger headquarters, Janss is waiting for them, hoping to learn more about what might have happened to Stelter. Tom more or less accuses Janss of Stelter's death because he believes that Janss has the most to gain by throwing suspicion on someone else. Janss tells Tom he is barking up the wrong tree and leaves.

Janss decides to search Stelter's room himself and warns his new clerk not to tell anyone. Shortly after entering Stelter's room, Janss hears someone at the window and hides behind a door. Janss watches as the second-story man enters the room and finds a small hidden bottle. Janss pulls his gun and takes the burglar by surprise. After learning that the bottle contains an explosive, Janss takes the burglar down to his office.

Janss has his new clerk cover the burglar while he assures the clerk that "this second-story man is going to do some first-class talking." The burglar refuses to talk, but Janss spots Zaroff's initials on the explosive's bottle cap. He locks the explosive in his desk drawer and goes to confront Zaroff.

At ranger headquarters, the coroner confirms that Stelter was dead at least two hours before the rangers found him. Since his prime suspect is dead, Tom decides that he should make a thorough search of Stelter's room. Tom and Tony head for Janss's store.

Janss confronts Zaroff accusing him of trying to drive the Indians off the reservation and throwing the blame on him. Zaroff turns on his intercom and Carlton overhears everything. Janss tells Zaroff he wants to be cut in on his scheme, and they agree to team up for their mutual benefit.

When Tom arrives at Janss's store, the new clerk takes him to Stelter's room. While they are upstairs, one of Zaroff's men arrives to free the man being held in Janss's office. The clerk goes back downstairs and hears someone in the office. He enters, and Zaroff's men subdue him, break into the desk to get the bottle of X-94 explosive, and leave through the window.

Tom hears the scuffle downstairs and finds Janss's new clerk on the floor. Tom goes to the window and sees the bad guys riding off. He leaves the store, jumps on Tony, and rides off in hot pursuit. Zaroff's men come to a fence and go around it, but Tom and Tony jump the fence to close the distance. They have a running gun battle on horseback. One of the bad guys' horses stumbles, throwing him. The rider is unable to catch his horse, so both of Zaroff's men decide to shoot it out with Tom from the cover of the rocks.

Zaroff's men soon begin to run out of ammunition. Tom continues to draw their fire by putting his Stetson on a stick. Finally, Zaroff's men are down to their last bullet. Tom tells them to surrender, but they refuse to as long as they have the bottle of X-94. Tom tells them to "come out with your hands up." Instead, they throw the bottle of X-94, which explodes right in front of Tom. Will Tom survive to reappear in chapter 9?

Chapter 9

"The Silver Band" opens with Tom shooting the bottle of X-94 in midair. Tom is blinded by the explosion, and Zaroff's men ride off, assuming he is dead. Tom whistles for Tony and tells him to take him back to ranger headquarters.

As soon as Tom arrives, the rangers see that Tom has been blinded, and they send for a doctor. The doctor carefully examines Tom's eyes and discovers that the wounds are superficial; Tom has been only temporarily blinded. The doctor tells Tom that he should regain his eyesight in two or three hours.

Zaroff's men return to his ranch and tell him they have blown Tom to pieces. Janss says, "I'll believe that Tom Morgan is dead when I get an invitation to his funeral!" Zaroff tells Janss that there were enough explosives in that bottle to kill 10 Tom Morgans.

Zaroff and Janss come up with a plot to drive the Ravenhead Indians off their reservation. They plan to make it look as if Indians have raided Janss's store and stolen several bolts of valuable silk. Longboat will plant the stolen goods in one of the Indian huts. The townspeople will start a riot and drive the Indians off.

For evidence, Longboat comes up with a silver band (bracelet) that he has taken from Featherfoot's hut. He will drop the bracelet in Janss's store and put the bolts of silk in Featherfoot's hut. At about the time Featherfoot is leaving Janss's store with a new pair of shoes, Janss and Brunner, one of Zaroff's men, are going to Indian agent Adams, reporting that Janss's store has been raided by the Indians.

At the store, Adams, Janss, Brunner, and Ruth examine the damage and find the silver bracelet. Adams recognizes the bracelet as belonging to Featherfoot. They descend upon Featherfoot at his hut and find him wearing a matching bracelet on the other wrist. Brunner finds the bolts of silk hidden behind a curtain. Adams urges restraint, locks Featherfoot in a back room at the agency, and talks Janss and Brunner into driving him into town to get Tom to investigate the charges. On the way to town, Brunner manually chokes the car, causing it to stall.

Longboat goes to his secret telephone in the rocks and phones Zaroff, letting him know that Featherfoot has been locked up in a back room at the agency office. Zaroff recognizes this as a golden opportunity and sends several of his henchmen out as townspeople to lynch Featherfoot, thereby increasing hostilities.

Ruth spots Zaroff's men approaching, breaks the door lock at the agency, and convinces Featherfoot he must escape to save his life. The two ride off into the hills but are spotted by Zaroff's men, who ride out after them. To throw them off the trail, Ruth and Featherfoot swap horses, and Ruth leads Zaroff's men up a blind canyon. Zaroff's men take a shortcut to get ahead of Ruth, thinking that she is Featherfoot. They string a rope across her path and trip her horse, throwing her for a loop. Will Ruth be OK? See chapter 10, "Signal Fires," next week to find out.

Chapter 10

When Zaroff's men discover they have knocked Ruth unconscious, they decide to leave before she comes to and recognizes them. Featherfoot, who is suffering from total exhaustion, falls off his horse. Ruth comes to and rides off to find Featherfoot, who hears her coming and signals his location to her with a birdcall. Ruth tells Featherfoot to stay put until she can get Tom, but Featherfoot wants to return to the reservation.

After Ruth leaves, Featherfoot builds a signal fire. Ruth finds Tom and Adams at ranger headquarters and fills them in on what has happened. Tom, Ruth, and rangers Burnet and Rogers ride out to find and help Featherfoot.

In the meantime, Longboat sees the signal fire and finds Featherfoot. Featherfoot tells Longboat he wants to return to the reservation, but Longboat convinces him that the white men will kill him if he returns to the reservation. Longboat convinces Featherfoot to take refuge in a mountain hideout and tells him he is going to get help.

Tom, Ruth and the rangers find the signal fire still burning, but Featherfoot is gone. They ponder Featherfoot's fate.

Meanwhile, back at the lab, Metzger is demonstrating to Zaroff that X-94 can be transformed into a motor fuel twice as powerful as gasoline. Metzger speeds up a compressor motor to a dangerously high level and Zaroff has him quickly shut it down. Zaroff is elated—X-94 is the motor fuel of the future. Now, he will surely control world power that other men have only dreamed of.

Longboat arrives at Zaroff's and tells him he found Featherfoot and took him to the mountain hideout. Zaroff tells Longboat to go back to the reservation and tell Adams and the Indians that Featherfoot has been killed by white men. Zaroff hopes to stir up the Indians to the point they will want to leave the reservation.

Zaroff sends his men out again to get Featherfoot. However, Featherfoot sees the men coming and bolts the door to the cabin. Zaroff's men start firing at him and the locked door, and Tom, Ruth, and the rangers hear the shots. Tom sends the rangers after Zaroff's men as he and Ruth stop to help Featherfoot. Featherfoot lets Tom and Ruth in, and they begin to realize that Longboat may be a traitor.

Meanwhile, at the Indian agency, Longboat is telling Adams and the Indians that the white men have killed Featherfoot. He insists that Adams leave the reservation at once, and a fight breaks out. Longboat grabs Adams's pistol.

Tom arrives in time to hear the ruckus at the agency office and enters with Ruth, leaving Featherfoot outside. In a brief struggle, Tom disarms Longboat. Longboat insists that the white men have killed Featherfoot. Ruth signals for Featherfoot to come inside.

Featherfoot accuses Longboat of being a cowardly traitor, and a fight ensues between Longboat and Featherfoot. Featherfoot is knocked down and Tom pulls Longboat off him. While Tom is helping Featherfoot, Longboat escapes on Ruth's horse. Tom jumps on Tony and rides off after Longboat.

Longboat heads to Zaroff's lab and dismounts behind it. Janss and Zaroff are in the lab discussing the potential of X-94 as the world's most powerful motor fuel. Suddenly, they spot Longboat with Tom in hot pursuit.

Zaroff locks the door between the lab and the toolshed so that neither man can get into the lab. Longboat enters the shed and hides behind the compressor. Tom enters, and Longboat jumps him when his back is turned. As the two men are fighting, Zaroff puts some X-94 into the compressor motor and it speeds up until it explodes.

Will the traitor be the only one who dies in chapter 11?

Chapter 11

"A Traitor Dies" picks up with Tom and Longboat fighting. Tom knocks Longboat through a side door and is standing in the doorway when the compressor explodes. Tom is blown out the door and knocked to the ground. Longboat tries to escape in the cloud of smoke, but Tom goes after him, and the two fight violently. Tom is knocked to the ground, and Longboat is about to run him through with an iron rod when Janss shoots him. Janss, Metzger, and Zaroff have been watching the explosion and fight from the lab.

Janss comes out of the lab with Zaroff and tries to convince Tom he has just saved his life. Janss assumes he has killed Longboat, but Longboat is still alive. Zaroff volunteers to get some blankets while Janss offers to take Longboat back to the reservation in his car.

Tom attends to Longboat's injuries and Adams goes for the doctor. After the doctor arrives, Longboat regains consciousness and Longboat confesses: "My eyes are clear now like the eagles. For a long time I was blind. I helped the white men who were trying to drive my people from the reservation so that I could be chief of the Ravenheads." Before Tom and Ruth can get Longboat to tell them who the white men are, Longboat passes out.

The doctor tells Tom that Longboat should be all right in the morning. Janss's expression more or less gives him away when Longboat was on the verge of telling Tom who the white men were. After Janss leaves, Tom tells Ruth that they "better keep an eye on Longboat."

Janss goes back to his office, where he tells one of Zaroff's men that he needs to round up some others and go back to the reservation and take care of Longboat before he tells all. Zaroff's men recruits three others, and the four henchmen arrive at the reservation just as it gets dark.

Zaroff's men watch Longboat's cabin and see Ruth leaving. Thinking that Longboat is alone, Wolf sneaks into the cabin and stabs a dummy in the bed. Tom confronts Wolf, and Wolf throws the knife at him. Tom stops the knife with a wooden chair and they fight each other. Tom eventually subdues Wolf and puts on Wolf's clothes.

Tom goes back to the Indian agent's office, where Longboat has been moved, and makes sure that Longboat and Ruth are all right. Then he goes to join Zaroff's men in the dark, hoping to go with them as Wolf and find out who their leader is.

The henchmen, thinking that Wolf has killed Longboat, go back to Janss's office to report their progress. Tom stays outside to prevent being discovered. In the meanwhile, Wolf comes to and telephones Janss, telling him that Tom took his clothes.

Janss sends the three men looking for Tom under the pretext that he is going to pay them for a job well done. Janss plans to shoot Tom as soon as he walks through the door. However, Tom sneaks into Janss's store and gets the drop on Janss. Janss unexpectedly turns on the lights and the henchmen return to his office, firing at Tom but missing him.

Tom goes upstairs, and Janss sends one man outside to watch the upstairs window as the other three men follow Tom upstairs. Tom stalls the three men in the stairwell by throwing a barrel down the stairs at them. Tom is about to leave by the window when he spots the man outside. He hides in the room as the man outside puts a ladder up to the window and enters the room.

All four henchmen spot a black hat and what they believe to be Tom hiding behind some barrels and crates. They shoot through the barrels and crates in the direction of his hat.

A traitor did not really die in chapter 11. At first we might have wanted Longboat to die, but after his confession, we feel sorry for him and want him to live so that he can help Tom catch the rest of the dirty, rotten scoundrels.

Chapter 12

In "Danger Rides with Death," we see Zaroff's henchmen unloading their guns at what they think is Tom Morgan. After the volley ends, they look for Tom and can find only his black hat behind the barrels and crates.

Tom has escaped through the trapdoor in the floor. However, Janss remembers the trapdoor and has Zaroff's men cover it. They open the door, capture Tom, and take his gun. Janss sends Crossman and another hench-man to get a rope so they can tie up Tom.

Janss hears a car coming and he leaves. Tom is still being covered by one of Zaroff's henchmen and uses a spur to cut into a bag of flour on the floor. The henchman is distracted when the rangers arrive, and Tom kicks flour in his face and overpowers him. Then Tom goes after the two men who are looking for the rope.

Tom jumps Crossman and the other henchman as the rangers arrive and make their way into Janss's store. Three of Zaroff's men are arrested, but Janss gets away. Tom tells the rangers that he now has proof that Janss is behind the plot to force the Indians off their reservation.

Janss makes his way to the cave, where Zaroff's men have been mining X-94. One of the thugs calls Zaroff, telling him that the rangers are on to Janss and that Janss is at the cave. Zaroff, fearing that Tom may go to the cave, orders the two men at the cave to remove any X-94 and hide Janss in one of the oil trucks when it arrives. They plan to keep Janss undercover until things blow over and then get him out of the country.

Back at ranger headquarters, Crossman is brought in for questioning. Tom tells Crossman to confess where Janss is or hang himself for the death of Chief Black Wing. Eventually, Crossman tells Tom that Janss is headed for the Indian cave.

One of Zaroff's oil trucks arrives, and Morley, the driver, shows the two men in the cave a $5,000 reward poster for Janss. Morley takes Janss out to the truck, and when he returns, one of Zaroff's men knocks him out. The two men in the cave have decided that the $5,000 reward is just too tempting. They leave Morley and the bags of X-94 in the cave.

One of the thugs loads Janss into the tank of the oil truck, and they head for ranger headquarters to collect the reward. Meanwhile, Morley comes to in the cave and calls Zaroff's ranch. Zaroff and Carlton send out more men to head off the truck before it can get to ranger headquarters.

Then Tom and one of the rangers arrive at the deserted cave. They go in and find the wanted poster for Janss and the bags of X-94. Tom cuts open one of the bags but does not recognize what is in it. They decide to take some of the X-94 back to ranger headquarters to have it analyzed.

When Tom arrives at headquarters, he finds out that a bounty hunter is there trying to collect the reward for Janss. The man convinces Tom that his partner is holding Janss just a short distance outside of town. Tom, the bounty hunter, and some of the rangers ride out to arrest Janss.

Before the rangers can get there, two of Zaroff's men find the truck. Chapman sees them coming and hides in the brush. Zaroff's men think the bounty hunters have left with Janss and abandoned the truck. Janss hears the men and pounds on the side of the truck.

Zaroff's men draw their guns, open the hatch of the truck, and find Janss. They tell him to stay in the truck. One of the men, Vining, drives off with Janss and the truck while the other henchman takes the horses. Chapman has seen everything, but he stays hidden.

Finally, the rangers arrive and find the truck gone. The bounty hunter thinks Chapman has betrayed him, but Chapman comes out of the brush and tells the rangers that two men have taken the truck with Janss in it.

Tom rides after the truck. He takes a cross-country shortcut and is riding uphill but parallel to the truck when Vining spots him. Vining pulls his gun and shoots at Tom. Tom falls from his horse and rolls down a rough embankment as chapter 12 ends.

A setback maybe, but we know that Tom will survive and do his best to bring the villains to justice in chapter 13.

Chapter 13

"The Secret of X-94" starts with the same rough fall down the rocky slope. Tom recovers at the bottom of the hill and whistles for Tony to come. Tom apologizes to Tony and tells him that taking a fall is better than getting shot.

Tom and Tony ride out after the truck again. This time, Vining jumps out of the truck, and it crashes into an embankment. Janss is badly shaken, but he tries to crawl out the tank and collapses halfway out of the hatch. Tom pulls Janss out of the tank and goes to the Indian agent's office to call ranger headquarters.

Tom tells Ruth and Adams that he suspects there are others besides Janss involved in the plot to drive the Indians from their reservation, but he prefers not to accuse anyone until he has proof positive. Ruth leaves and heads for home.

Meanwhile, Vining calls Zaroff from a hidden phone at the grotto, and Zaroff tells him to get rid of the phone and go to Indian cave. Zaroff tells Vining he will send some men to help him pick up the X-94. Ruth spots Vining at the grotto and follows him to the cave. Zaroff sends a roadster with two men to the cave to help Vining load the X-94.

One of the rangers calls Zaroff to find out about the oil tanker used to hide Janss. Zaroff tells the rangers that the tanker was stolen from the garage the night before. Tom asks one of the rangers if the lab has had any luck in analyzing the bag of material found at Indian Cave. One of the lab chemists tells Tom that the material is a new type of superhigh explosive. Tom has a flashback and realizes that the bags must contain the same explosive that nearly blinded him.

Tom tells the rangers they need to go to Indian Cave and recover the bags of explosives before they get into the wrong hands. Tom leaves on Tony, and two other rangers take a station wagon to load up the explosives.

Ruth, who has followed Vining to Indian Cave, goes into the cave and hides. She sees Zaroff's men arrive and begin to load the explosives. The phone in the cave buzzes and flashes a light. Vining answers the phone, and Zaroff tells him to get the X-94 out of there in a hurry because the rangers will probably go to the cave as soon as they find out the material is a high explosive.

Ruth goes back into the cave and picks up the wireless phone. Zaroff tries to answer it, but Ruth hangs up. Zaroff calls the cave back to find out who tried to call him. Vining says that no one in the cave called. While Vining is on the phone, Ruth steals the roadster full of explosives.

Zaroff's men ride off after Ruth and the explosives. In the meantime, Tom, Tony, and the rangers in the station wagon are headed at breakneck speed for Indian Cave. Tom and Tony meet Ruth and the roadster head-on. The car swerves to avoid Tom and goes over a hill as Tom and Tony go down an embankment backward, and Tom is thrown to the ground.

Will the car crash and explode, killing Ruth in chapter 14?

Chapter 14

"Between Two Fires" starts with Zaroff's men watching Ruth and the car careening down the hill. Ruth jumps out of the car just before it comes to an abrupt stop in a sandy hill. Amazingly, the car does not explode.

The two rangers in the station wagon stop their car, and one goes to check on Tom while the other checks on Ruth. Tom and Tony are OK, but Ruth is apparently injured. They load her in the station wagon and head for town to take her to a doctor.

After the rangers leave, Zaroff's men go to the car, push it out of the sandbank, and take an alternate road to town, where they hide the car in an old barn and the explosives in an abandoned store.

Ruth regains consciousness in the station wagon and tells Tom she is all right. Tom has the rangers stop the car and Ruth tells them that she took the roadster and so-called X-94 that was loaded into it. She tells Tom that there was a secret phone in the cave and that someone had warned the men in the cave that the rangers were headed that way. Tom hopes that the wireless phone will lead him to the mastermind behind the attempts to scare the Indians off their reservation.

The rangers turn the station wagon around and go back to the cave to search for the wireless phone. Tom sends the rangers to look for more sacks of X-94 while he and Ruth look for the phone. Tom finds the wireless phone in a small opening hidden behind a rock. He tells the rangers to activate the call button at exactly 2 P.M., and he will be ready to get his man at the other end.

Tom then confides in his men that he has suspected Zaroff for some time. Tom tells his men that with the help of Ruth, he plans to sneak into Zaroff's study and be there when the wireless call arrives at 2 P.M.

In the meantime, Vining calls Zaroff to tell him that the Indian girl knows about the secret phone and the X-94. At about this time, a wireless message comes in on the big screen. The message says, "Quarter-million-dollar deposit pending delivery of last European shipment of X-94—Leon."

Zaroff is upset as he tells Carlton, "A fortune is waiting for me and my hands are tied by that interfering ranger." Morgan arrives at Zaroff's ranch, and Zaroff sends Metzger to the lab and Carlton to the door to let Morgan in.

Tom tells Zaroff that there has been an accident and that a young woman has been hurt; Tom needs Zaroff to take her to a doctor in his car. Tom and Tony lead Zaroff and his car to where Ruth is lying. After they load Ruth into Zaroff's car, Tom tells Zaroff that he will follow him, but instead Tom returns to Zaroff's ranch.

Zaroff takes Ruth to the doctor, finds out that she will be all right, then goes to the abandoned store to check on the X-94. Zaroff, suspicious of Tom from the start, says he needs to call Carlton at the ranch.

Carlton hears Tony whinny and goes to the window. Tom hides, and after Carlton leaves the den, Tom enters through the window. Suddenly, the phone rings and Tom hides behind the door. Carlton hears the phone ring and reenters the room to answer it. Tom gets the drop on Carlton and tells him to "answer the phone, but be careful what you say."

Zaroff tells Carlton the young woman is all right and he asks Carlton, "Are there any messages?" Carlton says, "Yes, that oil man is sending our supplies." Zaroff hangs up the phone and contemplates initials of words in the message: T.M.S.O.S.—Tom Morgan, SOS. "I knew it," Zaroff says, "Tom Morgan is at the ranch!"

Tom asks Carlton about the wireless phone, but he denies any knowledge of it. While Tom is questioning Carlton, Zaroff signals Metzger in the lab. Metzger goes to the ranch house with gun in hand. The wireless phone call is expected in five minutes.

When Metzger enters the den with gun aimed, Tom shoots the gun out of his hand. A fight ensues between Tom and Metzger and Carlton. While they are fighting, the crystal ball on Zaroff's desk flashes, indicating that the wireless call has been initiated.

Finally, Tom subdues Metzger and Carlton and sees the crystal ball flashing on the desk. As Tom looks for the hidden wireless phone, Zaroff, Vining, and another henchman arrive by car and enter the room. All three men draw their guns on Tom Morgan. Zaroff proudly exclaims, "Morgan, you're done."

How will Tom escape certain death in the final episode, "Justice Rides the Plains"?

Chapter 15

With Tom, Zaroff, and all of Zaroff's men present, another wireless message comes in on the giant display screen. This time the message reads,

Zaroff, how about giving a fellow a little lift back to ranger head-
?"

n walks up to the car with gun drawn, and Zaroff kicks Carlton out
h force that it knocks both Tom and Carlton to the ground. Tom's
s off, and Carlton wrestles with him as Zaroff starts the car and

n again takes a shortcut cross-country, riding Tony up a large hill
n a steep ravine to make his way back to the roadside ahead of
\s Zaroff approaches, Tom races Tony, pulls beside the car, and
to it. Tom and Zaroff are struggling as Tom looks up and sees that
s about to leave the road and go over a cliff.

n jumps off the car and rolls to safety. Zaroff tries to steer the car
, but it goes over the hill. The car flops over on Zaroff and explodes
hty blast, killing Zaroff.

he last scene, Tom is in the Indian agent's office with Ruth and
Adams is congratulating Tom on being appointed directed of In-
urs by the secretary of the interior, for his outstanding work with
ans. Adams and Tom are remarking that Zaroff could have been
nan if he had used his talents for good instead of evil.

n notices that Ruth is wistfully looking out the window and he goes
ier. "They [the Indians] are celebrating your promotion," she says.
out you?" says Tom. Ruth admits she is thinking about her slain
'om then invites Ruth to go with him to Washington; after all, he
l a secretary. Ruth is very happy and they seal the deal with a hardy
ke.

A Change in the Western Front

1ost everyone enjoyed the first few episodes of *The Miracle Rider*.
ers were awestruck by the rocket glider, the wireless telephone with
ing crystal ball, and the large-screen wireless radio display. They
d spellbound by Metzger, the evil genius at work in Zaroff's lab,
ng the Firebird and refining the X-94 high explosive. They felt
ietic toward the Indians and wanted Tom Morgan to prevail over
at the evil Zaroff and his henchmen.

ere were certain unforgettable scenes in *The Miracle Rider*: young
omising to follow in his father's footsteps; Tom being made a
:ad chief; the Firebird crashing; Ruth trapped in the burning
; Tom nearly blinded as he shoots the bottle of X-94 in midair;
iving a carload of X-94 down a dirt road at 60 miles per hour; and
ieeting his maker with a bang.

n at age 55, Tom had not lost his touch as an expert horseman,
iy Jr. was superbly trained. Cliff Lyons, who allegedly did most of

"Five million dollars is yours if you can send s
tions factory number 7—immediately—Leon.'
a rough idea of what X-94 means to me. If no
the most powerful man in the world." Tom 1
pliment.

Zaroff asks Tom if he, the condemned mar
Tom asks for a cigarette. As Tom starts rolling
away, telling Tom that he is on to that old tri
someone's face. As Zaroff says, "OK, boys, yo
blows the horn on Zaroff's car and distracts t

Tom kicks one henchmen's gun away as
the bad guys. Then he disarms Zaroff. Howev
lightly. He spins the large desk chair, knocking
Zaroff's men quickly recover their guns, but '

Before Zaroff's men can go after Tom, To
tion wagon. Zaroff's men open fire on them a
carefully makes his way to the rangers and tell:
the tear-gas grenades out of the truck."

Zaroff tells his men that he and Carlton w
going through the secret passageway to the
secret passageway door after he and Carlton I
men in the house and leaving them at the m

Then Tom takes an empty metal oil bari
using it as a shield. As soon as he is close enc
a couple of tear-gas grenades through the wind
by the secret passageway only to discover tha:
Zaroff and Carlton. The tear gas becomes un
ing, and the other henchman throw their gu
rangers.

Metzger, disillusioned by Zaroff's betra:
him how to get into the lab. When they exami
that Zaroff has taken all his papers, his worl
Tom that he was working on a synthetic for:
learn how to make out of something as simpl:
must be stopped.

Tom has the rangers take all the prison:
the station wagon as he and Tony take a cro
way back to ranger headquarters, Tom spots
binoculars and arrives at an oil-barrel loadir

Tom hides Tony in the trees and empti
way. Zaroff and Carlton hit the slick at hig!
of control and stalls to a halt. Zaroff ponders
on the road?" Tom steps out of hiding and

Tom's stunts for him, performed them as well as Tom could have done himself during his prime. Tom was still able to throw a rope, ride Tony like the wind, jump large obstacles in a single bound, and sit a horse as well as any man that has ever been in a saddle.

Some critics have said that Tom's voice "didn't record well" and that "his dialogue was unconvincing." Nat Levine thought that Tom had been shot in the mouth by a woman outlaw during Tom's early law enforcement days, so the Mascot producers supposedly had Tom's part of the script pared down to help save his voice. A new noise reduction circuit, developed by the International Sound Recording Company, also helped improve the overall sound track of *The Miracle Rider.*

However, according to Gene Autry, Tom "read poetry well and had a deep, rich voice that rumbled out of his throat like a train out of a tunnel. . . . His speech was what you would call deliberate." In *The Miracle Rider.* Tom's voice is quite audible, if somewhat ponderous in nature. Tom's voice may not be the reason he did not make it big in talkies.

In Bud Norris's *Tom Mix Book,* he points out that Mascot's *Miracle Rider* serial and Tom Mix set a number of important firsts. It was Mascot's first and only 15-chapter serial. At one million dollars, it was Mascot's highest grossing serial. It was Tom's only serial for Mascot, his longest motion picture, and his final film. If the serial made money for Mascot and Nat Levine, why did not Tom and Mascot team up in another film?

The answer is remarkably simple. In the twenties, Tom Mix was the King of the Cowboys. By the midthirties, Tom Mix was still King of the Cowboys, but western movies were in trouble. The serials were somewhat thin on plot and sparse on dialogue, and the moviegoing public was tiring of them. The little studios like Mascot and Monogram began losing big bucks. A new type of western was needed.

Nat Levine had a long-standing acquaintance with Herbert Yates, owner of American Records and Consolidated Film Labs. Yates would invest in a movie and 90 percent of the time would land the contract for processing the film. Moe Siegel, president of American Records, agreed with Yates that western movies needed a shot in the arm and that the Tom Mix–type action-western adventures were a thing of the past. Under the direction of Yates, Mascot, Liberty, Monogram, Majestic, Chesterfield, and Imperial merged, forming Republic Pictures.

The action-adventure cowboy was a character of the past. A young singer named Gene Autry would set new box-office records for Republic Pictures. From 1935 on, the western movies would have a new format: a decent story, good music, some comic relief, and a little action, including the classic fights and chases, and a little more romance.

Nat Levine continued to work at Mascot's North Hollywood studio, making films with Ann Rutherford and Gene Autry. Nat ended up as a

Republic producer managing his own film unit. Tom Mix was one of the last cowboys of the old shoot-'em-up era, and Gene Autry was one of the first of the singing-cowboy era. Tom Mix was one of the greatest showmen of all time. His films were strong on action, costume, and comedy, and he flew through his lighthearted westerns with the ease of a circus acrobat.

One exception of the new breed of singing cowboys was John Wayne. His films were high on action, adventure, romance, and realism. John was a man's man and a generation and a half younger than Tom Mix. Although their film careers overlapped, there was no doubt that Tom was a tired and aging player who was on the way out.

By contrast, John was a handsome, young, rugged actor who started his climb to the top in nonwesterns in 1928, became a star in his own right in 1932 and a top western hero by 1935. His popularity would continue long after the end of singing-cowboy era.

Only a few original 35mm copies of *The Miracle Rider* have survived to date. Most of the copies in current existence, which are frequently dubbed on VHS tape for western fans, at 16mm copies made from the original 35mm format.

Chapter 8

The Sawdust Trail: A Trail of Tears

The sawdust trail of the thirties turned out to be a rugged road and a trail of tears for Tom Mix, the former William Fox superstar. His accumulated wealth of the twenties was seriously depleted, and his movie future was uncertain at best. Tom Mix had a remarkable ability to bounce back after serious personal defeat, however, such as his FBO film disasters.

The Sells-Floto Circus

Because of Tom's immense popularity, the American Circus Corporation offered him a salary of $10,000 per week in 1929 to appear for three seasons with the Sells-Floto Circus. Tom organized his own Wild West troupe and appeared as a highlight attraction for the circus for their 1929–31 seasons. The Sells-Floto Circus was owned by the Bonfils-Tammen empire, which also owned the *Denver Post.* They wanted to capitalize on the popularity of the movies by putting Tom Mix on tour with their show. This was a first, a new tactic, and other circuses soon followed suit. Later in 1931, after the Ringling show consolidated, the Sells-Floto Circus closed.

Tom loved to appear before a live audience, and he let his friends and the audience know it. Perhaps the applauding crowds and happy children helped restore his faith in the future. Tom's Wild West exhibition, following the regular circus performances, was a premier show attraction that kept the audience in their seats until the end of the show.

To some, it might almost seem sinful that Tom Mix was paid $10,000 a week during the depression, when people were going hungry. Actually, the salary paid for Tom's Wild West troupe. The relationship of the wild west troupe to the rest of the circus is illustrated in the following February 28, 1930, article. From the wording of the article, it appears a special performance of the circus was staged for the writer (and others) at winter headquarters in Peru, Indiana.

169

SELLS-FLOTO PLUS TOM MIX
RECALL FOND MEMORIES
by Hope Halpin

Six syllable blurb, multicolored spectacle, infinitude of sound effects—in brief, the circus!

When the year's at the spring and we are beginning to tire of past season's plots and polite drama, this colossus of all amusements comes along and we go with a simple faith and a bag of sibilant popcorn to witness the fire eater, the sword swallower, and giant elephants toss spangled young ladies about—entertainment sold wholesale for the price of a single admission ticket. We all change into several Alices in Wonderland we were once upon a time as though the pink lemonade were the contents of the magic bottle labeled "Drink Me," and watch the 12-foot clown, the skating bears and the games of the seals with less skepticism than Alice herself.

This year, Sells-Floto have a sure fire draw in Tom Mix; most popular of all western stars, who has his own stable of some 20 to 25 horses including Tony. The cowboys with him and his several personal appearances under the big top point up the whole performance. The animal fair is headlined by Pallenberg's Wonder Bears who skate about the two stages as skillfully as any human, do some high bicycle riding that is considered a feat for man, and performa acrobatic tricks that are incredible. There are trained seals, ponies on revolving tables, three rings of Liberty drills, the pachyderm drill wherein young women put giant elephants through a routine of special tricks.

Then there are the acrobats, aerialists, contortionists, equilibrists and there is Mabel Pelke who tosses and twists herself on one arm 50 times in succession and there are the Three Flying Thrillers who offer some aerial feats that will send a thrill down your spine.

The space on the program given to the merry Andrews with their painted grins and chalk faces is slow business except, perhaps, for the Ford trick; that always rates a smile. Either circus clowning is on a decline or we are getting old.

Besides the Liberty drills and some good bareback acrobatics, there is not a lot of concentration on equestrianism which is doubtless due to Tom Mix's wild west show which follows hard upon the main performance. There is a brief Roman standing race, a tandem race and some yipping cowboys which dwindles off to the end of the performance.

Tom Mix has a band of yipping cowboys and an entertaining show that covers some rope work, rodeo riding, tricks with those formidable 52-foot bull whips, etc. all of which is diverting if Tom Mix's fans could keep their eyes off the bronzed, black haired, handsome favorite with his disarming smile. Tom, himself, stands around looking good natured and giving a hand now and then to help his boys entertain. He is a crack shot of course—all those bulls-eyes in films weren't fake—and proves it with six shooter and rifle. He rides Tony and various other of his horses and puts three little ponies through a clever routine in the ring. He is one star that justifies his reputation in a personal appearance.

As a whole the circus is a well run affair although a little slow in parts and shows an efficiency and sense of showmanship at headquarters. Fred Worrell, for many years with Ringling Bros., manager of Sells-Floto is a

The 1930-31 Sells-Floto Circus program photograph of Tom Mix. (Author's collection.)

former resident of South Bend. He has brought to this circus a distinction that it lacked in previous showing here, under other managements.

On March 28, 1930, Tom Mix took time off from his circus schedule to visit Georgie Wood, age 12, the son of Mr. and Mrs. George W. Wood of Peru, Indiana. In September 1929 the boy had been stricken with a spinal disease after being accidentally struck in the back. For over a year he was strapped to a steel bed frame so that he could not turn over. At this time, his doctors predicted it would be another year and a half before the boy would be able to get out of bed and learn to walk again. The boy's teacher, Helen Mullican, visited with him at his home three times a week to keep him up-to-date with his schooling, and, it was reported, the boy did exceptionally well and longed to return to school and his friends. He loved to read and he received outstanding grades on his tests.

Before being confined to his bed, Georgie had been an active boy; he was known as the life of the neighborhood. When he was accidentally struck on the back, his spine was badly bruised. He was taken to the Methodist Hospital in Indianapolis, where Dr. Mumford diagnosed the case and outlined the boy's therapy, which included daily ultraviolet-ray treatments.

Tom Mix was a hero to Georgie, so when Tom caught wind of the boy's plight from some of Georgie's friends, he dressed in his western finest and stopped by to see his young fan. Tom and Georgie spent a good 20 minutes together, and the two of them talked and joked with each other like a couple of old friends. Tom told Georgie about his wonderful horse, Tony, and the movies. Then Tom promised Georgie that he would come back in the fall and ride Tony on the lawn so Georgie could see them through his window. The boy's father replied, "I wouldn't care if Tom Mix brought Tony right into the house and put him in the other bed next to Georgie's— that's what I think of the big-hearted cowboy. He and Tony can come any time, day or night—they'll be welcome as long as I've got a home."

As Tom picked up his big white cowboy hat and was about to leave, Georgie said, "Thank you for coming." Tom replied, "You're going to get well, Georgie. I'm glad that I came. Good-bye till fall." Later Tom had a friend inquire to find out what magazines Georgie liked, and Tom arranged for the boy to have the subscription of his choice at Tom's expense.

The Sells-Floto Circus employed 100 to 125 performers and an additional 18 to 24 band members. Circus acts were called displays in the circus programs, and the Sells-Floto displays featured performing mules, trick riders, acrobats, clowns, trained seals, dancing horses, aerialists, high-jumping horses, and other novelty acts. There were three rings and two stages, with something going on every moment, and the name Tom Mix was a formidable drawing card.

Tom and Tony Jr. usually led the circus procession to open the big-top show. After the regular circus performances, he and his troupe of 40 expert riders and ropers put on a Wild West exhibition. The circus Wild West shows never failed to thrill the young and old alike and bring back memories of a bygone era. Tom was immensely popular with the younger generation, and frequently his admirers pressed so close into the arena that the show had to be stopped before Tom and his troupe could continue with their presentation.

When asked by a circus aide why he joined the Sells-Floto Circus, Tom replied, "I started out on the sawdust trail, and it does something to you. It gets into your blood and now in these years, the old longing has returned and, naturally, I returned to my first love. This I enjoy and this I can do better now that I've had a great deal of experience."

Circus aide Chester B. Hall said, "I only saw Tom angry once. His eyes became steel-like and seemed to turn to fire. He became tense and set, and the real smart-alecks moved away from him by backing up." The incident happened at one of the sideshow attractions called Queen of the South Sea Isles, which was staged in a 12-foot-by-12-foot section of tent that had a canvas bottom about three feet above the ground. In the rear of the tent were the living quarters for the queen, who was one inch under four feet in height and weighed about 75 pounds. The queen was very dark and was dressed in a beautiful scarlet gown with an intricate design. She sat in the middle of the canvas and handled all sorts of deadly snakes, permitting them to crawl over her. There were usually about 80 snakes on the canvas, most of them various species of rattlesnakes, with a few of the more exotic varieties thrown in.

A couple of snake handlers were in the process of adding a newly caught rattler to the group when two ruffians came up to the platform. They angered the rattlesnake with the handlers' sticks, and the snake struck at the queen, barely missing her. Tom rushed to the scene and shouted, "You two, beat it now!" Tom was angry and the two toughs knew it—they backed away silently and then hightailed it out of there.

The Queen of the South Sea Isles was a typical sideshow attraction: the queen was not really a queen, and she certainly was not from the South Sea Isles. "You can hardly imagine my surprise when I learned the queen was really a small, black boy of undeterminable age. Tom thought the world of that little fellow, Hall said.

The Sells-Floto Circus traveled mainly by rail, racking up 12,643 miles in 1929 and 13,271 miles in 1930. In 1931 they traveled 14,891 miles and were on tour for 177 days, excluding Sundays. The circus opened up in the Chicago Coliseum and toured St. Louis, Boston, San Francisco, Los Angeles, and other major cities.

Lawsuits and Injuries

The decade following the stock market crash presented many pitfalls, all of which took their toll on a man who, until this point, seemed to be filled with boundless energy and ambition. In the years that followed, Tom was plagued with illness, injury, marital problems, and numerous lawsuits.

On March 5, 1930, Tom was ordered to pay $175,000 in back taxes and penalties. Tom appeared in court in a brown dress suit and high-heeled boots. He carried his oversized Stetson in his hand and stood quietly while U.S. attorney Samuel McNabb told the court that he had received the authority to allow Mr. Mix to plead guilty and receive a routine fine. Judge James fined Mix $1,000 on each of three counts. During the court proceedings, it was explained that Mix's income statement had been prepared by Marjorie Berger, an income tax expert. Mix claimed that he did not know how Berger had handled his statement. She was sentenced to a term in a woman's federal prison for the falsification.

On June 10, 1930, Tom tried to prevent his 17-year-old daughter, Ruth Jane, from marrying Douglas Gilmore, an actor, when they eloped to Yuma, Arizona. Tom sent a telegram to the sheriff in Yuma, requesting that the marriage be stopped, but it arrived too late. When Ruth and Douglas were married, Tom cut off his daughter's $225 monthly allowance, which he had been paying to her since 1917. However, on July 2, 1930, Ruth sued her father for the right to keep her allowance on the basis that he had agreed to promote her career until she was 21 years old and a star in motion pictures. She stated that she had purchased a $13,000 home because she thought she could count on the allowance. Tom's lawyers contended that Ruth had lost her right to the allowance when she eloped to Yuma. On July 5, the court ruled that Tom did not have to pay the allowance any longer. Ironically, Ruth's marriage to Douglas Gilmore ended in an annulment on July 9, 1932.

On August 19, 1930, Tom was sued by an automobile dealer, John Berress, who alleged that he was attacked by Tom Mix when the Sells-Floto Circus appeared in Minneapolis. Berress was awarded several thousand dollars in damages because Tom had jumped the accuser on his way to the circus, was boisterously drunk, and shook his fist in the accuser's face, threatening him with bodily harm. Nothing was said about what the accuser might have done to provoke such personal attention from Tom.

On October 3, 1930, the press picked up a rumor that Tom Mix would buy the 101 Wild West Ranch Circus. On October 4, 1940, Colonel Zack Miller, the show owner, denied that Mix would buy the show. Those who knew Mix and Zack knew that Zack never forgave Tom for not making the 1929 show appearance. If Tom was the last man on earth, Zack would not have sold the show to him.

On November 4, 1930, Tom Mix was back in the hospital again for treatment of an old back injury. In October 1929, Tom had shattered his shoulder when his horse fell during a circus performance in Dallas, Texas, and the shoulder had to be wired together. Several weeks later, his shoulder bothered him so badly that it had to be rewired. On a Thursday Tom had been in Agua Caliente, Mexico, preparing to take a fast airplane ride to Natchez, Mississippi, to face a $50,000 breach-of-contract suit there on Friday. The Mississippi suit was brought by Zack Miller, who charged that

Mix broke an asserted agreement to stage an act with the show. Severe back pains forced cancellation of the flight and postponement of the trial. On Saturday night, Dr. R. Nicholas Smith sent Mix to a Hollywood hospital. The wire in Tom's shoulder had led to arthritis in his back and was finally removed on November 7, 1930.

On November 26, 1930, Victoria Forde Mix, Tom's wife, obtained a legal separation from Tom on the grounds of mental cruelty and Tom's unexplained absences from home. On December 15, 1930, it was revealed that mental cruelty would be the grounds for Tom and Vicky's upcoming divorce. According to the story, Tom frequently frightened Vicky by twirling a large loaded revolver on his finger. Tom filed a general denial of the charges but did not appear in court for the divorce proceedings, which were held in December 1930. As a result of the proceedings, Victoria obtained the custody of her nine-year-old daughter, Thomasina, and a property settlement. Under the agreement approved by the court, Thomasina was to spend half of her summer vacations with her father.

Adela Rogers St. Johns, who wrote several of Tom's screenplays, once wrote that when Tom's lucky love, Victoria Forde Mix, was with him, he could fail at nothing, but when Victoria left Tom, his landslide of trouble began. All the good luck and fortune that seemed to come with Vicky vanished when she divorced him.

In 1931, Tom was sued by Colonel Zack T. Miller of the 101 Ranch for breaking an oral agreement to appear with the 101 Ranch Wild West Show in 1929. When Tom took the stand, he openly admitted that he was not worth the $10,000 a week the circus had paid him; after all, he had worked for the Miller Brothers in 1908 for only seven dollars a week. Tom's was defended by John M. Kelly, probably a Ringling circus attorney, and the case went to trial in Erie, Pennsylvania. Miller was to receive a settlement of $60,000, but he never forgave Tom Mix for not appearing with the 101 Ranch Wild West Show in 1929. As a result of the depression, Ringling consolidated their assets in 1931, and the Sells-Floto Circus went off the circuit.

Late in 1931, Tom was given an even chance of recovery from peritonitis, the result of a ruptured appendix. There were unconfirmed rumors that Tom was shot by a former wife. A special serum was flown in by airplane from Stanford University to the Glendale airport on November 25, 1931, to help save the actor's life. From there, the serum was rushed by police escort to the Hollywood Hospital. Mix's condition was expected to remain critical for at least 48 hours from the time he had taken a turn for the worse after an emergency operation for appendicitis late on the 24th. Tom eventually made a full recovery.

Tom Mix recovering from peritonitis, one of his many problems circa 1931. (Author's collection.)

Tom Mix Talkies

On June 1, 1931, the *Berkshine Evening Eagle* in Pittsfield, Massachusetts, reported that Tom Mix was attempting to make a movie comeback. The article stated that Mix planned to sign a multipicture contract with Universal Pictures corporation. "I believe that the Universal company is better equipped than any other for my particular type of picture," Mix

Tom Mix in *Destry Rides Again,* **Universal, 1932. (Author's collection.)**

commented. These movies would be Mix's first talkies. Mix also voiced concerns about the prices theatres were charging to see movies and about the types of movies being produced.

After recovering from peritonitis, Tom made nine talking features for Universal Pictures. Although they were popular and in the true Mix tradition, they were not enhanced by sound because of Tom's unconvincing dialogue. Tony Jr., Tom's performing circus horse, made his movie debut in the Universal features. This time, the reviews were favorable, and Tom successfully avoided a second disastrous film flop.

The talking films made for Universal Studios and their release dates are shown below:

TITLE	RELEASE DATE
Destry Rides Again	April 17, 1932
The Rider of Death Valley	May 26, 1932
Texas Bad Man	June 30, 1932
My Pal, the King	August 4, 1932
The Fourth Horseman	September 29, 1931
Hidden Gold	November 3, 1932

TITLE	RELEASE DATE
Flaming Guns	December 22, 1932
The Terror Trail	February 2, 1933
Rustler's Roundup	March 3, 1933

Tom made only 9 talkies for Universal, not the 12 originally planned. Apparently, the six planned for the immediate future were filmed along with three additional films. I believe the series was cut short by three films because of the numerous injuries to Tom and Tony and the toll they had taken on horse and rider.

In his book *Life Is Too Short,* Mickey Rooney said,

> In my next flick I won my first starring role—costarring actually—with Tom Mix and his horse, Tony. My Pal, the King was a fantasy Western in which I played the seven-year-old King of Alvania, saved by Mix from the clutches of an evil count. The movie got me my first mention in the *New York Times,* whose reviewer spelled my name right, and said that I did quite well. Universal also paid me $250 for ten days of shooting. I was coming up in the movie world.

Mickey was actually 12 years old at the time.

In February 1932, Tom married Mabel Ward, an aerial performer with the Sells-Floto Circus, and on August 18, 1932, Tom again went to court. This time the dispute concerned the custody of his 10-year-old daughter, Thomasina. A hearing was held on September 7, 1932, and two days later newspapers reported that Mix and his ex-wife, Victoria DeAlazabel, had reached a satisfactory compromise.

Superior Court Judge, Ira Shinn, approved an agreement under which Mix would have custody of Thomasina for two months during the summer and on alternate holidays. Mrs. DeAlazabel also agreed to let Thomasina attend a Bay School instead of sending her to a convent for schooling.

"Nothing else in life meant more to him than his daughter, Thomasina," wrote Franc Dillon. His article went on to mention Tommy's first vacation back to the Beverly Hills estate to see her father after his divorce from Victoria. For her homecoming, a special pony was groomed, Sony the dog was given a bath, and the old nursery was transformed into an attractive apartment for 10-year-old Thomasina.

According to the article, Victoria had been granted full custody of the child, but for the past two years, Tom has been both mother and father to Thomasina. She had traveled with him and his circus and lived with her governess in his private car. Thomasina returned home with her father when he returned home to make pictures.

Then the past summer Thomasina had gone with her governess to visit her mother in San Francisco, hoping to return home to Tom in the fall, but her mother would not let her go. At that point, Tom began an unsuccessful

Tom has "the drop" on the evil count in *My Pal, the King,* **Universal, 1932. (Courtesy of Art Evans.)**

battle for her custody. Unfortunately, the press picked up on the story and accused Tom of using his daughter for another publicity stunt. However, letters from Thomasina to her father showed her loneliness, her sincere love for him, and her true sadness at being kept apart from him.

Tom also related to the reporter how he had sought the custody of Ruth so that he could give her a good education. Instead, he claimed his former wife, Olive, had neglected her education, sent her out on a vaudeville circuit where only her name kept her alive, and that now she too realized the importance of an education. Tom said he had sent Ruth's guardians $84,000 for the schooling she never received.

On October 22, 1932, Tom was injured when he was thrown from his horse, Tony, during the filming of a Universal feature. The accident happened near Lone Pines in the Mojave Desert when Tony stumbled on a five-foot embankment, went over the bank sideways, and rolled onto his master. Tom was unconscious for some time and suffered an injured right leg and a badly bruised side. In November, at the age of 23, Tony was retired to the Mix stables in Universal City. On Christmas Day 1932, after completing his work on *Rustler's Roundup*, Tom again retired from pictures.

The Sam B. Dill Circus

Tom Mix retired from pictures, but he could not retire from the only way of life he knew. In 1933, Tom Mix organized the Tom Mix Roundup with a group of circus friends from his Sells-Floto Circus days. The Tom Mix Roundup was considered a vaudeville unit and was made up of Tom and Tony Jr.; Dail (D. E.) Turney, manager; John Agee, master of ceremonies; cowboys Herman Nolan and Ed Hendershot; aerialists Irma and Mabel Ward, Tom's wife; Jack Knapp, rodeo clown; Joe Bowers, stage manager; Carl (C. O.) Robinson, band director; and a six-piece band. The show featured a liberty horse act, trick roping acts, and the Ward sisters' aerial act.

In his article "Tom Mix Was My Boss," C. O. Robinson recalls how the talkies and the depression had put many musicians out of work. He was grateful to Tom for giving him a job during those trying times and remembers that the Tom Mix Roundup troupe was treated with consideration at all times. "I will always remember the Christmas and birthday parties [Tom] gave us that winter."

Shortly after forming the Roundup, Tom began to talk about going into a partnership with Sam B. Dill, the owner and operator of a large, motorized three-ring circus that wintered in Dallas. The partnership was announced by *Billboard* on January 1, 1934, and the combined Sam B. Dill and Tom Mix Roundup show was born. The show opened in Hot Springs, Arkansas, on April 20, 1934.

According to Stuart Thayer in his article, "Tom Mix Circus and Wild West: The World's Newest Big Show," (*Bandwagon* March-April 1971), most of the vehicles were already five years old in 1934 and the show's meager menagerie consisted of only five truck-mounted cages and one whimsical elephant, Babe, that everyone loved. On the positive side, the show added 26 house trailers in 1934 so that only the band members had to sleep under a tent. The larger trailers housed workmen, ticket takers and staff, and the smaller trailers housed two, three, or four men each. Many of the trailers were painted with the familiar Tom Mix signature, making then an attractive display by themselves.

Show tents included a new big top, 120 feet long with three 40-foot rings; a new menagerie tent, 90 feet long with three 30-foot rings; and a new children's tent. Both big tents had to be replaced during the season because of the wear and tear caused by overflow crowds. The show also had 50 head of horses, mules, and ponies, which were housed in the menagerie tent at night.

Tom's pride and joy was a large General Motors $3,400 buslike automobile that became his home, office, and chief mode of transportation.

SAM B. DILL'S
BIG 3 RING
CIRCUS
FEATURING
TOM MIX AND TONY

C. A. LAWRENCE
GENERAL AGENT

SAM B. DILL'S 3 RING CIRCUS

Combined With
TOM MIX ROUND-UP

PERMANENT ADDRESS
STATE FAIR GROUNDS
DALLAS, TEXAS

TOM MIX
- in Person -
and TONY

SAM B. DILL'S ³ RING CIRCUS
FEATURING TOM MIX and TONY

DAN PYNE
GENL. PRESS REPRESENTATIVE

The 1934 Sam B. Dill Circus, featuring Tom Mix and Tony. (Courtesy Pfening Archives, Columbus, Ohio.)

Tom was so happy with the vehicle that he wouldn't allow anyone else to drive it when it was new.

If Tom lacked circus management skills, his new partner, Sam B. Dill, more than made up for it. Sam was a manager and assistant manager for the John Robinson Circus in the twenties, assistant manager for the Hegenbeck-Wallace Circus in 1928, the Sparks Circus in 1930, and the Gentry Brothers Circus (later renamed Robbins) in 1931. The later show became the Sam B. Dill Circus in 1932.

The 1934 Sam B. Dill Circus and Tom Mix Roundup was a hit from the start. Tom insisted on a good, clean show, and he made John Agee his

Tom with custom bus-van supplied by Sam B. Dill, 1934. (Courtesy of Pfening Archives, Columbus, Ohio.)

equestrian director. From the show's opening in Hot Springs, it went on to Tennessee, Kentucky, and Ohio. The rolling stock, all painted the same, made a beautiful sight lined up along the highways.

On May 23, 1934, when the show was in Ohio, Tom received word that the Pennsylvania Supreme Court had denied his appeal in the Zack Miller breach-of-contract suit. However, it soon became apparent that the magic of the Mix name was packing the tents, the show began to be publicized as Tom Mix and Tony heading Sam B. Dill's Three-Ring Circus.

The show hit a few snags in 1934 with the cancellation of a sold-out Sunday show by an Indiana minister and the destruction of the menagerie tent in Illinois by a tornado. Luckily, no one was hurt and all the show people pitched in to sew up the tent for the next day's performances.

By mid–July, when the show reached Davenport, Iowa, it had added 24 new Ford V-8 trucks. The continuous upgrading of the show tents and equipment gave the show the appearance of a first-rate outfit—and that was the way Tom wanted it, since his name was prominently displayed.

The show starred Tom Mix and Tony. The opening pageant featured young women, Indians, and Romans. Other 1934 displays included:

- Dogs and monkeys with Helen Ford and Mr. and Mrs. Roy Hilbert
- Acrobats—the Arbaugh and Jordan troupes, the Bell Brothers, and Wanda
- The Hobson Family riding act
- Single trips and muscle grinds with Joy Meyers and Ethyl Harris
- A clown-filled Ford
- The Herbert Beeson wire act
- A western concert announcement with Tom Mix, Tony, and the cast
- An elephant act with Mrs. Hilbert
- A pony act with Roy Hilbert and Helen Ford
- A clown baseball skit
- Walter, Jennifer, and Buddy, the trained seals
- The Tom Mix high school act—three horses
- The Flying Arbaughs and Flying Bells

The Wild West concert featured Tom Mix and Tony, trick riders Frank Gusky and Boots Sallee, Herman Nolan, Ralph Clark, Augie Gomez, and Ruth Gusky. In addition to the main show and western concert, the 1934 Sam B. Dill show had the following sideshow attractions:

- Magician W. E. DeBarrie
- Snakes with Ada Moore
- Mentalist act by Norma Estelle
- Bird circus with Mrs. DeBarrie
- Perkins Company Dancers
- Hillbilly Harold Riley
- Fan dancers Marie Martino and Dorothy Voss
- Minstrels by Regan and Company
- Rex Omar, lecturer

Movie stars, cowboys, and Wild West show performers were often featured with the circus in the decade following the depression. Some of the other stars who took to the sawdust trail from time to time were Colonel Tim McCoy with Ringling Brothers, Barnum and Bailey and, later, with his own show; Buck Jones with his own show; Ken Maynard with the Ringling Brothers and the Cole Brothers; Hoot Gibson with the Wallace Brothers; Jack Hoxie with the Downing Brothers and, later, his own show; Harry Carey, Reb Russell, William Desmond, Texas Ted Lewis, Rex Cole, and a host of others. None proved to be as popular as the Tom Mix show.

On August 11, 1934, on the way from Bristol to Kingsport, Tennessee, the Sam B. Dill Circus suffered its first tragedy. One of the semi trucks was forced off a mountain road by a bus, killing two roustabouts and injuring four others. The deceased were buried in Kingsport, and two of the more seriously injured workers remained in the local hospital. The Sam B. Dill

Circus also encountered excessive licensing fees and flooded circus lots. Two trucks were damaged while crossing the Smoky Mountain range. Sometimes other circuses traveling across the country at the same time adversely affected the box-office take.

The Sam B. Dill Circus played Texas for nine straight weeks and business flourished. The show played the Amarillo Fair, its best week of the season. Later, Tom was elected as a member at large of the Lions International at the Lions Club in Corpus Christi, Texas. While in Texas, hundreds of former Texas rangers, former soldiers, and ranchers flooded the lot, jawing about "the good old days" with Mix.

Dill wanted to winter in Texas, but Mix wanted to winter in California because he had laid the groundwork to film *The Miracle Rider,* the serial for Mascot Studios. The trip from Texas to California was a costly one, however. Business declined sharply in New Mexico and Arizona. To make matters worse, the state of Arizona forced the circus to buy 1934 license plates for all the trucks in the fleet, despite the fact that it was now November. Likewise, California had a poor showing.

On December 21, 1934, Tom Mix finally settled his lawsuit with Colonel Zack T. Miller, owner and operator of the 101 Ranch and 101 Ranch Circus. Tom allegedly paid $22,000 of a $66,000 judgment in an out-of-court settlement. Zack was not happy, but the case was settled once and for all.

In 1934, the Sam B. Dill Circus had made a successful 33-week tour, traveling 12,895 miles and making 222 stands in 16 states. Tom's share of the profits was estimated at $65,000. The show wintered at the Oil Exposition Company in Compton, California. But by the end of the 1934 season, Sam B. Dill, a heavy smoker, was a very sick man. He died that winter of lung cancer.

The Tom Mix Circus

After Dill's death, Mix acquired the circus as his own, at a cost of about $400,000, and took it out on the road as the Tom Mix Circus. With the exception of Buffalo Bill, no other circus owner was ever so well known before starting his circus career.

The 1935 Season

Tom came out of movie retirement in April 1935 to film *The Miracle Rider* serial for Mascot Studios. His official reason for returning to the screen was to fight crime and Communism; his unofficial reasons were to

Opposite: **Tom watches as elephant Babe pulls prop truck out of the mud, 1934. (Author's collection.)**

get some much needed publicity and money for his circus venture. As one reporter put it, "Tom's one fellow who will never have to worry about being shot for being too modest."

For the 1935 season, the Tom Mix Circus needed new grandstands, 11 new trucks, and new advertising material. Because the band was poorly housed in 1934, he purchased them their own semitrailer with 12 berths, clothes lockers, an instrument storage room, and running water.

Tom hoped to announce the arrival of the Tom Mix Circus in each city and town with a street parade. The horse and riders, costumed women, and gaily decorated trucks "put the town in the right frame of mind for the circus." The street parade was canceled in May when the show arrived in Seattle because of bad weather and heavy snows.

Management of the circus also changed when Daily Turney became general manager. Other members of the regular staff were Robert Brown, C. A. Lawrence, Pierce Williamson, Al Oaks, Harry Paine, H. C. Baker, John Agee, Denny Helms, Howard Payne, Jack Burslem, Nathan Alberts, Joe Ford, Ed Hendershot, J. Reece, Ray Garrett, Russell Kelly and J. C. Schnare.

The following displays were featured in the 1935 program:

- Historical pageant with 110 people, from covered wagon to automobile
- Presentation of the colors
- Dog act with Homer Hobson Sr. and Joe Bowers
- Cloud swings, swinging traps
- Riding acts by Herbert Hobson, Juanita Hobson, and Ella Linton
- Tom Mix and Tony Jr. — gun spinning and marksmanship
- Aerial revolves by Miss Zermer and Joy Myers
- Trapeze head balance by Charles Arley
- Comedy acrobats with the Ashton Trio, the Jordan Trio, and the Howard Bell Trio
- Western concert announcement
- Irma Ward, aerialist
- Perch act with Charles Arley
- Whirl revolves with Mildred Asher and Inez Hubbard
- Menagerie act with John Agee on Gowan
- Comedy mule act with Jack Knapp
- Jumping dogs with Homer Hobson and Helen Ford
- Babe the elephant and Inez Arlene
- Tom Mix and the Library Horse act
- Acrobats, gymnasts, and tumblers
- The Riding Hobsons
- The Flying Arbaughs
- Finale, "The Spirit of Progress"

The program shows the expansion that took place compared to the 1934 program. It was a strong show with lots of acts and a large cast.

The sideshow attractions were owned and supervised by Ted Metz, a trumpet player with the Carl Robinson Band (under contract with the Tom Mix Circus). William D. Heney was the bandleader.

The sideshow cast of characters included:

- The Man without Arms and Legs (an illusion)
- The Fat Lady
- The Pinhead
- The Skeleton
- The Midget
- The Frog Boy
- The Tattooed Man
- The Three-Legged Man (an illusion)
- Roberta-Ray, half-man, half-woman

The 1935 season opened in Compton, California, on March 6, 1935, and played a five-day engagement in Hollywood. During the season the show played to capacity crowds at Monterey, Salinas, and Eureka. The second day in Eureka was the biggest day's business in the history of the Mix show until that point. The Al G. Barnes show considered California their home territory, and they resented the Mix show intervention. In Fresno, billing crews from the Al G. Barnes and the Tom Mix Circuses got into a fistfight. The police jailed everyone and both shows agreed not to cover up the other show's posters.

After the California engagements, the show headed up the coast to Bellingham, Washington. The Mix show continued to play to capacity and turn away crowds in Portland, Oregon, and Tacoma, Washington. The show also did well in Helena and Butte, Montana, and Harding and Laramie, Wyoming, despite rain and hail. The Colorado stands were also substantial, but the intense heat began to affect show attendance in Nebraska. However, the Mix show was the first to play Omaha in two years, and there was an overwhelming turnout despite the intense heat.

On June 6, 1935, it was announced that Tom's daughter had eloped again, this time with Harry Knight, champion bronco buster from Canada. The lovebirds were married in Reno, Nevada. The outside world learned of the event when Knight sent a telegram to Tex Austin, a rodeo promoter.

The heat and rain also cut down on the attendance in Illinois, Indiana, and Michigan. At Saginaw, Michigan, new tents had to be ordered from the U.S. Tent and Awning Company. At Sandusky, Ohio, the Tom Mix Circus and the Cole Brothers Circus played simultaneous engagements without incident. As a matter of fact, each show helped advertise and promote the other. Executives and show performers had an unusual

opportunity to visit with each other between shots and at the end of the day.

The Tom Mix Circus ran into trouble on their first date in the state of Kentucky, just across the river from Ohio. Law enforcement officers there got greedy and started slapping fines on the circus as it was preparing to leave town. The fines were for minor motor vehicle infractions, such as not having rearview mirrors, which were not required in most states at that time. Tom considered the action a downright shakedown by the police. So while the town and their police officers slept, the circus split into three caravans. Amid the roar of truck motors and police sirens, the circus caravans crossed three different bridges into the neighboring state of Ohio. The drivers did not stop until they reached Seymore, Indiana, where the circus formed again.

This hasty departure cost the Tom Mix Circus several thousand dollars in lost box-office revenue, considerably more than the total dollar value of the fines. As far as Tom was concerned, however, it was the principle that mattered; he was not about to pay extortion money to anyone.

Business was poor in Missouri and Kansas due to heavy rain and flooded circus lots. A large amount of straw was laid down to salvage a good Labor Day showing at Lawrence, Kansas. Tom broke his leg on October 4, 1935, when his horse fell at a circus performance in Alva, Oklahoma. The record two-day jump of the 1935 tour was from Grand Junction, Colorado, to Las Vegas, Nevada, a distance of 634 miles.

The 1935 season ended with a night show at Barstow, California, and for a second time, the show wintered in Compton. The season had been successful, and payday was as regular as clockwork. The fast-moving Tom Mix Circus covered a lot of territory in 1935, playing 216 stands in 19 states and traveling 13,275 miles while on tour. Unlike other shows, the Mix show usually traveled during the daylight hours instead of at night. This allowed the performers to enjoy America the beautiful as they traveled from coast to coast.

The 1936 Season

The 1936 season opened in Compton and played 45 stands in California. Despite early friction with the Al G. Barnes show, business was good there. Mix reportedly left the show several times while it was in California and sometimes used a cowboy impersonator.

The 1936 show added new tents with white tops and red-and-white sides. The main tent was 150 feet long with three 50-foot rings. The Metz sideshow tent was 130 by 20 feet with gabled ends. A new light plant and

Opposite: **Tom Mix Circus sideshow attractions, at right, and main entrance to circus. (Courtesy of Circus World Museum, Baraboo, Wisconson.)**

Thomasina "Tommy" and Ruth Mix at circus winter headquarters, Compton, California, 1935. (Courtesy Leo Reed.)

office trailer were added. Grandstands were painted orange and blue, and a new colorful bandstand was constructed.

Two elephants were added to the show, and Tom bought a white Arabian horse named Warrior. The original Tony traveled with the show but was never ridden. Tony was retired from active duty in 1929, and treated as an old friend and respected celebrity. Alterations to the show included a new opening Parade of the Royal Mounted, some changes in the riding acts, and a substantial increase in clown acts and participation.

The Tom Mix Circus was the largest motorized circus on the road in 1936. The advance unit consisted of one car and five trucks. The main show fleet had 44 trucks, 8 cars, a bus, and 29 trailers. House trailers were used for the advance office, candy vendors, clown dressing room, ticket office, and a personal trailer for Tom Mix. Other trailers were used for the storage of candy stock, props, dog cages, hamburger stock, and the ladies' rest room. The best description of these vehicles, along with many photographs of them, is presented in part 2 of Stuart Thayer's article, which appeared in the May-June 1971 issue of Bandwagon Magazine.

The 1936 route book describes the circus opening as follows:

> Flashing away from Compton, CA where it had wintered and played an opening stand of a new season on March 11, the Tom Mix Circus in a glittering array of modern motor cars streaked northward along the Pacific shoreline on the first leg of the most sensational journey in circus history. A journey that was, in all truth, a veritable triumph from beginning to end. Roaring along cool mountain trails and across blazing drought land, through humble wayside hamlets and clamorous modern cities, buffeted by elemental vicissitudes, breasting always the ceaseless rush of traffic on bustling highways, Tom Mix and his circus swept forward to undying fame as the first of all motorized big shows to play an unbroken string of dates and length and breadth of our mighty nation.

Show attendance remained good in Oregon, but at Burley, Idaho, a furious windstorm struck the show on May 20, 1936, flattening the menagerie tent and doing considerable damage. During the storm the dust was so thick that visibility was reduced to less than 100 feet. All hands pitched in to help save the big top. Tom worked alongside the rest of his men, and he and three other employees received minor injuries when they were struck by flying debris while attempting to evacuate animals and load them into traveling trucks. A section of reserve seat flooring broke loose and hit Tom on the shoulder. After the storm, attendance was good in Idaho.

The crowds turned out in Wyoming, Colorado, and Kansas. Capacity crowds greeted the first appearance of the Tom Mix show in Kansas City, Missouri, and the press heaped praise on the show. Business was also good in Iowa and South Dakota, even though South Dakota was in the middle of a drought.

About halfway through the 1936 season, the Tom Mix Circus played a spectacular 10-day indoor engagement at the Chicago Coliseum. The circus was sponsored by the Goldblatt Brothers Stores, who reportedly paid the Tom Mix show $30,000 for its 10-day appearance and in return were allowed to sell tickets at a reduced rate in their stores. Actually, the Goldblatt stores gave away most of the tickets for the increased traffic they brought to the stores. The stores were decorated in a circus theme and they advertised in 24 newspapers. In addition, 12,000 sheets of advertising papers were posted and 200 billboards were used to promote the big event. Two million 42-page heralds were printed and distributed. About 103,000 people attended the big show during the 10-day period, despite the intense heat.

From Chicago, the show moved on through Ohio and Pennsylvania, making its debut in the state of New York, and business continued to be great. Finally, on August 10, 1936, the circus arrived in Stamford, Connecticut, gaining the distinction of becoming the first transcontinental motorized circus tour.

The circus did substantial business in Connecticut, Rhode Island, Massachusetts, and New Jersey. From there, they motored on to Pennsylvania, Maryland, Virginia, North Carolina, South Carolina, and Georgia. In Macon, Georgia, a polio epidemic kept children and adults away from crowds, so the show doubled back to Virginia, picking up Tennessee, Georgia, and closing on November 5, 1936, at Anniston, Alabama, where it set up winter quarters at a 47-acre complex that was the former location of the U.S. Pipe Company.

The 1936 Tom Mix Circus toured 25 states, made 217 stands, and traveled 12,235 miles. The 1936 season would turn out to be the best-ever season for the Tom Mix Circus.

The 1937 Season

On February 6, 1937, a fire at winter headquarters damaged trucks, the cook tent, other equipment. The same day, a flood hit Gadsen, Alabama, and the Mix show lent a top, a light plant, and 1,500 chairs in response to a Red Cross appeal.

The 1937 show had 29 horses, 8 ponies, 2 mules, 3 elephants, 3 zebras, a sun bear, and a llama. The displays for the 1937 season were similar to the 1936 season, with the Hanneford family riding act replacing the Hobson riding act. One new act, Ray Goody's Slide for Life, was added. Changes to the circus staff were as follows: J. Hervey, contract agent; Fred Emythe, press agent; Herb Duval, adjustor; William Flowers, connection; Fred Schaefer, menagerie boss.

It was about this time that Tom started having second thoughts about running a large, motorized unit. He began to think about the lower maintenance and shipping costs of a rail unit.

The 1937 show opened in Anniston, Alabama, on March 31. From there the show proceeded to Birmingham for a Shrine-sponsored show, then went on to Gadsen and Huntsville. Heavy floods in 1937 affected attendance in Arkansas, Tennessee, Illinois, Missouri, and Indiana. The show had to be canceled in Mansfield, Ohio, due to a wet lot, but gates were excellent in Akron and Youngstown, Ohio.

Business thrived through Pennsylvania and New York, despite heavy Ringling billing in Scranton. Through some clever planning the Mix show was the first show scheduled through New England from mid–May to late June, the crowds came despite the continuing wet weather. Rain and cold weather discouraged some circusgoers in Fall River and Lynn, Massachusetts. While in the Boston area, the performers took the opportunity to visit the big city for a little R and R, or at least a change of pace.

Show attendance was also good in Connecticut and New Hampshire. According to Dick Seiverling, in *Tom Mix: Portrait of a Superstar*, New Hampshire governor Francis Murphy and Mayor Lucier of Nashua were guests of Mix when the show played Nashua. At Concord, the circus staged

Photograph of Tom and Tony Jr. Tom Mix Circus, 1937 season. Note diamond-studded belt buckle. (Author's collection.)

a special show at the New Hampshire state prison, participating performers were dinner guests of the state prison officials.

In Portland, Maine, Tom found that his handbills had been covered over by those of a competitor's show, but, much to everyone's surprise, the Tom Mix Circus did its greatest single day's business of the season.

While the circus was in New England, the Congress of Industrial

Organizations tried to organize the circus performers several times. The union was unsuccessful in its attempts to organize the Mix show and too late to help several of the smaller shows that bit the dust in 1937. The consensus was that the union would have little effect on a show's ultimate fate, in any event.

After performing in wet lots in Maine and Vermont, the show returned to Glens Falls, New York, where it was warmly greeted in the hometown of the George Hanneford, who was with the Mix show at that time. Then, it was on to Oneida, New York, where the circus was the first show to play there after a two year period, assuring both a good crowd and brisk business.

Labor strikes and unrest and an accident en route from Butler to Washington dampened business in Pennsylvania. A car suddenly pulled onto the highway from a side road and stalled. One of the Mix circus trucks, pulling a trailer, swerved into a roadside ditch to avoid an accident. The trailer it was pulling broke loose and careened down a mountainside, demolishing it. It had contained office supplies and some of Tom's personal property, which was retrieved. The truck driver suffered only minor injuries.

The Tom Mix Circus celebrated the Fourth of July in East Liverpool, Ohio. For the entertainment of the troupe, a four-round boxing bout was held under the big top between shows.

Oppressive heat affected the attendance at the matinee shows in West Virginia, but the night shows played to good crowds. While in West Virginia, John Agee took over as equestrian director of the Mix show when Rhonda Royal resigned. On July 11, 1937, Tom and his wife traveled from Huntington, West Virginia, to Dover, Ohio, where they were the guests of honor at a Ringling show. On leaving West Virginia, the show made one performance in Tennessee and five in Virginia. While in Virginia, Tom learned that his mother had died of a lingering illness in the DuBois hospital.

After leaving Winchester, Virginia, the circus headed for Washington, D.C., where they were met on the historic Key Bridge by a police motorcycle escort. The Tom Mix Circus played its first engagement in the nation's capital on a new circus lot that had been established on Bennington Road and inaugurated manicured lawn-type circus lot next to the Anacosta River. The lot was made possible by the dreams and efforts of James E. Cooper of the Circus Fans Association (CFA). The show enjoyed record attendance during its three-day appearance. After the first night's performance, Melvin D. Hildreth, president of the CFA, had nothing but the highest praise for the Tom Mix Circus, its personnel, and the new circus lot. While in Washington, D.C., Tom visited the White House and War Department and had luncheon with a group of senators at the Capitol.

Business continued to thrive in Maryland, where the show played to straw houses and even turned away crowds. Advance publicity and advertising on radio station WIP made for a good, but seasonably hot, nine-day stand in the Philadelphia area.

Bad luck struck the show again on the morning of August 20, when three truck accidents occurred in the Pennsylvania mountains. While en route to West Pittston, Pennsylvania, one truck loaded with horses and zebras overturned when the driver lost control of his vehicle. In another accident, a truck carrying four zebras and a llama caught fire. A third truck, with a load of horses, broke down due to engine failure. However, the Pittston stand was made on time.

From Pennsylvania, the show toured Auburn, Geneva, North Tonawanda, and Niagara Falls, New York, then headed on to Toronto, Ontario, Canada and the 59th Annual Canadian National Exhibition. Newspaper coverage and advance publicity for the opening show on August 27 was excellent and the show probably would have played to record crowds had it not been for excessive heat and an outbreak of polio. Even so, the gates were average, contributing to a good 14-day engagement. While in Canada, Tom was a guest of the King Edward Hotel. He and his show personnel were treated like royalty, entertained by local dignitaries and private citizens alike during their extended stay in Canada.

The show reentered the United States through New York State and headed westward, making additional stands in Pennsylvania, Ohio, Indiana, and Illinois. Tom lost his Star Back truck in Ravena, Ohio, when it was demolished in a train accident; it was replaced when the show got to Akron. By now, the weather had turned cold, and poor attendance was noted on the westward trek.

Business remained weak until the show crossed the Mississippi River at Hannibal, Missouri, for a nine-day tour of the state. Large crowds came to see the Tom Mix Circus at Kansas City, Missouri, and the show played to overflow crowds at every performance. Continuing west and south, the Mix show rolled on into Kansas, Missouri again, and Arkansas. The two-day stand in Kansas City, Kansas, came up with four capacity-crowd stands. Despite wet weather in Arkansas, the rest of the stands brought average gates.

On November 6, 1937, the Tom Mix Circus played its last date of the season in El Dorado, Arkansas. The season marked the shortest mileage of any season, totaling only 10,521 miles and making only 195 stands. The season was rated as a good, but not great, for the Tom Mix Circus.

The 1938 Season

Optimism was high and the staff of the Tom Mix Circus looked with anticipation toward the 1938 season. The show added a few new, heavier trucks. Ruth Mix joined up with her father at the start of the season and received good billing. Little did anyone know nor could they predict that they were about to experience the worst year in circus history since 1875.

Colonel Tim McCoy's Real Wild West and the Parker and Watts Circus went out for the first time, and Atkins and Terrell put out a second railroad show. However, by the first week in May, *Billboard* was reporting poor crowds everywhere. The Tom Mix Circus experienced poor crowds in Texas, Oklahoma, and Missouri, even though it expanded to over two hours, its longest show ever.

On April 11, 1938, Tom Mix ended his 1933 contract with the Ralston Purina Company and signed a new contract to continue the youth-oriented radio programs, which followed the film-serial style. Tom endorsed the Ralston Purina products as helping to build a better and stronger youth, and the company held the boys and girls spellbound for 15 minutes every Monday, Wednesday, and Friday.

Tim McCoy's Wild West and Rough Riders of the World opened on April 14, 1938, in Chicago, at the International Amphitheater and closed 21 days later in Washington, D.C. Tim McCoy lost $300,000 and found himself flat broke and starting over. P. N. Branson joined up with the Mix show and became its general agent.

Poor showings were also experienced in Indiana, Ohio, and New York. By mid–May, Mix decided to call it quits. Tom put his daughter, Ruth, in charge of the show and he went on to Chicago to get ready for his European theater tour, which was to begin in September. Apparently, Tom had made a preliminary trip to London in May to secure the final arrangements for his European tour. Dail Turney continued to act as business manager.

The Downie Brothers show closed on May 31, and the Cole Brothers cut their salaries the same week. The Tom Mix Circus cut their admission price from 50 cents to 20 cents, hoping to break even. However, wages soon fell behind the gate, and the Mix show released 45 workers. There was a brief upturn in business in northern New York, and the best show of the season in Altoona, Pennsylvania, in mid–June. By this time, however, the show had been reduced to 50 performers and 11 band members.

It became obvious to Tom's staff that all the circuses were rapidly gathering in the East, so the Tom Mix show turned back, hoping to pick up business in the West. At this point they simply wanted to break even, but that did not happen. In late June, however, they did good business in Evanston, Illinois.

The first accident of the season occurred at Neenah, Wisconsin, on July 10, when gusty winds blew the big top down on a crowd of a thousand people watching the liberty drills. A falling pole broke a horse's back, and one of the riggers suffered a broken arm. The horse had to be shot, but no one in the audience was injured.

Business was poor in Wisconsin, Iowa, and Missouri. When the show arrived in Kansas City for its third appearance in as many years, 21,000 people stormed the ticket office, producing six overcapacity (straw) performances.

By the time the show hit Wichita on August 19, it had been cut to one ring, and performers and workers continued to drift away. Ruth Mix did all she could to hold the show together through Oklahoma and Texas, but it finally folded in Pecos on September 10, 1938.

There were many reasons why the large motorized circuses ran into financial difficulties and were forced to close. Their fate during the depression closely paralleled that of the large touring Wild West shows. There were just too many hungry mouths, both human and animal, to feed. Bad weather was always a problem—cars and trucks bogged down and maintenance costs skyrocketed, and the crowds did not come out.

There were other problems: disease among the animals, the death and injury of performers and animals, looting and rioting by hoodlums in unfriendly towns. In one Montana town, a group of thugs tore up every circus that came to town, and the Tom Mix Circus was no exception. After an evening performance, when all the tents had been taken down except the big menagerie tent, a group of young men gathered with the crowd and began throwing rocks at the tent. The superintendent of the circus blew his whistle and tried to disperse the crowd and send them home, but they refused to leave. The town hoodlums ducked under a rope tied to the menagerie tent and began slashing the canvas with knives. The superintendent blew his whistle again and suddenly the sides of the menagerie tent were dropped, revealing cowboys, roustabouts, and others on horseback with clubs and ax handles. At about the same time the cowboys began cracking heads, the elephant trainer had Babe the elephant pick up her chain and swing it in wide circles. This time the crowd cleared out in no time.

The town bullies did not give up easily and made repeat attacks on the circus. Every time they pressed their attack, they were spotted by a large revolving spotlight and driven back by the circus performers. Finally, the police, who had been conspicuously absent, arrived, complaining that several townspeople had been hospitalized. The fight had ended with the injury of the circus performers.

Such were the problems that plagued the Tom Mix Circus at one time or another. Tom tried to help his people whenever he could, but even he had to admit financial defeat in 1938.

During the late thirties, Tom also turned to drink to drown his sorrows. On one occasion, he slugged a spectator outside of his circus tent and was taken to court on aggravated assault charges. Those who loved Tom hated to see him drinking to excess and were reasonably successful

Tom Mix tips his hat to photographer. Ruth Mix in background, circa 1938. (Photo courtesy of Jimmie Dodd.)

in talking him into taking hold of his senses and returning to moderation.

In the end, the Tom Mix show equipment was put into the City-County Exposition Building in El Paso, Texas. From there it was widely dispersed for the payment of debts. A used-car dealer bought most of the trucks. The elephants, office wagon, and wardrobe were sold as partial payment for debts. The light plant and calliope were given to Dail Turney and C. W. Warrell, probably in lieu of back pay. J. W. Conklin, a carnival operator, became the major buyer of show equipment. Gladstone Shaw, the general superintendent, kept control of 20 head of horses. The Tom Mix Circus, which had brought entertainment and laughter to millions of people, was dealt its deathblow in the last days of the great depression. Ironically, the depression officially ended in 1939, and a great nationwide recovery began.

Chapter 9

The Fatal Crash
and Its Aftermath

The Resilient Character of Tom Mix

Tom Mix was a class act, a fighter who never accepted defeat. After his tremendously successful career with Fox, he suffered a severe setback with his FBO films, mainly due to the advent of the talkies. If this were not bad enough, the depression came along and knocked the props out from under him. His accumulated wealth of the twenties vanished in a very short time.

But Tom Mix did not give up. He made an astounding comeback as a circus performer during the midst of the depression and an unprecedented movie comeback with a successful series of talkies for Universal in 1932. Although his 1935 film serial, *The Miracle Rider,* may not have been the highlight of his film career, it was a box-office success and a money-maker for both him and the Mascot Film Studios. Best of all, a new generation of young Americans thrilled to the action and adventures of Tom Mix and the Old West.

The Tom Mix Circus was on the road only a few months in 1938 before Tom saw the handwriting on the wall. Almost immediately Tom handpicked a couple of members of his Wild West aggregation and made arrangements for a second European tour. Perhaps he thought he would bolster the finances of his faltering circus, but it was too little, too late, and his circus folded for good in 1938.

Sage of the Lasso

Tom and his press agents were never at a loss for words in the twenties and thirties. Tom spoke with great authority on everything from mom's apple pie to America's communist and drug threats. Many of these interviews attributed to Tom are highly entertaining and appear to be based on some of Tom's deep-seated beliefs.

In a June 3, 1934 newspaper article, Mix expressed opinions on a wide range of topics. Some of Mix's more interesting comments were about the roles of the sexes. Mix stated that "women may aspire to great things, but they never yet have achieved anything, without raising competition in a man who would do it better." Mix went on to declare that "It is up to the father to see that his family is well cared for and that they want for nothing."

1938 European Tour

England

In May 1938 Tom left for a second European tour. He arrived in England on May 20, and the police promptly took eight pistols and five rifles away from him because he had no import license. One reporter wrote that Tom's arrival in England "must have been the largest armed force that has tried to land on British soil since the last attempt by the Stuarts almost 200 years ago." Tom was in England about seven months.

In September, Tom and Tony II were big hits at the Birmingham Hippodrome Theater. Reviews of his performance noted Tom's unerring marksmanship as he split a bullet on the edge of a butcher's cleaver so that it smashed objects placed on either side of the cleaver.

In a September 23, 1938, interview with the *Birmingham Gazette,* both Tom and his wife, Mabel, discussed their professions and their lives together. When the reporter asked Mrs. Mix if she had ever worked on stage or in films, she got the feeling that neither Mrs. Mix nor her husband felt that both spouses should work in the same field. "I guess it doesn't kinder do for two married people to be tired at the same time. Neither is inclined to be so sympathetic to the other," said Tom.

In early December, Tom Mix, Jack Knapp, Tony II, and Joe Bowers arrived at Brighton to appear at the Brighton Hippodrome theater. Joe Bowers was acting as Tony II's caretaker and Tom's business manager. Hundreds of local children greeted them on their arrival, and when newsmen asked Tom if he had anything to say, Tom replied:

> Well, I wish the Brighton children a merry Christmas. I've got children of my own, and I'm very much interested in children in general. Wherever I go I always interest myself in their welfare, and I hope their parents and guardians take an interest in them too, and bring them up to be better citizens than we are. We've made our mistakes.

The local newspapers also noted that Tom appeared in great physical condition and that with his dark hair, excellent posture, and muscle tone did not appear to be those of a man of 58 years of age.

At the Hippodrome Tom demonstrated his skill with lasso and guns. He put on a rope spinning demonstration, followed by a sharpshooting act

Tom and Tony II in London, England, 1938. (Author's collection.)

with rifle and revolvers, breaking numerous spinning targets from a distance of 30 feet. He also split a bullet on the edge of a cleaver, as he had done many times before. After playing most of the big theaters in England, the Mix troupe left for the continent on April 1939.

Germany

Even though Tom Mix had over 5 million fans in Germany in the twenties and thirties, he did not revisit Germany during his second European tour. By now, dark war clouds threatened Europe. However, even Hitler could not ban Tom Mix because he had too many German admirers. According to Kurt Klotzbach, a German writer and dedicated Tom Mix fan, Hitler, while aboard the German battleship *Graf Spee*, invited Tom by telephone to tour Germany, but Tom replied, "I'll tour Germany again and see my fans—but only over your dead body." No one knows what Hitler's reply was—perhaps it was not fit to print. Tom was quick to recognize that Hitler's invitation was little more than a Nazi ploy to feed their war propaganda machine. Unfortunately, Tom died before Hitler did.

As strange as it may seem, Germany did produce a German and American Wild West show and circus hero, thanks to the influence of William F. "Buffalo Bill" Cody and the efforts of Tom Mix. Erich Rudolf Otto

Rosenthal later changed his name to Billy Jenkins and became known as "the German Buffalo Bill." Jenkins was five years younger than Mix, but he had a lot in common with Tom.

In 1890, at the age of five, one of Billy's uncles took him to see Buffalo Bill's Wild West Show when it toured Europe and Germany. The young boy was so thrilled by the show that he told his uncle he wanted to talk to Buffalo Bill. With a little luck and some political pull, his uncle was able to make arrangements for him to meet his hero. Buffalo Bill let the young boy ride a pony, gave him a ride on his lap, and presented him with an autographed picture. The boy shared his experience with all of his friends and he soon became known as Little Billy.

Billy never forgot Buffalo Bill nor gave up his desire to become an American cowboy. At the age of 15, he ran away from home, worked his way to Texas, and hired on as a cowboy at another uncle's ranch, the Heart Four Bar Ranch, near El Paso.

Later, Billy visited New York and was surprised to learn that his boyhood hero Buffalo Bill was appearing at Madison Square Garden. He looked up Buffalo Bill, who remembered him and extended an invitation for him to ride in the opening spectacle. After learning of Billy's firm resolve to be an American cowboy, Cody suggested that Billy learn the ropes and seek his fame and fortune at the Miller Brothers' 101 Ranch.

Zack Miller hired Billy and suggested he change his last name for showmanship purposes. It was then that Billy changed his last name from Rosenthal to Jenkins, the name of another uncle who had migrated to America. The name Billy Jenkins suited Zack Miller, and he assigned young Billy to one of his seasoned cowboys, Tom Mix. Billy Jenkins's feelings toward Tom Mix are best described in his 1950 Dortmund, Germany, interview with Kurt Klotzbach:

> From Tom Mix I learned all those cowboy tricks, especially how to handle a lasso. Soon I became so proficient with the lasso that Tom, my boss, one day envied my success as a lasso champion. The 101 Ranch employed me as a show rider, bull rider and bronco buster, but I had also worked as a sharp shooter and lasso champion. One day I said "Goodbye" to Miller's 101 and became a cadet of the Military Volunteer Cadet School. In 1907 I returned to Germany, but again I made a jump into the New World when the American circus, Ringling Brothers, made me an offer. From Ringling, I changed to Barnum & Bailey. Back in Germany again, I worked some years for the famous German circus, Hans Stosch Sarrasani. At last, I opened my own circus.

When Billy was asked how he felt about Tom Mix as a person, he replied:

> He was the toughest cowboy I have ever met, the straightest fellow and the best friend you can imagine, I have to thank him a lot for he was my best teacher. Without him, I am sure I never would have become a good cowboy or—Billy Jenkins. Yes, Tom was a very fine hombre!

Billy Jenkins and Tom Mix got together again at the Boy Scout conclave in Cologne when Tom made his European trip to Germany in 1925. Billy remembered Tom's signing autographs and handing out $125 Stetsons to various Boy Scout leaders.

Tom sent his last letter to Billy Jenkins when Billy was touring with his circus in Germany and Tom was touring with his circus in America in the late thirties.

> Do you still remember the grand old days at the 101 Ranch, Billy, it was a smashing time, wasn't it? You and I were encouraged by Buffalo Bill to become a cowboy when we saw his Wild West Show in our boyhood days. These times have passed now and will never return. . . .

Denmark

On March 17, 1939, Tom Mix entered into a contract with Mrs. M. Belli of the Circus Belli, traveling in Denmark. Tom agreed to appear with two assistants and his horse Tony II for trick shooting, rope spinning, and similar western acts. He would put on his show every night, along with Sunday and holiday matinees and three extra weekday matinees. According to Janus Barfoed of the Danish Film Museum, Tom signed the original Circus Belli contract in green ink, a little-known fact that might be of interest to Tom Mix trivia fans.

In the agreement, Tom also allowed himself to be interviewed and photographed while with the circus. Tom agreed to appear with the circus from April 29, 1939, through July 31, 1939, with the possible extension of the contract until October 1, 1939, if mutually agreeable.

Tom's salary was to be 650 Danish crowns ($3,250) a day and Belli agreed to pay all the fares and transportation costs for Mix, his assistants, and the livestock. Mix was to be paid daily, and Belli agreed to put a two-week deposit in a Copenhagen bank. There was only one day out of the whole season that the circus would not play and that was Whitsuntide, May 28; Tom would not be paid for that day. In case of war, strike, police harassment, and unforeseen acts of God, Tom's pay was to prorated for all performances given. Belli was to pay Fosters Agency, the booking agent, a 5 percent commission.

Tom accepted the contract, requesting first-class transportation for himself, four people, and the horses. He also asked that the circus cover local transportation and baggage costs and food for the horses. It was also his understanding that the 650 Danish crown salary was to be tax free. Apparently, the contract and its amendments were accepted by all parties. The daily salary was to cover Tom and his contingent. It represented an all-time-high payment for a contract of this nature.

Tom and his wife, Mabel, arrived in Horsens, Denmark, on April 18, 1939, where they were greeted by an enthusiastic crowd of over 10,000 people. Again, reporters noted that Tom's appearance had not changed much from his moviemaking days. Almost immediately, it became obvious to Belli that a larger circus tent would be needed to house the crowds that Tom was drawing. The circus was expanded to a six-mast tent capable of seating a crowd of 3,000 people at each performance. According to Janus Barfoed of the Danish Film Museum, Tom's popularity in Denmark was never greater.

Rumors of Tom's death had prematurely circulated in Denmark, to the consternation of Belli. There was some talk that the Tom Mix now appearing with Circus Belli was a fake. Fortunately for Belli and the circus, a man named Carl P. Nielson, who lived in Randers and had once worked for Tom in Hollywood, came forward. He identified himself to Belli and immediately recognized Tom and verified for the local news reporters that the real Tom Mix was indeed the star performer with Circus Belli.

Tom was said to be an imposing figure on his large white horse as he rode, swinging his hat and saluting the audience, into the arena. Tom performed his usual rope tricks and, in a variation to his act, shot at an ax blade, blowing out two candles. This, of course, is not much of a trick at all because if the two candles are placed in a box frame, a bullet passing anywhere through the frame will extinguish both candles.

During the Denmark circus tour, two writers, Henry Dahl and Willy Ulsing, accompanied Tom and took numerous photographs of him. Their work was published in a softbound book titled *Med Tom Mix Paa Circusturne*. Tom Mix impressed these writers as often moody and sometimes a lonely man. At times like this, Tom, like his boyhood hero, Buffalo Bill, seemed to find comfort in a good bottle of whiskey. Tom was more or less locked in his hotel room, away from any whiskey, when the circus was scheduled to put on a command performance for the king of Denmark.

Tom had managed to slip a bottle into his suitcase, and on the day of his royal presentation, he was found unconscious in his room, although he sobered up in time to make the royal presentation. While it was not his best performance, the king of Denmark gracefully saluted Tom Mix as he approached the royal balustrade. Most of the time, however, Tom remained sober and in complete control of his faculties.

Tom was also somewhat protective of his wife, Mabel, during his Denmark circus tour. On more than one occasion, he objected to photographers taking her picture; Tom considered his relationship with his wife a private matter, not one for the public record.

Tom Mix toured Denmark with Circus Belli until September 2, 1939, the day war broke out in Europe. Not wanting to be trapped in Europe for the duration of the war, Tom hastily left with his troupe and headed back to the United States with new hopes and ideas. Convinced that he was still popular, he felt another movie comeback might not be impossible.

Circus Belli program cover, Denmark, 1939. (Courtesy of Janus Barfoed.)

Tom's hopes for a comeback with his old employer, Fox Studios, were soon dashed. When he returned to the renamed 20th Century–Fox studios, Tom was warmly greeted by Fox's production manager, R. Lee "Lefty" Hough. Tom confided that he had lost about a million dollars with the Tom Mix Circus and still had credit problems. Lefty, somewhat sympathetic, took Tom to see his old friend, director John Ford, who was shooting *The Grapes of Wrath* at the time. Ford took Mix out for lunch, and the two had a pleasant chat, but the truth of the matter was that no one at Fox had any work for the 60-year-old cowboy.

The Last Days

The following sequence of events has been reconstructed based on a number of stories written by people who claimed they were with Tom Mix a few days before or on the actual day of his death. The author assumes that even a person as famous as Tom Mix can be in only one place at a time.

After returning from Europe, Tom moved his livestock back to his little ranch about 20 miles from Hollywood and was reportedly reorganizing his Wild West troupe and making a cross-country trip promoting a personal appearance tour in South America. He also had a contract or verbal agreement to make another movie, which he planned to complete before going to South America.

On his return trip, Tom went from New York city to Chicago and then headed south. He was in Alice, Texas, in early October when King Ranch photographer Jimmie Dodd snapped a close-up picture of Tom as he sat in front of his Cord roadster. The hood of his Cord was raised and Jimmie did not interview Tom or even think to ask him if he was having trouble with the Cord. Jimmie was just happy to have the opportunity to snap a picture of Tom before he continued his trip to El Paso.

Tom was in El Paso on October 9, 1940. He checked into the Ranchotel located on a dude ranch a few miles north of the city. There he renewed his acquaintances with a 17-year-old actor and artist named Gene Sterling, who had appeared as a child in a couple of Mix films. Sterling was working as a clerk and entertainer at the dude ranch hotel. Tom had stopped at the dude ranch because he wanted to talk to one of his former horse trainers, Slim Harris.

The next morning, Sterling asked Tom if he would give him a ride as far as Las Cruces, New Mexico, so that he could pick up one of his saddles at a repair shop. Tom agreed and offered to take him along to Tucson if he wanted to go. Sterling thanked Tom for the offer but told him he had to get back to work at the dude ranch. Sterling loaded the metal suitcases into the back of Tom's car, and they sped off down the road toward Las Cruces. According to Sterling, the Cord's speedometer pegged out at 150 mph on one stretch of the road. According to the manufacturer's specifications, the 170 horsepower supercharged Cord Model 812 had a top speed of 110 mph.

After dropping Sterling off, Tom arrived in Lordsburg, New Mexico, where he appeared as the grand marshal in their Fair Day Parade. Since Tom did not have a horse with him, a local horse named Smokey, who resembled old Tony, was selected as Tom Mix's parade horse that day. Smokey, a spirited mount, was a blue roan with three white boots. He was owned by F. B. Daniels, a Lordsburg agent for the Southern Pacific railroad.

One of the last photos of Tom Mix, October 1940. (Courtesy of Jimmie Dodd.)

The Fair Day Parade was a big event for Smokey—his first parade. Smokey held his head high and pranced to the music of the band as he carried America's King of the Cowboys along the parade route. The parade crossed town and ended at the fairgrounds; it was a short parade, the first for Smokey and the last for Tom Mix. After the parade, Tom visited old friends, Mr. and Mrs. John "Blackie" Baugh, then was off to Tucson, the next stop on his route.

While in Tucson, Tom called his old friend, Sheriff Ed Echols. In turn, Ed called their mutual friend Walt Coburn, a well-known western writer. Walt's wife left a message for him to read when he came in from his workshop and then headed for town. The message said that Ed Echols was bringing Tom Mix over that afternoon for a drink.

Walt Coburn made and spent a fortune writing western stories for the pulp magazines. He gave his wife full credit for salvaging enough money to buy a tract of land in the prestigious Catalina Foothills Estates. There, within view of all five local mountain ranges, Walt contracted builder John Murphey to construct a beautiful, sprawling Spanish-style adobe ranch house and workshop. This showplace home is fully described in Walt Coburn's article, "Tom Mix's Last Sundown."

On October 11, 1940, Sheriff Ed Echols picked Tom up at his hotel and drove him to Walt Coburn's ranch. Like a curious child, Tom periodically rang the old Spanish mission bell out front until Walt greeted them at the door. After a mutual exchange of greetings, Walt fixed drinks at the bar and, at Tom's insistence, gave Tom and Ed a one-hour guided tour of the house and workshop, or shed, as Walt called it. Then the men went to the large enclosed back porch where they rolled their own cigarettes and lit up. Comfortably seated with cigarettes and whisky, Tom Mix and Ed Echols began swapping yarns and telling tales about the good old days at the Miller Brothers' 101 Ranch and Wild West Show.

Tom recalled winning his early title as champion bulldogger at Seattle, in 1909, which brought back Ed's memories being the champion steer roper at the first Calgary Stampede in 1912. Both men talked about traveling as cowboys with Colonel Zack Miller and his famed 101 Ranch Wild West Show. Other alumni of the 101 Ranch that they talked about were Bill Pickett, Neal Hart, and Henry Grammar. Though neither of the men were witness to the event, they discussed the events leading up to the time when Henry Grammar shot a sheep shearer who had mistreated an old shepherd in a saloon ruckus in Malta around 1905. According to the story, Grammar pleaded self-defense because he was unarmed and had been attacked by the sheep shearer, who had a knife. Following a scuffle, Grammar managed to grab the bartender's gun and shoot the shearer. He was sentenced to serve three years in the penitentiary at Deer Lodge, but apparently got time off for good behavior.

Walt listened intently as the two men talked about the bull riders, bronco busters, bulldoggers, and trick ropers they had worked with in their days with the 101 Ranch Wild West Show. After the end of an enjoyable afternoon, Tom mentiond that he intended to stop in Florence to see his friend and former son-in-law Harry Knight, a former top bronco rider.

That evening the three men watched a spectacular fire-red Arizona sunset bring an end to a perfect day. It would be Tom Mix's last sundown.

Before Tom left, he gave Walt Colburn an autographed copy of his book, *Roping a Million*. In it, Tom described the number of wounds and injuries he received in his real life adventures and criticized scriptwriters and motion picture conferences that he felt unduly overburdened at the cost of the five-reel motion pictures. Tom felt he could save the studios a lot of money by being the star, the producer, and the director and by furnishing his own horse.

Ed Echols promised to bring Tom back the next day for lunch, so they left without a handshake. "So long, Walt. See you tomorrow," Tom said as they drove away. "So long until tomorrow," Walt replied. Walt had planned to serve Mexican beer and tenderloin steaks cooked over mesquite charcoal.

Sheriff Ed Echols took Tom back to the Santa Rita Hotel in Tucson but apparently Tom was not ready for bed. He joined Maurice Carl and other members of the hotel's band for a drink. Then Tom invited the group to his room, where it was rumored they partied until about three in the morning. At about that time, Tom put an end to the party by telling the boys he was tired and had to get up early the next morning and drive to Phoenix.

Sheriff Ed Echols returned to the hotel the next morning and talked briefly with Tom outside the hotel. Before Tom left, he asked the hotel to call Walt Coburn and let him know he would not be returning for lunch. The request was forgotten until several hours later, however.

Tom checked out of the hotel around noon, after talking that morning with Tucson police officer Dick Lease and hotel manager Nick Hall. Lease gave Tom directions and cleared the way for him as he left the hotel's parking lot.

After 2 P.M., Santa Rita Hotel manager Nick Hall called Walt Coburn to tell him about the misplaced message Tom had left, saying he would not be coming for lunch because he was headed to Florence to see his former son-in-law, Harry Knight. A short time later, Nick called Walt back again, informing him that Tom Mix had just been killed at about 2:15 P.M. in an automobile accident about 18 miles from Florence, Arizona.

On hearing the news, Echols left immediately for the site of Tom's fatal crash; an ambulance and the coroner followed him. Patrolman Dick Lease also heard about the accident and headed for the site. Hotel manager Nick Hall telephoned Tom's daughters and the Hollywood studios with the sad news. Walt Coburn found himself home alone, so he saddled up his horse, Tex, and rode off into the hills just to think things over and try to forget about the worries of the day.

Tom was alone in his cream-colored custom-built Cord roadster when he suddenly came upon a crew of highway workers. Hearing the unrelenting roar of a car's engine, John Adams, one of the workers, ran toward the

Workers examine Tom's wrecked car in garage shortly after the fatal accident. (Courtesy of Merle G. "Bud" Norris.)

speeding car, hoping to flag down the motorist, but it was too late. It was estimated that Tom was driving at a speed of about 80 miles per hour on Highway 89 just before the fatal accident occurred. Tom and his Cord crashed through a barricade and went down a dry wash; the car overturned, pinning him beneath the wreckage.

It is doubtful that Tom ever knew what hit him or that he suffered any pain. On impact, a metal suitcase in the back seat of the car flew forward, hitting Tom from behind and breaking his neck. Highway workers John Adams, of Oracle and E. A. Armeta of Casa Grande, Arizona, went to the overturned car and turned it upright, discovering the body of Tom Mix. Tom appeared to be sleeping peacefully; his cream-colored western dress suit was virtually unwrinkled. Coroner E. O. Divine said Mix had been killed instantly; there was no inquest.

News Releases

According to the various news releases, Tom died wearing his boots, his diamond-studded belt buckle, and white 10-gallon Stetson. His pockets contained $6,000 in cash and $1,500 in traveler's checks, and there were some jewels in the car.

Mabel Ward Mix, Tom's last wife, and Mary Stone, a friend, flew with stunt pilot Paul Mantz from Hollywood to Florence to claim the body. A small group of friends met the sleek red airplane on its return trip to the Union Air Terminal in Hollywood.

Although most of Tom's friends and relatives were rocked by the news of his tragic end, it was not a total shock, for Tom was known as a hard driver as well as a hard fighter and rider. In Hollywood, William S. Hart, one of Tom's friends, said, "It's just too awful. My recollections of Tom are still very vivid. He was wonderful." Mary Pickford, who was once a neighbor said, "I think he would have wanted it to come just as quickly as it did." In Madison Square Garden, Gene Autry paid tribute to Tom as one of the leading promoters of cowboy sports.

Tom's friends agreed that he wanted to be remembered first, last, and always as a cowboy. He had lived up to a cowboy's image—he rode hard, fought hard, and used his six-guns only when necessary.

A Lisbon newspaper reported on October 13, 1940, that the death of Tom Mix, the American motion picture star, had so deeply affected young Portuguese movie fans that Lisbon boys, members of the Tom Mix clubs, decided to go into mourning for two weeks—and not attend any picture shows for that period.

Funeral Arrangements

Tom's body was placed in the Pierce Brothers' Mortuary and his friends paid their last respects to him at the Little Church of Flowers. A Masonic ritual was read by Monte Blue, a close friend, and orchestra leader Rudy Vallee sang Tom's favorite song, "Empty Saddles." Other Hollywood notables, including William Fox, Carl Laemmle, Jack Warner, Cecil B. DeMille, Louis B. Mayer, Samuel Goldwyn, Hal Roach, Buster Keaton, Charlie Chaplin, Mickey Rooney, Clark Gable, George O'Brien, Wallace Beery, Hoot Gibson, Buck Jones, Harry Carey, William S. Hart, Gene Autry, and Gary Cooper attended the services. Sheriff Ed Echols was also there, of course. Tom was buried in a large bronze casket, dressed in his favorite white western dress suit.

Funeral services were conducted by the Reverend J. Whitcomb Bougher and Tom was laid to rest with full military and Masonic honors in Glendale's Forest Lawn Memorial Park, near the graves of Jean Harlow, Douglas Fairbanks, and Marie Dressler. Tom's pallbearers and close friends were Sheriff Eugene Biscailuz, cowboy star Monte Blue, director John Ford, lawyer Ivon D. Parker, cameraman Dan Clark, Herman Nowlin, Colonel Monte Stone, and director B. Reaves Easton.

The Will

During his lifetime, Tom earned over $6 million. But in spite of his great show of wealth in the twenties and the lavish funeral arrangements, at the time of his death Tom was reported to have only a modest estate, worth about $115,000.

According to the *South Bend Times,* Ralph Smith, Tom's attorney, estimated that the amount of Tom's estate might even be cut in half by the time the obligations to the estate were discharged.

The *Peru Daily Tribune* of October 19, 1940, revealed that according to the terms of Tom's will, four former wives and one daughter would be cut off without a penny. Tom's will, dated January 31, 1938, bequeathed the actor's entire estate to Mabel Ward Hubbell Mix and one of his two daughters, Thomasina Mix Matthews, age 19. A lifelong friend, Ivon D. Parker, received Tom's famous horse, old Tony, and all of Tom's western regalia.

Specific Terms

Tom's will is 15 pages long. Some of the specific terms of the will are listed below.

Under the subheading "Natural Heirs" Tom mentions his wife, Mabel Hubbell Mix, and his only two living children, his daughters Ruth Mix Knight and Thomasina Mix.

Under the subheading "Disinheritances," Tom excludes all former wives and his daughter, Ruth Mix Knight. While he did not name his former wives, his Hollywood obituary did: Grace Allen, Jewel Perrine, Olive Stokes, mother of Ruth Mix, and Victoria Forde, mother of Thomasina.

Under the subheading "Appointment of Executor," Tom named Ivon D. Parker at the Bank of American Building his duly appointed executor. Claude I. Parker, same address, was named as succeeding executor, should events require the appointment of one.

Under the subheading "Special Bequest," Tom bequeathed his faithful horse and pal, old Tony, to his treasured friend Ivon D. Parker. In his will, Tom also gave Parker all his western equipment and the paraphernalia used or employed by Tom in the making of western or frontier pictures.

Under the subheading "Residuary Estate," Tom left the remainder of his estate, in equal parts, to his beloved wife, Mabel Hubbell Mix, and his beloved daughter, Thomasina Mix. In a subparagraph, Tom left his minor daughter, Thomasina, with a monthly income of $500 for a broad education including foreign and domestic travel. After age 21, she was to receive the net income of the estate, and at age 25 she was to receive the balance of her inheritance. Mabel's sisters, Jessie Arbaul and Erm Arley, were named as surviving heirs to the estate.

Under the subheading "Guardian of Minor," Teresa Eason, Tom's business manager, was named as the guardian of the estate for Thomasina.

Under the subheading "Contest Provisions," Tom left the sum of $1.00 to anyone who contested his will or claimed to be a lawful heir to his estate.

The will was witnessed by Billie E. Adams, Catherine E. King, and Ralph W. Smith and dated 31 January 1938.

The western paraphernalia originally willed to Ivon D. Parker later became the essence of the Tom Mix Museum collection in Dewey, Oklahoma. Two large pieces of jewelry described in Parker's final accounting were a massive man's platinum diamond ring with Tom's initials on the sides and 38 small diamonds and one large diamond weighing 6.52 karats. His diamond-studded belt buckle was also described as gold and platinum, containing 247 diamonds and weighing 7.18 karats.

Tom may of course have left many other things to various friends and family members prior to the execution of his will.

Estate Problems

The existence of a will did not eliminate problems for Tom's estate. On November 24, 1940, a Hollywood newspaper reported that Mrs. Victoria de Olazabal, one of Mix's four ex-wives, was suing the Tom Mix Estate. Mrs. de Olazabal claimed that Mix had never paid five $10,000 promissory notes that he had given her in 1928 and 1929 for the support of herself and her daughter, Thomasina.

Fifteen years after the death of Tom Mix, his estate once again made headlines. Mabel Mix, Tom's fifth wife, and Thomasina Mix, Tom's daughter, were in court over plans to exploit Mix's name in films for TV and theater releases. Mabel Mix wanted to form a corporation under which she would hold 30 percent of the stock. She said that the corporation would help to put the Mix estate in the black. Thomasina Mix opposed the plan saying that she felt the Mix estate would profit more from the selling of Mix's story rights to a major studio.

Tony Joins His Master

On October 12, 1942, two years to the day following the death of Tom Mix, Tom's beloved horse Tony was humanely put to death. Tom and Tony had thrilled thousands of youngsters in hundreds of movies, but Tony was now pushing the age of 40 and could no longer enjoy a horse's life. Tony's teeth were so badly worn he could not chew alfalfa; he had to be fed a soft mash of grain and honey to sustain himself. Tom's friend and Tony's caretaker, Ivon D. Parker, had hesitated to put the horse to sleep for a couple of years. However, he now felt that the time was right for Tony to join his master in everlasting peace. Tom Mix, the King of the Cowboys, and Tony, the wonder horse, were united once again, this time in spirit.

Mabel Mix Continues the Circus Tradition

Tom's death did not bring an end to his wife Mabel's show business career. Mabel travelled and performed with the Bradley and Benson Show. In an August 1, 1945, interview Mabel reported, "I do a western act now. A little shooting, some trick rodeo riding and roping."

Thomasina Enters into Films

About a month later, a Hollywood newspaper article by Rosalind Shaffer carried a story about Tom's daughter, Thomasina Mix, who was then a 23-year-old, married mother of four children. At the time, Thomasina was trying to follow in her father's footsteps.

The article reported that Thomasina was "Under the friendly counsel of Sam Goldwyn...." Although she had not yet signed any contracts, Thomasina had landed a small role in the Danny Kaye picture, *The Kid from Brooklyn.*

The Riderless Pony

On December 5, 1947, a crowd of over three hundred people gathered as the Pinal County Historical Society of Florence, Arizona, dedicated a seven-foot statue of a riderless pony to mark the spot where Tom's fatal automobile accident occurred. Gene Autry and Ed Echols attended the ceremony, and Autry's rendition of "Empty Saddles in the Old Corral" brought tears to the eyes of many in attendance. The inscription on the monument, written by former society president A. W. Gressinger, reads as follows:

Jan. 6, 1880–Oct. 12, 1940
In memory of Tom Mix
whose spirit left his body on this spot
and whose characterizations and portrayals
in life served to better fix memories of
the Old West in the minds of living men.

Mabel Ward Mix spins a rope on the circus lot. (Courtesy Jimmie Dodd.)

A Car with a Life of Its Own

There have been many stories written about the Tom Mix Cord. Writers have said the color of the car was white, black, yellow, cigarette cream, green, and so forth; some say Tom had more than one Cord, a 1934 model and a 1937 model. The most reliable description of the Cord that Tom was driving at the time he was killed could be obtained only from the first man who restored it after the accident. That man was Raymond E. Nelson, a master mechanic, now deceased. Mr. Nelson stated that "The color of the car at the time of the accident was cigarette cream and the top was black mohair with a red piping around the front and rear edges."

Nelson first purchased the Cord in 1942 and restored it to its original condition. After using the car for 10 to 12 years, Nelson sold it to Chicago businessman, Robert Dusek. Mr. Dusek decided that he would rebuild the Cord and had it completely disassembled. Unfortunately for Dusek, the mechanic that started the project quit, and the car remained disassembled for many years.

In 1966, Mr. Nelson purchased the remains of the car, reassembled them, and again restored the car to its original condition.

Statue of a riderless pony at site of Mix's fatal crash. (Author's collection.)

At the time of the accident, the mileage on the Cord was 53,340. The engine number was FC2634, and the body number was 31910H. Both front fenders, the hood, and left door were badly damaged. The windshield and side window frames were also broken. RKO acquired the title to the vehicle and towed it back to Hollywood, where it was stored in a garage.

Nelson originally purchased the wrecked 1937 Model 812 super-charged Cord on October 2, 1942, from RKO for the sum of $100 and completely restored it in 1943. The cost of the customized car as purchased by Tom was about $3,000 which was an extraordinary sum of money in 1937. The Model 812 supercharged Cord was rated at 170 horsepower with a top speed of about 110 miles per hour.

As an honorary deputy sheriff under Sheriff Eugene Biscailuz of Beverly Hills, Tom was permitted to mount a siren and police emblem on the body of the car and a gun holster on the steering column. Naturally, the hand-carved leather holster bore the famous TM initials. The car also had an oversized gas pedal, designed to fit Mix's high-heeled boots, and hand-tooled leather fender guards. Nelson kept the original police equipment when he sold the car to the Tulsa dealer. Later, he added horseshoes to the restored car, which were given to him by a mutual friend of his and Tom's who claimed they originally belonged to Tom.

In January 1973, Nelson loaned the restored Cord to Universal Pictures for a 90-minute television movie pilot entitled *Partners in Crime,* starring Lee Grant.

Neil Haworth of California was the last auto buff to own and restore the Tom Mix Cord, which he claims nearly killed him also; seems that the restored Cord was unstable at high speeds. Who knows? Maybe the original automobile was also unstable at high speeds. After becoming leery about the safety of the automobile, Neil sold it to the Imperial Palace Auto Collection, where it is now on display in Las Vegas, Nevada.

Chapter 10

Long Live the King
of the Cowboys

Tom Mix Baseball Cards

Writer, artist, and baseball enthusiast Ken Haag wrote an article titled "Boyhood Gods Come Calling," in the February 15, 1991, issue of the *Sports Collectors Digest.* Tom appears as the subject of two baseball cards designed by Haag. One card shows Tom in a baseball uniform and is titled "Tom Mix Barnstorming, 1927" and a second card shows Tom, with guns drawn, and Babe Ruth and is titled "Tom Mix and Babe Ruth, Ultimate Swat Team, 1932." This pair of cards were two of a 15-card series published in 1985. Since only five hundred sets were published, they were soon sold out and are now a collector's item.

Haag's article goes on to say,

> The next hero to visit [St. Paul, Minnesota] was none other than Tom Mix. He had appeared at the Minnesota Orpheum Theater with horse Tony to hype a movie before, but now in 1933 he came to Lake Phalen and Gillette Hospital to visit the crippled children's hospital. ...
>
> Well, the strict rules of fear of the nurses wrath prevailed as Tom moved through the double building flashing his silver six shooters and jangling his spurs as the children stood silent. He smiled and waved but no response was given. The children, part awe-struck, part fearful of being punished, were models of "drill squad" attention. Tom Mix left with a smile and total bewilderment. Silent movies were his forte, Silent fans were a first! ... and only in St. Paul.

Few people probably realize that one genuine baseball player and respectable actor is also considered a Tom Mix lookalike. During John Berardino's baseball career, he played for the St. Louis Browns and the Cleveland Indians. During his acting career, he portrayed Dr. Steve Hardy on *General Hospital* for 30 years. Today, he is still a dead ringer for Tom Mix. Here is Ken Haag's story of John Berardino.

218

JOHN BERARDINO—THE WOULD-BE TOM MIX
by Ken Haag

Growing up near the back lots of Hollywood Studios, John Berardino as a boy had cowboy whims. He learned to ride horseback and would even get to wander into the old western sets and meander where the likes of Tom Mix, William S. Hart and Colonel Tim McCoy had kicked up the trail dust. It was John in dreamland!

As time and reality set in, John became quite a ball player, so good that by 1939 he was playing second base for the St. Louis Browns in the American League. Though he never hit for a high average, his play in the field was very credible—in fact, his fielding average for eleven seasons was .960; hall of famer Rogers Hornsby fielded .958!

John's best year was 1940 when he batted .258 and had 16 home runs. He played for St. Louis until early 1942, then lost 4 years to the war, serving in both the Army and the Navy. He never played more than 90 games a season after 1947 and went on to play with the Cleveland Indians. He ended his baseball career with the Pittsburgh Pirates in 1952.

John had an acting bug for sometime and even as he wound down his baseball playing days, he had bit parts in movies. Then all of a sudden, someone saw his handsome mug and noticed his *uncanny* resemblance to Tom Mix! Wheels or rather reels began turning.

It began when John got in touch with Tom Mix's widow, Mabel Ward Mix, and had done some preliminary work on a possible TV series. However, Mix's other wives and daughter were still around so the proposal soon became a tangled web.

Nonetheless, the powerful William Morris Agency had first rights on the Tom Mix life story for TV or Movies, so they embarked on their own ideas. Meanwhile, John Berardino, with Mabel's blessing, had gone to Mexico City to try to get a co-production deal co-starring the great Mexican actor, Defouso Bedoya (notorious Mexican bandit in the movie *The Treasure of the Sierra Madre*) with Berardino himself starring as Tom Mix. While John was pursuing all this, Mix's widow made a deal with the William Morris Agency—typical of Hollywood double dealing, and Berardino tossed in his spurs.

William Morris made a pilot for TV with one of their own clients, William Campbell, and it did not turn out well and was never sold as a Tom Mix feature.

The very sad part of this story is that Berardino, with such a close resemblance to Tom Mix, never got his chance to do a cowboy portrayal. Oh, he became very successful, very much so as *Dr. Steve Hardy* on TV's *General Hospital.* In fact, April 1993 marks his 30th year as Dr. Hardy and he was awarded his own Walk of Fame star near Mann's Theater on April 1, 1993.

So John shares only the facts, that in 1940 when Tom Mix died, John had his best season as a major league player, hitting 16 home runs and leading the league average in total chances at shortstop with 5.6. Somehow, John's tie-in legacy to Tom Mix should have been greater!

First Tom Mix Day Celebration

On October 17, 1966, I wrote to Governor Scranton of Pennsylvania inquiring as to why a highway memorial marker had never been erected to Tom Mix, one of Pennsylvania's most famous native sons. This letter was directed to the Pennsylvania Historical and Museum Commission, who at first thought a highway marker had been erected in Tom's honor. Later, the project was turned over to A. Henry Haas, field curator and, on September 5, 1967, the text of the proposed marker's inscription was sent to me for review and approval. The final inscription reads as follows:

TOM MIX

The famous cowboy star of silent motion pictures was born a short distance from here on January 6, 1880. He served as a soldier in the Spanish-American War, later becoming renowned for his "wild west" roles in cinema and circuses. Tom Mix died in an accident in Arizona on October 12, 1940.

On August 1, 1968, the *Emporium Independent,* a Pennsylvania newspaper, announced the first official Tom Mix Day celebration. The paper listed some of the events that were to coincide with the August 8 dedication of a roadside marker in honor of Mix.

The newspaper published a picture of Tom and his father, Ed, on horseback with the following caption: "Tom Mix is pictured on his wonder horse Tony with his father Ed Mix while the later was paying him a visit in Hollywood. Ed was a teamster and woodsman for John E. Dubois, and it was under his father's tutelage that Tom learned to love horses, and to become the fine equestrian he was."

The Pennsylvania Highway Memorial Marker to Tom Mix was officially dedicated on Thursday, August 8, 1968, at 2:30 P.M. I attended the dedication and assisted Mrs. Merle Bowser of the Cameron County Historical Society in breaking the traditional bottle of champagne on the marker because the ceremony was beginning to look like an episode of *Candid Camera.* Bowser had hit the marker half a dozen times, and the champagne bottle would not break. Finally, with the two of us gripping the bottle, aiming at the edge of the bronze marker and swinging with all our might, we were able to break it. What a relief!

The Tom Mix Memorial Dinner was held at 6:30 P.M. on Thursday, August 8, 1968, with authors John Nicholas, and his family, and Paul Mix and his family as guests of honor. Both authors made short after-dinner talks about their boyhood hero, Tom Mix, much to the delight of the audience. About 75 people attended the affair.

There was talk of making the Tom Mix Day an annual event, but the first celebration in Cameron County, Pennsylvania, soon faded into history.

It would not be until September 1980, when Dr. Richard F. Seiverling founded the National Tom Mix Festival, that western fans would begin to rally once more around their boyhood hero.

Fire Destroys Tom Mix Cabin

On November 1, 1981, the *Los Angeles Herald Examiner* reported that Tom Mix's log cabin in Laurel Canyon had been destroyed by fire. Apparently, drifters had used the cabin as a crash pad.

> An enormous log-cabin type house built by silent cowboy film star Tom Mix in Laurel Canyon more than 60 years ago, and later a notorious crash pad for drifters, was destroyed yesterday by fire.
> By the time Los Angeles city firefighters arrived, the structure—built as a hunting lodge by Mix in 1915 at the corner of Laurel Canyon Boulevard and Lookout Mountain Drive—was "completely involved" in a fire that started in the basement and consumed the building like a tinderbox, fire officials said.
> At the beginning it wasn't so bad," said a dazed Diane Yeakey, 27, who had been sleeping in her rented room at the house when the fire broke out at 6:63 A.M. "Years ago, a friend of mine said if it caught on fire it would go like that," she said, snapping her fingers. "It did."
> Yeakey was one of about eight persons, including a mother and young baby, living in the 18 room cabin, built of railroad ties and split logs, at the time of the blaze. All escaped injury except Art Windsor, who suffered minor burns trying to battle the flames with a garden hose.
> "I always was careful about fire," said Fania Pearson, 67, an ordained minister and educator who has owned the house since 1959. "I always made sure I could find my book and stamp collections in the front room of the house, so if a fire started I could get them out quickly."
> Yesterday, however, Pearson escaped with only her two small dogs, Cookie and Tippy, leaving her belongings—the antiques, five pianos, valuable paintings and rare books—in the charred rubble.

Illustrator and Artist

Few men have done more to perpetuate the visual image of Tom Mix than artist and illustrator Andy Woytowich. Andy was born in Allentown, Pennsylvania, and grew up in Yonkers, New York; he is a retired Yonkers commercial artist. Since the commemorative revival of Tom Mix in 1980, Andy has spent most of his free time sketching Tom Mix, his boyhood hero. The year 1980 marked the 100th anniversary of the birth of Tom Mix and the 40th anniversary of his death. As a youngster, Andy faithfully listened to *Tom Mix and His Ralston Straight Shooters* and collected many of the radio premiums that were offered for a box top, or a box top and ten cents.

Andy uses few drafting or drawing aids, which make his finely detailed work even more noteworthy. Andy likes the Believe-or-Not style of drawing where each drawing tells a mini-story in itself. Two of his popular series of drawings are *Tom Mix Gems* and *Star Magic*. His drawings seem to capture the spirit of Tom Mix better than any of his contemporaries have. Andy Woytowich's Tom Mix drawings have appeared on the cover and inside several specialty booklets and western newsletters, including *The Tom Mix International Fan Club* (Tom Mix nostalgia newsletter); *Western Legends* (newsletter); *Tom Mix Highlights* (booklet); *Tom Mix: The Formative Years* (booklet); and *The Tom Mix Coloring Book* (booklet). In addition to these, Andy has donated many of his drawings to the National Tom Mix Festival and the Tom Mix International Fan Club promoters and founders for their unrestricted use in their Tom Mix promotions.

The number of Andy's pen-and-ink drawings since 1980 now exceeds the total number of films made by Tom Mix. Most of Andy's work is currently distributed by PM Publications, of Austin, Texas.

An Avid Memorabilia Collector

Art Evans is an avid Tom Mix fan and memorabilia dealer who has been collecting western keepsakes since his childhood. Evans and his wife, Ramona, have filled their home with his large collection of cowboy movie star souvenirs. "Tom Mix is my special hero," said Evans in a 1990 news story by Marilee Miller. "He was my idol as a boy. If I find any Tom Mix stuff I don't already own, I want it!"

Art Evans has been a great help to the author in obtaining unique Tom Mix photos for this book as well as helping to expand his personal Tom Mix Western comic book collection over the past several years.

An Independent Video Producer

Jim Harmon is a video producer specializing in video movie serials. He wrote a book published in 1992 by McFarland & Company, Inc., titled *Radio Mystery and Adventure and Its Appearances in Film, Television and Other Media.* According to Jim, this book contains 80 pages or so on Tom Mix and the Tom Mix radio series.

Jim has also produced his own radio adaption of Tom's movie serial, *The Miracle Rider,* and from time to time, Jim has offered audiocassettes of the *Ralston Straight Shooters* show, extra copies of Ralston's Tom Mix Comics, VHS copies of Tom Mix movies, Ralston pinback buttons, cereal boxes, movie viewers, and horseshoe nail rings, Tom Mix makeup kits, and the like. Harmon has copyrighted many of the abandoned *Tom Mix and*

His Ralston Straight Shooters shows and now believes he may have a claim to that format.

Harmon also had a unique relationship with Curley Bradley, the Tom Mix of Radio. Curley was Jim's boyhood idol and later became Jim's close friend and business partner for more than 10 years. See chapter 6 for more information on the Jim Harmon/Curley Bradley relationship.

The Stolen Horse

On April 12, 1989, the Associated Press reported that someone had stolen the iron statue of a horse from the Tom Mix memorial near Florence, Arizona. Unfortunately, both the highway memorial marker in Pennsylvania and the statue of the riderless pony in Arizona have been damaged by vandals on several occasions. The marker in Pennsylvania was shot numerous times with high-powered rifles. The only tribute to Tom now is at the Tom Mix Birth Site Park across the river from the original highway marker location.

On February 18, 1994, the *Yuma Daily Sun* proudly proclaimed, "Tom Mix's Horse Back—Sort Of." The article reported that a 30-by-27-inch metal statue of a horse was going to be mounted atop a new monument at the Pinal County Historical Society in Florence, Arizona.

The statue, which was originally on the Tom Mix memorial along U.S. 89, was stolen in 1980 and then anonymously returned.

Tom Mix Music

In 1935, the M. M. Cole Publishing Company produced a 64-page music book titled *Tom Mix Western Songs,* which contained 25 original songs and 21 others approved for publication by Tom Mix.

In the foreword, "A Word from Tom Mix," Tom writes:

> In rounding up material for this collection I have endeavored to assemble a wide variety of western songs with themes of moonlit prairies, desert springtime and winding trails; novelty songs of the tenderfoot, the two-gun cowman, the card sharp, the yodeler, chuck-wagon cook, etc. The collection also includes songs of the range, the old cow-pony, the night herder and other characters covering various phases of range life.
>
> I wish to kindly acknowledge the special help and assistance of Will Livernash in compiling this collection, and for his careful and patient efforts in preparing the piano accompaniments, the arrangements of ukulele, banjo, guitar and general musical presentation.
>
> I earnestly hope that my humble offering of *Tom Mix Western Songs* will merit the approval of all my friends and movie fans and that some of the songs will strike a responsive chord in the hearts of the music-loving public and become a lasting pleasure to them.
>
> Good luck and best wishes,
>
> (signed) Tom E. Mix

Songs in the book are:

I Love Those Saddle Songs (That We Sang in the Sweet Long Ago)
Old Pal of My Saddle Days
Sing Me a Cowboy Song
My Desert Rose
The Arizona Yodeler
The Cowboy's Lullaby (or Lie Low)
When the Roundup Is Over
I Want to Be a Real Cowboy Girl
Rootin', Tootin', Two-Gun Shootin' Cowman
My Sweetheart of the Range
The Ballad of Big Pete Moran (The Tale of a Poker Game in Song)
Chuck Wagon Bill
When It's Springtime in the Desert
When It's Branding Time in Texas
The Trail to Happiness
The Night Herder's Song
The Cowboy's Warning
The Modern Cowboy
Out Thar in the Beautiful Hills (A Romantic Cowboy Travesty)
When It's Moonlight on the Mesa
The Dying Cowboy's Request
My Old Cow Pony
The Dude at the Crescent and Star
When the Pale Moon Shines on the Prairie
Chuck Wagon Blues

Tom is credited with having written the words to "I Love Those Saddle Songs" and "Old Pal of My Saddle Days."

In the center of the music book is an abbreviated biography of Tom Mix, by Boris Randolph. This biography was obviously based on Tom's previous movie and circus biographies, containing most of the legendary tales previously mentioned. The biographical sketch also contains three pages of pictures, with the last page of pictures from the Mascot serial *The Miracle Rider*. The publication of the music book probably followed shortly after the release of *The Miracle Rider* films.

National Tom Mix Festival

For the past 12 years, the greatest promoter of Tom Mix Americana has undoubtedly been Dr. Richard F. Seiverling, the founder and president of the National Tom Mix Festival. According to his book, *Portrait of a Superstar,* Dr. Seiverling has been a Tom Mix fan ever since he scribbled the name of his hero on the top of his mother's recipe for chocolate cake. Dick was about seven years old at the time, and from then on, Mom's chocolate cake was known as Tom Mix chocolate cake.

Dick's interest in Tom Mix continued as he collected penny arcade cards and played cowboys and Indians with the neighborhood children; Dick, of course, always wanted to be Tom Mix. The culmination of Dick's boyhood dreams was realized at the age of 19 when Dick, a cub reporter for the *Ephrata Ensign,* interviewed his boyhood hero, Tom Mix, at Mount Gretna Park on July 4, 1940.

Dick learned that Tom was born in Texas, had 1,700 to 2,000 horses at his ranch in Arizona, had two married daughters, Ruth and Thomasina, no sons, and that Tom liked to play polo on his Arizona ranch. Dick also learned that Tom had a striking signature, was against compulsory military service, and was still married to the same wife he brought to Hollywood.

Dick stayed to see Tom's show and his sharpshooting act. He was soon convinced that Tom was a dead shot on little glass plates and that he could indeed split a bullet on the edge of a meat cleaver, breaking small glass plates on either side of it.

The National Tom Mix Festival began in DuBois, Pennsylvania, in 1980 and remained there until 1990. In 1990, there were two Tom Mix festivals, one in DuBois and the other in Las Vegas. Dick Seiverling, the founder and chairman of the National Tom Mix Festival, was the promoter of the Las Vegas festival; local promoters organized the DuBois festival. The Tom Mix Cord (death car) was a featured display at the 1990 Las Vegas festival. In 1991 and 1992, the national festival moved to Guthrie, Oklahoma, where it was combined with their Autumn Magic festival. Guthrie may become the new permanent home of the National Tom Mix festival.

The original National Tom Mix Festival committee staff consisted of Dr. Richard F. Seiverling, founder and chairman; Merle "Bud" Norris, Tom Mix author and memorabilia collector; Allen "Slim" Binkley, circus valet to Tom Mix; Ted and Ruth Reinhart, country-western entertainers; R. William Uhler, photographer and film projectionist (deceased); and Serge "Tom Morgan" Darrigrand, the "National Tom Mix Lookalike."

Some of the Tom Mix relatives who have visited one or more of the National Tom Mix festivals are Gordon Hill, grandson; Vicky Matthews, granddaughter; Dan Matthews, grandson; Rusty Hill, great-grandson; Nancy Rohrback, great-niece; Janet Bastendorf, great-niece; Mr. and Mrs. Keith Mix, cousin; and Mr. and Mrs. Paul Mix, cousin.

A typical Tom Mix festival features Tom Mix movies and sometimes movies by the other four members of the Big Five movie cowboys, a memorabilia room for the display, trading, and selling of Tom Mix memorabilia, light comedy and a shooting demonstration by Tom Morgan (Serge Darrigrand) and his wife, Brenda, and musical entertainment by Ted and Ruth Reinhart.

The festivals are often combined with other community activities such as a street parade, a Tom Mix lookalike contest, street merchants, antique or craft shows, an antique car display, a pet show, children's activities, a banquet or reception, a rodeo or Wild West show, an old time saloon, and the like.

Allen "Slim" Binkley, personal attendant to Tom Mix, Tom Mix Circus. (Courtesy Allen R. Binkley.)

In Guthrie, Oklahoma, the Tom Mix Festival is an integral part of Guthrie's Autumn Magic Celebration. The 1992 celebration featured:

- 13th Annual International Tom Mix Festival
- Territorial Gunfighters (local Guthrie group)
- Cimarron River Settlers Association (living history group)
- Fifth U.S. Cavalry, L-troop (horseback patrol)

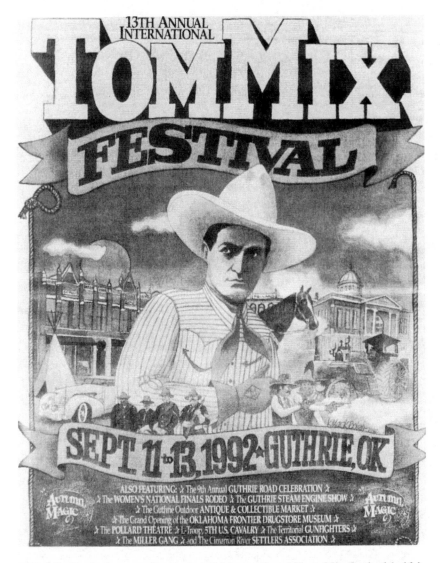

Tom Mix festival poster from second international Tom Mix festival held in Guthrie, Oklahoma. (K. Mack Boles, poster artist.) (Author's collection.)

- Annual Guthrie Outdoor Antique and Collectible Market
- Women's National Finals Rodeo
- Oklahoma Frontier Drugstore Museum
- Ninth Annual Guthrie Road Celebration (antique autos)
- Autumn Magic Parade (Saturday at 3 P.M.)
- *The Best Little Whorehouse in Texas* (play at the Pollard theater)

Psychologist with a Heart

John Samorajczyk is the founder of the Tom Mix International Fan Club. Here is how John first became interested in Tom Mix, one of his boyhood heroes.

From the time I was seven, one of the fondest sounds of my childhood was the voice of the announcer telling me that the *Tom Mix Straight Shooters Program* was on the air. When it neared time to tune into the next episode of "The Secret Mission" or "The Mystery of the Double X Ranch," I would run home from wherever I was and plant myself firmly in front of the radio.

When Jane asked me to join the Tom Mix Club, and Pecos told me about the premiums and comic books, I eagerly wrote down the "Checkerboard Square" address. When Tom himself spoke, I listened. How full of anticipation I became when I heard him say words like: "I'll send you my pocket knife *free*," or "I'll *give* you this ring," or "I'll send you this exact wooden replica of my favorite six-shooter. It's a brand new, never before offered, ivory-handled, steel-black gun. Yes, you can own a real cowboy gun just like mine for only one Ralston box top and 10 cents in coin ... to cover postage and handling. But, you must *hurry*. This is a limited time offer."

I am sure that there are a lot of people reading this who remember what that feeling of excitement was like. While it is true that we cannot go back to our childhood, at least we can try to recapture some of those wonderful memories. Sharing these memories is what inspired me to found the Tom Mix International Fan Club. A real boost was given to our club when Dr. Richard F. Seiverling, Mix historian and founder of the National Tom Mix Festival, encouraged me to expand the club. He invited me to participate in the Tom Mix Festival, then held in Tom's hometown of DuBois, Pennsylvania, and to help promote Tom Mix in particular and our western heritage in general.

In the ensuing years, the club has grown in volume and output. There are now 14 issues of the *Tom Mix Nostalgia* series (vol. 1) and 16 issues of the *Tom Mix Archives* (vol. 2). In our issues, we have reprinted reviews of Mix-related events, premiums, manuals, Ralston comics, photographs, stories, and more. Some of the members have created their own premiums, clubs, and other memorabilia. Perhaps one day these, too, will be collector's items. The most personally rewarding contributions for me have been our members' re-creations of their own childhood ... memories that they have shared with us. It is gratifying to know that there are so many others out there who remember what it was like and can still experience the uplifting feeling of getting in touch with the past.

Club members are stationed all over the world. We are currently in the process of having our newsletters, bulletins, and pictorials translated into Polish. They will be part of a Klub Filmowy exhibition of European and American publications on film memorabilia. Members of the Polish Film Society have joined not only our Tom Mix Club, but also our Lone Ranger and Air Heroes clubs. Information on our publications are now a part of their reference material for film studies. The Tom Mix legend will hopefully inspire our Polish Straight Shooters just as it has inspired (and continues to inspire) us. Tomasz Mix bedzie zyc zawsze.

Some of the fan clubs founded and managed by John Samorajczyk are Tom Mix (Miracle Rider); Captain Midnight; Inner Circle; Lone Ranger; Buck Rogers; Sea Hound.

John Samorajczyk's profession is psychotherapy, and he often works with youngsters. John makes it a point to give the kids a free membership in the Tom Mix International Fan Club, complete with membership card, picture, and certificate. The kids really appreciate the membership card and in turn pledge to shoot straight with John, their psychotherapist, and with their parents, a unique and wonderful way to pass along the idealism and heritage of the Tom Mix story.

Tom Mix Western Comics

In addition to the Ralston Tom Mix comic books mentioned in chapter 6, Tom Mix appeared in a number of comic book publications such as *Popular Comics* (145 issues) and *Crackajack Funnies* (43 issues) by Dell Publishing. Tom Mix first appeared in issue 5 of *Popular Comics*, June 1936, and may have appeared through the end of the series with the number 145 issue in July–September 1948. Tom Mix appeared in the *Crackajack Funnies* from June 1938 until January 1942.

Starting with issue 70 in September 1948, Fawcett Publication changed the name of *Wow Comics* series to *Real Western hero* comics, which featured Tom Mix and three other heroes through issue 75, which ended in February 1949. This series was followed by Fawcett's *Western Hero* series, beginning with issue 76 in March 1949 and ending with issue 112 in March 1952.

Fawcett Publications also published 61 issues of the *Tom Mix Western* comics from January 1947 through May 1953. The number of pages in each issue were 36 or 52, with issues 18, 22, 26, 30, 34, 38, 41, and 43–60 being 36 pages. It is interesting to note that this series of comic books corresponds to the recovery period following World War II through to the good times of the early fifties.

Tom Mix also appeared in 38 issues of Fawcett's *Master Comics* series in the early fifties, starting with issue 95 and ending with the last issue, 133 in April 1953.

Between the Dell and Fawcett publishing companies, comics including sections featuring Tom Mix were more or less continuously in print from about June 1936, four years prior to Tom Mix's death, until June 1953, some 12½ years after Tom Mix's death. However, only the Ralston *Tom Mix Comics/Commandos* series and Fawcett *Tom Mix Western* comics exclusively featured Tom Mix.

Comics mentioned above can range in price from a few dollars to as much as $575 each, depending on scarcity and condition. Anyone interested in purchasing old comic books should consult a book on the subject, such as *The Official Overstreet Comic Book Guide*, by Robert M. Overstreet.

Rails 'n' Trails Festival

Las Vegas, New Mexico, has a population of 14,750 people, a Wild West heritage, and some nine hundred historic buildings. Frontier era storefronts can be found on both sides of the main street, which even boasts an old-fashioned ice cream parlor.

Every year, during Memorial Day weekend, the town celebrates their Rails 'n' Trails festival commemorating the Santa Fe Trail, which ran through town, and the arrival of the Atchison, Topeka and Santa Fe Railroad in the 1870s.

Some of the activities for the weekend include a Tom Mix film festival, working cowboys' rodeo, western parade, western writers' reception, antique show, model railroaders' exhibit, quilt show, charity auction, old time photo booth, pancake breakfast, Victorian melodrama, arts and crafts booths, food booths, western shootout, western dance, cow chip throwing contest, children's petting zoo with miniature animals, storytelling, city-wide barbecue, and historic trolley tours from the old 1920s roundhouse. In the 1920s, the roundhouse was the repair and maintenance shed for steam locomotives.

Most of the weekend events are staged in the old roundhouse area, with the Tom Mix film festival, antique show, Victorian melodrama, and model railroading exhibit staged at the local college. Locations are subject to change slightly from year to year.

One of the highlights of the weekend is the children's parade and the regular parade, starting at 10 A.M. on Saturday. For the Rails 'n' Trails theme, youngsters portray settlers, Indians, and even trains. For 1992, actor Ike McFadden, from the *Young Riders* and Wells Fargo commercials, and Tom Mix lookalike Serge Darrigrand were scheduled to be the parade marshals. Typical horse-drawn vehicles include hearses, buggies, buckboards, bandwagons, and prairie schooners. In addition, the parade features trick riders, floats, entertainment, Old West cavalry groups, Indian dancers, and vintage cars.

Tom Mix Birthplace Park

In the mideighties, Raymond and Eva Flaugh obtained the original land where Tom's birthplace home stood. Almost immediately they set about to build a birthplace park and museum to honor one of Pennsylvania's native sons. Tom's valet, "Slim" Binkley, and his wife, Ruth, also supplied many hours of labor, helping to clean up the grounds, fix fences, and add reproductions of the old Mix homestead water well and outhouse. Finally, a small museum building was added to house Tom Mix memorabilia.

Funds were also raised for the preservation effort by selling certificates of ownership to one square inch of the Tom Mix birthplace property. With these certificates, the original purchasers received a souvenir rock from either the foundation of the old Mix home or the stable area out back. Also, ownership in the property guaranteed sponsors free visitation and picnic use rights.

Originally, the monies collected were intended for use in building a monument dedicated to Tom Mix and to replace the highway monument, which was vandalized a number of times and eventually abandoned by the Pennsylvania Historical Society. The monument to Tom Mix consists of a list of names of birthplace park contributors inside the museum. On January 14, 1987, President Ronald Reagan made a hundred-dollar donation to the Tom Mix Birthplace Park. The little museum contains family history, Tom Mix books, photos, pins, radio premiums, firearms, and various memorabilia.

The season for visiting the park is from about mid–April through mid–October. Events are planned throughout the year, with the Tom Mix Roundup in late July a featured event. Simulated dramatic events have been added to the Roundup, such as a shootout, jail break, hanging a woman on horseback, and a shotgun wedding. Events at the park, such as the roundup and grinnin' and pickin' (country-western music and dances) are advertised by the Cameron County Tourist Promotion Agency.

Tom Mix Museum, Dewey, Oklahoma

On June 30, 1966, a group of Washington County, Oklahoma, residents left for California to buy Tom Mix's western regalia collection. The collection, once insured for $1 million, was purchased for $40,000 from Milton Uhler of Van Nuys, California. The memorabilia was left to Uhler by his late uncle, Ivon Parker. Parker had been written into Tom's will because he had taken care of old Tony after the horse was retired. It was also rumored that Parker had helped Tom financially with his circus ventures. Tom's personal property had been put into storage for about 25 years prior to its purchase by the Oklahoma group.

The money to purchase Tom's collection was raised by the Dewey, Oklahoma, Jaycees in ten days. A nonprofit civic corporation, known as the Tom Mix Museum, Inc., was then formed by Dewey and Bartlesville,

Author's son, Tom, on Tom Mix Museum replica of Tony, June 1968. (Author's collection.)

Oklahoma, citizens. The real work began with the construction of a large block-and-brick museum building, two blocks west of Dewey's main intersection. Edgar Weston, the museum curator, went to work inside the building constructing glass showcases to display the collection.

Members of the civic corporation picked up a 50-year-old horse mannequin from the Woolaroc Museum. Years ago, the mannequin had been used by a saddle shop to display goods. With considerable artistic talent, Geraldine Weston began to reshape the mannequin into a likeness of old Tony. She added about 150 pounds of asbestos fiber, dry glue, pottery plaster, and paint. The countless hours of work invested by Weston were well worth the effort, however, because the Tom Mix Museum now proudly displays a full-size, lifelike replica of Tony, the famed "wonder horse." A 25-foot high sign was also erected in front of the building just prior to the museum's grand opening.

The Tom Mix Museum had its grand opening on June 1, 1968. Tom's daughter, Ruth Mix Hill, and grandson, Hickman Hill, took part in the ribbon-cutting ceremony, and Monty Montana, a friend of Tom's, autographed hundreds of white souvenir hats bearing the famous TM Bar brand. Monty also starred in a western show that was held Saturday night at the Dewey Rodeo Arena. Despite threatening clouds, the grand opening proved a great success.

Included in the museum collection are about 20 saddles, 15 pistols, 18 rifles, 5,000 photographs, Tom's honorable discharge, a Texas Ranger certificate, many of his motion picture and circus costumes, and the suitcase responsible for his death. At one time, the museum had hoped to add Tom's 1937 supercharged Cord roadster to their collection, but the death car is now on display at the Imperial Palace Antique Car Museum in Las Vegas, Nevada.

Tom Mix Rangers of Virginia

The Tom Mix Rangers of Virginia are an active family group of parade riders and trail riders who can stage an Old West shootout better than Bruce Willis and James Garner, at least in the movie *Sunset*.

Mitch Toney, acting vice-president of the Tom Mix Rangers of Virginia describes when and how the rangers were formed in his article titled "Riding with the Rangers."

> Around 1985, what was formerly the Cameron County Bridle and Saddle Club (among other horse clubs in the Sinnemahoning Area), changed their name to The Tom Mix Rangers. This group, along with the new Tom Mix birthplace owner, Raymond Flaugh, and other Cameron countians, formed the Annual Tom Mix Roundups. This event features nine miles of parade and nine miles of trail riding, shooting exhibitions, and country music dances.
>
> My dad [Bob Toney] and I found out about the Roundups from Tom Mix himself, at least the current Tom Mix anyway—Mr. Serge Darrigrand. Serge has been a supporter of the Virginia Rangers and a true inspiration (thanks, Serge). We were so impressed with the events of the 1988 Roundup that we felt it was a shame that there was nothing like this at, or near, home. So, in true Tom Mix fashion, we decided to do something about it.
>
> We set our game plan, laid out our first newsletter and recruited our riding buddies to help get the ball going. At Buckingham County Day, in May 1989, four members of the newly formed Virginia Rangers rode away with a First Place trophy in the horse entry. Since that time, with advertising, parade appearances and good old word of mouth, the Virginia Rangers have grown at a steady pace and now have a one hundred plus membership. . . .
>
> But the Rangers are more than just parades. We've held mock gunfights in South Carolina and at nursing homes and a retirement village in our own state and plans are underway to do them in other states. . . .
>
> Perhaps the most important event of the year was when our Rangers dispatched a unit of horses to help state and local authorities locate an ill man who had wondered off and was missing for two and a half days. The Rangers covered in a matter of hours with horses what would have taken an entire day to cover on foot by three times as many people. The ill man was found and in good health and the Tom Mix Rangers of Virginia had become one of only two mounted search and rescue teams in the entire state of Virginia.

Tom Mix was a man of action, and in that spirit, The Tom Mix Rangers ride.

The Tom Mix Rangers of Virginia participate in many community holiday events and parades, putting the name of Tom Mix in the public eye in a favorable light.

The head ranger of the Tom Mix Rangers of Virginia is Bob Toney (Tom Mix), who has a horse (Rose) that resembles Tom Mix's horses, Tony and Tony Jr. Tony was a chestnut with white stockings on his back legs and a white blaze, ending with a diamond shape on his forehead and nose; Tony Jr. was a chestnut with four white stockings and a wider white blaze — I think. I love horses, but do not profess to be an expert rider or expert on horseflesh.

Mitch Toney (Bob's son) and Jay Lester of the Tom Mix Rangers of Virginia appear in the movie *Somersby,* starring Richard Gere and Jody Foster. See the movie and try to recognize the bearded gunslingers Mitch Toney and Jay Lester.

Sources of Information

The following persons and organizations listed below are actively engaged in promoting the spirit of the Old West in general and Tom Mix in particular. Most of them have material for sale relating to Tom Mix. Please contact the person or organization listed for current prices on available items.

PM Publications
P.O. Box 180182
Austin, TX 78718-0182
Available information and materials: *Tom Mix Highlights,* booklet by Andy Woytowich; *Tom Mix: The Formative Years,* booklet by Paul Mix; *Tom Mix Coloring Book,* by Andy Woytowich; *Star Magic,* booklet by Andy Woytowich; Tom Mix pinback buttons; *Western Legends Newsletter;* Tom Mix stills; Tom Mix memorabilia; Color laser reproductions of Tom Mix comic book covers.

Art Evans
52 North Dean

Coquille, OR 96423
Available information and materials: Tom Mix comics; Tom Mix memorabilia; Tom Mix photos.

Jim Harmon
634 S. Orchard Dr.
Burbank, CA 91506
Available information and materials: Tom Mix movies; Tom Mix videos; Tom Mix audio tapes; Tom Mix memorabilia; Movie serials on VHS; Color laser reproductions of Tom Mix Comic Covers.

Autumn Magic/Tom Mix Festival
P.O. Box 995

Guthrie, OK 73044
Available information and materials: Schedule of activities for Autumn Magic Festival; Schedule of activities for National Tom Mix Festival; TM memorabilia sold at the festival.

Dr. Richard F. Seiverling
326 Ridge Rd.
Hershey, PA 17033
Available information and materials: National Tom Mix Festival information; Tom Mix photos; Tom Mix memorabilia; Tom Mix books; *Tom Mix: Portrait of a Superstar,* by Dr. Richard F. Seiverling.

Merle G. "Bud" Norris
1324 N. Hague Ave.
Columbis, OH 43204
Available information and materials: National Tom Mix Festival information; Tom Mix memorabilia; Tom Mix books; Tom Mix photos; Tom Mix 16mm movies; Tom Mix VHS movies; *The Tom Mix Book,* by Merle G. Norris.

Old Pard Video Productions
P.O. Box 446
Muscatine, IA 52761
Available information and materials: Tom Mix T-shirts, cups, caps, clocks, plaques; Tom Mix pinback buttons; Tom Mix VHS movies; country-western VHS tapes.

Tom Mix International Fan Club
19205 Seneca Ridge Ct.
Gaithersburg, MD 20829-3135
Available information and materials: Membership in Tom Mix International Fan Club; Membership in other fan clubs mentioned above; Newsletters for each of the fan clubs; Reproductions of Tom Mix Ralston comics.

Big Slim's Western Museum
61 Park Avenue
Rutherford, NJ 07070
Available information and materials: Information on quality western wear; Information on the western museum.

Rails 'n' Trails/Tom Mix Festival
P.O. Box 148
Las Vegas, NM 87701
Available information and materials: Information on festival activities; Memorabilia sold at the festival.

Tom Mix Birthplace Park
RD #1
Driftwood, PA 15832
Available information and materials: Schedule of park activities.

Tom Mix Museum
721 N. Delaware
Dewey, OK 74029-2307
Available information and materials: Schedule of museum activities.

Tom Mix Rangers of Virginia
Rt. 1, Box 130
New Canton, VA 23123
Available information and materials: Membership information and newsletter; Schedule of activities; Memorabilia offered through club.

Appendix 1

Chronology of Tom Mix's Military Service

April 25, 1898	Start of Spanish-American War. Thomas E. Mix has physical at Washington Barracks, D.C.
April 26, 1898	Tom enlists at Washington Barracks, D.C.; assigned to Battery M, Fourth Regiment.
May 1, 1898	Battery M assigned to guard the DuPont Powder Works at Montchanin, Delaware.
May 5, 1898	Battery M ordered to Wilmington, Delaware (a short distance from Montchanin).
May 28, 1898	Battery M leaves camp at Montchanin and returns to Washington Barracks.
June 13, 1898	Battery M leaves for duty at Battery Point, Delaware.
July 1, 1898	Thomas E. Mix is promoted to the rank of corporal.
July 31, 1898	For all practical purposes, Spanish-American War hostilities end by this date.
September 7, 1898	Battery M assigned to detached duty at Fort Delaware, Delaware.
September 12, 1898	Battery M returns to Battery Point.
November 22, 1898	Battery M leaves Battery Point, to take up stations at Fort Constitution, New Hampshire.
November 24, 1898	Battery M arrives at Fort Constitution, after 429 miles rail travel.
December 10, 1898	Spanish-American War officially ends with the signing of the Treaty of Paris.
December 31, 1898	Corporal Thomas E. Mix is promoted to the rank of sergeant.
February 4, 1899	Start of Philippine Insurrection.
April 14, 1899	Sergeant Mix transfers from Battery M at Fort Constitution to Battery O, same regiment, and reports to Fort Monroe, Virginia.
April 18, 1899	Tom starts duty at Fort Monroe.
July 12, 1899	Tom appointed quartermaster sergeant.
August 5, 1899	Battery O leaves Fort Monroe by steamer due to an outbreak of yellow fever at the Old Soldier's Home and goes to Fort Terry, New York.

September 12, 1899	Battery O leaves Fort Terry.
September 13, 1899	Battery O returns to Fort Monroe.
November 18, 1899	Tom promoted to first sergeant.
February 8, 1900	Battery O leaves Fort Monroe by steamer and goes to Washington, D.C., to attend the funeral of Major General Henry Lawton.
February 10, 1900	Battery O returns to Fort Monroe.
June 1900	Boxer Uprising starts.
June 25, 1900	Battery O leaves Fort Monroe and takes up permanent stations at Fort Hancock, New Jersey.
June 26, 1900	Battery O arrives at Fort Hancock.
September 1900	Boxer Uprising ends.
November 12, 1900	Tom takes furlough to DuBois, Pennsylvania.
December 11, 1900	Tom's furlough ends and he returns to Fort Hancock.
March 1901	Philippine Insurrection ends, but Boer War has already started.
April 25, 1901	First Sergeant Thomas E. Mix honorably discharged at Fort Hancock.
April 26, 1901	Tom passes physical exam and reenlists.
May 1, 1901	Tom takes furlough to Norfolk, Virginia.
May 11, 1901	Returns from furlough.
May 31, 1902	Boer War ends with the signing of the Treaty of Vereeniging.
July 12, 1902	Tom takes furlough to Fort Monrie and goes to Norfolk.
July 18, 1902	Thomas E. Mix marries Grace I. Allin (Allen).
July 25, 1902	Tom's furlough and honeymoon ends, and he returns to Fort Hancock.
July 29, 1902	48th Company Artillery leaves for Fort Terry with three officers and 99 enlisted men.
July 30, 1902	48th Company arrives at Fort Terry.
September 14, 1902	48th Company leaves Fort Terry.
September 15, 1902	48th Company arrives back at Fort Hancock.
October 20, 1902	Tom takes furlough to Pittsburgh (takes wife, Grace, to Guthrie, Oklahoma, sometime later).
October 24, 1902	Tom's furlough ends, but he does not return to Fort Hancock.
October 25, 1902	Tom is officially listed as AWOL (absent without leave).
November 4, 1902	AWOL period ends. Thomas E. Mix is listed as an army deserter.

Appendix 2

Newspaper Headline Chronology

September 1928	Tom Mix, Screen Star, Calls on Master Georgie Wood, Little Sick Boy
October 29, 1929	Star's Shoulder to Be Rewired
March 5, 1930	Tom Mix Pays $175,000 on Income Taxes
June 10, 1930	Tom Mix Fails to Prevent Marriage
June 27, 1930	Mix to End Daughter's Allowance
July 2, 1930	Mix's Daughter Sues for Rights; Fights Attempt to Cancel Agreement on Monthly Checks
July 5, 1930	Mix Wins Allowance Suit; Court Rules Actor Does Not Have to Pay Daughter
August 19, 1930	Tom Mix Is Sued by Auto Dealer
October 3, 1930	Famed Cowboy May Buy Circus in Peru Deny Tom Mix Will Buy Circus
October 4, 1930	Sale to Mix Denied by Owner of Show
November 4, 1930	Tom Mix in Hospital; Injured Back Prevents Him from Attending Mississippi Suit
November 7, 1930	Mix Faces Operation; Doctor Will Remove Wire Holding Broken Shoulder
November 8, 1930	Tom Mix Undergoes Operation
November 26, 1930	Mix's Wife Obtains Legal Separation
December 15, 1930	Pistol Scares Mrs. Mix
December 25, 1930	Divorces Tom Mix; Film Cowboy's Second Wife in Los Angeles Suit Charges Cruelty
June 1, 1931	Famous Cowpuncher Actor, Touring Country with Sells-Floto; Will Return to Screen for 12 Pictures—Decries Prevalence of Gangster Movies
November 25, 1931	Tom Mix, Veteran Film Star, Wages Fight Against Death in Hospital at Hollywood; Rush Serum by Plane to Save Life of Noted Cowboy
July 9, 1932	Mix's Daughter Ends Marriage
August 18, 1932	Mix Girl's Case in Court September 7
September 9, 1932	Tom Mix Given Custody of Girl for Two Months
October 22, 1932	Tom Mix Hurt When Tossed by His Horse
May 23, 1934	Tom Mix Loses Contract Suit

August 11, 1934	Two Circus Workers Killed in Accident
December 21, 1934	Tom Mix Settles Suit
April 20, 1935	Mix Runs Back to Save Nation
June 6, 1935	Tom Mix's Daughter Elopes
October 4, 1935	Horse Breaks Tom Mix's Leg
November 11, 1935	Mix, Tired of Ease, to Seek Hard Life in South America
May 20, 1936	Tom Mix Is Injured When Gale Hits His Circus
November 1, 1937	Ruth Mix Rides Range Again; Tom's Daughter at Last Gets Chance in Spirited Western; Tired of Playing Silly Parts in Blonde Wig and Fine Clothes
May 20, 1938	Tom Mix on Vaudeville Tour in England
July 10, 1938	Gusty Winds Flatten Big Top
October 12, 1940	Tom Mix Dead: Failed to See Bridge Detour
	Tom Mix Is Killed as Car Pins Him
	Tom Mix and Tony Hit the Road "Three Years with Sells-Floto Circus"
October 13, 1940	Tom Mix Cowboy Hero Is Killed, Pinned Under Overturned Auto
	Born a Cowboy, Lived a Cowboy, Died a Cowboy
	Tom Mix Breaks Neck as Car Upsets in Arizona; Body Removed to California
	Tom Mix, Circus Star, Is Killed in Wreck
	Tom Mix, Rider, Dies under Auto; Circus and Screen Equestrian, Cowboy Idol of Youth Killed in Arizona Car Upset
October 14, 1940	Tom Mix's Body in Hollywood
	Tom Mix Came Home Yesterday
	Last Rites For Tom Mix on Wednesday
August 8, 1945	Nostalgic Days of "Big Top" Recaptured
September 12, 1945	Former Mrs. Mix (Victoria Mix Robinson) Gets 3rd Divorce
September 18, 1945	Thomasina Starts Career in Films
February 22, 1951	Tom Mix Rated Tops by Veteran of 750 Westerns; Bob Kortman Says Tom Mix Was the Greatest Cowboy of Them All
December 11, 1953	Mix's Daughter (Thomasina) to Wed Major
March 1, 1955	Testimony Set in Tom Mix Exploitation Case
December 22, 1955	Daughter of Mix (Mrs. John Allen Andre) Sues for Divorce
December 28, 1963	Grandson of Tom Mix Appears in *Gunsmoke* (mentions Hickman Hill's debut in television)
June 22, 1966	King Midas Myth Is Sculptor (mentions that Charles De Temple of London is son of TM)
November 17, 1983	Firm Lists Actor's Home at $299,500 (Tom's cost was about $200,000)

Filmography

Selig Polyscope Company

1909

Ranch Life in the Great Southwest, August 9, 1909. A one-reel Selig documentary. *Note:* There is some question as to whether this movie was made in Oklahoma or Missouri. Most film historians believe it was shot on a ranch near Dewey, Oklahoma.

Ad Story: The greatest western picture ever put before the public. *Ranch Life in the Great Southwest* showing champion celebrities of the great southwest in deeds of daring that make the hair stand on end. The most reckless dare-devils in the world. See Pat Long, Champion at Steer Bull Dogging. Charles Fuqua and Johnny Mullins, the Champion Ropers. Tom Mix, ex–United States Marshall, the Bronco Expert. Harry Grammar, Champion of the World, throwing and tying a steer in 14½ seconds.

Watch the infuriated bulls as they are thrown by these dare-devil cowboys.

A chance of a lifetime. The greatest ensemble of passing characters in the world.

You will never see their likes again.

(Admission was five cents.)

Cast: See Ad Story.

Credits: Written and produced by William Selig, directed by Frank Boggs.

On the Little Big Horn, or Custer's Last Stand, November 27, 1909. A one-reel Selig drama.

Cast: Hobart Bosworth, Betty Harte, Tom Mix, and Frank Maish.

Credits: Produced by William Selig, directed by Frank Boggs, and written by Lannier Bartlett.

In the Days of Daring. A Selig western featuring Tom Mix.

Credits: Produced by William Selig and directed by Tom Mix.

1910

Taming Wild Animals. A one-reel Selig adventure featuring Tom Mix.

Credits: Produced by William Selig and directed by Frank Boggs.

Up San Juan Hill. A one-reel Selig western featuring Tom Mix. *Note:* Filmed along the Des Plains River, near Chicago.

Cast: Tom Mix, Betty Harte, and Tom Santschi.

Credits: Produced by William Selig, directed by Frank Boggs, and written by Edward McWade.

Pride of the Range. A one-reel Selig western comedy featuring Tom Mix.

Cast: Tom Mix, Tom Santschi, Betty Harte, Hoot Gibson, Milt Brown and Al Green.

Credits: Produced by William Selig and directed by Frank Boggs.

The Pony Express. A one-reel Selig western featuring Tom Mix.

The Millionaire Cowboy. A one-reel Selig western comedy featuring Tom

Century Theatre—Tonight!

Greatest WESTERN PICTURE

Selig, 1910.

Ever put before the public.

Ranch Life in the Great Southwest

Showing champion celebrities of the great southwest in deeds of daring that make the hair stand on end. The most reckless dare-devils in the world.

See PAT LONG, Champion at Steer Bull Dodging.

CHAS. FUQUA and JOHNNY MULLINS, the Champion Ropers.

TOM MIX, ex-United States Marshal, the Broncho Expert.

HARRY GRAMMAR, Champion of the World, throwing and tying a steer in $14\frac{1}{2}$ Seconds.

Watch the infuriated bulls as they are thrown by these dare-devil cowboys.

A chance of a lifetime. The greatest ensemble of the past passing characters of the world.

You will never see their like again.

MISS CAROLINE DAVIES

The Kentucky Nightingale, will be heard tonight in her latest success, southern lullaby, entitled
Pals of Mine Goodby.

5c

WITH BRIDGES BURNED
Dramatic.

MUSIC HATH CHARMS
Comedy

Coming Monday—Great Comedy Quartette—Opening season of vaudeville.

Mix. *Note:* Filmed on the shores of Lake Michigan.
Credits: Produced by William Selig, directed by Frank Boggs, and written by Lanier Bartlett.

Briton and Boer. A one-reel Selig drama featuring Tom Mix. *Note:* Filmed along the Des Plains River, near Chicago.
Credits: Produced, directed, and written by William Selig.

An Indian Wife's Devotion. A one-reel Selig western featuring Tom Mix.
Credits: Produced by William Selig.

The Trimming of Paradise Gulch, June 2, 1910. A one-reel Selig western featuring Tom Mix.
Credits: Produced by William Selig, directed by Frank Boggs, and written by Lanier Bartlett.

The Range Riders, June 9, 1910. A one-reel Selig western featuring Tom Mix. *Note:* Advertised June 14, 1910, as Selig's greatest feature, greatest western drama of the year featuring bronco busting, lassoing, and a cattle stampede. And appearing for the first time in motion pictures—Olive Stokes Mix of Bartlesville, Oklahoma.
Cast: Tom Mix, Myrtle Stedman, William V. Mong, and Olive Stokes.
Credits: Produced by William Selig and directed by Lynn Reynolds.

1911

In Old California, When the Gringos Came. A one-reel Selig western featuring Tom Mix.
Cast: Kathlyn Williams, Tom Santschi, and Tom Mix.
Credits: Produced by William Selig, directed by Frank Boggs, and written by Lanier Bartlett.

In the Days of Gold. A one-reel Selig western.
Cast: Hobart Bosworth, Betty Harte, Roy Watson, Frank Richardson, Tom Santschi, and Tom Mix.

Credits: Produced by Hobart Bosworth and F. E. Montgomery, directed by Frank Boggs, and written by Hobart Bosworth and F. E. Montgomery.

The Schoolmaster of Mariposa. A one-reel Selig western.
Cast: Hobart Bosworth, Betty Harte, and Tom Mix.
Credits: Produced by William Selig, directed by Frank Boggs, and written by Lanier Bartlett.

Rescued by Her Lions. A one-reel Selig adventure.
Cast: Kathlyn Williams, Tom Santschi, Charles Clary, and Tom Mix.
Credits: Produced by William Selig, directed by Frank Boggs, and written by Edward McWade.

The Totem Mark. A one-reel Selig western.
Cast: Kathlyn Williams, Tom Santschi, Charles Clary, Tom Mix, and Joseph Girard.
Credits: Produced by William Selig, directed by Frank Boggs, and written by Edward McWade.

Kit Carson's Wooing. A one-reel Selig western.
Cast: Hobart Bosworth, Betty Harte, Tom Mix, and Tom Santschi.
Credits: Produced by William Selig, directed by Frank Boggs, and written by Lanier Bartlett.

Lost in the Arctic. A one-reel Selig adventure.
Cast: Kathlyn Williams, Tom Santschi, Charles Clary, and Tom Mix.
Credits: Produced by William Selig, directed by Frank Boggs, and written by Edward McWade.

Lost in the Jungle. A one-reel Selig adventure.
Cast: Kathlyn Williams, Tom Santschi, Charles Clary, and Tom Mix.
Credits: Produced by William Selig, directed by Frank Boggs, and written by Edward McWade.

Opposite: **Only known ad of Tom's first Selig film. (Courtesy Francis P. Clark.)**

The Cowboy and the Shrew, April 10, 1911. A short Selig western drama featuring Tom Mix.
Cast: Tom Mix and Herbert Rawlinson.

Wheels of Justice, May 11, 1911. A one-reel Selig western.
Cast: Kathlyn Williams, Tom Santschi, Charles Clay, Tom Mix, and Joseph Girard.
Credits: Directed by Frank Boggs and written by Edward McWade.

Back to the Primitive, May 11, 1911. A one-reel Selig nature adventure.
Cast: Tom Mix, Kathlyn Williams, Charles Clary, and Joseph Girard.
Credits: Produced by William Selig, directed by Frank Boggs, and written by Edward McWade.

The Rose of Old St. Augustine, June 1, 1911. A one-reel Selig drama.
Cast: Kathlyn Williams, W. H. Stowell, Charles Clary, Tom Mix, Frank Weed, Vera Hamilton, True Broadman, and Harrison Gray.
Credits: Directed by Otis Turner.

Captain Kate, July 13, 1911. A one-reel Selig adventure.
Cast: Kathlyn Williams, Tom Santschi, Charles Clary, Tom Mix, Frank Weed, Frank Smith, and Tom Anderson.
Credits: Produced by William Selig, directed by Frank Boggs, and written by Edward McWade.

Saved by the Pony Express, July 29, 1911. A one-reel Selig western featuring Tom Mix.
Cast: Tom Mix as the Pony Express Rider.

Dad's Girls, September 12, 1911. A one-reel Selig western.
Cast: Kathlyn Williams, Frank Weed, Olive Stokes, Tom Mix, Stan Twist, Charles Clary, William Stowell, and Louis Fierce.
Credits: Directed and written by Otis Turner.

Told in Colorado, October 10, 1911. A one-reel Selig western.

Cast: William Duncan, T. J. Carrigan, Myrtle Stedman, Tom Mix, Olive Stokes, and Otis B. Thayer.
Credits: Directed and written by Joseph A. Golden.

Why the Sheriff Is a Bachelor, October 24, 1911. A one-reel Selig western featuring Tom Mix.
Cast: Tom Mix, Myrtle Stedman, T. J. Carrigan, O. B. Thayer, William Duncan, George Hooker, Olive Stokes, and George Allen.
Credits: Directed and written by Joseph A. Golden.

Western Hearts, November 7, 1911. A one-reel Selig western featuring Tom Mix.
Cast: Tom Mix, T. J. Carrigan, Otis B. Thayer, Myrtle Stedman, William Duncan, Ralph Kennedy, and Dick Trethwick.
Credits: Directed and written by Joseph A. Golden.

The Tell-Tale Knife, November 25, 1911. A one-reel Selig adventure featuring Tom Mix.
Cast: Tom Mix, William Duncan, Rex de Rosselli, Myrtle Stedman, Charles Tipton, and Leon Watson.
Credits: Produced and directed by William Duncan.

A Romance of the Rio Grande, December 12, 1911. A one-reel Selig western featuring Tom Mix.
Cast: Tom Mix, Betty Harte, William Duncan, Myrtle Stedman, and George Hooker.
Credits: Produced and directed by Colin Campbell, written by Lanier Bartlett.

The Bully of Bingo Gulch, December 26, 1911. A one-reel Selig western.
Cast: William Duncan, Tom Mix, Charles Farra, Myrtle Stedman, and Rex de Rosselli.
Credits: Directed and written by Otis B. Thayer.

1912

Outlaw Reward. A one-reel Selig western featuring Tom Mix.

The Cowboy's Best Girl, January 16, 1912. A one-reel Selig western.
Cast: Myrtle Stedman, Rex de Rosselli, William Duncan, Tom Mix, Olive Mix, Robert Perry, Francis Carroll, Charles Canterbury, and Florence Dye.
Credits: Directed by O. B. Thayer and written by Everitt McNeil.

The Diamond S Ranch, February 29, 1912. A one-reel Selig western featuring Tom Mix. *Note:* May be a re-release of a 1909 film. The film was advertised as the first film to show Tom Mix or anyone else bulldogging a steer from a speeding auto.
Cast: Tom Mix, Frank Maish, and Olive Stokes Mix.
Credits: Produced by William Selig, directed by Otis B. Thayer.

A Reconstructed Rebel, May 1912. A one-reel Selig western featuring Tom Mix.
Cast: Tom Mix, Hobart Bosworth, Betty Harte, and Tom Santschi.
Credits: Produced by William Selig, directed by Colin Campbell, and written by Lanier Bartlett.

1913

How It Happened, January 31, 1913. A one-reel Selig adventure.
Cast: William Duncan, Tom Mix, Myrtle Stedman, and Lester Cuneo.
Credits: Produced, directed, and written by William Duncan.

Cowboy Millionaire (parts 1 and 2), January 31, 1913. A four-reel Selig western comedy featuring Tom Mix.
Credits: Produced by William Selig and directed by Tom Mix.

The Range Law, February 14, 1913. A one-reel Selig western.
Cast: William Duncan, Myrtle Stedman, Tom Mix, and Lester Cuneo.
Credits: Produced by William Selig, directed and written by William Duncan.

Juggling with Fate, March 3, 1913. A one-reel Selig drama featuring Tom Mix. *Note:* Mix played the dual role of Andrews, the marshal, and Morgan, the masked outlaw.
Cast: Tom Mix, Myrtle Stedman, Lester Cuneo, and Rex de Rosselli.
Credits: Produced by William Selig, directed by Tom Mix, and written by Edward McWade.

The Sheriff of Yavapai County, March 21, 1913. A one-reel Selig western. *Note:* Tom played the part of a gambler.
Cast: William Duncan, Myrtle Stedman, Tom Mix, Lester Cuneo, and Rex de Rosselli.
Credits: Produced, directed, and written by William Duncan.

Pauline Cushman, the Federal Spy (parts 1 and 2), March 27, 1913. A two-reel Selig adventure.
Cast: Charles Clary, T. J. Commerford, Winifred Greenwood, Lafayette McKee, Harry Lonsdale, Grant Forman, Walter Roberts, and Tom Mix.
Credits: Produced by William Selig and written by Charles O. Nixon.

The Life-Timer, March 27, 1913. A one-reel Selig action adventure.
Cast: William Duncan, Myrtle Stedman, Tom Mix, Florence Dye, and Lester Cuneo.
Credits: Produced, directed, and written by William Duncan.

The Shotgun Man and the Stage Driver, April 3, 1913. A one-reel Selig western. *Note:* Tom played the part of the stage driver.
Cast: William Duncan, Tom Mix, Myrtle Stedman, and Florence Dye.
Credits: Produced, directed, and written by William Duncan.

A Prisoner of Cabansas, April 3, 1913. A one-reel Selig adventure featuring Tom Mix.
Cast: Tom Mix, Tom Santschi, and Bessie Eyton.
Credits: Produced and directed by Colin Campbell, written by R. L. Terwilliger.

That Mail Order Suit, April 18, 1913. A one-reel Selig comedy.

Cast: Lester Cuneo, Tom Mix, and Myrtle Stedman.

Credits: Directed by William Duncan and written by Edgar Hungerford.

His Father's Deputy, May 17, 1913. A one-reel Selig action film.

Cast: William Duncan, Tom Mix, Lester Cuneo, Rex de Rosselli, and Marshal Stedman.

Credits: Produced, directed, and written by William Duncan.

The Noisy Six, May 21, 1913. A one-reel Selig action film featuring Tom Mix.

Cast: Tom Mix, Betty Harte, and Bessie Eyton.

Credits: Produced and directed by Colin Campbell, written by O. A. Nelson.

Religion and Gun Practice, May 26, 1913. A one-reel Selig western. *Note:* Tom plays the part of gunslinger Kil Kullen.

Cast: William Duncan, Myrtle Stedman, Tom Mix, Rex de Rosselli, and Lester Cuneo.

Credits: Produced and directed by William Duncan, written by A. W. Corey.

The Wordless Message, May 29, 1913. A one-reel Selig drama featuring Tom Mix.

Cast: Tom Mix and Tom Santschi.

Credits: Produced and directed by Colin Campbell, written by Hettie Gray Baker.

Taming of a Tenderfoot, June 7, 1913. A one-reel Selig western.

Cast: Lester Cuneo, Tom Mix, Myrtle Stedman, and Florence Dye.

Credits: Directed by William Duncan and written by Cornelius Shea.

The Law and the Outlaw, June 7, 1913. A two-reel Selig western.

Cast: William Duncan, Tom Mix, Myrtle Stedman, Lester Cuneo, and J. Edgar Hungerford.

Credits: Produced and directed by William Duncan, written by Tom Mix and U. E. Hungerford.

Made a Coward, June 11, 1913. A one-reel Selig western.

Cast: William Duncan, Tom Mix, Lester Cuneo, Rex de Rosselli, Myrtle Stedman, and Florence Dye.

Credits: Produced and directed by William Duncan, written by A. W. Colins.

Songs of Truce, June 28, 1913. A one-reel Selig adventure featuring Tom Mix.

Cast: Tom Mix, Tom Santschi, and Kathlyn Williams.

Credits: Produced and directed by Colin Campbell, written by Hettie Gray Baker.

The Marshal's Capture, June 28, 1913. A one-reel Selig western. *Note:* Tom played the part of a half-breed.

Cast: William Duncan, Tom Mix, Lester Cuneo, and Myrtle Stedman.

Credits: Produced and directed by William Duncan, written by Elizabeth Frazer.

Sallie's Sure Shot, July 4, 1913. A one-reel Selig western. *Note:* Tom played the part of half-breed Injun Sam.

Cast: William Duncan, Tom Mix, Lester Cuneo, and Myrtle Stedman.

Credits: Produced and directed by William Duncan, written by Cornelius Shea.

Bud Doble Comes Back, July 11, 1913. A one-reel Selig action-adventure featuring Tom Mix.

Cast: Tom Mix and Tom Santschi.

Credits: Produced and directed by Colin Campbell, written by Frank Clark.

The Only Chance, July 14, 1913. A one-reel Selig drama. *Note:* Tom plays the part of a railroad engineer.

Cast: William Duncan, Lester Cuneo, Tom Mix, and Rex de Rosselli.

Credits: Directed by William Duncan and written by C. Chester Wesley.

The Taming of Texas Pete, July 24, 1913. A one-reel Selig western. *Note:* Tom plays the part of a half-breed.

Cast: William Duncan, Tom Mix, Betty Kastner, and Myrtle Stedman.

Credits: Produced and directed by William Duncan, written by Joseph F. Poland.

The Stolen Moccasins, July 26, 1913. A one-reel Selig western. *Note:* Tom Mix plays the part of an Indian.

Cast: William Duncan, Myrtle Stedman, Tom Mix, and Lester Cuneo.

Credits: Produced and directed by William Duncan, written by Cornelius Shea.

An Apache's Gratitude, August 1, 1913. A one-reel Selig western. *Note:* Tom plays the part of Tonto, an Indian.

Cast: William Duncan, Myrtle Stedman, Tom Mix, Jim Robson, and Rex de Rosselli.

Credits: Produced, directed, and written by William Duncan.

The Good Indian: A Saving Service Rewarded, August 22, 1913. A one-reel Selig western. *Note:* Tom plays the part of the Good Indian.

Cast: William Duncan, Tom Mix, and Myrtle Stedman.

Credits: Produced by William Selig, directed by William Duncan, and written by Ethel C. Unland.

How Betty Made Good, August 27, 1913. A one-reel Selig western. *Note:* Tom plays the part of the ranch foreman.

Cast: Lester Cuneo, Myrtle Stedman, Tom Mix, Rex de Rosselli, Howard Farrell, Sid Jordan, and Vic Frith.

Credits: Directed by William Duncan and written by Ethel C. Unland.

Howlin' Jones, September 4, 1913. A one-reel Selig western. *Note:* Tom plays the part of Robledo.

Cast: William Duncan, Rex de Rosselli, Tom Mix, Sid Jordan, Vic Frith, Florence Dye, Myrtle Stedman, and George Panky.

Credits: Directed by William Duncan and written by O. H. Nelson.

Tobias Wants Out, September 11, 1913. A one-reel Selig adventure featuring Tom Mix.

Credits: Produced and directed by Oscar Eagle, written by Arthur P. Hankins.

The Rejected Lover's Luck, September 19, 1913. A one-reel Selig western. *Note:* Tom plays the part of an Indian.

Cast: Lester Cuneo, Rex de Rosselli, Tom Mix, Myrtle Stedman, and Vic Frith.

Credits: Directed by William Duncan and written by Cornelius Shea.

The Cattle Thief's Escape, October 1, 1913. A half-reel Selig western. *Note:* Tom plays the part of a half-breed.

Cast: William Duncan, Rex de Rosselli, Tom Mix, Myrtle Stedman, and Lester Cuneo.

Credits: Directed by William Duncan and written by R. E. Hicks.

Saved from the Vigilantes, October 9, 1913. A one-reel Selig western. *Note:* Tom plays the part of Squire Beasley.

Cast: William Duncan, Myrtle Stedman, Tom Mix, Hugh Mosher, Olive Stokes Mix, and Rex de Rosselli.

Credits: Directed by William Duncan and written by Malcolm Douglass.

The Silver Grindstone, October 14, 1913. A one-reel Selig drama.

Cast: William Duncan, Myrtle Stedman, Florence Dye, Tom Mix, Lester Cuneo, and Rex de Rosselli.

Credits: Directed by William Duncan and written by Eugene P. Lyle.

Dishwash Dick's Counterfeit, October 21, 1913. A one-reel Selig western. *Note:* Tom plays the part of a cattle rustler.

Cast: Rex de Rosselli, Myrtle Stedman, Tom Mix, and Lester Cuneo.

Credits: Directed by William Duncan and B. Williams.

A Muddle in Horse Thieves, October 25, 1913. A one-reel Selig western featuring Tom Mix.

Credits: Produced by William Selig, directed by Tom Mix, and written by Elizabeth Frazer.

The Sheriff and the Rustler, November 1913. A two-reel Selig western. *Note:* Tom played the part of the Rustler.

Cast: Lester Cuneo, Tom Mix, George Panky, Rex de Rosselli, Neil Broaded, Vic Frith, and B. L. Jones.

Credits: Produced and directed by William Duncan, written by Tom Mix.

The Schoolmarm's Shooting Match, November 7, 1913. A half-reel Selig western comedy.
Cast: William Duncan, Myrtle Stedman, Lester Cuneo, Rex de Rosselli, Tom Mix, Hugh Mosier, and William Jones.
Credits: Directed by William Duncan and written by Cornelius Shea.

The Child of the Prairies, November 13, 1913. A one-reel Selig western featuring Tom Mix.
Cast: Tom Mix, Lester Cuneo, Florence Dye, Myrtle Stedman, Vic Frith, Hugh Mosier, and Sid Jordan.
Credits: Produced by William Duncan, and written by Tom Mix.

The Escape of Jim Dolan, November 13, 1913. A one-reel Selig western featuring Tom Mix.
Cast: Tom Mix, Betty Harte, Tom Santschi, Lester Cuneo, Nip Van, Myrtle Stedman, Rex de Rosselli, Vic Frith, Sid Jordan, and Hugh Mosier.
Credits: Produced by William Selig, directed by Colin Campbell, and written by Tom Mix.

Local Color, November 21, 1913. A one-reel Selig western comedy featuring Tom Mix.
Credits: Produced by William Selig, directed and written by Tom Mix.

Cupid in the Cow Camp, November 26, 1913. A one-reel Selig western comedy featuring Tom Mix.
Cast: Tom Mix, Myrtle Stedman, Lester Cuneo, Vic Frith, Sid Jordan, Rex de Rosselli, Art Cook, and Marshall Stedman.

Physical Culture on the Quarter Circle V Bar, December 11, 1913. A one-reel Selig western.
Cast: William Duncan, Rex de Rosselli, Tom Mix, Lester Cuneo, Myrtle Stedman, Florence Dye, and Hugh Mosher.
Credits: Directed by William Duncan, and written by Edwin Ray Coffin.

Buster's Little Game, December 17, 1913. A one-reel Selig western.

Cast: William Duncan, Lester Cuneo, Myrtle Stedman, Florence Dye, Rex de Rosselli, and Tom Mix.
Credits: Produced and directed by William Duncan, written by C. W. Vansant.

Mother Love vs. Gold, December 23, 1913. A one-reel Selig drama.
Cast: William Duncan, Myrtle Stedman, Lester Cuneo, Tom Mix, Florence Dye and Rex de Rosselli.
Credits: Produced and directed by William Duncan; written by John M. Kiskadden.

1914

The Sheriff's Girl. A one-reel Selig western featuring Tom Mix.
Credits: Produced by William Selig.

Buffalo Hunting. A one-reel Selig western featuring Tom Mix.
Credits: Produced by William Selig, directed by F. J. Grandon, and written by Gilson Willets.

Single Shot Parker. A one-reel Selig western featuring Tom Mix.
Credits: Produced by William Selig.

By Unseen Hand, January 7, 1914. A one-reel Selig drama.
Cast: William Duncan, Lester Cuneo, Rex de Rosselli, Tom Mix, Myrtle Stedman, and Marshall Stedman.
Credits: Produced and directed by William Duncan, written by Hardee Kirkland.

A Friend in Need, January 22, 1914. A one-reel Selig western.
Cast: William Duncan, Florence Dye, Eleanor Blevins, Lester Cuneo, Tom Mix, and Charles Wheelock.
Credits: Produced, directed, and written by William Duncan.

The Little Sister, February 5, 1914. A one-reel Selig drama featuring Tom Mix.
Cast: Tom Mix (one of the big brothers), William Duncan, Grace Tregarthen, Lester Cuneo, and Charles Wheelock.
Credits: Produced by William Duncan,

Tom's first *Single Shot Parker* film originated in 1914. (Courtesy of Art Evans.)

directed by William Selig, and written by Merla Marion Metcalfe.

Shotgun Jones, April 14, 1914. A two-reel Selig western featuring Tom Mix.
Credits: Produced and directed by Colin Campbell, written by Bertrand W. Sinclair and Bertha M. Bower.

Me an' Bill, June 6, 1914. A two-reel Selig western featuring Tom Mix.
Cast: Tom Mix, and Tom Santschi.
Credits: Produced by William Selig, directed, and written by Colin Campbell.

When the Cook Fell Ill, June 9, 1914. A one-reel Selig western comedy featuring Tom Mix.
Cast: Tom Mix, Wheeler Oakman, Frank Clark, and Frank Feehan.
Credits: Produced and directed by Colin Campbell, written by B. M. Bower.

The Leopard's Foundling, June 11, 1914. A one-reel Selig action film.
Cast: Kathlyn Williams and Tom Mix.

Credits: Produced by Kathlyn Williams, directed by Colin Campbell, and written by Mabel Heckes Justice.

In Defiance of the Law, June 13, 1914. A three-reel feature starring Tom Mix and Bessie Eyton.
Cast: Tom Mix, Wheeler Oakman, Bessie Eyton, Joe King, Frank Clark, Baby Lillian Wade, and Lillian Hayward.
Credits: Produced and directed by Colin Campbell, written by James Oliver Curwood.

The Wilderness Trail, June 26, 1914. A one-reel Selig western featuring Tom Mix. *Note:* Tom plays the part of an outlaw.
Cast: Wheeler Oakman, Joe King, Tom Mix, Kathlyn Williams, Bessie Eyton, Lillian Hayward, and Frank Clark.
Credits: Produced and directed by Colin Campbell, written by James Oliver Curwood.

Wiggs Takes the Rest Cure, June 26, 1914. A one-reel Selig drama featuring Tom Mix.
Credits: Produced and directed by F. J. Grandon, written by W. E. Wing.

Lure of the Ladies, July 7, 1914. A one-reel Selig drama featuring Tom Mix.
Credits: Produced and directed by Oscar Eagle, written by Will M. Hough.

Etienne of the Glad Heart, July 15, 1914. A two-reel Selig adventure featuring Tom Mix.
Cast: Tom Mix, Wheeler Oakman, Bessie Eyton, Frank Clark, and Lillian Hayward.
Credits: Produced and directed by Colin Campbell, written by Mabel Heckes Justice.

His Fight, July 20, 1914. A one-reel Selig action film featuring Tom Mix.
Cast: Tom Mix, Tom Santschi, and Kathlyn Williams.
Credits: Produced and directed by Colin Campbell, written by James Oliver Curwood.

The Reveler, July 31, 1914. A one-reel Selig adventure featuring Tom Mix.
Credits: Produced and directed by Colin Campbell, written by B. M. Bower.

When the West Was Young, August 1914. A two-reel Selig western. *Note:* Tom plays the part of an Indian chief.
Cast: Bessie Eyton, Wheeler Oakman, Jack McDonald, Gertrude Ryan, Frank Clark, Tom Mix, and Harry Lonsdale.
Credits: Produced and directed by Colin Campbell, written by Cyrus Townsend Brady.

The White Mouse, August 4, 1914. A two-reel Selig drama featuring Tom Mix.
Cast: Tom Mix, Wheeler Oakman, Bessie Eyton, and Joe King.
Credits: Produced and directed by Colin Campbell, written by James Oliver Curwood.

Chip of the Flying U, August 17, 1914. A three-reel Selig action film featuring Tom Mix.
Cast: Tom Mix, Kathlyn Williams,

Frank Clark, Wheeler Oakman, Bessie Eyton, and Fred Huntley.
Credits: Directed by Colin Campbell, written by B. M. Bower.

To Be Called For, August 19, 1914. A one-reel Selig adventure featuring Tom Mix.
Credits: Produced and directed by F. J. Grandon, written by Wallace C. Clifton.

The Fifth Man, August 22, 1914. A three-reel Selig adventure featuring Tom Mix.
Cast: Tom Mix, Tom Santschi, Frank Walsh, Charles Clary, Bessie Eyton, Lafe McKee, and Roy Watson.
Credits: Produced and directed by F. J. Grandon, written by James Oliver Curwood.

Jim, September 2, 1914. A one-reel Selig drama featuring Tom Mix.
Credits: Produced and directed by F. J. Grandon, written by Wallace C. Clifton.

The Lonesome Trail, September 2, 1914. A one-reel Selig western featuring Tom Mix.
Cast: Tom Mix and Kathlyn Williams.
Credits: Produced and directed by Colin Campbell, written by B. M. Bower.

The Livid Flame, September 3, 1914. A two-reel Selig drama featuring Tom Mix.
Credits: Produced and directed by F. J. Grandon, written by Walter E. Wing.

Four Minutes Late, September 9, 1914. A one-reel Selig adventure featuring Tom Mix.
Credits: Produced and directed by F. J. Grandon, written by James Oliver Curwood.

The Real Thing in Cowboys, September 10, 1914. A one-reel Selig western featuring Tom Mix.
Cast: Tom Mix, Goldie Colwell, and Miss Townsend.
Credits: Produced and directed by Tom Mix, written by Hettie Gray Baker.

Hearts and Masks, September 15, 1914. A three-reel Selig action film featuring Tom Mix.

Cast: Tom Mix and Kathlyn Williams.
Credits: Produced and directed by Colin Campbell, written by Harold McGrath.

The Way of the Red Man, September 16, 1914. A one-reel Selig western featuring Tom Mix. May be a re-release of a 1910 film.
Cast: Tom Mix, Leo Maloney, Goldie Colwell, and Roy Watson.
Credits: Directed and written by Tom Mix.

The Moving Picture Cowboy (parts 1 and 2), September 16, 1914. Two one-reel Selig western comedy films starring Tom Mix.
Cast: Tom Mix, Ellinor Blevins, Lester Cuneo, Sid Jordan, W. L. Lewis, Charles Wheelock, and Bobby Murdock.
Credits: Produced by Lester Cuneo, directed and written by Tom Mix.

The Mexican, September 24, 1914. A one-reel Selig western featuring Tom Mix. *Note:* Tom Mix played the part of the Mexican.
Cast: Tom Mix, Lillian Wade, Leo Maloney, and Goldie Colwell.
Credits: Produced and directed by Tom Mix, written by Lynn Reynolds.

The Going of the White Swan, September 28, 1914. A two-reel Selig drama with Tom Mix.
Cast: Bessie Eyton, Wheeler Oakman, Tom Mix, Frank Clark, Roy Clark, and Joe King.
Credits: Produced and directed by Colin Campbell, written by Gilbert Parker.

Jimmy Hayes and Muriel, September 30, 1914. A one-reel Selig drama featuring Tom Mix.
Cast: Tom Mix, Goldie Colwell, Leo Maloney, and Roy Watson.
Credits: Produced and directed by Tom Mix, written by Sidney Porter.

Why the Sheriff Is a Bachelor (2d version), October 10, 1914. A one-reel Selig western comedy featuring Tom Mix.
Cast: Tom Mix, Leo Maloney, Goldie Colwell, and Roy Watson.

Credits: Produced, directed, and written by Tom Mix.

Garrison's Finish, October 10, 1914. A three-reel Selig action film featuring Tom Mix.
Credits: Produced and directed by F. J. Grandon, written by B. M. Ferguson.

The Losing Fight, October 15, 1914. A one-reel Selig action film featuring Tom Mix.
Credits: Produced, directed, and written by Colin Campbell.

The Ranger's Romance, October 15, 1914. A one-reel Selig western featuring Tom Mix.
Cast: Tom Mix, Goldie Colwell, Roy Watson, and Inez Walker.
Credits: Directed and written by Tom Mix.

The Tell-Tale Knife (2d version), October 15, 1914. A one-reel Selig adventure film featuring Tom Mix.
Cast: Tom Mix, Goldie Colwell, Harry Loverin, Leo Maloney, and Hoot Gibson.
Credits: Produced, directed, and written by Tom Mix.

Out of Petticoat Lane, October 24, 1914. A two-reel Selig comedy featuring Tom Mix.
Credits: Produced, directed, and written by F. J. Grandon.

The Sheriff's Reward, October 24, 1914. A one-reel Selig western featuring Tom Mix.
Cast: Tom Mix, Goldie Colwell, Leo Maloney, and Roy Watson.
Credits: Produced, directed, and written by Tom Mix.

The Scapegoat, October 24, 1914. A one-reel Selig western featuring Tom Mix.
Cast: Tom Mix, Goldie Colwell, and Leo Maloney.
Credits: Directed, produced, and written by Tom Mix.

If I Were Young Again, October 24, 1914. A two-reel Selig drama featuring Tom Mix.

Credits: Produced and directed by F. J. Grandon, written by Gilson Willets.

Young Girl and Mine, October 31, 1914. A Selig women's suffrage play.
Cast: Kathlyn Williams and Tom Mix.
Credits: Directed by F. J. Grandon and written by Gilson Willets.

The Tell-Tale Knife (3d version), November 7, 1914. A one-reel Selig adventure featuring Tom Mix.
Cast: Tom Mix, Goldie Colwell, Roy Watson, and Inez Walker.
Credits: Produced, directed, and written by Tom Mix.

Saved by a Watch, November 11, 1914. A one-reel Selig western featuring Tom Mix.
Cast: Tom Mix, Goldie Colwell, Leo Maloney, and Inez Walker.
Credits: Produced, directed, and written by Tom Mix.

The Rival Stage Lines, November 12, 1914. A one-reel Selig western featuring Tom Mix.
Cast: Tom Mix, Goldie Colwell, Leo Maloney, Sid Jordan, Inez Walker, and Lynn F. Reynolds.
Credits: Produced and directed by Tom Mix, written by Allen A. Martin.

In the Days of the Thundering Herd, November 12, 1914. A five-reel Selig western featuring Tom Mix. *Note:* The movie was filmed at Pawnee Bill's Ranch at Pawnee, Oklahoma.
Story: The Indians still hunt the great buffalo herd while defending their hunting grounds against the ever-westward expansion. The film shows a complete Indian village, dozens of prairie schooners, and hundreds of horses.

Tom and Sally are crossing the plains to join Sally's father in the California gold fields. The wagon train is wiped out by Indians, and only Tom and Sally are spared because the Indian Chief and his sister takes a liking to them. They finally escape their captors and join a band of buffalo hunters. In turn, the buffalo hunters are almost wiped out by the Indians, but the Cavalry arrives in the nick of time. Tom and Sally are rescued and finally join her father in California.
Cast: Tom Mix, Bessie Eyton, Red Wing, Wheeler Oakman, John Bowers, and Major Gordon Lillie (Pawnee Bill).
Credits: Produced by William Selig, directed by Colin Campbell, and written by Gilson Willets.

The Soul Mate, November 14, 1914. A one-reel Selig western featuring Tom Mix.
Cast: Tom Mix and Kathlyn Williams.
Credits: Produced and directed by F. J. Grandon, written by Mark Reardon.

Lure of the Windigo, November 28, 1914. A two-reel Selig drama featuring Tom Mix.
Credits: Produced by William Selig, directed by F. J. Grandon, and written by Mabel Heckes Justice.

The Man from the East, November 28, 1914. A one-reel Selig western featuring Tom Mix.
Cast: Tom Mix, Goldie Colwell, Leo Maloney, Pat Chrisman, Inez Walker, Hoot Gibson, R. H. Kelly, C. W. Bachman, Ed Jones, and Susie Morella.
Credits: Produced by William Selig, directed and written by Tom Mix.

Wade Brent Pays, December 8, 1914. A one-reel Selig drama featuring Tom Mix.
Cast: Tom Mix and Tom Santschi.
Credits: Directed by F. J. Grandon, written by Marie Wing and F. J. Grandon.

Cactus Jake, Heart Breaker, December 10, 1914. A one-reel Selig comedy featuring Tom Mix.
Cast: Tom Mix, Goldie Colwell, Leo Maloney, and Josephine Miller.
Credits: Directed by Tom Mix, written by Edwin Ray Coffin.

Flower of Faith, December 10, 1914. A two-reel Selig drama.
Cast: Kathlyn Williams and Tom Mix.
Credits: Produced and directed by F. J. Grandon, written by Will M. Hough.

A Militant School Ma'am, December 28, 1914. A one-reel Selig comedy featuring Tom Mix.

Cast: Tom Mix, Goldie Colwell, and Leo Maloney.

Credits: Produced by William Selig, directed by Tom Mix, and written by Edwin Ray Coffin.

1915

Weary Goes Wooing. A one-reel Selig western featuring Tom Mix.

Cactus Jim. A one-reel Selig western featuring Tom Mix.

Cast: Tom Mix, Goldie Colwell, and Lynn Reynolds.

Western Justice (re-released). A patched-up 1907 Selig film with rodeo shots of Tom added. Other than Tom, cast and credits unknown.

Harold's Bad Man—A Story of Luck and Love, January 1, 1915. A one-reel Selig western comedy featuring Tom Mix.

Cast: Tom Mix, Goldie Colwell, Leo Maloney, Pat Chrisman, Sid Jordan, and Ed Jones.

Credits: Produced and directed by Tom Mix, written by Edwin Ray Coffin.

Cactus Jim's Shop Girl, January 9, 1915. A one-reel Selig western featuring Tom Mix.

Cast: Tom Mix, Goldie Colwell, Lynn Reynolds, and Sid Jordan.

Credits: Produced by William Selig, directed by Tom Mix, and written by Edwin Ray Coffin.

Heart's Desire, January 13, 1915. A one-reel Selig drama featuring Tom Mix.

Credits: Produced by William Selig, directed by F. J. Grandon, and written by Wallace C. Clifton.

The Grizzly Gulch Chariot Race, January 13, 1915. A one-reel Selig western featuring Tom Mix.

Cast: Tom Mix, Inez Walker, Sid Jordan, Dick Crawford, and Roy Watson.

Credits: Produced by William Selig, directed by Tom Mix, and written by O. A. Nelson.

Forked Trails, January 16, 1915. A one-reel Selig action film featuring Tom

Mix. *Note:* Critics noted good photography with a weak plot. In one scene, the heroine lays her gun down on a table so that she can tie the hands of a Mexican bandit. He quickly reverses the tables on her.

Cast: Tom Mix, Goldie Colwell, Sid Jordan, and Pat Chrisman.

Credits: Produced by William Selig, directed by Tom Mix, and written by William McLeod Raine.

Roping a Bride, January 26, 1915. A one-reel Selig western featuring Tom Mix.

Cast: Tom Mix, Goldie Colwell, Sid Jordan, C. W. Bachman, Roy Watson, and Inez Walker.

Credits: Produced and directed by Tom Mix, written by E. Lynn Summers.

Bill Haywood, Producer, February 1, 1915. A one-reel Selig comedy featuring Tom Mix.

Story: In this film, Tom, a cowboy, takes over the direction of a stranded motion picture crew. He starts out by writing his own script, then goes about trying to put it on film. He tells the actors what he expects of them, then has them take their places.

When everyone is ready, Tom pulls out his gun and fires a shot in the air. The shot spooks the livestock, who stampede and promptly tear up the set, leading to chaos.

Cast: Tom Mix, Mabel van Buren, Sid Jordan, Goldie Colwell, Roy Watson, George Fawcett, Pat Chrisman, Dick Hunter, Dick Crawford, and Ed Jones.

Credits: Produced by William Selig, directed by Tom Mix, and written by Cecille B. Peterson.

Hearts of the Jungle, February 11, 1915. A one-reel Selig adventure featuring Tom Mix.

Credits: Produced by William Selig, directed by F. J. Grandon, and written by Wallace C. Clifton.

Slim Higgins, February 11, 1915. A one-reel Selig western featuring Tom Mix.

Cast: Tom Mix, Goldie Colwell, Roy Watson, and Pat Chrisman.

The Man from Texas originated in February 1915. (Courtesy of Art Evans.)

Credits: Produced, directed, and written by Tom Mix.

A Child of the Prairie (2d version), February 24, 1915. A two-reel Selig western featuring Tom Mix.

Cast: Tom Mix, Louella Maxam, Baby Norma Maxam, Ed J. Brady, Fay Robinson, and Rose Robinson.

Credits: Produced by William Selig, directed and written by Tom Mix.

The Man from Texas, February 24, 1915. A two-reel Selig western featuring Tom Mix.

Story: Tom (the man from Texas) receives a letter from his sister saying that she is sick and fears that she will never see him again. Her heart has been broken by a man who has broken his promise and left her all alone. She encloses a picture of the low-life character.

Tom leaves the ranch to avenge his sister, but he is assured by the ranch owner that he will have a job if he ever

needs one. Meanwhile, Tom Hargrave, the man who failed to keep his promise, leaves the sick, heartbroken sister and hires on as a card dealer at the local bar.

Tom has a nightmare on the trail and awakens at the same moment his loving sister dies. Meanwhile, Moya Dalton, daughter of the West, comes to town to pick up her mail. Tom Hargrave sees her drop a letter, retrieves it for her, and walks her home. Tom arrives in town only to find out that Hargrave left his sister a couple of days before she died.

Tom stays on Hargrave's trail even as he and Moya go for a morning ride. On the trail, Hargrave tries to have his way with Moya, but her screams are heard by Tom, who rushes to her rescue. Tom runs Hargrave off before he recognizes him from the picture his sister sent.

Hargrave goes to safe ground, then tries to shoot Tom, but the bullet puts only a neat hole in his hat. Tom pursues Hargrave back to town, and Hargrave again draws his gun to shoot Tom in the back. Tom hears the click of the hammer, turns, and fires, killing Hargrave on the spot.

Tom then turns himself into the sheriff Frank Scott (Sid Jordan), but he is cleared as witnesses testify it was a matter of self-defense. Tom finds Moya a sympathetic listener as he tells her about his sister and Hargrave.

Later, the ex-sheriff becomes Tom's rival for Moya's affections. Tom writes a letter asking Moya to a dance, but Sid beats the mail and gets Moya to agree to go to the dance with him. Tom is saddened when he gets his reply from Moya saying she has already accepted a dance invitation from Frank Scott.

On the night of the dance, Moya asks Frank why Tom has not come to the dance, and Frank plants seeds of doubt in Moya's mind concerning Tom's love and affection for her. Later, Moya and Frank decide to get married, but Moya's father insists that Frank earn at least two thousand dollars before he can have his daughter's hand.

At the local bar, Mexican Joe tells Frank he knows how he can make a quick two thousand dollars, and the two begin to make plans to rob the overland stage. Unbeknownst to Frank, Tom and Moya are out riding when the stage is held up, and they are witnesses to the robbery. Tom and Moya take cover, but Frank also takes cover at the same spot. Tom and Frank have a fierce fight, but Tom wins and takes Frank and his share of the loot back to town.

Meanwhile, Moya is informed that one of the ranch hands has broken his arm and needs help. She leaves Tom a note and rides out to help him. She assists him getting on a horse and later, after aid does not arrive, goes to a sheepherder's cabin in search of food.

Mexican Joe arrives at the sheepherder's cabin, and Moya surprises him and takes his gun. As she is attempting to tie him up, he gets away from her and ties her up. Tom arrives and upsets a table just as Mexican Joe fires at him. Tom captures Mexican Joe and is elected sheriff.

Months later, in the ranch owner's absence, the ranch foreman presses his unwanted attentions on Moya. She gets him fired, and he organizes a group of rustlers in vengeance. Tom forms a posse to catch the rustlers, who eventually capture Moya. She marks the trail for Tom, however, and he follows her to an abandoned shack, where he is taken by surprise and wounded while trying to rescue her.

Tom's posse arrives in the nick of time, and Moya now realizes that Tom is the only man for her. After recovering from his wounds, the two ride off in a wagon. Tom kisses and hugs Moya as the movie ends.

Cast: Tom Mix, Leo Maloney, Sid Jordan, Hoot Gibson, Goldie Colwell, Louella Maxam, and Ed Brady.

Credits: Produced, directed, and written by Tom Mix.

The Stagecoach Driver and the Girl, February 26, 1915. A one-reel Selig western featuring Tom Mix. May have been re-released by Avwon as *The Stage Coach Driver.*

Cast: Tom Mix, Goldie Colwell, Louella Maxam, Sid Jordan, Ed Brady, and Ed Jones.

Credits: Produced, directed, and written by Tom Mix.

Jack's Pals, March 3, 1915. A one-reel Selig drama featuring Tom Mix.

Credits: Produced and directed by F. J. Grandon, written by C. B. Murphy.

The Puny Soul of Peter Rand, March 6, 1915. A one-reel Selig adventure featuring Tom Mix.

Cast: Tom Mix and Tom Santschi.

Credits: Directed by F. J. Grandon, story by Walter E. Wing.

Sagebrush Tom, March 8, 1915. A one-reel Selig western featuring Tom Mix.

Cast: Tom Mix, Myrtle Stedman, Goldie Colwell, and Ed J. Brady.

Credits: Produced, directed, and written by Tom Mix.

The Outlaw's Bride, March 13, 1915. A one-reel Selig western featuring Tom Mix.

The Stagecoach Driver and the Girl originated in February 1915. (Courtesy of Art Evans.)

Cast: Tom Mix, Eugenia Forde, Ed J. Brady, and Pat Chrisman.

Credits: Produced by William Selig, directed by Tom Mix, and written by Cornelius Shea.

Ma's Girls, March 20, 1915. A one-reel Selig comedy featuring Tom Mix.

Cast: Tom Mix, Eugenie Forde, Goldie Colwell, Ed J. Brady, and Louella Maxam.

Credits: Produced, directed, and written by Tom Mix.

The Legal Light, March 20, 1915. A one-reel Selig adventure featuring Tom Mix.

Cast: Tom Mix, Eugenia Forde, and Ed J. Brady.

Credits: Produced by William Selig, directed by Tom Mix, and written by Edwin Ray Coffin.

Getting a Start in Life, March 29, 1915. A one-reel Selig western comedy featuring Tom Mix.

Cast: Tom Mix, Louella Maxam, and Sid Jordan.

Credits: Produced and directed by Tom Mix, written by James Oliver Curwood.

Mrs. Murphy's Cooks, April 3, 1915. A one-reel Selig western comedy featuring Tom Mix.

Cast: Tom Mix, Louella Maxam, and Anna Dodge.

Credits: Produced, directed, and written by Tom Mix.

The Face at the Window, April 10, 1915. A one-reel Selig drama featuring Tom Mix.

Credits: Produced and directed by F. J. Grandon, written by Wallace C. Clifton.

The Conversion of Smiling Tom, April 10, 1915. A one-reel Selig western featuring Tom Mix.

Cast: Tom Mix, Sid Jordan, Louella Maxam, Eugenia Forde, and William Brunton.

Credits: Produced and directed by Tom

Mix; written by Emma Bell (Tom's sister?).

An Arizona Wooing, April 26, 1915. A one-reel Selig western featuring Tom Mix.

Story: Mix plays the role of a cowboy unpopular with the local ranchers because he is raising sheep on a cattle ranch. He is equally disliked by Mexican Joe, who is vying with him for the love of a girl named Jean.

Some unfriendly cowboys stake out Tom on the desert, and Mexican Joe finds him and tortures him. Jean arrives on the scene and reluctantly agrees to marry the Mexican in order to save Tom.

Jean's father finds Tom and unties him. Together they round up some of the cowboys to go after Jean and the Mexican. After a brief gunfight, the Mexican is captured; he witnesses the marriage of Tom and Jean.

Cast: Tom Mix, Bessie Eyton, Sid Jordan, Pat Chrisman, Louella Maxam, and Billy Brunton.

Credits: Produced and directed by Tom Mix, written by William McLeod Raine.

A Matrimonial Boomerang, April 30, 1915. A one-reel Selig comedy featuring Tom Mix.

Cast: Tom Mix, Louella Maxam, Pat Chrisman, and Howard Farrell.

Credits: Produced by William Selig, directed by Tom Mix, and written by Edith Blumer.

Saved by Her Horse, May 26, 1915. A one-reel Selig adventure featuring Tom Mix. *Note:* The heroine rides Tony in this film.

Cast: Tom Mix, Louella Maxam, Sid Jordan, and Pat Chrisman.

Credits: Produced and directed by Tom Mix, written by Cornelius Shea.

Pals in Blue, May 26, 1915. A three-reel Selig western featuring Tom Mix. May be a re-release of a 1910 film.

Story: Two pals find themselves stranded and broke in a town after their Wild West show leaves, They are put in jail for not paying their bills. When they get out, they decide to join the army and are sent to Arizona.

The commander of the post sends them and a minor officer whose wife the commander desires on an assignment that puts their lives in danger from raiding Indians. Jerry is killed. Tom reaches the fort in time to send reinforcements to save the company. He also shoots the ruthless commander who is holding the other man's wife in his arms.

Cast: Tom Mix, Ada Gleason, Sid Jordan, Howard Farrell, Pat Chrisman, Edward Bradley, Bob Anderson, Al Merrill, and Eugenia Forde.

Credits: Produced by William Selig, directed and written by Tom Mix.

The Heart of the Sheriff, June 8, 1915. A one-reel Selig western featuring Tom Mix.

Cast: Tom Mix, Sid Jordan, and Louella Maxam.

Credits: Produced, directed, and written by Tom Mix.

The Girl of Gold Gulch, June 10, 1915. A one-reel Selig western starring Tom Mix and Victoria Forde.

Cast: Tom Mix, Victoria Forde, Joe Ryan, and Ed Jones.

Credits: Produced and directed by Tom Mix, written by Cornelius Shea.

The Parson Who Fled West, July 3, 1915. A one-reel Selig western comedy featuring Tom Mix.

Credits: Produced and directed by Burton L. King, written by Malcolm Douglas.

The Foreman of the Bar Z Ranch, July 15, 1915 (believed filmed in Las Vegas, New Mexico). A one-reel Selig western featuring Tom Mix.

Cast: Tom Mix, Louella Maxam, and Pat Chrisman.

Credits: Produced and directed by Tom Mix, written by Wallace C. Clifton.

The Child, the Dog and the Villain, July 17, 1915 (believed filmed in Las Vegas, New Mexico) or *The Girl, the Villain and the Dog.* A one-reel Selig western featuring Tom Mix.

Cast: Tom Mix, Louella Maxam, Sid Jordan, Pat Chrisman, Leo Maloney, and Pearl Hoxie, the little girl, with Teddy, the Selig dog.

Credits: Produced and directed by Tom Mix, written by Campbell McCullock.

The Taking of Mustang Pete, July 24, 1915 (believed filmed in Las Vegas, New Mexico). A one-reel Selig western featuring Tom Mix.
Cast: Tom Mix, Louella Maxam, Pat Chrisman, Leo Maloney, and Henry Pagett.
Credits: Produced and directed by Tom Mix, written by Emma Bell.

The Gold Dust and the Squaw, July 31, 1915 (believed filmed in Las Vegas, New Mexico). A one-reel Selig western featuring Tom Mix.
Cast: Tom Mix, Betty O'Neal, Sid Jordan, Leo Maloney, Pat Chrisman, and Bob Anderson.
Credits: Produced and directed by Tom Mix, written by Cornelius Shea.

The Lucky Deal, August 7, 1915 (believed filmed in Las Vegas, New Mexico). A one-reel Selig adventure featuring Tom Mix.
Cast: Tom Mix, Betty O'Neal, Sid Jordan, Leo Maloney, and Pat Chrisman.
Credits: Produced, directed, and written by Tom Mix.

Never Again, August 8, 1915 (believed filmed in Las Vegas, New Mexico). A one-reel Selig western featuring Tom Mix. *Note:* The story deals with a temperance theme.
Cast: Tom Mix, Victoria Forde, Sid Jordan, and Leo Maloney.
Credits: Produced, directed, and written by Tom Mix.

Rancher's Daughter (believed filmed in Las Vegas, New Mexico). *Note:* Possibly a working title or never released.

Country Drugstore (believed filmed in Las Vegas, New Mexico). *Note:* Possibly a working title or never released.

How Weary Went Wooing, or *Weary Goes A-Wooing,* September 4, 1915 (believed filmed in Las Vegas, New Mexico). A one-reel Selig western comedy featuring Tom Mix.
Cast: Tom Mix, Victoria Forde, Sid Jordan, and Leo Maloney.

Credits: Produced and directed by Tom Mix, written by B. M. Bower.

Never Again (2d version), September 11, 1915 (believed filmed in Las Vegas, New Mexico). A one-reel Selig western featuring Tom Mix.
Cast: Tom Mix, Victoria Forde, Sid Jordan, and Leo Maloney.
Credits: Produced, directed, and written by Tom Mix.

The Range Girl and the Cowboy, September 11, 1915 (believed filmed in Las Vegas, New Mexico). A one-reel Selig western featuring Tom Mix.
Cast: Tom Mix, Victoria Forde, Leo Maloney, and Sid Jordan.
Credits: Produced, directed, and written by Tom Mix.

The Auction Sale of Run-Down Ranch, September 11, 1915 (believed filmed in Las Vegas, New Mexico). A one-reel Selig western featuring Tom Mix.
Cast: Tom Mix, Victoria Forde, Pat Chrisman, Leo Maloney, and Joe Simkins.
Credits: Produced and directed by Tom Mix, written by Cornelius Shea.

Her Slight Mistake, September 18, 1915 (believed filmed in Las Vegas, New Mexico). A one-reel Selig drama featuring Tom Mix.
Cast: Tom Mix, Howard Farrell, Leo Maloney, Pat Chrisman, and Ethelyn Chrisman.
Credits: Produced and directed by Tom Mix, written by E. Winthrop Sargent.

The Girl and the Mail Bag, September 25, 1915 (believed filmed in Las Vegas, New Mexico). A one-reel Selig western featuring Tom Mix.
Cast: Tom Mix, Victoria Forde, Leo Maloney, and Sid Jordan.
Credits: Produced and directed by Tom Mix, written by Cornelius Shea.

The Stagecoach Guard, October 9, 1915 (believed filmed in Las Vegas, New Mexico). A one-reel Selig western featuring Tom Mix.
Cast: Tom Mix, Victoria Forde, and Sid Jordan.

Credits: Produced, directed, and written by Tom Mix.

The Brave Deserve the Fair, October 9, 1915 (believed filmed in Las Vegas, New Mexico). A two-reel Selig adventure featuring Tom Mix.
Cast: Tom Mix, Leo Maloney, Victoria Forde, and Sid Jordan.
Credits: Produced by William Selig, directed and written by Tom Mix.

The Race for a Gold Mine, October 16, 1915 (believed filmed in Las Vegas, New Mexico). A one-reel Selig western featuring Tom Mix.
Story: Tom and Nell arrive first and show Sid several gold nuggets. Sid makes Tom a partner in the mine and Tom embraces Nell.
Cast: Tom Mix, Victoria Forde, Sid Jordan, and Pat Chrisman.
Credits: Produced and directed by Tom Mix, written by Cornelius Shea.

The Foreman's Choice, October 20, 1915 (believed filmed in Las Vegas, New Mexico). A one-reel Selig western featuring Tom Mix.
Cast: Tom Mix, Victoria Forde, Pat Chrisman, Sid Jordan, and Howard Farrell.
Credits: Produced and directed by Tom Mix, written by Cornelius Shea.

Athletic Ambitions, October 23, 1915 (believed filmed in Las Vegas, New Mexico). A one-reel Selig western comedy featuring Tom Mix.
Cast: Tom Mix, Victoria Forde, Pat Chrisman, Sid Jordan, and Howard Farrell.
Credits: Produced, directed, and written by Tom Mix.

The Tenderfoot's Triumph, October 29, 1915 (believed filmed in Las Vegas, New Mexico). A one-reel Selig comedy featuring Tom Mix.
Cast: Tom Mix, Hazel Daly, Joe Simkins, Sid Jordan, and Pat Chrisman.
Credits: Produced and directed by Tom Mix, written by Cornelius Shea.

The Chef at Circle G, October 30, 1915 (believed filmed in Las Vegas, New Mexico). A one-reel Selig comedy featuring Tom Mix.
Cast: Tom Mix, Hazel Page, Pat Chrisman, and Sid Jordan.
Credits: Produced by William Selig, directed by Tom Mix, and written by Edwin Ray Coffin.

The Impersonation of Tom, November 6, 1915 (believed filmed in Las Vegas, New Mexico). A one-reel Selig western comedy featuring Tom Mix.
Cast: Tom Mix, Hazel Daly, Sid Jordan, Pat Chrisman, and Babe Chrisman.
Credits: Produced and directed by Tom Mix, written by Cornelius Shea.

With the Aid of the Law, November 11, 1915 (believed filmed in Las Vegas, New Mexico). A one-reel Selig western featuring Tom Mix.
Credits: Produced and directed by Tom Mix, written by Marshal E. Gamon.

Bad Man Bobbs, November 13, 1915 (believed filmed in Las Vegas, New Mexico). A one-reel Selig comedy featuring Tom Mix.
Cast: Tom Mix, Ethelyn Chrisman, Sid Jordan, and Pat Chrisman.
Credits: Produced and directed by Tom Mix, written by Edwin Ray Coffin.

On the Eagle's Trail, November 27, 1915 (believed filmed in Las Vegas, New Mexico). A one-reel Selig western featuring Tom Mix.
Cast: Tom Mix, Victoria Forde, Joe Simkins, and Sid Jordan.
Credits: Produced and directed by Tom Mix, written by Cornelius Shea.

1916

The Wagon Trail. A one-reel Selig western featuring Tom Mix.
Review: The Wagon Trail, a colorful western romance in which Tom Mix displays to wonderful advantage his shooting, fighting, and riding ability. Patrons will find *The Wagon Trail* much to their liking.

The Long Trail. A one-reel Selig western featuring Tom Mix.

Cast: Tom Mix and Frank Walsh.
Credits: Produced by William Selig, directed by Frank Boggs, and written by Tom Mix.

The Desert Calls Its Own, January 1, 1916. A one-reel Selig western featuring Tom Mix.
Cast: Tom Mix, Victoria Forde, Ethelyn Chrisman, Sid Jordan, and Pat Chrisman.

A Mix-up in the Movies, January 22, 1916. A one-reel Selig comedy featuring Tom Mix.
Cast: Tom Mix, Pat Chrisman, Babe Chrisman, Joe Simkins, and Sid Jordan.
Credits: Produced, directed, and written by Tom Mix.

Making Good, January 23, 1916. A one-reel Selig action film featuring Tom Mix.
Cast: Tom Mix, Victoria Forde, Pat Chrisman, and Joe Ryan.
Credits: Produced, directed, and written by Tom Mix.

The Passing of Pete, February 11, 1916. A one-reel Selig western picture with Tom Mix.
Cast: Tom Mix, Victoria Forde, Ethelyn Chrisman, Sid Jordan, and Betty Keller.
Credits: Produced, directed, and written by Tom Mix.

A $5,000 Elopement, March 3, 1916. A one-reel Selig western featuring Tom Mix.
Cast: Tom Mix, Victoria Forde, Sid Jordan, Joe Ryan, and Chet Ryan.
Credits: Produced and directed by Tom Mix, written by Cornelius Shea.

Trilby's Love Disaster, March 4, 1916. A one-reel Selig drama featuring Tom Mix.
Cast: Tom Mix, Victoria Forde, Ethelyn Chrisman, Joe Ryan, and Betty Keller.
Credits: Produced, directed, and written by Tom Mix.

Along the Border, March 18, 1916. A one-reel Selig western featuring Tom Mix.

Story: Grace, the daughter of Jim, a ranch owner, and Tom, a Texas Ranger, are in love. Buck is the disappointed rival who swears to get revenge. He plans with Delgado, an outlaw, to capture Grace and her father and hold them for ransom. Grace makes a sensational escape and tells Tom and his pals about the outlaw's plans. Tom and the rangers capture Delgado and his outlaw band and rescue Grace's father.
Cast: Tom Mix, Victoria Forde, Sid Jordan, Joe Ryan, and Joe Simkins.
Credits: Produced, directed, and written by Tom Mix.

Too Many Chefs, April 1, 1916. A one-reel Selig adventure featuring Tom Mix.
Cast: Tom Mix, Victoria Forde, and Joe Ryan.
Credits: Produced, directed, and written by Tom Mix.

The Man Within, April 15, 1916. A three-reel Selig western featuring Tom Mix.
Cast: Tom Mix, Victoria Forde, Sid Jordan, Pat Chrisman, and Joe Ryan.
Credits: Produced by William Selig, directed by Tom Mix, and written by E. Lynn Summers.

The Sheriff's Duty, April 22, 1916. A one-reel Selig western drama featuring Tom Mix.
Cast: Tom Mix, Betty Keller, Pat Chrisman, Sid Jordan, and Joe Ryan.
Credits: Produced, directed, and written by Tom Mix.

Crooked Trails, May 13, 1916. A one-reel Selig adventure featuring Tom Mix.
Story: Irene returns to the ranch from boarding school. She sees Dick, the ranch foreman, defeat Poncho, a half-breed, in a bucking bronco contest. She admires Dick's ability as a rider and a friendship springs up between them. Poncho, who also loves Irene, is outraged.
Robertson, a cattle buyer, visits the ranch with a large sum of money. Poncho and a friend capture Irene and Robertson, but Irene makes a sensational escape. Dick and the cowboys see Poncho

"A $5,000 ELOPEMENT"—Selig Western Drama Featuring TOM MIX.
"THE BATTLE"—Vitagraph Comedy, With HUGHIE MACK.

A $5,000 Elopement. **(Author's collection.)**

chasing Irene and capture him. They then go after the other outlaws and surround them. Dick is wounded in the gun battle, but the outlaws are defeated.

Cast: Tom Mix, Victoria Forde, Pat Chrisman, Sid Jordan, and Joe Ryan.

Credits: Produced, directed, and written by Tom Mix.

Going West to Make Good, May 13, 1916. A one-reel Selig western drama, featuring that capable player Tom Mix.

Story: Tom is a wealthy easterner in love with Vicky. Vicky refuses to marry Tom, hoping to find real romance in the West. She goes west to visit her uncle, who owns a ranch. Tom follows Vicky but gets there first and becomes a cowboy.

When Vicky is about to arrive, three bandits hold up the stage. They kill the stagecoach driver and the horses run off with Vicky. Tom sees the runaway stage, overtakes it, and saves Vicky, who realizes

that Tom is a true cowboy in every sense of the word.

Cast: Tom Mix, Victoria Forde, and Joe Ryan.

Credits: Produced, directed, and written by Tom Mix.

The Cowpuncher's Peril, May 26, 1916. A one-reel Selig western featuring Tom Mix.

Cast: Tom Mix, Victoria Forde, Pat Chrisman, and Joe Ryan.

Credits: Produced, directed, and written by Tom Mix.

Taking a Chance, June 3, 1916. A one-reel Selig western drama featuring Tom Mix.

Cast: Tom Mix, Victoria Forde, Pat Chrisman, and Joe Ryan.

Credits: Produced, directed, and written by Tom Mix.

Some Duel, June 17, 1916. A one-reel Selig western featuring Tom Mix.

Cast: Tom Mix, Victoria Forde, Joe Ryan, Sid Jordan, and Pat Chrisman.

Credits: Produced, directed, and written by Tom Mix.

Legal Advice, June 24, 1916. A one-reel Selig western comedy featuring Tom Mix.

Story: A new lady lawyer comes to town, and the cowboys go all out, breaking the laws in hopes of securing her legal advice. When Tom finally gets his day in court, he finds out that the pretty young lawyer is wed to an elderly gent. It is more than Tom can stand, and he puts an end to his own miserable life.

Cast: Tom Mix, Sid Jordan, Victoria Forde, Pat Chrisman, Joe Ryan, and George Panky.

Credits: Produced, directed, and written by Tom Mix.

Shooting Up the Movies, July 1, 1916. A two-reel Selig western comedy featuring Tom Mix.

Cast: Tom Mix, Victoria Forde, Sid Jordan, Howard Farrell, Hazel Daly, and Joe Ryan.

Credits: Produced, directed, and written by Tom Mix.

Local Color (2d version), July 7, 1916 (believed filmed in Las Vegas, New Mexico).

Story: The word is out at the ranch that a young woman writer, Vicky, is coming from the East to get some local color for a new book. The cowboys decide they should cooperate, so they organize all sorts of activities they think are typical of a lawless West—they want to make sure that their visitor gets plenty of local color.

They even trick Vicky into a fake wedding with Tom, but the laughs on Tom and the cowboys because the fake minister turns out to be a real one.

Cast: Tom Mix, Victoria Forde, Sid Jordan, Joe Simkins, and Joe Ryan.

Credits: Produced, directed, and written by Tom Mix.

An Angelic Attitude, July 15, 1916. A one-reel Selig western comedy featuring Tom Mix.

Story: Al calls an old friend, Dan, to let him know that a pretty young lady named Grace wants to come West and sketch some real western scenery. Grace is to arrive at Dan's ranch in a few days. Dan is elderly, but the sight of Grace arouses youthful emotions. Dan's son, Tom, also admires the pretty girl.

Tom and Grace fall in love, but the old man is always interrupting them. Grace cons the old man into believing she wants to paint a picture of an angel. As the old man is left hanging helplessly from a tree, Tom and Grace sneak off to enjoy a few hours alone.

Cast: Tom Mix, Victoria Forde, Joe Ryan, and Sid Jordan.

Credits: Produced and directed by Tom Mix, written by Edwin Ray Coffin.

A Western Masquerade, July 22, 1916. A one-reel Selig western comedy featuring Tom Mix. *Note:* Tom Mix appears dressed as a woman in one scene.

Cast: Tom Mix, Victoria Forde, Sid Jordan, and Joe Ryan.

Credits: Produced, directed, and written by Tom Mix.

A Bear of a Story, July 29, 1916. A one-reel Selig western comedy with Tom Mix.

Story: Tom is engaged to Vicky. Vicky's best friend has a pet bear. Vicky insists that Tom get her a pet bear too.

Tom and Sid crawl into a bear's den, trying to get a cub, and are run out by an angry mother bear. The bear chases Tom up a tree and goes up after him. Sid goes back to the ranch house to get a saw. Tom saws off the branch holding the bear, and the bear hits the ground running. The bear tries to attack Tom's and Sid's horses. Finally, against the bear's best wishes, Tom and Sid rope her and run her down a hill to the ranch house.

By the time Tom and Sid get the bear to the ranch house, the pet bear has scratched Vicky's finger, and Vicky wants nothing more to do with bears. After risking their lives to get the bear, Tom and Sid faint, slumping gradually to the ground.

Cast: Tom Mix, Victoria Forde, Sid Jordan, and Betty Keller.

Ad for *Going West to Make Good*. (Courtesy of Francis P. Clark.)

Credits: Produced, directed, and written by Tom Mix.

Roping a Sweetheart, August 5, 1916. A one-reel Selig western comedy featuring Tom Mix.
Cast: Tom Mix, Victoria Forde, Sid Jordan, and Pat Chrisman.
Credits: Produced, directed, and written by Tom Mix.

Tom's Strategy, August 12, 1916. A one-reel Selig western featuring Tom Mix.
Cast: Tom Mix, Victoria Forde, Betty Keller, and Howard Farrell.
Credits: Produced, directed, and written by Tom Mix.

The Taming of Grouchy Bill, August 19, 1916. A one-reel Selig western comedy featuring Tom Mix.
Cast: Tom Mix, Victoria Forde, Sid Jordan, Pat Chrisman, and Joe Ryan.
Credits: Produced, directed, and written by Tom Mix.

The Pony Express Rider, August 26, 1916. A two-reel Selig western featuring Tom Mix.
Cast: Tom Mix, Pat Chrisman, Sid Jordan, Victoria Forde, and Joe Ryan.

Credits: Produced, directed, and written by Tom Mix.

A Corner in Water, September 2, 1916. A one-reel Selig western drama featuring Tom Mix.
Cast: Tom Mix, Victoria Forde, Pat Chrisman, Joe Ryan, and Chet Ryan.
Credits: Produced, directed, and written by Tom Mix.

The Raiders, September 9, 1916. A one-reel Selig western drama featuring Tom Mix.
Cast: Tom Mix, Victoria Forde, Pat Chrisman, and Sid Jordan.
Credits: Produced, directed, and written by Tom Mix.

The Canby Hill Outlaws, September 10, 1916. A one-reel Selig western featuring Tom Mix.
Cast: Tom Mix, Pat Chrisman, Victoria Forde, and Sid Jordan.
Credits: Produced, directed, and written by Tom Mix.

A Mistake in Rustlers, September 23, 1916. A one-reel Selig western featuring Tom Mix.
Cast: Tom Mix, Victoria Forde, Leo Maloney, Sid Jordan, and Pat Chrisman.

Credits: Produced, directed, and written by Tom Mix.

An Eventful Evening, September 30, 1916. A one-reel Selig adventure featuring Tom Mix.
Cast: Tom Mix, Victoria Forde, Betty Keller, and Pat Chrisman.
Credits: Produced and directed by Tom Mix, written by Victoria Forde.

The Way of the Red Man (2d version), October 3, 1916. A one-reel Selig western featuring Tom Mix.
Credits: Directed and written by Tom Mix.

A Close Call, October 7, 1916. A one-reel Selig adventure featuring Tom Mix.
Cast: Tom Mix, Victoria Forde, Pat Chrisman, Joe Ryan, and Sid Jordan.
Credits: Produced, directed, and written by Tom Mix.

Tom's Sacrifice, October 14, 1916. A one-reel Selig western featuring Tom Mix.
Cast: Tom Mix, Victoria Forde, Joe Ryan, Howard Farrell, Joe Simkins, and Sid Jordan.
Credits: Produced and written by Victoria Forde.

When Cupid Slipped, October 21, 1916. A one-reel Selig action comedy featuring Tom Mix.
Cast: Tom Mix, Pat Chrisman, Victoria Forde, and Sid Jordan.
Credits: Produced and written by Victoria Forde.

The Sheriff's Blunder, November 4, 1916. A two-reel Selig western featuring Tom Mix.
Cast: Tom Mix, Sid Jordan, and Victoria Forde.
Credits: Produced, directed, and written by Tom Mix.

Mistakes Will Happen, November 11, 1916. A one-reel Selig comedy featuring Tom Mix.
Cast: Tom Mix, Victoria Forde, Pat Chrisman, and Sid Jordan.
Credits: Produced, directed, and written by Tom Mix.

The Golden Thought, December 9, 1916. A two-reel Selig western featuring Tom Mix.
Cast: Tom Mix, Victoria Forde, Sid Jordan, Earl Deming, Alice Burke, Barney Furey, Lily Clark, and Pat Chrisman.
Credits: Produced and directed by Tom Mix, written by J. A. Lacy.

Twisted Trails, December 11, 1916. A three-reel Selig drama of the west featuring Tom Mix.
Ad Story: Twisted Trails is an unusual drama of the West. The Selig Co. asserts that *Twisted Trails* is one of the most thrilling and meritorious films that has been released in some time. An exceptional cast including Tom Mix, Bessie Eyton, Eugenie Besserer, Al W. Filson, and William Machin, is featured in the play.

Tom Mix presents one of the most thrilling action scenes ever seen on the motion picture screen. In order to escape from his pursuers, Tom and his galloping horse dash across a narrow log bridge which spans a chasm. Should his horse have made one misstep, both horse and rider would have plunged onto the rocks hundreds of feet below.
Review: Not only is *Twisted Trails* a feature drama in every detail, but there is some unusual photography contained therein, notably a rain storm, accompanied by vivid flashes of lightning. The photoplay is replete with exciting situations and dramatic climaxes.
Cast: See story; including Pat Chrisman and Sid Jordan.
Credits: Produced and directed by Tom Mix, written by Edwin Ray Coffin.

Starring in Western Stuff, December 23, 1916. A one-reel Selig western featuring Tom Mix.
Cast: Tom Mix, Victoria Forde, Sid Jordan, Pat Chrisman, Ethelyn Chrisman, and Pete Bender.
Credits: Produced, directed, and written by Tom Mix.

1917

The Saddle Girth, January 23, 1917. A one-reel Selig western featuring Tom Mix.

Tom's first *Heart of Texas Ryan* **film originated in February 1917. (Courtesy of Art Evans.)**

Cast: Tom Mix, Louella Maxam, and Sid Jordan.

Credits: Produced, directed, and written by Tom Mix.

The Luck That Jealousy Brought, January 24, 1917. A one-reel Selig action comedy featuring Tom Mix.

Cast: Tom Mix, Louella Maxam, Sid Jordan, and Pat Chrisman.

Credits: Produced and directed by Tom Mix, written by Cornelius Shea.

The Heart of Texas Ryan, February 2, 1917. A five-reel Selig western featuring Tom Mix as Jack Parker. *Note:* This film was released in 1923 by Exclusive Features and retitled *Single Shot Parker,* not to be confused with the 1914 Selig original of the same title.

Cast: Tom Mix, Bessie Eyton, George Fawcett, Goldie Colwell, Frank Campeau, William Rhyno, Leo Maloney, Charles Gerard, and Sid Jordan.

Fox

1917

Hearts and Saddles, March 11, 1917. A two-reel western comedy featuring Tom Mix and Tony.

Cast: Tom Mix, Victoria Forde, Sid Jordan, Pat Chrisman, Victor Portez, and George Panky.

Credits: Produced by William Fox, directed by Tom Mix and Bob Eddy, written by Tom Mix.

A Roman Cowboy, May 6, 1917. A two-reel western comedy featuring Tom Mix and Tony.

Six-Shooter Andy, **Fox, 1918. (Author's collection.)**

Cast: Tom Mix, Sid Jordan, Victoria Forde, and Vic Frith.

Credits: Produced by William Fox, directed and written by Tom Mix.

Six-Cylinder Love, June 10, 1917. A two-reel action comedy featuring Tom Mix and Tony.

Cast: Tom Mix, Victoria Forde, and Sid Jordan.

Credits: Produced by William Fox, directed and written by Tom Mix.

A Soft Tenderfoot, July 5, 1917. A two-reel western comedy featuring Tom Mix and Tony.

Cast: Tom Mix, Victoria Forde, Pat Chrisman, Sid Jordan, and Billy Mason.

Credits: Produced by William Fox, directed and written by Tom Mix.

Durand of the Badlands, August 12, 1917. A five-reel western featuring Dustin Farnum.

Cast: Dustin Farnum, Tom Mix,

Winifred Kingston, Frankie Lee, Babe Chrisman, Lee Morris, Amy Jerome, and Tony as Black Bess.

Credits: Produced by William Fox, directed by Richard Stanton, and written by Maibelle H. Justice.

Tom and Jerry Mix, September 2, 1917. A two-reel western featuring Tom Mix and Tony.

Cast: Tom Mix, Victoria Forde, Sid Jordan, Pat Chrisman, and Floyd Anderson.

Credits: Produced, directed, and written by Tom Mix.

1918

Cupid's Round-up, January 13, 1918. A five-reel western featuring Tom Mix and Tony.

Cast: Tom Mix, Wanda Petit, Roy Watson, E. B. Tilton, Edwin Booth, Verne Mersereau, Al Padgett, and Eugenia Ford.

Credits: Produced by William Fox, directed by Edward LeSaint, and written by Charles Kenyon; based on a story by George Scarborough.

Six-Shooter Andy, February 24, 1918. A five-reel western featuring Tom Mix and Tony.

Cast: Tom Mix, Pat Chrisman, Enid Markey, Sam DeGrasse, Bert Woodruff, Bob Fleming, Jack Planck, Ben Kammer, George Stone, Lewis Sargent, Buddy Messinger, Raymond Lee, Virginia Lee Corbin, Violet Radcliff, Beulah Burns, Thelma Burns, Charles Stevens, Vivian Planck, and Dick Hunter.

Credits: Produced by William Fox, directed by Chester and Sidney Franklin, and written by Bernard McConville.

Western Blood, April 14, 1918. A five-reel western featuring Tom Mix and Tony.

Cast: Tom Mix, Victoria Forde, Barney Furey, Pat Chrisman, Frank Clark, and Buck Jones.

Credits: Produced by William Fox, directed and written by Lynn Reynolds; based on a story by Tom Mix.

Ace High, June 9, 1918. A five-reel western featuring Tom Mix and Tony.

Cast: Tom Mix, Lawrence Payton, Virginia Lee Corbin, Pat Chrisman, Kathleen O'Connor, Lloyd Pearl, Lewis Sargent, Colin Chase, Jay Horley, and Georgie Johnson.

Credits: Produced by William Fox, directed and written by Lynn Reynolds.

Who Is Your Father? July 7, 1918. A two-reel comedy drama featuring Tom Mix and Tony.

Cast: Tom Mix.

Credits: Produced by William Fox and Henry Lehrmann, directed and written by Tom Mix.

Mr. Logan, U.S.A., September 8, 1918. A five-reel western featuring Tom Mix and Tony.

Cast: Tom Mix, Kathleen O'Connor, Smoke Turner, Dick Le Reno, Val Paul, Maude Emory, Charles LeMoyne, and Jack Dill.

Credits: Produced by William Fox, directed and written by Lynn Reynolds.

Fame and Fortune, November 8, 1918. A five-reel western featuring Tom Mix and Tony.

Story: The film tells of a town that has driven out certain men because they are too good for it. These men gather in a new place and only await a leader to take vengeance on their persecutors. About this time, Tom returns home after an absence of many years, comes to town, and finds that every effort has been made to cheat him out of his inheritance. He becomes a leader of men for the new town, and when a woman he loves is stolen by the leader of the old town, the action begins to pile up. From there on, thrilling things happen. This is said to be the most exciting photoplay Mr. Mix has ever appeared in.

Cast: Tom Mix, Kathleen O'Connor, Virginia Lee Corbin, Jay Morley, Pat Chrisman, Lawrence Peyton, Colin Chase, Virginia Brown Faire, Lewi Sargent, George Nicholls, Charles McHugh, Annette DeFoe, Val Paul, Jack Dill, E. N. Wallock, and Clarence Burton.

Credits: Produced by William Fox, directed by Lynn Reynolds, and written by Bennett Cole; based on a story by Charles A. Seltzer.

1919

Treat 'Em Rough, January 5, 1919. A five-reel western featuring Tom Mix and Tony. *Note:* Tom bulldogs a steer to split a stampeding herd, thereby saving his and the heroine's life.

Cast: Tom Mix, Jane Novak, Smoke Turner, Jack Curtis, Charles LeMoyne, and Val Paul.

Credits: Produced by William Fox, directed and written by Lynn Reynolds; based on a story by Charles A. Seltzer.

Hell Roaring Reform, February 16, 1919. A five-reel western featuring Tom Mix and Tony.

Cast: Tom Mix, Kathleen O'Connor, Smoke Turner, George Berrell, Jack Curtis, and Cupid Morgan.

Tom Mix with bear in *Fighting for Gold*, Fox, 1919. (Author's collection.)

Credits: Produced by William Fox, directed by Edward LeSaint, and written by Charles Kenyon; based on a story by Anthony Roach.

Fighting for Gold, March 30, 1919. A five-reel western featuring Tom Mix and Tony.

Story: Tom is an English miner working a claim in the United States. To prevent trouble, Tom must look after a wayward partner and prevent a British firm working the land next to him from jumping his claim. Falling in love adds new troubles.

Tom is accused of a crime he didn't commit and he finds he must continuously fight against overwhelming odds to keep his mine and the girl he loves. Tom triumphs in the end.

Cast: Tom Mix, Lucille Young, Teddy Sampson, Sid Jordan, George Nichols, Jack Nelson, Harry Lonsdale, Robert Dunbar, Frank Clark, and Hattie Buskirk.

Credits: Produced by William Fox, directed by Edward LeSaint, and written by Charles Kenyon; based on a story by W. McLeod Raine.

The Coming of the Law, May 11, 1919. A five-reel western featuring Tom Mix and Tony.

Cast: Tom Mix, Jane Novak, Brownie Vernon, George Nichols, Jack Curtis, Sid Jordan, Smoke Turner, Charles Le Moyne, Pat Chrisman, Lewis Sargent, Jack Dill, Harry Dunkinson, Banty Caldwell, Earl Simpson, Dick Hunter, Buck Jones, Pedro Leone, and Vic Frith.

Credits: Produced by William Fox, directed by A. Rosen, and written by Denison Clift; based on a story by Charles A. Seltzer.

The Wilderness Trail, July 6, 1919. A five-reel western featuring Tom Mix and Tony.

Cast: Tom Mix, Colleen Moore, Sid Jordan, Frank M. Clark, Lulu Warrenton, Pat Chrisman, and Jack Nelson.

Credits: Produced by William Fox, directed by Edward LeSaint, written by Charles Kenyon; based on a story by Frank Williams.

Rough Riding Romance, August 24, 1919. A five-reel western featuring Tom Mix and Tony.

Cast: Tom Mix, Sid Jordan, Juanita Hansen, Pat Chrisman, Jack Nelson, Spottiswood Aitken, and Frankie Lee.

Credits: Produced by William Fox, directed by Arthur Rosson, and written by Charles Kenyon.

The Speed Maniac, October 19, 1919. A five-reel action film featuring Tom Mix and Tony.

News Story: The biggest, most daring auto race ever filmed for a motion picture—a real race over the course at Santa Monica, California—is shown in Tom Mix's new Fox photoplay, *The Speed Maniac,* with Mix himself driving the car that is wrecked in the contest. The picture is to be shown at the Victoria theater tonight.

Thousands of people were lined up along the course to watch this race. They did not know that the steering knuckle on the car that Mix drove had been weakened, and never dreamed that the star was taking neck-breaking chances. When his car turned a complete somersault and he was thrown out on the road, a cry went up from a thousand throats, "He's killed!"

But nothing serious ever happens to Tom Mix, no matter how great the risk he takes, because besides being a man of brawn, he is a man of brain. He reasons out his death-defying feats, timing and calculating them to a hair breath. Indeed, Mix seems to be possessed of a life-preserving instinct in the midst of the greatest danger.

This wonderful scene, the most realistic race ever filmed, is only one of the many sensations in *The Speed Maniac.*

Cast: Tom Mix, Eva Novak, Buck Jones, Charles K. French, Ernest Shields, Jack Curtis, Helen Wright, Charles Miles, Maynard Mack, Pat Harmon, Lee Shumway, George E. Stone, and George Hackathorne.

Credits: Produced by William Fox, directed by Edward LeSaint, and written by Denison Clift; based on a story by H. H. van Loan.

1920

The Feud, January 25, 1920. A five-reel drama featuring Tom Mix and Tony. *Note:* Tom plays a dual roles as Jere Lynch and John Smith; Eva Novak plays dual role as Betty Summers and Betty Brown.

Story: The film is set in the days of hoop skirts, crinolines, men quick on the trigger, chivalry, and beautiful women.

For generations a feud has existed between two families. The fathers clash on sight, and even the servants of the rival clans hate each other.

But one Lynch and one Summers did not share the heritage of hate. Jere Lynch and Betty Summers, secretly in love and afraid of precipitating a shooting affray, make the cabin of Nancy, a kindly black woman, their secret rendezvous. As Nancy tells their fortunes, she predicts the union of a Lynch and a Summers— but not till death had visited one of the families.

Betty's father and mother have set their hearts on marrying Betty to Cal Brown (Joseph Bennett), a distant relative who visited the Summers to further his suit. But his wooing has made slow progress.

While Betty's father and brother and Cal Brown are out driving, the horses run away. Jere stops the runaways but is knocked unconscious. The Summers, out of gratitude, revive him, but they find Betty's picture in a locket tied with ribbon around his neck. The Summers deliver the unconscious Jere to his home. There the fathers clash, each of them vowing to shoot Jere if the love affair continues.

Jere and Betty, therefore, plan to elope. But Jere's visit to the minister is discovered, which precipitates a shooting affray. Ben Summers (Lloyd Bacon) kills Jere's father and Jere shoots Ben.

Jere rides, with a posse in pursuit, to the cabin where Betty is waiting for him. He has time only to tell Betty he is going out West and to beg of her to wait till he can send for her. Then he rides for his life.

On the Santa Fe trail, Jere and a pal leave the emigrants' wagon train to ride after a herd of buffalo. In the hunt Jere injures his leg. In the midst of the desert he meets Ray Saunders (Jean Calhoun), an emigrant girl whose father has just perished in the desert. Ray dresses Jere's leg and carries her to the wagon train.

Jere and Betty are still in love, but Jere's sister, in enmity, plans to end that by withholding Jere's letter enclosed to her for Betty, then telling Betty that Jere is dead and writing to Jere that Betty has married Cal Brown.

As time goes on and neither Jere nor Betty hears from the other, the sister's machinations have the desired effect. Jere gradually falls in love with Ray.

Later Jere achieves a wagon train of his own, which he guides over the Santa Fe trail, carrying with him his wife, Ray, and their infant son. The train is attacked by Indians. Jere decides to break through in a desperate attempt to bring troops from the fort. Jere and a comrade made the attempt, but Jere's horse is shot under him. Then his pal is shot. Jere, on the second horse, reaches the fort, badly wounded and barely conscious, hanging from the saddle horn.

That night, back home, Betty is married to Cal Brown. Jere dies of his wounds.

The troops reached the scene of the settler's last stand the next morning. The only person left alive is the infant son of Jere and Ray.

Thirty years later, John Smith, the grown son of Jere and Ray, is one of the participants in the Western land rush. Among the other land seekers are Betty Summers Brown, daughter of Betty and Cal Brown.

Betty asks a claim that caught the eye of Bill Brady (Sid Jordan), a passing ruffian. Bill was attempting to preempt the claim by force when John Smith saves the day. The acquaintance thus quickly ripened into love.

Betty and John Smith are married, but the rift in the lute comes when Betty's grandmother arrives, for she promptly recognizes John Smith as a Lynch, and the home is broken up.

Some time later a friend informs John Smith that his wife has a male guest at her home of whom she seems very fond. John rides over, ready to kill the intruder, only to find that the male guest is his own son, newly born. The couple reconciles, and the marriage of a Summers and a Lynch becomes a happy one.

Cast: Tom Mix, Eva Novak, Claire McDowell, J. Arthur Mackey, John Cossar, Molly McConnell, Lloyd Bacon, Sid Jordan, Lucretia Harris, Guy Eakins, Jean Calhoun, Joseph Bennett, Frank Thorne, and Nelson McDowell.

Credits: Produced by William Fox, directed by Edward Le Saint, and written by Charles Kenyon; based on a story by Charles Kenyon.

The Cyclone, January 25, 1920. A five-reel western featuring Tom Mix and Tony. *Note:* The stunt in this film was cleverly staged using lightly plastered chicken-fire floors. The floors were weak enough for horse and riders to crash through but strong enough to break their falls and prevent injury.

Story: Sergeant Tom is a champion rider and marksman for the Northwest Mounted Police. Tom investigates the death of another policeman who was hot on the trail of a band of smugglers. Tom discovers the head of the gang is the range boss for the father of his sweetheart. The range boss is smuggling Chinese refugees and their valuables to Vancouver.

The boss escapes at the border and returns to the ranch to capture the heroine. Tom follows the range boss to the ranch and arrests him. However, as Tom is backing up, he falls off the porch. Every time Tom tries to get up, the range boss kicks him, knocking him back down. The range boss escapes with the girl and takes her to his hideout in Vancouver's Chinatown. Tom follows the range boss to the hideout, rides up three floors of stairs, rescues the girl, and falls through two floors to the ground level. The mounties arrive on cue and arrest the range boss and his gang.

Cast: Tom Mix, Colleen Moore, William Ellingford, Buck Jones, and Henry Herbert.

Credits: Produced by William Fox, directed by Cliff Smith, and written by J. Anthony Roach.

The Dare-Devil, March 7, 1920. A five-reel western featuring Tom Mix and Tony.

Pressbook cover of *The Dare Devil*, Fox, 1920. (Author's collection.)

Story: A western ranch owner is enjoying his pipe in the cool of the evening when queer things begin to happen to the shack of the cowboys.

Seizing his gun, he rushes over in time to see his foreman come head over heels out the door. Then the side of the house is shattered by a mass of cowboys and the roof caves in.

Surrounded by the debris stands "Anything Once" Atkinson (Tom), son of the railway president.

A word from the ranch owner, and the cowboys close in on Atkinson, who, after a desperate struggle, is tied up and sent back to his despairing and discouraged father, who had hoped the ranch would make an industrious man of his son.

His father refuses to see him, but Atkinson is determined. He crashes through the glass fanlight of his father's office, lands at his feet, and begs for one more chance.

Buchanan Atkinson (George Hernandez) then sends his son to Calm City, Arizona, and wires the superintendent there of his intention. Gilroy Blake (Lee Shumway), a dispatcher, arranges a reception for the train, but on the arrival of the train, Atkinson is a minus quantity, having become mixed up in a fight with the porters and making his escape from the top of the train half a mile from the station.

Atkinson walks into town just in time to see a celebration in honor of John Barleycorn, who is to be buried by law at midnight the same night.

The sight of a tenderfoot is the signal for the cowboys to start the fun. They shoot at the feet of the young man without effect. Finally one of them shoots in half the cane carried by Atkinson, who, failing to get satisfaction by word of mouth, promptly hands the cowboy the coup de grace.

Turning, Atkinson comes face to face with Superintendent Spencer (Charles K. French), his daughter, and Gilroy Blake. He is not cordially welcomed by the superintendent or dispatcher, but Alice Spencer (Eva Novak) greets him kindly.

Atkinson is impressed by the delightful daughter of the West, and makes better progress in his efforts to entertain her than in his work, and thus displeases Blake, who has secretly loved Alice.

Spencer's position as superintendent is in jeopardy owing to a series of train robberies in his division by Black Donlin's gang. The sheriff is unable to find out anything about the bandits.

Urged by Alice, who tells him that her father's position is threatened, Atkinson sets out on the trail of the bandits and agrees to represent himself as Slim Higgins, a notorious outlaw, in order to get in with the band and capture them.

Atkinson invades the outlaw's cave, hidden behind the waterfall. He passes himself off to Black Donlin as Slim Higgins and quickly learns their secrets.

Donlin, however, learns from Blake, with whom he plans the robberies of the bullion on the trains, the identity of the newcomer. On Donlin's return to his secret headquarters, Atkinson barely escapes with his life.

Alice Spencer is kidnapped by Blake and put aboard the train, which is to be held up by the gang, but Atkinson, racing through a shortcut, reaches the side of the moving train. Galloping along, he shoots the lock from the side of the car in which the girl is a prisoner, seizes her and swings her onto his saddle. He tells her to ride for the sheriff, grasps the side of the moving train, and jumps aboard to guard the treasure from the outlaws. The train is held up. As the outlaw chief opens the door, Atkinson's powerful right knocks him backward.

Atkinson's fierce singlehanded fight against tremendous odds is ended by the arrival of Alice Spencer with the sheriff's posse. The bandits flee, keeping up a running fight with their pursuers and take refuge in a shack. Atkinson, with the assistance of the cowboys, breaks in the walls of the building and captures the desperadoes.

The news of Atkinson's capture of the outlaws spreads rapidly. It reaches his father at the same time the news of his marriage to Alice Spencer does.

With his bride, Atkinson returns to receive his father's blessing. Throwing a

The Terror, **Fox, 1920. (Author's collection.)**

rope to a window near the roof of the building, he climbs up and into the window, thus completing an exciting episode in the career of a tenderfoot who was helped by a woman's love, and won his spurs in the lawless West.

Cast: Tom Mix, Eva Novak, Lucille Young, Pat Chrisman, Charles K. French, Lee Shumway, Sid Jordan, Harry Dunkinson, Lafe McKee, and George Hernandez.

Credits: Produced by William Fox, directed and written by Tom Mix.

Desert Love, April 11, 1920. A five-reel western featuring Tom Mix and Tony.

Cast: Tom Mix, Eva Novak, Francelia Billington, Lester Cuneo, Charles K. French, and Jack Curtis.

Credits: Produced by William Fox, directed and written by Jacques Jaccard; story by Tom Mix.

The Terror, May 16, 1920. A five-reel western featuring Tom Mix and Tony.

Cast: Tom Mix, Lester Cuneo, Francelia Billington, Lucille Young, Joseph Bennett, Charles K. French, and Wilbur Higby.

Credits: Produced by William Fox, directed and written by Jacques Jaccard; story by Tom Mix.

Three Gold Coins, July 4, 1920. A five-reel western featuring Tom Mix and Tony. *Note:* Filmed in Prescott, Arizona.

Story: The happy-go-lucky owner of six hundred acres of apparently worthless land, Bob Fleming (Tom), his funds exhausted, partakes of his last meal. While doing so, however, he hears an extravagant offer of three dollars to anyone who dares to ride and keep his seat on a bucking and unbroken horse. Undaunted by its contortions, Bob approaches the beast and mounts it skillfully, retaining his seat despite the horse's convolutions and desperate attempts to dislodge him.

With his hard-earned spoils, Fleming makes his way to a roulette table at which he wins, but the croupier suspends the game when Bob stakes above the prescribed limit. He demands his winnings, and the place is soon in an uproar, but Bob gains the upper hand and keeps his assailants at bay with a hose, then rides away into the hills to ruminate.

Disturbed by the sound of a motor, Bob discerns a high-powered car winding through the valley. He sees Black Duncan (Pat Chrisman), a notorious outlaw, and his men hold up the occupants. Riding furiously to the rescue, Fleming is too late to be of assistance, and the passengers, fearing that he is another bandit, make all possible speed. A puncture enables Bob, who is joined in the chase by Spike (Walt Robbins) and Boots (Sid Jordan), two of his companions, to draw level with the automobile. He quickly assures the travelers, James Reed (Frank Whitson) and his romance-seeking daughter Betty (Margaret Leomis), of his honorable intentions and restores to the blushing Betty a dainty piece of lingerie that had blown from the car during the chase.

As protection against further highwaymen, Bob is invited by Betty to accompany the party to Four Corners. Her wildly fantastic taste is roused with the pleasurable offerings of the town, and she persuades her father to prolong their stay. Reed, enthusiastic about Bob's skill with a lasso, sets him the task of shooting three gold coins from a fence with three successive shots. His marksmanship proves to be on a par wit his prowess with a rope, and Reed presents Bob with three gold coins and some seasoned advice on success. Betty becomes enamored of Bob's dexterity, and he joyfully agrees to teach her to use a gun.

Two mysterious strangers, Ballinger (B. Hadley) and Berry (Dick Rush), whose presence in town has been a source of speculation, acquaint Fleming with the possibility that he could become a millionaire. His "worthless" land, he is told, is simply oozing with oil, and the two propose a scheme to form a company as Bob's partners.

The following day Four Corners is immersed in the subject of oil, and all members of the community invest in the project. Bob is elected treasurer. Since the town has no bank, the money is placed for security in the safe of the local store.

The same day Reed and his daughter prepare to leave and invite Bob to pay them a visit should he ever have business in their city. With the departure of Betty, Four Corners becomes like a wilderness to Bob, but he hurries forward the boring and drilling operations on his land.

Rumors concerning Ballinger and Berry reach James Reed, whose inquiries result in a detective's information that they are notorious swindlers. Betty, overhearing the conversation, wires Bob to visit her. Despite his desire to remain at work on the oil field, Bob, is persuaded by his partners to make the journey.

Following his departure the pair try to gain possession of the shareholder's money, but the store's manager refuses to part with it. They then decide to call in the assistance of Black Duncan and his outlaw followers.

On his arrival at Reed's residence, Bob learns about the swindle and the steps about to be taken to expose the impostors. He succumbs to Betty's persuasions to leave the matter in the hands of her father.

At a late hour in Four Corners, Black Duncan's men raid the store, but their presence is discovered and they are beaten off. The money chest, however, is found to be empty. The crafty Berry and his accomplice succeed in casting suspicion on the absent Fleming.

Unknown even to Bob, the money is in safekeeping with his friends Spike and Boots, who had had a foreboding of evil intent on the part of the suspicious promoters.

Returning to Four Corners, Bob is arrested for the theft and put in prison to await trial. Work at the oil wells goes steadily forward, the promoters having secured fresh investments from new stockholders. Despite his efforts to delay the trial until the arrival of Reed and officers of the law, Fleming is hauled before the court.

As Berry and Ballinger are preparing to leave camp with the new funds, the long-awaited evidence arrives and the pair are arrested. The attention of the court is attracted to the oil fields, where a gusher commences to flow. Bob makes his escape by crashing through a window and climbing to the roof. He swings perilously from one building to another by means of a rope from a flagpole. Eventually, a well-directed shot severs the halyard, and Fleming drops, jumps into the saddle of a horse, and dashes furiously away. Spike and Boots acquaint the shareholders of the whereabouts of their money while a party sets out to bring Bob back. Others of the community teach the swindlers a lesson by ducking them in a lake of oil before exhorting the pair to flee the country.

Bob needs violent persuasion to convince him that all is well and returns to Four Corners to be complimented by Betty and her father on the success of his business venture. Taking Betty in his arms, Bob tells her that the three gold coins have indeed brought him luck, and she shows full agreement with this by consenting to be his wife.

Cast: Tom Mix, Sid Jordan, Pat Chrisman, Margaret Loomis, Bert Hadley, Frank Whitson, Bonnie Hill, Walt Robbins, Sylvia Jocelyn, Dick Rush, Margaret Collington, and Frank Weed.

Credits: Produced by William Fox, directed by Clifford Smith, written by Alvin Weitz, story by H. H. van Loan.

The Untamed, September 5, 1920. A six-reel action film featuring Tom Mix and Tony.

Cast: Tom Mix, Pauline Starke, Sid Jordan, George Siegman, Philo McCullough, James Barrows, Charles K. French, Pat Chrisman, Gloria Hope, Frank Clark, Major J. A. McGuire, Joe Connelly, and Buster, a horse.

Credits: Produced by William Fox, directed and written by Emmett J. Flynn; story by Max Brand.

The Texan, October 31, 1920. A five-reel western featuring Tom Mix and Tony.

Cast: Tom Mix, Sid Jordan, Gloria Hope, Robert Walker, Charles K. French, Ben Corbett, and Pat Chrisman.

Credits: Produced by William Fox, directed by Lynn Reynolds, written by Lynn Reynolds and Jules Furthmann; story by J. B. Hendrix.

Prairie Trails, December 20, 1920. A five-reel western featuring Tom Mix and Tony.

Cast: Tom Mix, Kathleen O'Connor, Robert Walker, Charles K. French, Sid Gordan, Gloria Hope, William Elmer, and Harry Dunkinson.

Credits: Produced by William Fox, directed by George Marshall, written by Frank H. Clark; story by J. B. Hendrix.

1921

The Road Demon, February 20, 1921. A five-reel action film featuring Tom Mix and Tony.

News Story: Tom Mix comes back to the New Symphony again. Finding that horses in Western pictures were a bit slow, and wishing to modernize his films, Mix mixes racing cars with his latest picture, which is called *The Road Demon.*

Mix made his reputation on thrills and speedy pictures, and *The Road Demon* is claimed to be the fastest of them all. However, for all the title, the picture is a Western with autos put in for good measure. The story is replete with new laughs and from the moment Mix obtains the car on the trade, finds that the steering gear is broken and uses his lariat to guide the rattletrap, there is one laugh after another.

Local interest attaches to the picture because Barney Oldfield's racing car, that was once used in winning races in Indianapolis and at Sheepshead Bay, furnishes some of the thrills of the picture. The car is one of the old-fashioned racers, but it still has the speed and even after the hard usage Mix gave it, it was still in running condition.

Racing drivers who helped Mix put the

picture over include such famous racers as Ralph De Palma, Bennie Hill, Jimmie Murphy, Tommy Milton, Eddie O'Donnell, Eddie Hearn and Joe Thomas.

Cast: Tom Mix, Sid Jordan, Claire Andersen, Charles K. French, Lloyd Bacon, George Hernandez, Charles Arling, Harold Goodwin, Billy Elmer, Lee Phelps, and Frank Tokawaja.

Credits: Produced by William Fox, directed and written by Lynn Reynolds.

Hands Off, April 3, 1921. A five-reel western featuring Tom Mix and Tony.

Cast: Tom Mix, Pauline Curley, Charles K. French, Lloyd Bacon, Frank Clark, Sid Jordan, William McCormick, Virginia Warwick, J. Webster Dill, and Marvin Loback.

Credits: Produced by William Fox, directed by George Marshall, and written by Frank H. Clark; story by William MacLeod Raine.

A Ridin' Romeo, May 22, 1921. A five-reel western comedy featuring Tom Mix and Tony.

Cast: Tom Mix, Sid Jordan, Pat Chrisman, Rhea Mitchell, Harry Dunkinson, and Eugenie Ford.

Credits: Produced by William Fox, directed and written by George Marshall; story by Tom Mix.

Big Town Round-up, July 3, 1921. A five-reel western featuring Tom Mix and Tony.

Cast: Tom Mix, Ora Carew, Gilbert Holmes, Harry Dunkinson, Laura La Plante, William Buckley, William Elmer, and William Crinley.

Credits: Produced by William Fox, directed and written by Lynn Reynolds; story by William MacLeod Raine.

After Your Own Heart, August 7, 1921. A five-reel western featuring Tom Mix and Tony.

Cast: Tom Mix, Ora Carew, George Hernandez, William Buckley, Sid Jordan, Betty Jewel, Charles K. French, Duke Lee, James Mason, J. Gordon Russell, Bill Ward, and E. C. Robinson.

Credits: Produced by William Fox, directed by George Marshall, written by

John Montague and Tom Mix; story by W. W. Cook.

The Night Horseman, September 18, 1921. A five-reel western featuring Tom Mix and Tony.

Cast: Tom Mix, Mary Hopkins, Harry Lonsdale, Joseph Bennett, Sid Jordan, Cap Anderson, Bert Sprotte, Lon Poff, and Charles K. French.

Credits: Produced by William Fox, directed and written by Lynn Reynolds.

The Rough Diamond, October 30, 1921. A five-reel action film featuring Tom Mix and Tony.

Cast: Tom Mix, Sid Jordan, Eva Novak, Hector Sarno, and Edwyn Brady.

Credits: Produced by William Fox, directed and written by Edward Sedwick; story by Tom Mix.

Trailin', December 11, 1921. A five-reel western featuring Tom Mix and Tony.

Cast: Tom Mix, Sid Jordan, Eva Novak, Bert Sprotte, James Gordon, Duke Lee, William Duvall, Harry Dunkinson, Al Fremont, J. Farrell MacDonald, Bert Hadley, and Caroll Halloway.

Credits: Produced by William Fox, directed and written by Lynn Reynolds, story by Max Brand.

1922

Sky High, January 15, 1922. A five-reel action film featuring Tom Mix and Tony. *Note:* Filmed in Arizona's Grand Canyon.

Cast: Tom Mix, Sid Jordan, Eva Novak, J. Farrell MacDonald, William Buckley, Pat Chrisman, and Adele Warner, and Wynn Mace.

Credits: Produced by William Fox, directed and written by Lynn Reynolds.

Chasing the Moon, February 26, 1922. A five-reel western featuring Tom Mix and Tony.

Cast: Tom Mix, Eva Novak, William Buckley, Sid Jordan, Elsie Danbric, and Wynn Mace.

Credits: Produced by William Fox, directed and written by Edward Sedgwick;

***The Texan,* Fox, 1920. (Courtesy of Art Evans.)**

story by Tom Mix and Edward Sedgwick.

Up and Going, April 2, 1922. A five-reel action film featuring Tom Mix and Tony.

Cast: Tom Mix, Eva Novak, Sid Jordan, Patsy Ruth Miller, Bert Sprotte, Joe Harris, Al Fremont, Earl Simpson, William Conklin, Tom O'Brien, Pat Chrisman, and Paul Weigel.

Credits: Produced by William Fox, directed and written by Lynn Reynolds; story by Tom Mix.

The Fighting Streak, May 14, 1922. A five-reel western featuring Tom Mix and Tony.

Cast: Tom Mix, Patsy Ruth Miller, Gerald Pring, Al Fremont, Bert Sprotte, Robert Fleming, and Sid Jordan.

Credits: Produced by William Fox, directed and written by Arthur Rosson; story by G. Owen Baxter.

For Big Stakes, June 18, 1922. A five-reel western featuring Tom Mix and Tony.

Cast: Tom Mix, Patsy Ruth Miller, Sid Jordan, Bert Sprotte, Joe Harris, Al Fremont, and Earl Simpson.

Credits: Produced by William Fox, directed and written by Lynn Reynolds.

Just Tony, August 20, 1922. A five-reel western featuring Tom Mix and Tony.

Story: In this movie, Tony is the leader of a band of wild mustangs who enjoy the freedom of the plains. Tony is captured by a cruel Mexican and treated badly. He escapes his captor and returns to his band of horses. As a wild horse, Tony saves several lives, establishing himself as a real movie hero. Tom sets out to recapture Tony. It takes several attempts before Tom can win Tony's friendship, but in the end he does. *Note:* Local newsboys

The Rough Diamond, **Fox, 1921. (Author's collection.)**

were invited to see a sneak preview of *Just Tony* and tell promoters what they liked and disliked about the movie. The movie was a big hit with the newsboys.

Cast: Tom Mix, Claire Adams, J. P. Lockney, Duke Lee, Frank Campeau, and Walt Robbins.

Credits: Produced by William Fox, directed and written by Lynn Reynolds; story by Max Brand.

Do and Dare, October 1, 1922. A five-reel western featuring Tom Mix and Tony.

Cast: Tom Mix, Claire Adams, Dulcie Cooper, Claude Peyton, Jack Robbins, Hector Sarno, Wilbur Higby, Bob Klein, and Gretchen Hartman.

Credits: Produced by William Fox, directed and written by Edward Sedgwick; story by Marion Brooks.

Tom Mix in Arabia, November 5, 1922. A five-reel action film featuring Tom Mix.

Story: A girl is en route with her father

and brother to Arabia, and Tom acts as her guide while she is in Arizona. The cowboy takes life pretty easy on his ranch and is very upset when a speeding roadster comes by, hurling him out of his hammock. The driver of the car is an Arabian prince who claims that some of his people are after him because he wants to marry against their wishes. Looking very much like Tom, the prince persuades Tom to double for him so that he can make good his escape. Tom does so by sitting in the wrecked car, but the prince's pursuers refuse to listen to his story and carry him off to the Orient, where the girl will also be found.

Here the pretender to the throne has carried off the heroine while her father and brother are in the hands of the terrorists. Tom rescues the prisoners in a dramatic conclusion and is saved from an awkward situation by the arrival of the real prince. All ends happily.

Cast: Tom Mix, Claire Adams, Norman Shelby, George Hernandez, Edward

Peil, Ralph Yearsley, Eugene Corey, Hector Sarno, and Barbara Bedford.

Credits: Produced by William Fox, directed and written by Lynn Reynolds.

Catch My Smoke, December 31, 1922. A five-reel western featuring Tom Mix and Tony.

Cast: Tom Mix, Lillian Rich, Claude Peyton, Gordon Griffith, Harry Griffith, Robert Milash, Pat Chrisman, Cap Anderson, and Ruby LaFayette.

Credits: Produced by William Fox, directed by William Beaudine, and written by Jack Strumwasser; story by J. B. Adams.

1923

Romance Land, February 3, 1923. A five-reel lyric western featuring Tom Mix and Tony.

Story: Pep Hawkins (Tom) lives in a rancher's hut on the western plains. The only other occupant is White Eagle (Pat Chrisman), a full-blooded Indian. Together they herd a small string of longhorn cattle. The outside of the cabin is little different from any other shack that shelters cattlemen, but the interior is decidedly unusual in appointments. There are suits of medieval armor, pictures of people famous in the sixteenth century, notably Sir Walter Raleigh, and many books of fiction that describe the golden age of romance, among them Scott's *Ivanhoe.* The furniture is fashioned of the same period. Rapiers and broadswords are used for decoration.

In this atmosphere, Pep reads his books and becomes imbued with the spirit of Raleigh. He fancies himself as Ivanhoe, riding forth, squired by White Eagle, to rescue the fair flower of his heart. Whether his attendance is upon the queen or some imprisoned damsel, the glowing face of Nan Harvess (Barbara Bedford) always dances before his eyes. Nan has been bequeathed her father's ranch, the largest in the territory. But Pep does not hold her dear because of her wealth; her radiance and charm make him her willing knight. And like the heroes of yore, Pep fences daily with rapier and broadsword.

In the town of Red Dog, within riding distance of Hawkins's ranch, Nan Harvess lives with her uncle. The tale of King Arthur so engrossed her that she cares nothing for modern fiction. Nan's uncle has misappropriated some of her property, but only one other person knows it: Counterfeit Bill (George Webb), ranch foreman, who is in league with the uncle, "Scrub" Hazen (Frank Brownlee). Hazen has chosen Bill to marry his ward, Nan.

Dazzled by Nan's wealth and smitten by her charm, he is naturally elated with the proposed union. Nan does not dislike Bill, but to her romantic nature he makes little appeal. Hazen tells Nan she is approaching a marriageable age, and that the choice of a husband should be made soon. The girl replies that the man whom she would wed must first prove himself 100 percent man. Hazen suggests a tournament to decide the eligibility of her suitor. Nan, inspired by tales of knights who braved death to win their lady's favor, approves the plan.

Besides tourneys, other feats of prowess are bronco busting, chariot driving, and stagecoach racing. Scrub Hazen tips Bill off, and between the two they plan to fix the judges and insure success.

The contest is announced to tell the men in the district, and excitement runs high. White Eagle comes to Red Dog for supplies, hears the news, and tells Pep. Hawkins comes at once to Red Dog and, after maneuvering, enters his name in the tourney.

The great day finally dawns. Pep pays his homage to Nan. She is elated by his gallantry and impressed with his spectacular performance. Although allotted the worst "outlaw" horse available, Pep shows that he is the master of the game. His work compels the judges to declare him winner. The next event is the chariot race. Pep wins the race but is disqualified on a technicality. Thereafter comes the stagecoach race. Pep wins after being fouled. The marriage is announced for that evening at the opera house, and in celebration there is to be a masquerade.

Tom Mix and Patsy Miller in *The Fighting Streak*, Fox, 1922. (Author's collection.)

Hazen arranges to have Pep ambushed. But Pep, his armor buckled on for the masquerade, breaks through. In the dressing room Nan is forced to give her costume to Nita, her Indian maid. The ceremony is almost over when Nan escapes and warns Pep of the deception.

Bill and Hazen kidnap Nan, taking her to a minister who lives on top of a cliff. Pep follows. Nan steps out of the house to consult with the minister. Pep, with the help of others, topples the old cabin, including Bill and Hazen, over the cliff. The troublemakers gone, Nan and Pep are married by the minister—and start their great adventure in "Romance Land."

***Do and Dare*, Fox, 1922. (Author's collection.)**

Review: Mix Has Thrilling Flight a Hundred Feet in Midair — Swaying a hundred feet above a river in a tool bucket less than six feet in its greatest measurement, rocking with the swing of the cable as it tossed from side to side, Tom Mix forged ahead in midair for more than three hundred yards. When he climbed to safety he had still another dangerous task before him — that of freeing a girl from the hands of kidnappers. This is one of many exciting scenes in *Romance Land*, a William Fox production.

Cast: Tom Mix, Pat Chrisman, Barbara Bedford, Frank Brownlee, George Webb, and Wynn Mace.

Credits: Produced by William Fox, directed by Edward Sedgwick, and written by Joseph F. Poland; story by Kenneth Perkins.

Three Jumps Ahead, March 25, 1923. A five-reel action film featuring Tom Mix and Tony.

Cast: Tom Mix, Alma Bennett, Edward Peil, Joe Girard, Virginia True Boardman, Margaret Joslin, Harry Todd, Franke Forde, and Earl Simpson.

Credits: Produced by William Fox, directed and written by John Ford.

Stepping Fast, May 13, 1923. A five-reel western featuring Tom Mix and Tony.

Story: The action starts in the ruins of the cliffdwellers who formerly lived in the Arizona desert. Mix plays the role of a young cowboy who goes to the aid of a scientist who has been attacked by three men.

Learning of the existence of a treasure map, he works his way to China as a stoker, expecting to find the chart in Hong Kong. There he meets and saves the life of the girl whose father entrusted him with the secrets of the treasure.

He and his lovely heroine escape from a dungeon in darkest China when Tom lassos a mouse, ties a "help" message around its neck, and puts it out the window. Back across the Pacific they dash in a speedy yacht and race the blackguards to the hidden treasure.

Cast: Tom Mix, Claire Adams, Donald McDonald, Hector Sarno, George Siegmann, Edward Peil, Tom Squire, Edward

Romance Land, **Fox, 1923. (Courtesy of Art Evans.)**

Jobson, Ethel Wales, Minna Redman, and Earl Simson.

Credits: Produced by William Fox, directed by Joseph J. Franz, and written by Bernard McConville; story by Bernard McConville.

Soft Boiled, August 18, 1923. An eight-reel action comedy featuring Tom Mix and Tony.

Cast: Tom Mix, Billie Dove, Joseph Girard, Tom Wilson, Lee Shumway, Frank Beal, Jack Curtis, Charles H.

Soft Boiled, Fox, 1923. (Courtesy of Art Evans.)

Mailes, Harry Dunkinson, and Wilson Hummel.

Credits: Produced by William Fox, directed and written by J. G. Blystone; story by Edward Moran.

North of Hudson Bay, September 10, 1923. A five-reel action film featuring Tom Mix.

Cast: Tom Mix, Kathleen Key, Jennie Lee, Frank Campeau, Eugene Pallette, Will Walling, Frank Leigh, and Fred Kohler.

Credits: Produced by William Fox, directed by John Ford, and written by Jules Furthman.

The Lone Star Ranger, October 15, 1923. A six-reel western featuring Tom Mix and Tony.

Cast: Tom Mix, Billie Dove, Lee Shumway, Stanton Heck, Edward Peil, Frank Clark, Minna Redman, Francis Carpenter, William Conklin, and Tom Lingham.

Credits: Produced by William Fox, directed and written by William Hillyer.

Mile-a-Minute Rodeo, November 18, 1923. A six-reel western comedy featuring Tom Mix and Tony.

Cast: Tom Mix, Betty Jewel, J. Gordon Russell, James Mason, Duke Lee, and James Quinn.

Credits: Produced by William Fox, directed by Lambert Hillyer, and written by Robert N. Lee; story by Max Brand.

Eyes of the Forest, December 28, 1923. A five-reel western featuring Tom Mix and Tony. *Note:* Tom and Tony were injured on the trail by a poorly timed explosion during the filming of this feature.

Cast: Tom Mix, Pauline Starke, Sid Jordan, Buster Gardner, J. P. Lockney, Tom Lingham, and Edwin Wallock.

Credits: Produced by William Fox, directed by Lambert Hillyer, and written by LeRoy Stone; story by Shannon Fife.

Eyes of the Forest, **Fox, 1923. (Courtesy of Kurt Klotzbach.)**

1924

Ladies to Board, February 3, 1924. A six-reel western featuring Tom Mix and Tony.

Cast: Tom Mix, Gertrude Olmstead, Philo McCullough, Pee Wee Holmes, Gertrude Claire, and Dolores Rousse.

Credits: Produced by William Fox, directed by J. G. Blystone, and written by Donald W. Lee; story by Dudley Pelley.

The Trouble Shooter, May 6, 1924. A six-reel action film featuring Tom Mix and Tony.

Cast: Tom Mix, Frank Currier, Kathleen Key, J. Gunnis Davis, Mike Donlin, Dolores Rousse, Al Fremont, Charles McHugh, Earl Fox, and Howard Truesdel.

Credits: Produced by William Fox, directed by Jack Conway, and written by Frederic and Fanny Hatton.

The Heart Buster, June 20, 1924. A five-reel western featuring Tom Mix and Tony.

Cast: Tom Mix, Esther Ralston, Cyril

Chadwick, William Courtwright, Frank Currier, and Tom Wilson.

Credits: Produced by William Fox, directed by Jack Conway, and written by John Stone; story by George Scarborough.

The Last of the Duanes, June 30, 1924. A seven-reel western featuring Tom Mix and Tony. *Note:* Tom plays the part of Buck Duane, an outlaw.

Cast: Tom Mix, Marion Nixon, Brinsley Shaw, Frank Nelson, Lucy Beaumont, and Harry Lonsdale.

Credits: Produced by William Fox, directed by Lynn Reynolds, and written by Edward Montayne; story by Zane Grey.

Oh, You Tony! September 5, 1924. A seven-reel western featuring Tom Mix and Tony.

Cast: Tom Mix, Claire Adams, Dick La Reno, Earl Fox, Dolores Rousse, Charles K. French, Pat Chrisman, Miles McCarthy, Matilda Brundage, and May Wallace.

Credits: Produced by William Fox,

directed by J. G. Blystone, and written by Donald W. Lee.

Teeth, November 3, 1924. A seven-reel western featuring Tom Mix and Tony.
Cast: Tom Mix, Lucy Fox, Edward Peil, George Bancroft, Lucien Littlefield, and Duke the dog.
Credits: Produced by William Fox, directed by John Blystone, and written by Donald W. Lee; story by Clinton Stagge.

The Deadwood Coach, December 6, 1924. A seven-reel western featuring Tom Mix and Tony.
Cast: Tom Mix, Doris May, George Bancroft, DeWitt Jennings, Bustern Gardner, Lucien Littlefield, Norman Wills, Nora Cecil, Clyde Kinney, Frank Coffyn, and Sid Jordan.
Credits: Produced by William Fox, directed and written by Lynn Reynolds; story by Clarence E. Mulford.

1925

Dick Turpin, February 1, 1925. A seven-reel action drama featuring Tom Mix.
Ad Story: Dick Turpin (Tom), the notorious British highwayman, steals from the rich and gives to the poor. Tom falls in love with an aristocrat's daughter, who is about to be wed to a cad. He puts his life in danger to rescue her. Finally, he outwits his enemies and eludes his pursuers.
Cast: Tom Mix, Kathleen Meyers, Philo McCullough, James Marcus, Lucille Hutton, Alan Hale, Bull Montana, Fay Holderness, Jack Herrick, and Fred Kohler.
Credits: Produced by William Fox, directed by J. G. Blystone, and written by Charles Kenyon; story by Charles Kenyon and Charles Darnton.

Riders of the Purple Sage, March 8, 1925. A six-reel western featuring Tom Mix and Tony.
Story: A Texas Ranger pursues the kidnappers of his sister. He encounters a youth who is about to be whipped by rustlers and rescues him. The youth becomes the manager of a young woman's ranch, and romance follows.
The ranger discovers the outlaws' hideout, and the youth captures their young woman leader. He falls in love with her. Since the bandits outnumber the ranger, they chase him and the woman rancher into a valley from which they cannot escape. The ranger and the young woman prepare to spend the rest of their days together.
Cast: Tom Mix, Beatrice Burnham, Arthur Morrison, Seesel Ann Johnson, Warner Oland, Fred Kohler, Joe Rickson, Charles Le Moyne, Marion Dixson, Dawn O'Day, Charles Newton, Mabel Ballin, Harold Goodwin, and Wilfred Lucas.
Credits: Produced by William Fox, directed by Lynn Reynolds, and written by Edfrid Bingham; story by Zane Grey.

The Rainbow Trail, April 19, 1925. A six-reel western featuring Tom Mix and Tony.
Cast: Tom Mix, Anne Cornwall, George Bancroft, Lucien Littlefield, Mark Hamilton, Thomas Delmar, Vivian Oakland, Steve Clemento, Fred de Silva, Doc Roberts, Carol Holloway, Diana Miller, and Fred Dillon.
Credits: Produced by William Fox, directed and written by Lynn Reynolds; story by Zane Grey.

The Lucky Horseshoe, August 23, 1925. A five-reel western featuring Tom Mix and Tony.
Cast: Tom Mix, Billie Dove, Malcolm Waite, J. Farrell MacDonald, Clarrisa Selwynne, Ann Pennington, and J. Gunnis Davis.
Credits: Produced by William Fox, directed by J. G. Blystone, and written by John Stone; story by Robert Lord.

The Everlasting Whisper, October 4, 1925. A six-reel western featuring Tom Mix and Tony.
Cast: Tom Mix, Alice Calhoun, Robert Cain, George Berrell, Walter James, Virginia Madison, and Karl Dane.
Credits: Produced by William Fox, directed by J. G. Blystone, and written by Wyndham Gittens; story by J. Gregory.

The Deadwood Coach, **Fox, 1924. (Courtesy of Art Evans.)**

The Best Bad Man, November 15, 1925. A five-reel western featuring Tom Mix and Tony.

Story: Tom, disguised as a bandit, visits his Colorado property. He finds his agent, Dunlap, cheating homesteaders and trying to ruin an old man whose daughter, Peggy, he covets. Dunlap is supposed to be building a dam, but he is doing all he can to hamper the work. When Tom exposes his plans and ruins his schemes, Dunlap blows up the dam. Tom saves Peggy from the ensuing flood, and Tony carries Tom and Peggy to safety. Then they are married.

Cast: Tom Mix, Clara Bow, Buster Gardner, Cyril Chadwick, Tom Kennedy, Frank Beal, Judy King, Tom Wilson, and Paul Panzer.

Credits: Produced by William Fox, directed by J. G. Blystone, and written by Lillie Hayward; story by Max Brand.

The Yankee Señor, December 27, 1925. A five-reel action film featuring Tom Mix and Tony.

Press Book: With many of its gorgeous scenes reproduced in technicolor, *The Yankee Señor,* Tom Mix's latest screen attraction, offers a real treat to the nation's moviegoers.

It is a fast moving story of old Mexico, with Tom and Tony racing through every foot of it in a way that will leave you breathless. You'll revel in its beauties, its thrilling situations and tense dramatic moments.

Cast: Tom Mix, Olive Borden, Tom Kennedy, Francis McDonald, Joseph Franz, Margaret Livingston, Alec B. Francis, Kathryn Hill, Martha Mattox, Raymond Wells, Eugene Pallette, and Harry Seymore.

Credits: Produced by William Fox, directed by Emmett Flynn, and written by Eve Unsell; story by Katherine F. Gerould.

1926

My Own Pal, February 14, 1926. A five-reel western featuring Tom Mix and Tony.

The Rainbow Trail, **sequel to** *Riders of the Purple Sage,* **Fox, 1925. (Courtesy of Art Evans.)**

Cast: Tom Mix, Olive Bordon, Tom Santschi, Virginia Marshall, Bardson Bard, Hedda Nova, William Colvin, Virginia Warwick, Jay Hunt, Helen Lynch, Tom McGuire, and Jacques Rollens.

Credits: Produced by William Fox, directed by J. G. Blystone, and written by Lillie Hayward; story by Gerald Beaumont.

Tony Runs Wild, April 11, 1926. A six-reel western featuring Tom Mix and Tony.

Cast: Tom Mix, Lawford Davidson, Jacqueline Logan, Duke Lee, Vivian Oakland, Edward Martindel, Raymond Wells, Lucien Littlefield, Jack Padjan, Tony, Marion Harlan, Richard Carter, and Arthur Morrison.

Credits: Produced by William Fox, directed by Thomas Buckingham, written by Edfrid Bingham and Robert Lord; story by H. H. Knibbs.

Hard Boiled, August 8, 1926. A six-reel western featuring Tom Mix and Tony.

Cast: Tom Mix, Helen Chadwick, William Lawrence, Charles Conklin, Emily Fitzroy, Phyllis Haver, Dan Mason, Walter O'Donnell, Ethel Grey Terry, Edward Sturgis, Eddie Boland, and Emmett Wagner.

Credits: Produced by William Fox, directed by J. G. Blystone, and written by Charles Darnton and John Stone; story by Shannon Fife.

No Man's Gold, August 8, 1926. A six-reel western featuring Tom Mix and Tony. *Note:* Same story line as *The Rider of Death Valley.*

Cast: Tom Mix, Eva Novak, Frank Campeau, Forrest Taylor, Harry Grippe, Malcolm Waite, Mickey Moore, and Tom Santschi.

Credits: Produced by William Fox, directed by Lewis Seiler, and written by John Stone; story by J. A. Dunn.

The Great K & A Train Robbery,
October 25, 1926. A five-reel western featuring Tom Mix and Tony.

Ad Story: Tom and Tony will once again ride into your heart in this cyclonic thriller that'll chill you to the marrow. Watch the Star of the West riding amid a rain of bullets in running down a gang of railroad desperadoes. See him swim under water to the bandit's lair. Watch his lasso jerk a pal from the wheels of death. And see him steal the heart of a beautiful girl. It's 22-carat entertainment—every second of it!

Cast: Tom Mix, Dorothy Dwan, William Walling, Henry Grippe, Carl Miller, Edward Piel, and Curtis McHenry.

Credits: Produced by William Fox, directed by Lewis Seiler, and written by John Stone; story by Paul J. Ford.

The Canyon of Light, December 5, 1926. A six-reel western featuring Tom Mix and Tony.

Cast: Tom Mix, Dorothy Dwan, Carl Miller, Ralph Sipperly, Barry Norton, Carmelita Geraghty, William Walling, and Duke Lee.

Credits: Produced by William Fox, directed by Benjamin Stoloff, and written by John Stone; story by Kenneth Perkins.

1927

The Last Trail, January 16, 1927. A six-reel western featuring Tom Mix and Tony.

Cast: Tom Mix, Carmelita Geraghty, William Davidson, Frank Hagney, Lee Shumway, Robert Brower, Jerry the Giant, and Oliver Eckhardt.

Credits: Directed by Lewis Seiler and written by John Stone; story by Zane Grey.

The Bronco Twister, March 13, 1927. A six-reel western featuring Tom Mix and Tony.

Cast: Tom Mix, Helene Costello, George Irving, Dorothy Kitchen, Paul Nicholson, Doris Lloyd, Malcolm Waite, Jack Pennick, and Otto Fries.

Credits: Produced by William Fox, directed by Orville O. Dull, and written by

John Stone; story by Adela Rogers St. Johns.

The Circus Ace, June 12, 1927. A five-reel western featuring Tom Mix and Tony.

Cast: Tom Mix, Natalie Joyce, Jack Baston, Duke Lee, James Bradbury, Stanley Blystone, Dudley Smith, Buster Gardner, and Clarence the Kangaroo.

Credits: Produced by William Fox, directed by Ben Stoloff, and written by Jack Jungmeyer; story by Harold Shumate.

Tumbling River, August 14, 1927. A five-reel action film featuring Tom Mix and Tony.

Cast: Tom Mix, Dorothy Dwan, Edward Peil, William Conklin, Stella Essex, Elmo Billings, Wallace MacDonald, Buster Gardner, Harry Grippe, and Tom's horse, Buster.

Credits: Produced by William Fox, directed by Lewis Seiler, and written by Jack Jungmeyer; story by J. E. Grinstead.

Outlaws of Red River, August 17, 1927. A six-reel western featuring Tom Mix and Tony.

Cast: Tom Mix, Marjorie Daw, Arthur Clayton, William Conklin, Duke Lee, Johnny Downs, Francis McDonald, and Virginia Marshall.

Credits: Produced by William Fox, directed by Lewis Seiler, and written by Harold Shumate; story by Gerald Beaumont.

Silver Valley, October 2, 1927. A five-reel western featuring Tom Mix and Tony.

Cast: Tom Mix, Tom Kennedy, Dorothy Dwan, Philo McCullough, Jocky Hoefli, Lon Poff, Harry Dunkinson, and Clark Comstock.

Credits: Produced by William Fox, directed by Ben Stoloff, and written by Harold Blipsitz; story by Harry S. Drago.

The Arizona Wildcat, November 7, 1927. A five-reel western featuring Tom Mix and Tony.

Cast: Tom Mix, Dorothy Sebastian, Ben Bard, Gordon Elliot, Monty Collins Jr., Cissy Fitzgerald, Doris Dawson, and Marcella Daly.

No Man's Gold, Fox, 1926. (Courtesy of Art Evans.)

Credits: Produced by William Fox, directed by R. William Neill, and written by John Stone; story by Adela Rogers St. Johns.

1928

Daredevil's Reward, January 27, 1928. A five-reel western featuring Tom Mix and Tony.

Cast: Tom Mix, Natalie Joyce, Lawford Davidson, Billy Bletcher, Harry Cording, and William Welch.

Credits: Produced by William Fox, directed by Eugene Ford, and written by John Stone; story by John Stone.

Horseman of the Plains, February 2, 1928. A five-reel western featuring Tom Mix and Tony.

Cast: Tom Mix, Sally Blaine, Heime Conklin, Charles Byer, Lew Harvey, Grace Marvin, and William Ryno.

Credits: Produced by William Fox, di-

rected by Ben Stoloff, and written by Fred Myton; story by Harry S. Drago.

Hello, Cheyenne, March 29, 1928. A five-reel western featuring Tom Mix and Tony.

Ad Story: Tom shows a new bag of tricks in this story of two telephone companies and a thrilling race for supremacy. A long-distance Western classic showing Tom at his best.

Cast: Tom Mix, Carol Lincoln, Jack Baston, Martin Faust, Joseph Girard, Al St. John, and William Caress.

Credits: Directed by Eugene Ford and written by Fred K. Myton; story by Harry S. Drago.

Painted Post, June 1, 1928. A five-reel western featuring Tom Mix and Tony.

Cast: Tom Mix, Natalie Kingston, Philo McCullough, Al St. John, and Fred Gamble.

Credits: Produced by William Fox, directed by Eugene Ford, and written by Buckleigh F. Oxford; story by Harry S. Drago.

The Canyon of Light, Fox, 1926. (Coutesy of Art Evans.)

FBO Films

Son of the Golden West, October 1, 1928. A six-reel western featuring Tom Mix and Tony.

Cast: Tom Mix, Sharon Lynn, Lee Shumway, Tom Lingham, Fritzi Ridgeway, Duke Lee, Joie Ray, Wynn Mace, and Mark Hamilton.

Credits: Produced by Joseph Kennedy, directed by Eugene Forde, and written by George Pyper.

King Cowboy, November 5, 1928. A seven-reel western featuring Tom Mix and Tony.

Press Story: In a setting far removed from the great open spaces of the West in which he has been seen upholding the right and punishing "bad men" on the screen, Tom Mix is presented in *King Cowboy,* his latest production.

Although the action of the interesting story takes place in the country of the Riffs in northern Africa and the background is picturesquely adorned with Moorish mosques and ancient towering buildings, Tom and his wonder horse "Tony" play their familiar roles of riding, roping and hair-raising stunts that have made them famous the world over.

But the troupe of cowboys and riders at whose head Mix appears is augmented by a company of Arab horsemen in robes and turbans who add much to the scenic effects of the photoplay.

The action of *King Cowboy* is said to be speedy and gripping and concerns the experience of a party of American cowboys who visit Morocco as a "Wild West Show" but are really in search of the owner of their ranch, who is held captive by the Riffs.

The Westerners are captured by the tribesmen, discover their imprisoned employer and eventually fight their way

Top: Horseman of the Plains, Fox, 1928. (Courtesy of Art Evans.) *Bottom: Hello, Cheyenne*, Fox, 1928. (Courtesy of Art Evans.)

to freedom. Sally Blaine is said to appear very attractive as the captive ranch owner's daughter who conducts the cowboy party to Morocco.

Review: "Mr. Mix, don't do anything like this again."

Cast: Tom Mix, Sally Blaine, Lew Meehan, Wynn Mace, Barney Furey, Robert Fleming, and Frank Leigh.

Credits: Produced by Joseph Kennedy, directed by Robert De Lacey, and written by Frank Clark; story by S. E. V. Taylor.

1929

Outlawed, January 1, 1929. A seven-reel western featuring Tom Mix and Tony.

Ad Story: Stunt on Stunt—The Ace of Outdoor Stars Crashing Through a Riot A-teeming with Western Thrills—Daring and Doing—Living and Loving—As Only Your Favorite Can.

Review: Not so hot, Mr. Mix, not so hot. The saddle girths are slipping under the "King of the Cowboys." He'll do well to lay low 'til he gets some new gags under his high hat. Here's the same old thing, only worse, without enough sparks, color or action to keep an eight year old boy awake. Another flop like this and the juvenile clientele, with the critical precocity of modern infants, will shout a lusty "Applesauce."

Cast: Tom Mix, Sally Blaine, Ethan Laidlaw, Frank Clark, Barney Furey, Al Smith, and Al Ferguson.

Credits: Produced by Joseph Kennedy, directed by Eugene Forde, and written by George Pyper.

The Drifter, February 25, 1929. A six-reel western featuring Tom Mix and Tony.

Press Story: The thrills include Tom's courageous ride on the wings of an airplane; his fight to keep possession of a mysterious white mule, the only living being which knows the way to a hidden mine; and his fistic encounters with a gang of desperadoes who secretly are a group of narcotic smugglers.

To cope with his ruthless adversaries, Tom is required to perform miraculous feats of horsemanship in which he has the graceful cooperation of Tony.

The climax of the film is reached when Tom makes a flying tackle off the wing of a soaring airplane, in which the pilot has sought to abandon him; catches the pilot about the waist and thus shares a parachute with him in a perilous drop to the ground.

Review: Tom Mix is bowing out. The jingle of his spurs will soon be an echo, the sight of his ten-gallon hat just a memory. Vaudeville is calling him. He'll probably break little glass balls with a rifle. *The Drifter* is his cinema swan song—his last picture on his last contract. Unfortunately, it won't emblazon the famous Mix initials in film history. Just another western, but send the kids anyway, just to see the airplane.

Cast: Tom Mix, Dorothy Dwan, Wynn Mace, Barney Furey, Al Smith, Frank Austin, Ernest Wilson, and Joe Rickson.

Credits: Produced by Joseph Kennedy, directed by Robert De Lacey, and written by George Pyper; story by Oliver Drake and Robert De Lacey.

The Big Diamond Robbery, May 13, 1929. A seven-reel western featuring Tom Mix and Tony. *Note:* The worst reviews seemed to be reserved for Tom's final FBO film, *The Big Diamond Robbery.* It had weak plot, numerous character changes, and featured impossible and unbelievable stunts. As a result, Tom expected this film to be his last motion picture.

Cast: Tom Mix, Kathryn McGuire, Frank Beal, Ethan Laidlaw, Barney Furey, Martha Mattox, and Ernest Hilliard.

Credits: Produced by Joseph Kennedy, directed by Eugene Forde, written by John Twist; story by Frank Clark.

Top: **King Cowboy,** FBO, 1928. (Courtesy of Art Evans.) *Bottom:* **The Big Diamond Robbery,** FBO, 1929. (Courtesy of Art Evans.)

Universal Pictures

1932

Destry Rides Again, April 4, 1932. A six-reel western featuring Tom Mix and Tony Jr.

News Story: "Destry Rides Again," and so does Tom Mix, much to the delight of the Mix supporters.

For a time it looked doubtful if the virile 52-year-old star of Western films would ever be seen again, much less ride. Picture followers are well familiar with the battle for life that Mix put up during his recent appendicitis operation.

Not only will Mix be seen again but this time he will be heard, for *Destry Rides Again* marks Tom's talking debut. Yes, and you will hear Tony neigh, for it is also the first sound film for Tom's pal in horseflesh.

The Max Brand novel of a wildcat cowboy who was framed to prison by a ring of unscrupulous politicians and who emerged from behind the bars, years later, to pay his debt to each member of the jury, is a perfect vehicle for the hemanish Mix.

Mix films were always noted for their action and the current talkie is no exception. With the saddle star Claudia Dell, Zasu Pitts, Earle Foxe and others.

If you go for Western pictures, this will appeal, for it is out of the ordinary run of this type of entertainment.

Cast: Tom Mix, Claudia Dell, Earl Fox, Zasu Pitts, Stanley Fields, Francis Ford, Charles K. French, Edward J. LeSaint, Edward Piel Sr., Frederick Howard, Robert Ruffner, John Ince, George Ernest, Ed Brady, and Chris Martin.

Credits: Produced by Carl Laemmle Jr., directed by Ben Stoloff, and written by Richard Schayer and Isador Bernstein; story by Max Brand.

The Rider of Death Valley, May 20, 1932. A seven-reel western featuring Tom Mix and Tony Jr.

News Story: Filmed almost in its entirety in the wastes of the southwestern desert, the picture offers pictorial beauty seldom surpassed, it is said.

The theme concerns a beautiful girl, a gold mind and a heroic cowboy who rescues both from the clutches of a group of cowtown villains. Lois Wilson is the girl and others in the cast are Fred Kohler, Mae Busch, Otis Harlan and, of course, Tony, Tom's horse pal.

Review: Action, thrills, and a good old-fashioned western drama are promised in Tom Mix's latest screen effort, entitled *The Rider of Death Valley.*

Cast: Tom Mix, Lois Wilson, Fred Kohler Sr., Mae Busch, Edmund Cobb, Williard Robertson, Edith Fellows, Forrest Stanley, Pete Morrison, Iron Eyes Cody, Otis Harlan, and Francis Ford.

Credits: Produced by Carl Laemmle, Jr., directed by Al Rogel, and written by Jack Cunningham; story by Max Brand.

Texas Badman, June 18, 1932. A six-reel western featuring Tom Mix and Tony Jr.

News Story: The Texas Bad Man is a story which pictures the western star in the disguise of a bold, bad bandit, an original written by Jack Cunningham.

Supporting Mix are villainous Fred Kohler, Lucille Powers, Williard Robertson, and, of course, Tony, for what Mix picture would be complete without the horse.

The story boasts stage coach holdups, if you care for them, desperate chases and daring rescues. Franklyn Farnum, remembered from the old silent days, will be seen in a role, as will other lesser knowns.

It will be interesting to many to learn that Tony, the star's intelligent horse, recently celebrated his twenty-second anniversary since the day Mix bought him from an Arizona farmer for $12.50.

Review: In *The Texas Bad Man,* Tom Mix appears in the leading role as a Texas Ranger in the disguise of a bandit. Lucille Powers appears as the heroine, Williard Robertson gives his interpretation of a dual-natured crook, and Fred Kohler has the heavy role.

Cast: Tom Mix, Lucille Powers, Fred

Riders of Death Valley, **Universal, 1932. (Courtesy of Art Evans.)**

Kohler Sr., Edward J. LeSaint, Williard Robertson, Franklyn Farnum, Dick Alexander, Bud Osborne, Joseph Girard, Lynton Brent, Buck Bucko, and Tetsu Komai.

Credits: Produced by Carl Laemmle Jr., directed by Edward Laemmle, and written by Jack Cunningham.

My Pal, the King, August 1, 1932. A seven-reel western featuring Tom Mix, and Tony Jr. *Note:* In his book *Life's Too Short,* Mickey Rooney gives Tom credit for giving him his first big break in a major motion picture.

Story: Tom's Wild West Show visits the small make-believe European country of Olvania. Mickey, the boy king, slips away from his court, catches the eye of Tom, and gets to ride with Tom on Tony Jr. in the opening parade. Later, he and his aunt are special guests at Tom's Wild West show. However, when word reaches Tom that the boy king has disappeared, Tom and his boys ride to Mickey's

rescue. With the aid of his lasso, Tom scales the wall of the evil count's castle. As the guards are about to shoot him, he swings through a window and encounters the evil count, who has put Mickey in a flooded dungeon. The count gets the drop on Tom, but when he is distracted, Tom shoots the gun out of his hand. Then Tom rescues Mickey and his tutor, who have been trapped in the flooded dungeon. A couple of Tom's cowboys give the evil count a taste of his own medicine.

Cast: Tom Mix, Mickey Rooney, Noel Francis, Paul Hurst, Stuart Holmes, Jim Thorpe, Finis Barton, Ferdinand Schumman-Heink, James Kirkwood, Wallis Clark, Christian Frank, and Clarissa Selwynne.

Credits: Produced by Carl Laemmle Jr., directed by Kurt Neumann, and written by Richard Schayer.

The Fourth Horseman, September 22, 1932. A six-reel western featuring Tom Mix and Tony Jr.

Tom chokes bad guy, Fred Kohler, in *Texas Bad Man,* Universal, 1932. (Courtesy of Art Evans.)

Story: An abandoned mining town is about to become a boomtown with new settlers arriving daily. Kohler and his gang see an opportunity to run the town by taking over all the saloons, gambling joints, and dance halls. The heroine owns almost all the land in town but is unaware that it is about to be sold for taxes. Kohler and his gang plan to pay the taxes and take the land. Tom discovers the plot and helps save the day for the girl and the settlers. The settlers ride into town and engage the gang in a furious gun battle. Tom beats Kohler in a rip-roaring one-on-one fistfight.

Cast: Tom Mix, Margaret Lindsay, Fred Kohler Sr., Raymond Hatton, Buddy Roosevelt, Edmund Cobb, Rosita Marstini, Richard Cramer, Duke Lee, Grace Cunard, Hank Mann, Fred Burns, Bud Osborne, Walter Brennan, Harry Allen, Herman Nowlin, Paul Shawham,

Frederick Howard, Helen Millard, Captain Anderson and Martha Mattox.

Credits: Produced by Carl Laemmle Jr., directed by Hamilton McFadden, and written by Jack Cunningham; story by Nina Putnam.

Hidden Gold, October 19, 1932. A six-reel western featuring Tom Mix and Tony Jr. *Note:* Tom plays the part of a local boxing champ. The climax is filmed against the background of a realistic forest-fire scene.

Cast: Tom Mix, Raymond Hatton, Judith Barrie, Eddie Gribbon, Willis Clarke, Donald Kirke, and Roy Moore.

Credits: Produced by Carl Laemmle Jr., directed by Art Rosson, and written by Jack Natteford and Jim Milhauser; story by Jack Natteford.

Flaming Guns, December 17, 1932. A six-reel western comedy featuring Tom

Top: **Paul Hurst with Tom Mix between scenes in** *My Pal, the King,* **Universal, 1932. (Courtesy of Janus Barfoed.)** *Bottom: The Fourth Horseman,* **Universal, 1932. (Courtesy of Art Evans).**

Tom helps defend Naomi Judge in ***Terror Trail,*** **Universal, 1933. (Courtesy of Art Evans.)**

Mix and Tony Jr. *Note:* Tom returns from the service as a retired army sergeant.

Cast: Tom Mix, Ruth Hall, William Farnum, Bud Osborne, Duke Lee, George Hackathorne, Pee Wee Holmes, Clarence Wilson, Slim Whitaker, Clyde Kinney, Fred Burns, Jimmy Shannon, William Steele, Walter Patterson, and Robert Ruffner.

Credits: Produced by Carl Laemmle Jr., directed by Art Rosson, and written by Jack Cunningham; story by Peter Kyne.

1933

Terror Trail, January 24, 1933. A six-reel western featuring Tom Mix and Tony Jr.

Story: Rustlers, known as the Painted Horse Gang, are stealing cattle and horses and shooting innocent cowboys

and ranchers. A reward for their capture rapidly rises to $5,000. Bernie Laird (Arthur Rankin), who wrangles horses for the outlaws, strongly objects to the needless murder. Finally, the ranchers telegraph the governor that Silver County is in the hands of cutthroats and thieves. The governor notifies the sheriff (Lafe McKee) that he is sending Tom Munroe (Tom) to clean up the situation.

Colonel Ormsby (John St. Polls) is head of the vigilantes, and it soon becomes obvious that with the sheriff, he is also the head of the Painted Horse Gang. Almost immediately, Ormsby makes plans to get rid of Tom Munroe, who was a former U.S. marshal in Indian territory.

On the way to town, Tom captures four rustlers caught in the act near the Red Rock Indian Reservation. Lucky Dawson (Ray Hatton) makes a quick bet that the rustlers will be out of jail before dark. Ormsby arrives at the sheriff's office and meets Tom. Ormsby then goes to the jail cells and chews the thieves out for being caught by just "one man."

Munroe is tired, hungry, and looking for a place to catch some sleep. The sheriff directs him to the local stable and hotel. Tom puts Tony Jr. up, then retires to his room for a hot bath. Someone shoots at Tom while he is in the stable, but they miss him.

Tom gets his bathwater ready, then puts his bed against the door and closes his blind. In the meantime, the crooks are being released from the jail. As Tom is getting ready for his bath, shooting from downstairs hits his tub and almost him. It turns out to be Lucky Dawson, the gambler, who is drunk. Tom gets his guns and puts an end to the nonsense. On his way back to his room, he bumps into Norma Laird (Naomi Judge). Tom does not realize he is without his pants, but Norma does.

The thieves steal most of the horses out of the stable on their way out of town. They steal Tom's and Lucky's horses but leave Ormsby's pinto behind. Ormsby lends his horse to Tom and goes to get the sheriff to organize a posse. Lucky bets Tom that he can take him close to where the stolen horses are. They go to Norma Laird's ranch and have dinner there. Norma has several head of horses in the corral that need breaking.

While having dinner, Tom hears Tony Jr.'s neigh and captures Norma's brother Bernie with some of the stolen horses, which he says were abandoned by the thieves when the posse chased them.

The next day a rider arrives in town firing warning shots and announcing that the stagecoach has just been held up. Tom rides out after the thieves, finds the abandoned stagecoach, empty money bag and boot heel. Then he spots about 16 riders making their getaway.

The thieves swap their painted horses for other horses and Bernie pads their hooves and takes them to a hideout in a cave. Tom goes to a nearby cabin, where he finds a wet horse blanket. He goes inside for a drink and discovers one occupant has lost a heel on his boot. As the crooks are distracted by a coffeepot boiling over, Tom gets the drop on them and finds Bernie hiding out of sight. He takes the four men in.

The rest of the Painted Horse Gang rides into town to release the prisoners. The sheriff gives guns to the locked-up men and lets them lock him up. Ormsby and Bernie ride off to Norma's ranch. Bernie admits he has been wrangling horses for the thieves.

The gang surrounds the ranch and begin to shoot it up, fearing Bernie will spill the beans. Ormsby walks out of the house to talk to some of the men, whom he says he recognizes. Bernie confesses that Ormsby is the leader of the band.

Tom calls for Tony and lets him into the ranch house. Amid a hail of bullets, he heads for the corral, where he spots the thieves' getaway horses along with the unbroken horses.

Tom sends some of the ranch hands to meet Lucky Dawson, who is on his way with help. Another ranch hand helps him put the thieves' saddles on the unbroken horses. As the thieves hear the reinforcements arriving, they break up and head for the corral. They mount the unbroken horses and have the ride of their lives. They are quickly taken in tow by the ranch hands.

Two of the gang try to escape on a painted horse. Tom rides after them, lassos both, and drags them back to the ranch. Ormsby shows up and congratulates Tom for catching the thieves. Tom handcuffs Ormsby and takes him to jail.

As Tom and Norma are having dinner again, Lucky Dawson is betting that they will be married within the month. Tom and Norma swap bits of cake.

Cast: Tom Mix, Naomi Judge, Raymond Hatton, Arthur Rankin, Francis McDonald, Lafe McKee, Bob Kortman, Hank Bell, John St. Polls, Frank Brownlee, Jay Wilsey, Henry Tenbrook, W. J. Holmes, Leonard Trainer, and Jim Corley.

Credits: Produced by Carl Laemmle Jr., directed by Armand Schaefer, and written by Jack Cunningham; story by Gran Taylor.

Noah Beery Jr. and Tom Mix in *Rustler's Roundup,* **Universal, 1933. (Courtesy of Art Evans.)**

Rustler's Roundup, February 23, 1933. A six-reel western featuring Tom Mix and Tony Jr.

Story: This one follows the tried-and-true formula without any signs of originality, but it is handled with a snap and punch and crowded with exciting incident. Of course with Tom Mix in evidence practically all the time, it is in the bag for the thrill fans.

Tom does the bandit act in order to save the girl's property, which the villainous foreman of the ranch is trying to take away from her. Later he comes to a showdown with the foreman, whose gang has been rustling the girl's cattle in order to force her to relinquish the ranch.

There is also some exciting stuff with a rodeo, in which Mr. Mix does his well-known equestrian stunts, taking all the honors from his rival, who is also the villain. The movie works up to a big slap-bang climax with plenty of action and all kinds of fighting and gun play.

Cast: Tom Mix, Noah Beery Jr., Diane Sinclair, William Desmond, Nelson McDowell, Douglas Dumbrille, Bud Osborne, Roy Stewart, Pee Wee Holmes, William Wagner, Frank Lackteen, and Walter Brennan.

Credits: Produced by Carl Laemmle Jr., directed by Henry MacRae, and written by Frank Howard Clark and Jack Cunningham; story by Ella O'Neill.

Mascot Studios

The Miracle Rider. A 15-episode western serial featuring Tom Mix and Tony Jr.

Story: In this novel story of the modern West, Tom Mix plays a Texas Ranger who braves a thousand deaths to unravel

Tom Mix takes time to reload revolver in *The Miracle Rider*, 1935. (Author's collection.)

the plot to force his Indian friends off their reservation. Helping Tom display his tricks is his famous horse, Tony Jr.

Chapter 1	*The Vanishing Indian,* 5 reels	
Chapter 2	*The Firebird Strikes,* 2 reels	
Chapter 3	*The Flying Knife,* 2 reels	
Chapter 4	*A Race with Death,* 2 reels	
Chapter 5	*Double-Barreled Doom,* 2 reels	
Chapter 6	*Thundering Hoofs,* 2 reels	
Chapter 7	*The Dragnet,* 2 reels	
Chapter 8	*Guerilla Warfare,* 2 reels	
Chapter 9	*The Silver Band,* 2 reels	
Chapter 10	*Signal Fires,* 2 reels	
Chapter 11	*A Traitor Dies,* 2 reels	

Chapter 12 *Danger Rides with Death*, 2 reels
Chapter 13 *The Secret of X-94*, 2 reels
Chapter 14 *Between Two Fires*, 2 reels
Chapter 15 *Justice Rides the Plains*, 2 reels

Cast:

Tom Morgan . . . . Tom Mix
Ruth. .Joan Gale
Zaroff. . . . . Charles Middleton
Carlton . . . . Jason Robards
Janss . . . . Edward Hearn
Stelter . . . . Ernie Adams
Adams. . . . . .Edward Earle
Sewell . . . . Tom London
Metzger . . . . Niles Welsh
Vining. . . . . .Edmund Cobb
Morley . . . . Max Wagner
Hatton . . . . Charles King
Crossman. . . . . George Chesebro
Chapman. . . . . .Stanley Price
Mort . . . . George Burton

Rogers . . . . Jack Rockwell
Black Wing. . . . . .Bob Frazer
Longboat . . . . Bob Kortman
Tony Jr. as himself

Other Players:

Pat O'Malley   Dick Curtis
Jay Wilsey   Dick Alexander
Frand Ellis   Lafe McKee
Earl Dwire   Slim Whitaker
Hank Bell   Chief Big Tree
Art Artigan   Fred Burns
Forrest Taylor

Credits: The Miracle Rider was supervised by Victor Zobel, directed by Armand Schaefer and B. Reeves Eason; based on a story by Gerald Gerahty, Barney Sarecky, and Wellyn Totman; screenplay by John Rathmell; film editor, Dick Fantl; photography, Ernest Miller and William Nobles; supervising editor, Joseph Lewis; sound engineer, Terry Kellum.

Bibliography

The following books and articles provide additional information about Tom Mix and the people and events that helped shape his life. Reprints of some articles and back issues of some magazines may be available from the publishers. Consult your local library for the availability of books and other materials.

Articles and Magazines

Achor, John. "The Golden Age of Radio . . . and Box Tops." *Good Old Days,* September 1992.

Ackworth, Robert. "Cowboy Legend of the Silver Screen." *Signature,* 1967.

"Albert McBride—King of the Oil Drillers," *Western Frontier,* November 1977.

Bartlesville Examiner-Enterprise. "Tom Mix Museum Souvenir Edition." May 27, 1968.

Binkley, Allen. "Tom Mix Tent #148." *Favorite Westerns and Serial World,* no. 27, 1988.

Birchard, Robert. "Sid Jordan: Friend to Mix." *Classic Film Collector,* fall 1966.

_____. "Motion Picture Vignettes." *Frontier Times,* February-March 1970.

_____. "Motion Picture Vignettes: Sid Jordan—From Real Deputy to Reel Outlaw," *Frontier Times,* April-May 1970.

_____. "Tom Mix: Budding Western Star." Publication and date unknown.

Boy's Cinema. "Tom Mix at Work and Play." March 17, 1923.

Borden, Hal. "Smokey Never Forgot First Parade When Tom Mix Took His Last Ride." *El Paso Times,* May 14, 1967.

Brown, Johnny Mack. "Tom Mix—The Greatest Fighting Man I Ever Knew." Publication and date unknown.

Cantrell, Don. "Tom Mix—His Last Ride." *Real West,* September 1975.

Cary, Diana Serra. "The Hollywood Posse: The Story of a Gallant Band of Horsemen Who Made Movie History." *True West,* July-August 1976.

Coburn, Walt. "Tom Mix's Last Sundown." *Frontier Times,* August-September 1968.

Coville, Gary W. "Revisiting the Legend of Tom Mix." *Antique Trader Weekly,* March 18, 1992.

Christy, Jack. "A Man Never Dies Who Leaves Behind a Friend: Tom Mix" (interview with Major Monte Stone). *Song and Saddle,* August 1947.

Daniszewski, John. "Cowboy Tom Mix Rides on in Hearts of His Many Fans." *Philadelphia Inquirer,* September 24, 1981.

DeMarco, Mario A. "Tom Mix: Mr. Action." *Real West.* Date unknown.

_____. "The Big Five." *Real West Hall of Fame.* Date unknown.

_____. "The Sawdust Trail." Publication and date unknown.

Dillon, Franc. "Tom Mix's Fight for Thomasina." Publication unknown, 1925.

Dodge, Matt. "Tom Mix in Arizona." *Real West,* summer 1979.

Dowd, Maureen. "The Man with the President's Ear." *Time,* August 8, 1983.

Dumont, Lou. "Tom Mix: Historical Tape Recordings." *Hobbies,* September 1983.

Earle, Jim. "Tom Mix's Colt." *Arms Gazette,* December 1976.

Echols, Lee E. "I Never Knew an Echols Who Was Worth a Damn." *True West,* January-February 1978.

Franklin, Grady. "The Western Trail." *Favorite Westerns,* no. 4, 1981.

Goodwin, Tony. "Ghost Trails of the Sentinels." *Adirondack Life,* November-December 1990.

Green, Lisa. "Who Gets the Most Out of Marriage? The Stars Express Frank Opinions." Publication unknown, 1932.

Greenwalt, Julie. "America's Picasso of Car Designers, Gordon Buehrig, Rolls Out a $130,000 Custom-Bodied Dream Car." *People,* March 8, 1982.

Hall, John. "There Was a Cowboy!" *ACD Newsletter,* October 1967.

————. "The Life and Times of Tom Mix." Unpublished, 1968.

Harmon, Jim. "Tom Mix, The Miracle Rider." Publication and date unknown.

Harper, William, Teresa Harper, and Jon Lundin. "The Legendary Tom Mix in Comics." *Under Western Skies,* no. 23, March 1983. (This issue also contains newspaper stories by Bob Dvorchak and Doug Morris.)

Hinkle, Milt. "Swashbuckler Tom Mix." *True West,* July-August 1967.

Henderson, Sam. "The Film Cowboys: Heroes, Who Were for Real." *Frontier West,* June 1973.

————. "The Real Saddlemates of Tom Mix." *Oldtimers Wild West,* December 1977.

————. "Hey There, Straight Shooters!! Let's Saddle Up and Ride the Oklahoma High Country with the One and Only Tom Mix." Parts 1 and 2. *Oklahoma Today,* March-April 1984.

————. "When Silent Screen Cowboy Fans Saw Double!" Publication and date unknown.

Hornback, Randall. "Curley Bradley." Publication and date unknown.

Lewis, Jack. "The Tom Mix I Knew and Loved." *Horse and Horseman,* June 1982.

"The Life of Tom Mix." *Song and Saddle,* August 1947.

Koller, Joe. "Tom Mix—Soldier of Fortune." Publication and date unknown.

Mix, Paul E. "Open Letter to People of DuBois on Tom Mix Festival." *Under Western Skies,* no. 18, March 1982.

————. "One Mix's Opinion about the Movie *Sunset.*" *Westerns and Serials, Favorite Westerns,* no. 29, 1988.

————. "The Great Calgary Stampede Dispute." *Westerns and Serials,* no. 37, 1991.

Mix, Tom. "The Coconut Grove." *Life,* October 13, 1927.

Nelson, Raymond E. *Auburn Cord Duesenberg Club Newsletter,* Special Feature Edition, The Tom Mix Cord, October 1967.

Pontes, Bob. "An Interview with Allen "Slim" Binkley, Valet to Tom Mix." *Favorite Westerns,* no. 25, 1986.

Roberts, Wendell. "How Tom Mix Backed into the Movies." *Southland Magazine,* February 16, 1964.

Robinson, C. O. "Tom Mix Was My Boss." *Frontier Times,* June-July 1969.

Rosen, Sid. "Tom Mix, the Greatest Cowboy of the West." *Under Western Skies,* no. 9, March 1980 (with filmography).

Rutherford, John A. "Tom Mix as the Miracle Rider." *Under Western Skies,* no. 31, 1985.

St. Johns, Adela Rogers. "Lucky and Unlucky Loves of Hero Tom Mix." *American Weekly,* 1940.

Seiverling, Dr. Richard F. "Rare Memorabilia to Be Displayed at Tom Mix Festival." *Under Western Skies,* 1989.

————. "Tom Mix Festival Chairman Validates Hero's Biography for *World Book Encyclopedia.*" *Under Western Skies,* 1989.

————. "Rare Rediscovered Films to Be Premiered at Vegas Tom Mix Festival." *Westerns and Serials,* no. 35, 1990.

Singer, Mark. "Keepers of the Flame." *New Yorker,* June 3, 1991.

Stryker, Steven. "The Singing Sweethearts of Western Music." *Westerns and Serials,* no. 36, 1991.

Stumpf, Charles K. "DuBois Honors Its Native Cowboy." *Under Western Skies,* September 22, 1982.

Thayer, Stuart. "Tom Mix Circus and Wild West." *Bandwagon,* March-April 1971.

"Tom Mix," *Cooper's Hero Hobby,* 1968.

"Tom Mix: Flicker-Wise or War-Wise, He Was Happiest When Fighting, 'Cause Fighting Was in His Blood."

Virgines, George E. "The Guns of Tom Mix." *Guns Magazine,* February 1970.

Wallace, Michael, and John Gibson Phillips Jr. "Oil Man: The Story of Frank Phillips and the Birth of Phillips Petroleum." *Doubleday,* 1988.

Wardlow, Jean. "Tom Mix: Puritanical Hero of the Plains." *Today Magazine,* April 4, 1971.

"What??? Real-Life Gunslingers on Movie Screens?" *Western Frontier,* 1976.

Wright, Ed. "Elk Meat from Tom Mix." *True West,* January-February 1976.

Books and Booklets

Autry, Gene, with Mickey Herskowitz. *Back in the Saddle Again.* New York: Doubleday and Company, 1978.

Birchard, Robert S. *King Cowboy: Tom Mix and the Movies.* Burbank, CA: Riverwood Press, 1993.

Christenson, H. M., and F. M. Christenson. *Tony and His Pals.* Albert Whitman, 1938.

Collins, Ellsworth, and Alma Miller England. *The 101 Ranch.* Norman: University of Oklahoma Press, 1937, 1971.

DeMarco, Mario. *Photostory of the Screen's Greatest Cowboy Star, Tom Mix.* Mario DeMarco, n.d.

E. I. Dupont Company. *DuPont: The Autobiography of an American Enterprise.* New York: Charles Scribner, 1952.

Everson, William K., and George N. Fenin. *The Western, from Silents to Cinerama.* Crown Publishers, 1962.

————. *A Pictorial History of the Western Film.* Citadel Press, 1969.

Fernett, Gene. *Next Time Drive Off the Cliff!* Cinememories Publishing, 1968.

Harmon, Jim. *Radio Mystery and Adventure and Its Appearances in Film, Television and Other Media.* McFarland, 1992.

Hinkle, Milt. *A Texan Hits the Pampas* (booklet). Old West, 1967.

Irving, Clifford. *Tom Mix and Pancho Villa.* St. Martin's Press, 1982.

Little, W. T. *Roundup* (booklet). *Cannon City Daily Record,* mid–1960s.

McCoy, Tim, with Ronald McCoy. *Tim McCoy Remembers the West.* Norman: University of Nebraska Press, 1977, 1988.

Matthews, Leonard. *History of Western Movies.* Crescent Books, 1984.

Meyer, William R. *The Making of the Great Westerns.* Arlington House, 1979.

Mix, Olive Stokes, with Eric Heath. *The Fabulous Tom Mix.* Prentice-Hall, 1957.

Mix, Paul E. *The Life and Legend of Tom Mix.* A. S. Barnes, 1972; 2d ed., with filmography, 1981.

————. *Tom Mix, the Formative Years* (booklet). PM Publications, 1990.

Moore, Colleen. *Silent Star Colleen Moore Talks about Her Hollywood.* Doubleday and Co., 1968.

Nicholas, John H. *Riding Up to Glory: The Life of Tom Mix.* E. J. Kneip, 1969; reprint, Persimmon Hill, 1978.

Norris, M. G. "Bud." *The Tom Mix Book* (with filmography). World of Yesterday, 1989.

Overstreet, Robert M. *Official Comic Book Price Guide Companion.* House of Collectibles, 1990.

Pfeufer, Carl. *Tom Mix Western Original Art Catalog* (booklet—black and white comic book). William Harper, 1981.

Ponicsan, Darryl. *Tom Mix Died for Your Sins.* Delacorte Press, 1975.

Rainey, Buck. *The Life and Films of Buck Jones: The Silent Era.* World of Yesterday, 1988.

Rasmussen, Henry. *Imperial Palace Auto Collection.* Motorbooks International, n.d.

Ricci, Mark, Boris Zmijewsky, and Steve Zmijewsky. *The Films of John Wayne.* Citadel Press, 1979.

Richards, Norman V. *Cowboy Movies.* Bison Books, 1984.

Rooney, Mickey. *Life Is Too Short.* Villard Books, Random House, 1991.

Rothel, David. *The Singing Cowboys.* A. S. Barnes, 1978.

Schickel, Richard, and Allen Hurlburt. *The Stars.* Bonanza Books, 1962.

Seiverling, Dr. Richard F. *Tom Mix: Portrait of a Superstar* (with filmography). Keystone Enterprises, 1991.

Stansbury, Kathryn. *Lucille Mulhall: Wild West Cowgirl.* Homestead Heirlooms Publishing Co., 1992.

Stern, Jane, and Michael Stern. *Way Out West.* Harper Collins Publishers, 1993.

Time-Life Editors. *America, 1920–1930. Time-Life* Books, 1969.

Tumbusch, Tom. *Illustrated Radio Premium Catalog and Price Guide.* Tomart Publications, 1989.

Wayne, Aissa. *John Wayne, My Father.* New York: Random House, 1991.

Wayne, Pilar, with Alex Thorleifson. *John Wayne: My Life with the Duke.* McGraw-Hill, 1987.

Wheatley, Reg. *Tom Mix Rides Again. Wrangler's Roost* no. 62, Christmas 1981.

Woytowich, Andy. *Tom Mix Highlights* (booklet). Empire Publishing, 1989.

_____. *Tom Mix Coloring Book* (booklet). PM Publications, 1991.

Wyatt, Edgar M. *More Than a Cowboy: The Life and Films of Fred Thompson and Silver King.* Wyatt Classics, 1988.

Interviews and Miscellaneous Sources

Alabama
Captain Bijou, Toney

Arizona
Donald "Ike" McFadden, Camp Verde

Austria
Peter A. Schauer, Vienna

California
Patrick Bousquet, Simi Valley
Gary E. Brown, Visalia
Earl Ehrenberg, San Diego
Gene Autry Western Heritage Museum, Los Angeles
Alex Gordon, Golden West Broadcasters, Hollywood
Jim Harmon, Burbank
Vickie Matthews, Ojai
Daniel P. Matthews, Lakewood
Jim Mecate, City of Industry

Leo Reed, Santee
Robert G. Wolter, Reseda

Canada
Gerald Saunders, Baie Verte, Newfoundland

Colorado
Denver Public Library, Western History Department, Denver

Connecticut
Samuel B. Walker, Deep River

Delaware
Elutherian Mills Historical Library, Wilmington
Hagley Foundation

Denmark
Janus Barfoed, Charlottenlud

England
Colin Momber, Wrangler's Roost, Bristol
John M. Hall, Birmingham

Florida
George Siessel, Altoona

Germany
Kurt Klotzbach, Dortmund

Illinois
George V. Krauss, Buffalo Grove
George F. Zalabak, Lyons

Iowa
Gene Bell, Old Pard Video Productions, Muscatine

Kansas
John Birdeno, Inman
Ruth Schnarr, Wichita
Charles L. Warnock, Independence
Joseph L. Warnock, Independence

Maine
Walter Kern, Methuen

Maryland
James E. Murray, Severn
John Samorajczyk, Gaithersburg
Bob Wallace, Silver Springs

Michigan
Serge A. Darrigrand, Onsted

Minnesota
Ken Haag, St. Paul

Missouri
Ralston Purina Company, St. Louis

New Jersey
Big Slim's Western Museum, Rutherford
Ferdinand R. Petrie, Rutherford
Thomas J. Hoffman, Sandy Hook Park Historian, Highland

New Mexico
Dan Hutchins, Santa Fe
Las Vegas Chamber of Commerce, Las Vegas
Boyd Mager, Albuquerque
Rails 'n' Trails/Tom Mix Festival Committee, Las Vegas
Jack R. Smith, Albuquerque
Alan Tobin, Las Vegas

New York
Matthew Adams, Ithaca
Robert D. Barron, Elmira
Andy Woytowich, Yonkers

North Carolina
Ed Wyatt, Wyatt Classics, Raleigh

Ohio
Merle G. "Bud" Norris, Columbus
Fred D. Pfening, Jr., *Bandwagon,* Columbus

Oklahoma
Autumn Magic/Tom Mix Festival Committee, Guthrie
Jack C. Baskin, Ponca City
Guthrie Chamber of Commerce, Guthrie
Ray and Velma Falconer, Ponca City
Tom Mix Museum, Dewey
University of Oklahoma, Western History Collections, Norman

Oregon
Art Evans, Coquille
Jim Yaple, Portland

Pennsylvania
Janet Bastendorf, Lancaster
Allen "Slim" Binkley, Annville
Frank Buccigrossi, North Versailles
Frankie Barr Caldwell, Driftwood
Raymond Flaugh, Tom Mix Birthplace Park, Driftwood
Richard L. Mix, Williamsport
Ted Reinhart, Alexandria
Dr. Richard F. Seiverling, Hershey
U.S. Army Military History Institute, Carlisle
DuBois Chamber of Commerce, DuBois

Texas
K. Mack Boles, Dallas
Frank Galindo, San Antonio
Jack M. Haden, Austin
Dixie L. Mix, Austin
Dr. Carl R. and Dolores Ruthstrom, Katy

Virginia
Matthew L. Adams, Springfield
Tom Mix Rangers of Virginia, New Canton
Bob Toney, New Canton
Mitch Toney, New Canton

Washington, D.C.
U.S. Army Center of Military History
National Archives and Records Service

Wisconsin
Circus World Museum, Baraboo

Index